Wine secrets

Wine Secrets

by

Dennis Overstreet

&

Ava Overstreet

Illustrations
by
Jorge
Irribarren

Grosset & Dunlap
A Filmways Company
Publishers
New York

To my parents, Jackie and Archie—in love and peace.
D.O.

Secrets! . . . Who holds without failure the magic secrets when cautiously delivered by nose and tongue? Dennis Overstreet's knowledge in the field of wine, emphasized by each line of his book, brings a tangible dimension to the delicate chase for bouquet.

Philippe de Rothschild

Introduction

Voilà des années que l'enthousiasme de mon ami Dennis Overstreet m'enchante où il soit, d'une manière générale, le signe de son tempérament naturel ou plus précisément celui de son amour pour le vin.

C'est toujours une constation émouvante, pour un viticulteur, lorsqu'il voyage loin du climat où s'épanouit sa vigne, que de trouver de tels promoteurs de son vin. Car il faut une foi et une curiosité de tous les instants pour cerner la personnalité du vin dans toute sa diversité, pour distinguer "l'âme du vin." Aujourd'hui je me régouis de voir que Dennis fait usage d'une nouvelle facette de son client pour servir le vin, le vin de France en particulier, le vin de Bordeaux parmi les vins de France, et parmi ces derniers il ne manque pas de faire au Sauternes la place qui lui revient.

J'apprécie, et je pense que les lecteurs en feront autant, l'angle soit lequel est appréhendé un sujet qui a déjà tenté tant de plumes. Une oeuvre d'art ne justifie pas le prix qu'on lui attache par les efforts musculaires ou intellectuels de son auteur. Il faut pour la juger, faire abstraction des considérations de sa production, si originale soit elle, si contraignante qu'elle puisse être. Il faut se laisser en toute innocence à l'impression qu'elle suscite, à l'émotion qu'elle crée. De la même façon, le vin est fait pour être bu. Cette oeuvre d'art née de la nature et du travail des hommes, est destinée à être consommée. De quelle façon? C'est un domaine d'expériences sans fin, un procès dont on aime à reprendre perpetuellement les pièces pour mieux les examiner.

J'apprécie également dans cet ouvrage que soit presenté le métier de ceux qui diffusent le vin, comme un artisanat complémentaire de celui du viticulteur.

Le négociant est le prolongement du vigneron. Il représente un maillon entre le producteur et le dégustateur final, absolument indispensable, tant pour ce consommateur que pour ceux qui sont en amont, en particulier le viticulteur. Cette formule doit permettre la circulation d'une information éprouvée, relativement à un produit qui est différent chaque année, et qui évolue dans le temps et bien sûr dans l'espace. Si elle ne circule pas, ou si elle est altérée, le viticulteur en souffre comme d'une trahison.

Or cette transmission de l'information existe. Nous en avons pour preuve les nombreux professionnels qui viennent sans cesse nous rendre visite à Bordeaux, aux risques de devenir des amis, voire des confidents. Ils savent rester des critiques exigeants et observateurs. Certains se sont installés à Bordeaux, on ne sait plus à quel siècle. Au coeur du sujet ils sont désormais les touts premiers acteurs de la diffusion du vin de Bordeaux et sa renommée est pour beaucoup leur oeuvre. Le vin de Bordeaux, et ceux qui l'aiment, peuvent se réjouir de cette vigilence. C'est la garantie que le merveilleux potentiel de cette région bénie des dieux sera toujours respecté comme il l'a toujours été au cours des ages. C'est la confirmation que le vin de Bordeaux sera toujours fidèle à sa vocation.

Sans tomber dans le travers d'un code rigoureux et intangible, il faut admettre qu'il y a certaines règles, certains usages qui ont leur raison d'être, qui glorifient le vin, à moins que ce ne soit lui qui mette en valeur les mets avec lesquels on le marie le plus volontiers.

Il y a aussi des états de grâce pour apprécier le vin. Il faut savoir les créer, de même qu'une belle fête ne se conçoit pas sans beaux habits, le vin s'apprécie mieux si on lui dresse son décor. Il faut savoir créer les conditions d'une bonne dégustation. C'est aussi à cause de cette harmonie qu'il suscite, qu'il réclame, qu'on peut dire que le vin est objet de civilisation. Dennis, un bon Californien, est un ami de la vigne. Il fait tout cela, il le dit avec talent.

Il me semble, un observateur reciproque des États-Unis, que ce livre vient à point pour satisfaire la curiosité d'un public jeune, enthousiaste, sans préjugés, que Dennis a déjà séduit dans son merveilleux temple du vin qu'est le "Wine Merchant." Dionysos lui en sera reconnaissant. Nous aussi . . .

Comte A. de Lur-Saluces
Château d'Yquem

Introduction

For years I have been enchanted by my friend Dennis Overstreet's enthusiasm: It is the sign of his natural temperament and, more precisely, the sign of his love for wine.

It is the realization of a dream for a wine-grower to find such a promoter of his wine when he travels far from the clime where his vineyard blooms. Dennis makes every moment of his involvement with wine an act of faith and curiosity, in order to capture the personality of the wine in all its diversity and seek out "the soul of the wine." I am glad to see that Dennis has made use of a new way to present wine—the wines of France in particular, the wines of Bordeaux among them. And among the wines of Bordeaux, I note, he never fails to return to the Sauternes.

I appreciate, and I believe the reader will, Dennis's fresh approach to a subject that already has been treated by so many writers. A work of art does not justify its price by the physical or intellectual effort expended by its creator. It is necessary to leave aside any such considerations regarding its production, no matter how original or compelling. We must be allowed to abandon ourselves to it in all innocence, open to the impression it conveys and the emotions it creates. By the same token, wine is made to be drunk.

This work of art, born of nature and the efforts of men, is meant to be consumed. The question is, how? The answer is in the exploration of a realm of endless experiences, a process of discovery for the wine-lover.

I am also pleased to see in this book the attention paid to the work of the *négociant,* whose craft is complementary to that of the wine-grower. The negociant is an extension of the wine-grower. He represents a link between the maker and the final taster, and is equally indispensable to producer and consumer. His work permits the circulation of reliable information about a product that is different each year, and will continue to evolve with time. If this information is not made known—or if it is altered—the wine-grower is betrayed.

This information is indeed made known, by the professionals who are constantly coming to visit us in Bordeaux. They have become our friends and even our confidants, but they remain exacting critics and observers. Certain of their firms have been active in Bordeaux for generations, and they have been prime movers in making Bordeaux wine popular. Its renown owes much to their work. Bordeaux wine and those who love if rejoice over their vigilance. It is the guarantee that the wonderful potential of this region blessed by the gods will always be respected as it has been over the centuries. It is confirmation that the wine of Bordeaux will always be true to its vocation.

Without falling into the morass of a rigorous and artificial code, we have to acknowledge that with wine there are certain practices, certain customs, that have their reasons—they glorify the wine, making it more than merely an enhancement for the dishes with which they so pleasantly combine. There are "states of grace" for the appreciation of wine, and one must know how to create them. As an elegant party with inelegant dress is inconceivable, so wine is better enjoyed if one "dresses" it with proper surroundings. We must create the conditions for a good tasting. Wine excites, and demands, a certain harmony, and thus one might say that wine is an artifact of civilization. Dennis, a good Californian, is a friend of the vine. He understands all this, and he writes about it with appreciation.

It seems to me, in my turn an observer of the United States, that this book appears at the right moment to satisfy the curiosity of a young, enthusiastic, and unprejudiced public, some of whom Dennis has already seduced in his marvelous temple of wine, The Wine Merchant. Dionysos will be grateful to him, and so will we.

Count A. de Lur-Saluces
Château d'Yquem

Contents

Acknowledgments

We wish to express our appreciation to those who offered positive advice and valuable suggestions in the preparation of *Wine Secrets*, in some cases reading and commenting on the manuscript in whole or in part. We are grateful to Richard Bloch, Chairman of the Board, Filmways Corporation; Dr. Floyd E. Bloom, Director of the Arthur V. Davis Center for Behavioral Neurobiology, Salk Institute; Arthur Bone of the Wine & Spirit Education Trust Limited; John Boys of the Institute of Masters of Wine; Christie's Wine Department; David Courtney-Clack; Lucille Dash; Alan Haufrecht; Dr. Arthur P. Kowell; Dr. Robert Matthews; Michelin Tire Corporation; Moët-Hennessy Corporation; Robert Mondavi Winery; the executive staff of Château Mouton-Rothschild; Samuel Patterson, Sr.; our daughter, Tara Leigh.

Special thanks are due to Dr. A. D. Webb, Chairman of the Department of Enology, University of California, who painstakingly read some technical chapters, assisting us with his incredible knowledge; to our editor, Nancy Brooks, whose editorial skills are nonpareil; to Mary Milanese, Grosset & Dunlap's supremely capable managing editor; and to Bob Markel, editor-in-chief.

We would also like to thank our celebrity friends who took the time to gather their thoughts on wine and to share them with us. We salute Mel Brooks, Yul Brynner, Henry Ford II, Gene Kelly, Walter Matthau, Burgess Meredith, Dan Rowan, Al Stewart, and Gene Wilder.

Wine
Secrets

How
to Buy
Wine

It may be flattering to be told, "If *you* like it, then it's a good wine," but that's nonsense. There is a better and a worse to wine, as with anything else, and appreciation of the difference is discernible to anyone who has taken the time to acquire knowledge and experience.

Ideally, you should have a good wine merchant to guide you, one who stocks a wide range of wines of different variety, quality, and diversity of price. It is he who has a regard for your level of appreciation, your pocketbook, and your degree of wine interest and knowledge. You can rely on him not only to guide you in your selection of wines for the many different social occasions in your life but to respond personally to your special needs by ordering wines at your request. He keeps abreast with the current trends and is able to pass on to you, in his newsletters of fact and opinion, his best advice on the most recent vintage. And if you want to start a cellar, taking into your account your age, your income, and the space you have available, he can competently advise you on buying potentially great wine in its youth.

If you haven't found him yet, don't despair. You don't have to be at the mercy of the liquor store clerk, Madison Avenue, or esoteric wine journalese. The following three points will teach you to see beyond hype:

Point one: *Quality in wine is dependent on good grapes.* You cannot make good wine from bad grapes, and good grapes are produced in good vintages. This first principle has always guaranteed success to every reputable wine merchant, regardless of claims to the contrary. But how do *you,* the consumer, gain information about quality wines? First,

you must learn about the various vintages in order to decide what constitutes the best value. There is no grand mystery involved. The information is as readily accessible to you as it is to the wine merchant or the columnist who reviews wines in the gourmet section of the newspaper.

Some of the sources to which you can subscribe are the numerous newsletters and promotional brochures issued by the wineries, the wine institutes, and the various regulatory and trade boards of different wine-producing countries (addresses can be found in the Appendix).

Weather plays a vital role because each grape varietal responds differently to factors affecting each vintage. One year's climatic conditions may be favorable to the Cabernet Sauvignon while disastrous to the Pinot Noir.

And because the weather, and therefore the growing conditions, is so unpredictable, established European wine producers adhere to strict production standards determined by law to protect and assure the high quality of their wines. Certain varietals are permitted to grow only in those areas that have been analyzed as favorable to that type, where the soil and climate are sympathetic to its production.

Newer wine-growing regions of the world, like California and Australia, are still experimenting with what grows best, and laws regulating the variety of grape that can be grown and the quantity of wine that can be produced do not as yet exist. Bearing this in mind, it is up to you to know what type of temperature creates specific kinds of conditions and how this affects the various grape types.

Cool temperature during the growing season will cause the grape to be high in acid. Warm temperature will produce higher levels of sugar and low acidity. Acid in white wine is responsible for its fresh crispness as a young wine and for its creamy softness and bouquet when aged. In a red wine, the exact same amount of acid will make it unpalatable, bitter, sour, and vegetative in aroma. Excess ripeness will make the wine taste rubbery, alcoholic, and its aroma will be burnt or raisiny. Rain at harvest time will bloat the grapes, causing a thin, diluted wine.

Knowing the growing-season conditions of a particular wine will be a help to you when shopping in the marketplace because you'll know exactly how much to expect from a particular wine.

Learning about the various climatic zones of California and Europe will acquaint you with which grapes grow more suitably in different climates. The University of California at Davis devised a system of classifying the wine-producing areas of the world into five regions of similar climate, ranging from the coolest (Region 1) to the warmest (Region 5). In *Region 1:* Santa Cruz, California; Germany; Champagne and Burgundy, France; *Region 2:* Lower Napa, Sonoma, Monterey, California; Bordeaux, France; *Region 3:* Livermore Valley, California; the Rhône Valley, France; Italy; *Region 4:* Ukiah/Lodi, California; Rioja, Spain; and *Region 5:* San Joaquin Valley, California; Jerez, Spain.

Varietals such as Chardonnay and Pinot Noir do best in Region 1, the coolest climate. And while they may not produce their most positive traits in warmer climates, due to popularity and pressing economic factors winemakers can be induced to produce them.

Since the Europeans have been in the commercial winemaking business longer than we, they have created laws that deal with greed and sudden fads, limiting the number of abuses that can exist for any length of time. Château Mouton-Rothschild, for example, is not required to state the kinds of grapes used in their blend or *encépagement* because European law specifies that the grapes used in a château's wine must come from that château's property—and nowhere else. Thus, when you buy any château-bottled wine from a French vineyard, the grapes must have originated on that vineyard's soil. However, this is not the case with California wines, and the laws are more flexible as to the kinds of grapes that can be blended together. That is why you must examine the California wine label closely. Even though the wine may have been made in Napa Valley, that is no guarantee that the grapes were grown there.

Point two: *Be on constant watch for fraud and deception.* This is not paranoia, this is the real world.

Please listen to me when I tell you that right now, somewhere in the world, someone is trying to sell you a fraudulent bottle of wine.

European wine-producing countries have set up elaborate regulations preventing frauds of their wines. These rules aren't generally known by the drinking public. But if you know how the game is played, you'll be one step ahead of the unscrupulous producer, shipper, and wholesaler.

Look out for the obvious. If you are fond of Chardonnay and you are browsing through the racks at your local wine shop and suddenly see an unknown label bearing the name of a shipper you've never heard of and find that it is marked considerably less than a more well-known brand, don't think you've struck gold. More likely the so-called Chardonnay is something else altogether. In other words, rely on reputable brands and shippers. The percentages favor the familiar over the unknown.

When you buy a bottle of imported wine, make sure it is sealed with a closure, whether cork, capsule, or screw top, that is nonreusable. In addition, the name and address of the bottler or the code number under which he operates should be printed on the cork or on the capsule and accompanied by the phrase: *Bottled by.*

If you acquire a wine whose contents are suspect, make an inquiry by sending a copy of the label and the name and identity number of the bottler to the trade commission office representing the country of wine origin. If you don't find this information readily available in your telephone book, contact the nearest consulate or embassy for that country and ask them to put you in touch with their trade commissioner or to give you an address where you can write the authorities. In France, there is a fraud squad that looks into these kinds of scandals, and any information you give will help to stop this type of illegal practice.

If you have a dispute with someone regarding the vintage, use this trick to verify the vintage date of the wine: The lead capsule or brightly colored aluminum foil wrapper will slip off the bottle neck when twisted upward firmly. The cork will then be exposed along with the branded vintage date.

Wines shipped in boxes that do not clearly identify the winery or château should be scrutinized for possible chicanery. Most wineries and shippers are proud of their products and, whenever possible, display their names on the outside of the containers.

Free ports like Amsterdam and Liverpool are hubs of commerce for illegal operations in which wines are relabeled and shipped to merchants greedy for popular wines and undemanding of documentation certifying the origin of the shipment.

One of the quickest ways for you to spot this common and unlawful practice is to take the bottle of wine, turn it around and look at the label from the backside. A label that has been applied by a machine will generally wrap smoothly against the surface of the bottle. A fraudulent bottle, however, will commonly show only the two ends of the label glued, and the reason is because this procedure is done quickly and by hand.

Another clue as to the wine's condition is the amount of *ullage,* the air space between the wine and cork. If you see more than a half-inch of space between wine and cork, become concerned and find out how your wine merchant has been storing the wine or under what conditions he bought the shipment.

Point three: *Paying top dollar doesn't guarantee superiority.* Simply because a usually high-priced wine has been discounted, don't be so sure that you're getting a bargain until you're aware of what the fair price is for this wine. An excellent barometer of the wine's worth is the price it is fetching at an auction, and just as Wall Street reflects the economy's ups and downs, so does the auction house bear witness to what the wine will bring in currency on the marketplace.

You can write to the following prestigious auction houses for information:

Christie's Wine Department
8 Kings Street, St. James
London, S.W. IY 6QT England

Sotheby Parke Bernet
34–35 New Bond Street
London WIA, 2AA England

These two reputable houses are responsible for major sales of wine throughout the world. Their newsletters and catalogs are valuable sources of information that will give you an accurate picture of market trends that may not immediately be reflected in your area.

Knowing when to buy always is important because the law of supply and demand will certainly affect the availability and price of certain wines.

Buy wine for a useful purpose—drinking, not speculating—and try to restrain your impulse to buy thirty cases of a particularly good one when five or six cases will do. It may be tempting to envision yourself making a killing on a particular wine that's "bound to go up," but if it doesn't, you'll be the one who will have to consume it all.

If you enjoy a sweet Sauternes after dinner or with pâté, and if you don't often drink it with your meals, try buying half bottles. This means that none of the wine will be wasted—and you will have the pleasure of opening a fresh bottle each time.

Wines bought in magnum or larger-sized bottles take longer to develop, but the extra aging time definitely develops qualities that are unattainable in smaller sizes.

Don't become a slave to a passing fad. After learning the lessons that I will give you in this book, I'd like to see you buying less, but better-quality, wine than more of mediocre types. Have confidence in your own judgment and buy the wines that you find interesting rather than merely aping what others consider quality. A good example is Dom Pérignon. Although I think the Moët-Chandon people are making good Champagne, I also think they are geniuses at merchandising. There are other equally fine Champagne houses, and buying Dom Pérignon merely because it is the thing to do is only for those who are insecure about their own good taste. That's not you.

When buying old wines, be especially wary. Price and scarcity are highly volatile factors when it comes to rare bottles of wine, and the merchant who buys and sells these old wines is the player holding the cards. Make sure he's reputable and that you know what you're buying. Remember, it's a gamble because some wines can be kept a bit more *too* long.

As more and more interesting wine areas develop, don't hesitate to request these new wines from your retailer. If you find that he's not interested, ask him for the winery's name and address. Write to the winery and ask them to make the wine available in your area. A reputable wine merchant, however, should be happy to make an attempt to locate the particular wine you want and not sell you merely the wine he has on hand.

Wines usually become available in either spring or fall, and since there is only one vintage per year, knowing its potential is important. Keep in mind that, for aging purposes, red wines are released two years after the vintage; white wines, six months to a year after that date. Start making queries just before wines are released for sale, organizing your stock and budget needs.

It may sound discriminatory or unfair, but the best wineries most often will deal only with the best wine shops, and at the best values. If you live in a remote area, save your money and make an annual trip to the nearest big city with a decent wine or liquor store. The only exception is a resort area, or a small-town store owned by a wine nut.

It might be a good idea to call or write to the owner of the wine shop where you are going on your

CLIMATE REGIONS

1 Very cool

2 Cool

3 Moderate

4 Warm

5 Very warm

FRANCE

PARIS

Champagne

1

1

Alsace

1

Loire Valley

Burgundy

2

1

Jura

CREPY

SEYSSEL

LYON

Savoie

Bordeaux

2

BERGERAC

MONBAZILLAC

Cotes du Rhone

2

3

3

Languedoc

2

Cotes de
Provence

Southwest

MINERVOIS

CORBIERES

RIVESALTES

FRONTIGNAN

CASSIS

BANDOL

NICE

MARSEILLE

Roussillon

CALIFORNIA

MENDOCINO

4

3

1

2

4

SONOMA

1

3

2

NAPA

4

SACRAMENTO

4

SAN FRANCISCO

MODESTO

2

MERCED

1

MADERA

2

3

5

FRESNO

SAN BENITO

1

MONTEREY

5

KERN

SANTA BARBARA

1

2

SAN BERNARDINO

5

LOS ANGELES

4

SAN DIEGO

N

W — E

S

The deeper the roots, the better the wine. Why? Because more essential nutrients will be found at more profound depths. The root system searches for water, oxygen, and soil elements. If the water level is very high, as in the center illustration, the root will not find proper nourishment. The overhead view of the vine shows how the root system spreads out in its search for nourishment. The ideal soil, on the left, shows how each layer offers new life to the ever-expanding root system.

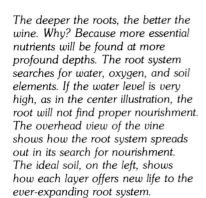

Top layer (5 feet deep) is a combination of gravel, clay, and loam.

Rust color from iron oxidation in soil is a good clue that soil is well aerated.

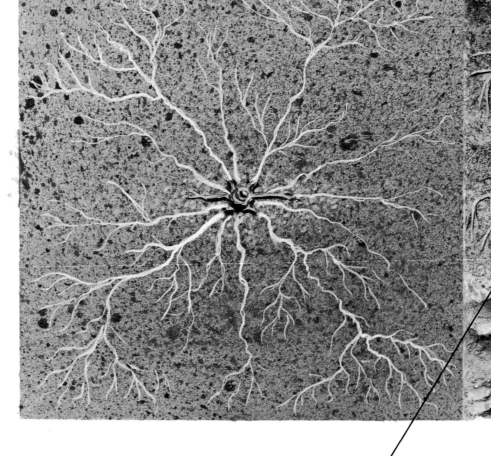

Roots anchor the vines to the soil. Tap roots follow the path of least resistance, seeking essential minerals: phosphorus, potassium, nitrogen, sulfur, calcium, and magnesium. Irrigated soil makes the roots' job easier. Rainfall washing down the vine, increasing the growth of the roots, is preferred to irrigation in Europe. Fluctuating water tables can cause uneven development.

Next layer is a combination of sand and humus.

Tap root goes down about 30 feet.

Rocky bottom lay

Clouds are an insulating blanket over the fields.

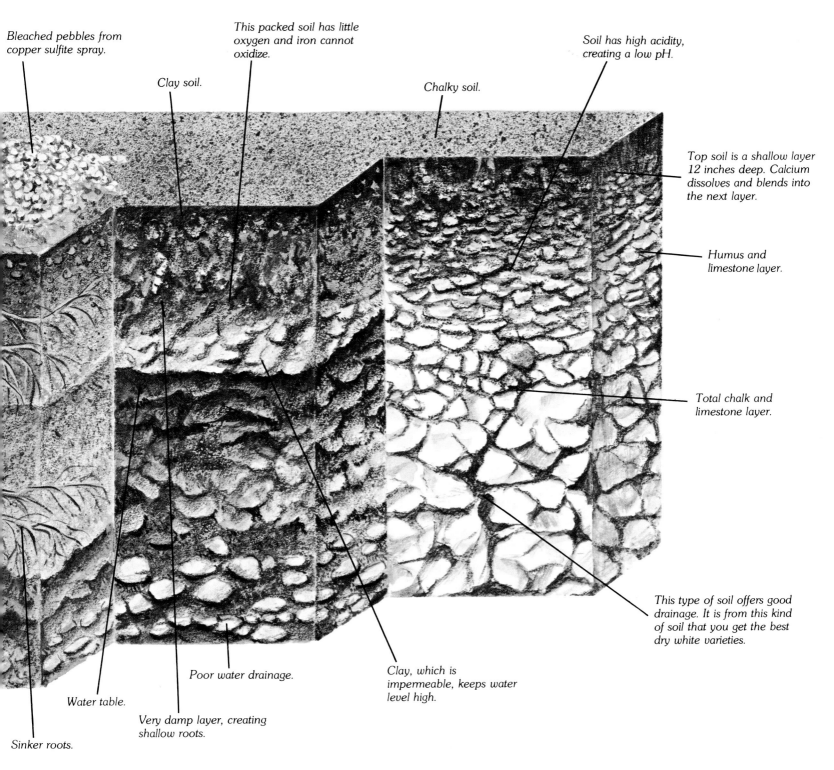

Bleached pebbles from copper sulfite spray.

This packed soil has little oxygen and iron cannot oxidize.

Clay soil.

Chalky soil.

Soil has high acidity, creating a low pH.

Top soil is a shallow layer 12 inches deep. Calcium dissolves and blends into the next layer.

Humus and limestone layer.

Total chalk and limestone layer.

This type of soil offers good drainage. It is from this kind of soil that you get the best dry white varieties.

Poor water drainage.

Clay, which is impermeable, keeps water level high.

Water table.

Very damp layer, creating shallow roots.

Sinker roots.

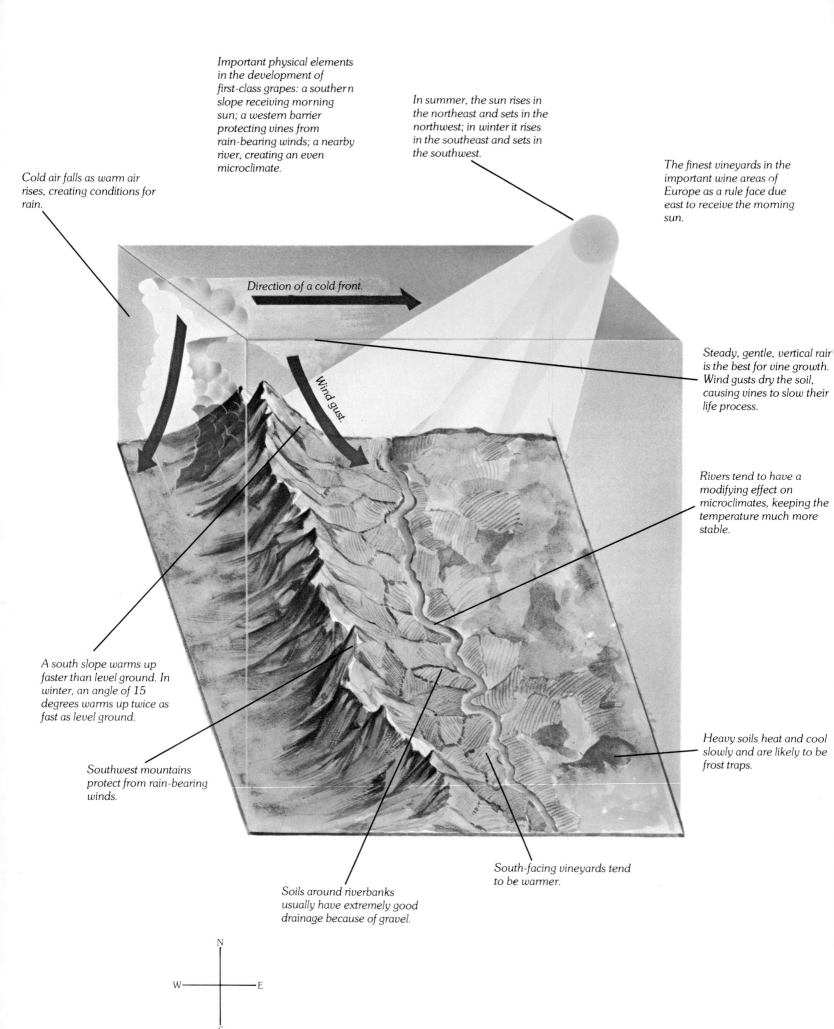

Important physical elements in the development of first-class grapes: a southern slope receiving morning sun; a western barrier protecting vines from rain-bearing winds; a nearby river, creating an even microclimate.

In summer, the sun rises in the northeast and sets in the northwest; in winter it rises in the southeast and sets in the southwest.

The finest vineyards in the important wine areas of Europe as a rule face due east to receive the morning sun.

Cold air falls as warm air rises, creating conditions for rain.

Direction of a cold front.

Wind gust.

Steady, gentle, vertical rain is the best for vine growth. Wind gusts dry the soil, causing vines to slow their life process.

Rivers tend to have a modifying effect on microclimates, keeping the temperature much more stable.

A south slope warms up faster than level ground. In winter, an angle of 15 degrees warms up twice as fast as level ground.

Southwest mountains protect from rain-bearing winds.

Heavy soils heat and cool slowly and are likely to be frost traps.

South-facing vineyards tend to be warmer.

Soils around riverbanks usually have extremely good drainage because of gravel.

N
W — E
S

annual shopping spree. He will be flattered to know that you are coming to see him from such a distance (at least I am) and will probably give you more of his time and expertise in making your selections.

Whether your allotment is $40, $50, $100, or more, start saving and then purchase at one time. This will allow you to obtain the maximum leverage for your dollar because of the discount factor and the fact that a great vintage will not lessen in value as time goes by but will escalate in price.

If the vintage in a particular type is disappointing, don't buy. Continue saving your money and buy the next year's selection—but only if you decide investment in that vintage is worth it. Remember, you can buy your mediocre wine at the supermarket. Stocking up your best wine means that *you* must use good judgment and be informed about these three important factors: soil, weather, and grape—and buying the best possible quality for that year's dollar.

The Development of the Wine Trade

I think it is important for you to understand the diverse marketing patterns of France and California and their development. Differences between the two regions affect both the quality and quantity of the wine you buy.

Fulfillment of nature's requirements and skilled winemaking is not enough to enable a country to become a leader in producing great wine. Wine production must attract investment. Historically, this occurs when a fashionable leadership in society becomes intrigued with fine wines.

Very good wines were made in Greece of the Golden Age, in Imperial Rome, in fifteenth-century Spain—and in eighteenth-century France, when the strength of her wines was matched by her cultural and material wealth.

And the wine trade must be strong—strong enough, according to Dr. Emile Peynaud, former head of the Bordeaux Oenological Station, to cross over from domestic to international markets, imposing its country's wines on the rest of the world.

Dr. Peynaud believes that California wines, especially those of the Napa Valley, are equal to and, in some cases, may even surpass the wines of France. But California has not taken the lead in the world of wines—yet. How did France achieve her dominance? How will California?

I believe that if California is to step forward she must develop, as did France, a network of middlemen—brokers, *négociants*, shippers—who will provide the checks and balances necessary to encourage world trade and quality wine production.

The California wine trade today is extremely limited. Most California wine is sold in California; it is not even distributed in Wyoming or Montana, and still less is sold throughout Europe and Japan. Small or boutique wineries, producing less than 20,000 cases a year, cannot interest large distributors who want to be guaranteed substantial quantity and a range of prices. Thus the small wineries are immediately eliminated from major markets and must sell directly to specific retailers. Large wineries make exclusive arrangements with wholesalers or distributors in particular marketing areas—which does disseminate the product, but the exclusive nature of the agreement works against competition. What this means is that for California wineries, large or small, the cost is controlled by the immediate needs at the source—the winery—rather than by a world marketplace.

And the needs of the wineries, especially the small ones, are great. There is a tremendous cash flow problem and a need for capital. Unlike the producer of liquor or soft drinks, a winery is limited to one harvest a year. A wine that has been aged, especially a red wine, will taste better and will consequently be able to command a higher price. Unfortunately, economics forces California wineries to sell rapidly after bottling. This means the wine is sold when young and not aged. The French middleman buys wine immediately after the harvest, but he doesn't move it out right away, so French growers get their money when they need it, right after the harvest, *and* the wine gets the bonus of more aging time. Most French châteaux are small, producing less than 20,000 cases a year, and make one or two varieties; California wineries, however, find it necessary to produce as many as nine or ten.

It would be wonderful if the wineries could, immediately after the harvest, get low-cost loans for their wines, enabling them to age some of their vintage for a period of time. But, given the economics of today, this is not so.

These problems aren't new, or unique, to California. But the French, particularly in Bordeaux, have developed over the centuries a marketing system that, for them, works effectively. Its operation has raised the quality of the top French wines and expanded their trade all over the world. Today, the *négociant* of French wines is more than a wholesaler; he is a wine man. He buys not exclusively but from different proprietors, thus developing his own list. He cellars the château-bottled wine he buys, and he makes his own regional blends from wines of different vineyards. His name is on the labels of the bottles he sells, and his reputation is on the line. This state of affairs took some time to establish itself, and the road was not always smooth.

French wineries originally sold young wine to foreign *négociants,* or shippers, who stored it in wood and gambled on its future as a great wine. Foreign shippers, however, had no time to scout the 'French countryside looking for sufficient quantities of the wines they wanted. The growers, responsible for each year's crop, could not both tend to the vineyards and sell their products abroad—they had no time to travel and promote their wines.

Enter the wine broker. Traditionally paid a 4 percent commission, he knew the territory but was not tied to the vineyards. The broker protected the growers from unscrupulous buyers (some of whom sailed away with the wines and later changed the terms of payment or claimed never to have received the wines at all). Everyone needed the broker, but it was easy to resent him. His only investment was his transportation, usually a horse and buggy. He led a pleasant life traveling from vineyard to vineyard, marking the qualities of the casks. The brokers knew their wines, and their reputations were impressive—sometimes, perhaps, exaggerated.

Cervantes wrote in *Don Quixote,* "The broker detected a faintly metallic taste in the cask, together with the suspicion of cardboard. When the cask was drained, in the bottom was found a metal key with a cardboard label." Brokers were feted and paid court to by the proprietors, much as wine writers are wooed today. If an owner dared to rub off the broker's chalk mark, no other broker would touch that wine. The brokers opened up the market, bringing together seller and buyer.

The trade of the brokers and *négociants* flourished. Who were these traders? Many of the earliest ones were Dutch. A Barton from Ireland came in 1725. The Johnstons, English, came in 1734; the

Schuylers, Germans, in 1739. Mestrezat came from Geneva in 1815; the Hanappiens from Orléans in 1816. Cruse came from Denmark in 1819; De Luze from Germany in 1820; Calvet from Hermitage in 1823; and Eschenauer from Alsace in 1831. These men marketed the wines of France all over the Continent and to England.

The Calvets, originally brokers, became a great shipping family, the first to go after the world wine trade. There were three brothers: Neil, who spoke German; George, who spoke Spanish; and John, who spoke English. Pursuing the wine trade the way the Rothschilds did banking, John went to England, George to South America, Neil to German-speaking countries—all of them built up the reputation of Calvet. Soon, if you saw the name Calvet on a bottle of Lafite or Latour, this was the Lafite or Latour you bought.

In 1855, in preparation for the Exposition Universelle de Paris, the brokers officially graded the wines of Bordeaux. Wine became fashionable. Bankers and noblemen began to buy wine estates, placing a manager or winemaker in charge who could run the property for the absentee owner. The demand for wine was great, and it led to temptation and abuses. Cider was mixed with vegetable dye and passed off as young, rough wine. Young claret (as the English call red Bordeaux) was doctored to masquerade as old; casks were often shipped two-thirds full, to be filled with a lesser wine at their destination. Brandy was added to wine of a poor vintage to give it body, and orris root to give it bouquet.

A broker would contract to buy all a grower could produce in the next five years, and needless to say, that grower's production would be augmented by various means to increase the yield. The Bishop of Toulouse reflected the prevailing attitude when he wrote that he believed that "new wines could resemble old wines; that aged wine treated badly could be restored to its pristine quality by adding alcohol; that two vintages could be blended together to make up for nature's deficiency. The only provision should be that the label show the description of at least 51 percent of the contents." In other words, as long as most of the wine in a bottle was of a given vintage, you could label the bottle by that vintage. If most of the wine in a blend was of one type, it could be labeled as such—if you blended Spanish wine with a major portion of Bordeaux wine, you could call your wine Bordeaux.

Today, people might say these standards are abominable, yet this description is the very same one that the Bureau of Alcohol, Tobacco and Firearms applies to California wines. Any wine with 51 percent of a varietal can now be labeled by that type (by 1983, the wine must contain 75 percent of the named grape). If the varietal comes from a particular county, you can name it after the county. If 75 percent comes from a particular vintage, you can label it with that vintage date. I believe that as the California trade becomes more sophisticated, we will have to learn, as the French did, that such conditions cannot be afforded. Quality controls must be established and enforced, even if it means telling growers what they can grow on a particular plot of land, how many gallons per acre they can produce, and what combinations of grape varietals they can blend.

The French realized that the conditions accepted by the good bishop, while not illegal, were destroying the trade. The *négociants* and brokers, who had themselves participated in the shenanigans, were the first to move to restore the integrity of the market. They began by going to Château Latour, classified a first growth in 1855, and saying, "We will buy 120 tonneaux (11,250 cases), your average production. If you produce anything over 120 tonneaux, we will pay you one half the price for that surplus." This was the beginning of concern for quality control, and today the French standard of truth in packaging, codified in the early 1900s in the Appellations Contrôlées and in the Appellations d'Origine, are the highest in the world.

When the phylloxera plague of the 1870s destroyed the vineyards of Europe, wines were immediately stored; good wines were hard to find, and prices skyrocketed. The brokers were without wine, and the growers started to move out of the Médoc region, migrating to Spain and Algeria. For the first time in history, wines came on the market that rivaled the wines of Bordeaux. Algeria became the favorite of connoisseurs. In 1915, according to wine critics, Algerian wines never were to be "so good and well deserved as now." By 1920, the important English market had decided that the Algerian wines were stronger and richer in color than Bordeaux wines, and they became quite voguish.

Bordeaux eventually recovered with the planting of hardy American rootstocks in French soil and the grafting of French vines onto American roots, which were resistant to the devastating phylloxera plague. At the same time, powerful personalities like Bernard Ginestet and Philippe de Rothschild imposed their own high standards of quality.

In the twenties, Baron Philippe de Rothschild of Mouton-Rothschild led the movement to château-bottling, which helped to prevent tampering with the wine after it leaves the château. Château-bottling also represented independence for the growers,

many of whom wanted to sell their wines directly rather than go through brokers and *négociants*.

At this time, across the Atlantic, Prohibition came to America. Growers who hadn't learned to sell their wine got rid of it, and profits plummeted. With the loss of the American market due to this economic disaster, the château owners realized they needed the commercial skills of the *négociants*, especially in bad times. The government was no help; it taxed heavily, and according to growers, put too many controls on the industry. When times were good, business was brisk and growers got their prices. But when times were bad, the situation disintegrated into chaos. Hardest hit were the small châteaux without a cultural identity and well-known name. The occasional drinker was inclined to buy the established-name lists, so if you weren't a classified growth you were in trouble during lean years. It was becoming apparent that it takes flair and salesmanship to sell wine, and the Bordeaux growers realized that *négociants* like Alexis Lichine and Frank Schoonmaker were responsible for maintaining their business in America.

Thus the château owners, though they were bottling their own wines, realized that if they wanted to be in the world marketplace they still needed the *négociant*. He understood the world marketplace; the owners didn't have the requisite commercial expertise. As the local merchant in Spain, California, and Japan recognizes the needs of his customers, the *négociant* knows what is going on worldwide and where he can move wine.

There always has been a certain tension between growers and *négociants*. French growers are always gloomy about prospects for a forthcoming vintage, hoping their pessimism will make price of the previous year's wine, still in cask, higher.

It is typical to read quarterly reports that claim the first quarter will not lead to anything; that the second quarter is being destroyed by night frost; the third quarter, by hail; and the fourth quarter, by rot. Then comes the miraculous "fifth quarter" and the actual harvest results in a wonderful vintage. A vintage is often mistakenly judged by these preliminary reports, which aren't always accurate.

But the *négociants* aren't fooled. They tour the Médoc, usually in a group, tasting at each château while remaining infuriatingly silent about their opinions.

Each wine vintage is generally sold in three *tranches*, or stages, in Bordeaux. The first group, one third, is sold from three to six months after the harvest; the second, six months later; and the last third is kept by the château for further aging. (In vintages of large production, some wine may be set aside for leaner times.) The first two sales, the château hopes, will pay for the entire cost of the vintage.

Each year, after the wine has been put in barrels, the major *négociants* for Bordeaux, as a group, make offers to the growers. The *négociants,* who have learned that it is not advantageous to deal exclusively, do business with all the châteaux. For example, although Mouton-Rothschild has an exclusive United States agent for Mouton-Cadet, its lesser wine, it will not give up Mouton-Rothschild to an exclusive agent. Baron Philippe de Rothschild believes that it is very important to maintain a relationship with merchants around the world. Most châteaux agree, and even if they have an exclusive agent in one country, they are always represented by a group of *négociants.*

The *négociants* are each offered a certain percentage of cases of each first-growth vintage, second-growth vintage, and so on. For instance: A Mouton-Rothschild vintage has produced 15,000 cases. The first offer by the château might consist of 5,000 cases, at a nonnegotiable price set by Mouton-Rothschild according to its judgment of what the wine is worth. All *négociants* have the opportunity to buy Mouton-Rothschild, in varying proportions: Some have the right to buy 10 percent, others only 5 percent. If a *négociant* thinks the price is too high, he will express his opinion to the other *négociants.* He may take his entire allocation with reluctance, or he may buy only 10 percent of it. If the offering does not receive the desired response, the château knows it has problems: A lack of enthusiasm on the part of the *négociants* indicates that the first price is too high. If a *négociant* does not take all of his allocation, the château will offer the remainder to his colleagues, and if another *négociant* buys it, his future allocation will be increased in forthcoming vintages.

The first offer made by the *négociants* is a very conservative one, but it is an opportunity for them to strike a bargain. A first growth will generally support a stable price on the international market. Lesser-known châteaux, however, have to be very shrewd when making their first offer; it must be realistic yet as profitable as they think they can obtain. They can make mistakes, because it is the *négociants,* not the growers, who know what the market will bear. But the growers have a second chance.

During the interim between the first two *tranches,* both sides evaluate the situation. The *négociants* hype up the vintage reports on the world market (although they won't falsely claim that it was a wonderful vintage when it was lousy), while the growers watch what other châteaux are doing in order to gauge the price at which the vintage can reasonably be sold in the marketplace. If the reception to the vintage is lukewarm, then the second and third offerings may be rejected by all or most of the *négociants* remaining in the château.

Let us say that the first offering, 5,000 cases, was set at $100 a case, and that all of the *négociants* take their allocations because there is a strong possibility that the wine is both a winner and a good value. After six months, at their second offering (normally higher than the first) the growers raise their prices approximately 20 percent. But while the grower may now be more aware of his bargaining position, at a 20 percent increase, not every *négociant* will choose to take his allocation. Those remaining still have a chance at the third offering, but if things proceed normally, the price demanded will be even higher. Why? One factor is that a price established at the first offering is unlikely to be followed by second and third prices that are lower, unless extremely unusual conditions exist, such as a world depression, giant scandal, and the like.

Let us take the example of Château Mouton-Rothschild, 1979. It has rained, and they've harvested the wine. It is still in the vat, fermenting. Now the traditional procedure is for the *négociant* to visit the château to taste and comment on this year's vintage of Château Mouton-Rothschild, of which he normally buys 10 percent. He, the *négociant,* will decide whether the wine still fermenting in the vat will produce a sound, a spectacular, or a mediocre vintage.

The *négociant*'s enthusiasm, or lack of it, will guide Château Mouton-Rothschild in determining what the fair market price will be. If Mouton-Rothschild asks $10 at the first offering, and Margaux offers $9, either the higher or lower price has to be vindicated in the marketplace. Otherwise someone will lose face, and the château's reputation will be affected by the price offered for its wine.

This system not only balances and normalizes the market, but it allows the grower protection during the bad harvests, which is the lot of all growers at one time or another. For example, let's say there is a bad vintage. Five thousand cases are offered. No *négociant* wants to buy wine from a bad vintage, but he knows that if he doesn't exercise his right to buy when times are bad, he will lose his right to buy the following vintage, which may turn out to be a great one. He wants to stay competitive, and he wants to keep an open channel to the château.

The checks and balances provided by the *négociant* system ensure competitive prices and an ever-expanding marketplace. Perhaps if it operated in this country, you would not have the present situation in which, for example, Chardonnay from Napa is in great demand while Chardonnay from Oregon is unattractive.

The *négociant* has had a great impact on the development of the Bordeaux and Burgundy wine regions, improving both quality and trade. He will also have to play a role in California if it is to find its place in the world of wine. The California winery owner, like his Bordeaux cousin, does not have the time, money, or marketing expertise to bridge domestic or international boundaries.

What responsibility do you, the consumer, have in this relationship of winemaker, winery owner, *négociant*/broker, wholesaler, retailer? We must learn to be more discerning and more cautious in our choices and not buy solely on the basis of vintage or a winery's name. If you buy traditionally excellent wine early in its development, you are either in a position to store it for a number of years or you're simply trying to impress someone. For immediate drinking, you need a wine that is going to be palatable that evening.

Select a wine merchant who is trying to establish a long-term business and is interested in your patronage for years to come. It is very important that he deal with only the best shippers. The wine business is built on reputation. In the long run, you will find it worth the slightly higher price by going with the well-known established shippers such as Latour,

Jadot, Drouhin, and Calvet among the respectable.

Louis Latour, the noted Burgundian shipper and *négociant,* made the point succinctly when he told me: "Burgundy has been made by shippers. The idea of cultivating vineyards on poor soil with a very low crop yield is something that requires high prices. To have high prices, you need someone who will take your wine from the farm in Burgundy and go to the north of Europe saying, 'This is good. You have to pay the price.' If we hadn't had people who were good enough, strong enough, and imaginative enough to travel as they did in the eighteenth century, going to the royalty of the time, we wouldn't have Burgundy existing right now. In Burgundy, we shippers have survived because we add something to the appellation. The appellation is scattered in many, many small parcels. If you want to select Nuits-St.-Georges, you wish to know who has bottled it. You have reliable shippers and unreliable shippers. You have reliable growers and unreliable growers. So you go to the best. We cover the whole range of appellations. And in addition, we are winegrowers and among the biggest in Burgundy. The so-called *négociant-propriétaires* are the Burgundy wine trade, and nobody can push them aside, because they have the tradition. They *know* what is a selection of wine. And their signature means something to a very, very large public. This is how we survive. The dividing line is very simple. And common sense is the dividing line between the good and the bad."

Grape, Vineyard, and the Making of Wine

Almost all the wines we know today—from Europe, California, South America, and Africa—began as the fruit of one species of one genus of a vast family of plants: the *vitis vinifera,* or the wine-producing vine. The varieties of *vinifera* can be counted in the thousands; those that concern you as a devotee of wine are fewer, about fifty, and of those, you will generally learn the intrinsic characteristics of not more than the twelve most popular. The names of these varieties are becoming more familiar to wine drinkers as California has become recognized as a fine wine-producing region, the quality of whose product can equal European wine in the same price bracket. American practice is to label wines by varietal name: Cabernet Sauvignon, Pinot Noir, Zinfandel. European wines are designated geographically, by the district in which the grapes are known: St.-Émilion, Rioja, Pouilly Fuissé.

The fruit of *vitis vinifera* is the berry, or grape. Each variety of *vinifera* has its own personality and characteristics, but despite individual differences, the anatomy of the grape is a structure both complex and orderly, following a distinct pattern.

Berry size and shape varies from the small, irregular, conical Cabernet Sauvignon to the Zinfandel grape, identified by its large cylindrical shape and distinguishing wing or shoulder. Look at a grape, feel it with your fingers. You will notice a waxy bloom on the skin that gives a pearly tint to the white grape, a bluish overtone to the black. The bloom protects the berry from sunburn, repels water, and gives off a faint, pleasant odor. This odor attracts the wild yeast *saccharomyces cerevisiae,* which will begin the process of fermentation when the grapes are crushed. Without yeast, wild or cultured, there is no fermentation; without fermentation there is no wine.

Peel the skin, hold it against the light. The skin is the repository of the greatest portion of aroma, coloring matter, and flavoring constituents that accumulate in the grape's last stages of maturity, but here too there are varietal differences: The Alicante-Bouschet grape, for example, has red pigment in both skin and pulp in the ripened stage. White wines can be obtained from red grapes by minimizing the skin's contact with the juice in the initial crushing stages. The recent surge in popularity of white wine means that many red grapes traditionally used to produce red wine are now being used to produce white.

The color of the berry is affected by many factors, one of which is temperature: Heat inhibits red and black pigment formation. Varieties with high acidity will show a reddish color; those with low acidity will be distinguished by a dull bluish tinge. The presence of iron will lend a violet hue. Tannin, an organic compound found primarily in the grape's skin, seeds, and stem, provides the wine with longevity and endurance and also affects its taste and color: A higher tannin content will increase the blue tint of certain varieties. The smaller the berry, the greater the skin-to-pulp ratio, which means more tannin and more color in the wine.

Now look at the seed. Most varieties have two of these small kernels; the Chardonnay has only one. As well as storing tannin, the seeds contain an oily resinous material that can make the wine unpalatable and enzymes that, if exposed to air, will turn a white wine brown (as a slice of apple left out will similarly discolor). Thus care must be taken at crushing time to minimize the release of these materials into the juice.

Discard both skin and seed and examine the

pulp. Its consistency may be juicy or tough; the pulp of one variety may freely release its juice, another may seem more reluctant. Taste it. It should taste both sweet and sharp. The pulp of an unripe grape tastes overly tart, while the meat of an overripe grape will lack acidity and thus taste flabby. If a good balance of sugar and acid has been reached, the grape has been picked at the right time. When the grapes are crushed, the amount and proportion of tannin is what makes the difference in the juice's zest. When too much tannin is present, the juice is astringent and puckery; if too little, the juice has a tired flavor. Tannin is quite noticeable in a grape with lower sugar content, while the same amount blends pleasantly with other elements in a sweeter grape.

The stem is the skeleton of the grape cluster and, in a mature grape, accounts for two to six percent of the total weight. California winemakers generally remove all the stems at the time of crushing. In Europe, some winemakers crush and ferment grapes with the stem, especially when a lot of tannin is desired in the finished wine.

Present in the juice of the grape are about two dozen natural fruit acids that will affect both the taste and color of the wine. The most prominent are tartaric acid and malic acid, accounting for approximately 90 percent of grape acid. Tartness of a wine is attributable to tartaric acid; a fresh, fruity taste is attributable to the presence and intensity of malic acid. The proportions and intensities of these acids vary in different varietals. Grapes from warmer climates contain more tartaric acid than those from colder regions. The characteristic taste of German wines, made from grapes grown in cooler temperatures, results from the predominance of malic acid.

A good wine grape must produce sugar (for both taste and the fermentation process) and juice. For sugar, a product of photosynthesis, the vine should have maximum exposure to sun, which is why many vineyards are terraced. The water that ends up in the pulp as juice—and in your glass as wine—is pumped by the roots from the soil. Grapes grow fairly well in many different soils, and although the deeper and more fertile soils will produce heavier crops, it will be the shallower soil that will give forth quality grapes. It is the complex soil with layers of gravel and sand that is light colored and often poor that is the best soil for most vineyards. This makes the ground penetrable and encourages the roots to grow long as they seek water and nourishment. The older the vine, the longer the roots as it seeks nourishment. Perhaps that is the secret of Romanée-Conti and Château Latour whose vines are more than thirty-five years old.

A shriveled berry indicates over-maturity—unless it is a berry that has been attacked by *Botrytis cinerea*, the "noble mold" known to the French as *pourriture noble* and to the Germans as Edelfäule. This mold gathers on the skins of certain grapes, but it does not rot them. Instead, it causes the skin to shrink and the juice to become concentrated. Loss of water increases the proportion of sugar and acid in these distinguished grapes, creating a shriveled, prunelike berry. The condition is rare, and it produces remarkable wine. The great dessert wines—the German *Trockenbeerenauslese* wines and the magnificent Château d'Yquem—are made from botrytized grapes.

The hedges are fully exposed to the sun's noon rays and the ground is shaded. The grapes will not ripen as quickly, but the rows planted in this fashion are far more suitable for mechanical harvesting in sloping terrain. This type of vineyard is more frequently seen in California.

N

W———E

S

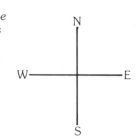

In this vineyard the sun exposure at noon will have the greatest effect on soil and leaves. The wind blows through in a westerly direction, hitting the vines. The best vineyards of Burgundy are planted in this manner, so that the soil receives maximum amount of sun and the rain does not erode the vine rows.

The harvesting of grapes is a hard and backbreaking business, a far cry from the romantic prose of Robert Louis Stevenson. I know. I've tried it. When I was new in the wine business, I decided that since I was in love with wine I should find out how it's made. I found a winery that would take my du-

16

bious services and talked a friend of a friend of a friend into hiring me as a picker.

I drove north into California wine country, eager to get started. It might have been smarter to enroll in a couple of courses at the University of California at Davis, but I felt the way Julia Child does about making pastry: *"Il faut mettre la main à la pâte!"*

My first shock was reveille: Five o'clock in the morning. This isn't the way it's done at Château Petrus! There, the owners, the Moueix family, don't allow the grapes to be picked until noon, when the morning mist has dissipated. Their theory is that the dampness of the morning air diminishes the quality of the grapes. Alas, when in California, you do as the Californians do, and at this winery it was believed that grapes should be picked when it is cool. If filled lugs or plastic pails remained unloaded at the end of a day's picking, they were left overnight in the field to be taken to the receiving area the following morning, when they were again cool.

So, half asleep, buckling my belt while stumbling through the damp fog, I joined the crew and was driven to the fields in a trailer-bed truck. We held our plastic pails tightly as the truck bounced along the ruts in the road. But I was not too sleepy to begin asking questions. Plastic pails, I learned, are the most sanitary receptacles for grapes and the easiest to maintain. Wooden boxes absorb stains from red grapes, making it possible for white grapes picked later to take on color.

When we arrived at the field, we were given clippers instead of the more usual knives; we were evidently going to be picking botrytized grapes. This is a rare condition in any vineyard, and I was excited to experience this situation my first day on the job. The foreman explained to us that we were to clip only the moldy, shriveled grapes, leaving the plump round ones intact on the vine, even if they were resting on the same cluster as the others.

As I clipped, I noticed the vineyardist holding an instrument in his hands while his assistant clipped samples of grapes from different clusters on various vines. Finally, unable to resist my curiosity (and happy to rest), I asked him what he was doing.

The vineyardist kindly explained that he was determining if the clusters were ready for picking. The moment of picking is crucial—the proper balance of sugar and acid in the grape must have been reached. He handed me the small narrow instrument, conveniently pocket-sized, and told me it was a refractometer, which registers the percentage of sugar in the grape in a range from 0 to 40 percent. Only a few drops of juice are needed for a reading,

and readings can be taken from several vines in a matter of minutes. But there was no time for further questions about sugar-acid balance—the foreman was threatening to fire me unless I joined the others and got on with it. And so, more hard endless picking. The temptation to load up the baskets with a few concealed heavier objects was strong indeed.

As the day went on, I learned more and more, as the vineyardist put up with my questions and I managed to keep in the good graces of the foreman.

After the harvest and before the new growing season, while the vines are dormant, they are pruned. The number of spurs left on each vine depends on the grape variety. Chenin Blanc and Ruby Cabernet vines are allowed not more than twelve spurs; French Colombard, fourteen; Barbera, ten. I learned that weeds can compete with vines for valuable nourishment and moisture, and thus are extremely undesirable. Vines need special protection during the morning frosts of March, April, and early May. Temperature differences exist between clean vineyards and those with weeds, and the variance can be as much as six degrees. A three- or four-degree difference between the air and the ground is enough to protect the vine's tender young buds from frost damage.

Vitis vinifera, I knew, is vulnerable to the dread phylloxera louse that destroyed millions of acres of vineyards in Europe in the late 1800s. But other American vines are resistant to it, and today in both Europe and California, the *vinifera* vines are grafted onto American rootstocks of other vine species. What about other insect pests? At the California winery where I worked, the methods to eliminate these were very ingenious, often depending on natural means rather than spraying. For instance, to combat the destructive leaf- hopper, blackberry bushes are planted. These provide refuge for wasp colonies, and the wasps, laying their eggs within the eggs of the leaf hoppers, prevent the pest from hatching. The weevil is enlisted to burrow into the germ of punctured vine seeds and prevent them from sprouting.

The nutritional needs of the vine stock are analyzed as it moves from youth to maturity by petiole analysis, examination of the stalk of the vine leaf. Soil is analyzed by core sampling, the extraction of a sample of a cross-section of earth. Soil textures may vary within a relatively small area, from fine or coarse sand to a very fertile, sandy loam. Thus different fertilizers are used, plot by plot, to match the requirements of the vine and the composition of the soil. No detail is too trivial when it comes to the

17

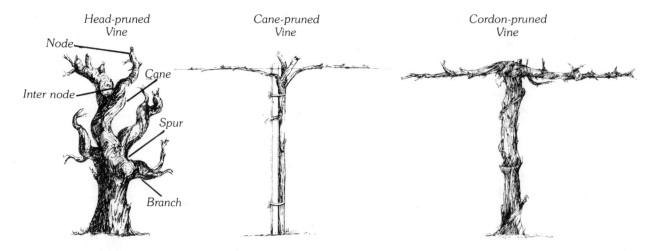

Head-pruned Vine

Node

Inter node

Cane

Spur

Branch

Cane-pruned Vine

Cordon-pruned Vine

grooming and care of the delicate vines. A healthy grapevine can thrive for eighty years or more, and with age will produce better grapes.

I was better at asking questions than at clipping grapes—which may or may not have been the reason I was promoted out of the field and into the winery. My first inside job was preparing red wine aging barrels for new wine. I loved my Yellow Submarine outfit, which was a rubber suit and huge boots that nearly spanned my waist.

My task consisted of filling barrels with a hot, alkaline solution to remove the bitter wood flavor constituents that taint wine. This alkaline solution was left in the wooden barrels for several days, and then I washed and steamed the barrels with clean water. It was a very watery job.

Most barrels show their point of origin: This can be the United States, the Côte d'Or of France, the Black Forest of Germany, Yugoslavia, even Japan. California winemakers sometimes prefer imported French oak to American oak because the air-dried French oak provides a more subtle oaky character to the wine. However, this is strictly a matter of personal taste and judgment on the part of the winemaker.

Barrels, like all other equipment in a winery, must be scrupulously cleaned and treated occasionally. The outside of the barrel is sprayed with linseed oil to protect the barrel from an insect known as the cask-borer. And it is because this insect is attracted to light that aging barrels are stored in dark areas of the winery.

Although my job was hardly glamorous, I did have a chance to see the winemaking process from start to finish, and I gained a real appreciation for the patience, skill, and attention to detail that is necessary to make fine wine.

Gondolas of grapes from the field are first weighed on platform scales, then emptied into the stemmer-crusher. In this machine the grapes are freed from their stems and lightly crushed, and all extraneous material, known to the winery staff as MOG (Material Other than Grapes), is eliminated; this can include such exotics as soda pop bottles and rocks. Sixty to seventy percent of the juice, or must, that will ultimately be obtained from the grapes is released in the crusher-stemmer; this is known as free-run juice.

More juice will be extracted by the additional pressure of the wine presses, of which there are many different types. The first press I saw in operation was a bag, or bladder, press. The must is poured into a slotted horizontal cylinder. The cylinder rotates, distributing the must around the periphery. A rubber bag along the axis of the cylinder is inflated by air pressure, forcing the must against the sides of the cylinder. The juice runs out through slots into a pan beneath the press. This juice is the press-run juice and has a higher level of tannin and other potentially undesirable extractives. Pressure is released, the cylinder is rotated again, and pressure is reapplied to improve the yield. The mass of skin, seeds, and stalks left in the press after the juice is extracted is known as pomace; it is sometimes used as fertilizer, or, in France, it is distilled and made into cheap brandy.

If white wine is being made, the pulpy free-run juice is separated from the grape skins in a drainer and transferred to a horizontal press. Rosé wine is similarly produced, except that the skins are left in contact with the juice a little longer before pressing a hint of pinkish color and flavor to the wine. Grapes for red wines, however, are fermented with their skins; the pigment in the skin provides color, the tannin provides the vitality desirable in red wines. Thus grapes for red wine are not pressed until after fermentation, and the crushed grapes are pumped directly from the trough of the crusher-stemmer into the fermentation vats.

Fermentation, the process by which grape sugar is converted to ethyl alcohol and carbon dioxide by the action of yeast, takes about 72 to 96 hours. As the must ferments, skins and pulp float to the top, forming a cap, or chapeau, which is vital to the red wine's development. The chapeau is constantly broken up and recirculated to maximize its contact with the juice.

The fermentation vats are usually of stainless steel or concrete, which, better than wood, protects the fermenting must from oxygen that would encourage the growth of undesirable microorganisms that would spoil the wine. As well as being porous, wood is difficult to insulate (important because of the delicate temperature control required) and harder to sterilize. Concrete can exhibit calcium pick-up that can affect the wine, and cracks or crevices can permit the entrance of microorganisms. At the winery where I worked, the fermenting vats were 1,000-gallon stainless steel tanks. Other wineries in the same district used a combination of oak ovals, concrete, and redwood tanks.

The fermenting must bubbles and boils as it gives off carbon dioxide. It is an impressive sight. Because of the natural affinity of grapes and wild yeasts for each other, wine has, of course, been made for centuries, but fermentation was long thought to be a spontaneous process. Not until Pasteur established, in 1854, that yeasts are the agents of fermentation—and more important, that strains of yeasts can be isolated and developed in the laboratory—was the winemaker no longer dependent solely on the wild yeast on the bloom of the grape. Today, both in Europe and California, laboratory-made yeast cultures are introduced into the must. (A notable exception here is in the making of Spanish sherry in Jerez, where the process of natural selection has so favored the flor yeast that no introduction of a cultured yeast strain is necessary.) These strains are carefully selected—no one strain works equally well in all areas, or for all varietals, and experiments with different cultures are constantly being explored.

Temperature control is crucial during fermentation. Warmth encourages the process, but once begun, fermentation itself generates heat, and at 90°F. the yeast can be injured; at 100° most will die. Fermentation is then "stuck"—a situation devastating to the winemaker. Here too varietal differences are apparent: Generally speaking, whites such as Sauvignon Blanc, French Colombard, and Chenin Blanc are far more sensitive to temperature than the lustier reds.

Larger wineries, especially those in warm climates, sometimes use high-capacity cooling systems. A common type consists of a large central mechanical refrigeration unit connected on one side of a heat exchanger; the fermenting must is pumped through the heat exchanger back to the fermenter, cooling it in the process. A small winery will likely use a smaller, portable unit with cooling coils that can be lowered into the fermenting vats.

If all goes well, fermentation will continue as long as conditions are favorable to the yeast, usually until all, or almost all, of the grape sugar is converted. The process naturally stops when, from the point of view of the yeast, too much alcohol is present—about 14 percent by volume. The sweetness of a wine can be due either to the high concentration of grape sugar in the must, as in the case of wine made from botrytized grapes, or to the stopping of fermentation by the addition of brandy. Thus, the wine retains a high sugar content, as with fortified wines like sherry and port, and the desired level of alcohol is reached by the addition of spirits.

The winemaker watches the process of fermentation carefully. One of his most important tools is a hydrometer, with which he checks the changing alcohol content in the must and the progress of the fermentation. When the process is complete, the wine—for such it is now, though new and raw—is carefully drained from under its chapeau into aging barrels such as the ones I cleaned. During the aging process, which for red wines takes normally six to thirty months (depending on the quality of the wine desired and the potential of the vintage), the wine is clarified of impurities in several stages and by several processes.

After the wine is first drained from the fermentation vat, it is allowed to stand while a major portion of the yeast cells and other fine suspended materials collect in the bottom of the container as sediment, or lees. Then the wine is drawn off, leaving the sediment behind. This first racking, as it is called, must be done carefully and quickly, since the yeast cells resting at the bottom can introduce off-flavors into the wine. Racking is repeated several times, the wine becoming clearer with each repetition. Until about a century ago, racking was traditionally done when the moon was full, the weather clear, and the wind to the north. I thought this was superstition, until I read Alexis Lichine's observation that these conditions imply high atmospheric pressures and hence a time when the wine is least active, the best time for the delicate job of racking.

In recent years, centrifuges have been used in clarifying wines. The wine is spun at high speed, and the fine solids are separated from the liquid in which they are suspended. Another modern clarification technique is filtration, in which wine is pumped under pressure through several porous layers of a filter. The pore sizes of the filtering material vary according to the wine's stage of development. Besides removing sediment, filtration also removes yeast, bacteria, and other unwanted substances, stabilizing the wine and protecting it from spoilage.

Fining, on the other hand, is a technique that has been known since the earliest days of winemaking. A precipitating agent is added to the wine: particles in the wine cling to it and then settle to the bottom, allowing the clarified wine to be drawn off. Over the years, many different fining agents have been used: egg white, isinglass, gelatine, skim milk, and ox blood. Today, the most common fining agents are a claylike mineral called bentonite and the nylon powders polyvinyl pyrrolidone and polyamide powder.

Modern consumers want wines that are free of any particles, and painstaking care to ensure crystal clear wine, especially whites, is common in California. The tartaric acid of the grape, which crystallizes in alcohol, produces a crust in the wine. This crust is disliked by the consumer, who sees it as sand or glass splinters. Most of the crust is removed by racking or cold stabilization, in which the wine is chilled to crystallize more of the excess tartrate, and then filtered to remove the precipitate.

During its first year of barrel aging, the wine in the cask evaporates somewhat, leaving an air space, or ullage, at the top of the cask. This is damaging to the wine. Certain microorganisms in the presence of air will act on the ethyl alcohol in wine, producing acetic acid—and in time, vinegar. There will, of course, always be some acetic acid in the wine you drink, but excessive exposure to air is to be avoided. Thus the casks are regularly topped off with fill wine so that there is no air space at the top of the cask.

Before the wine from the casks is to be bottled, the winemaker may choose to blend some of the different casks into a large tank, for further aging, and then the wines will undergo final fining.

Wines undergo a final polishing before they are sent to the bottling room. Most bottles used in the United States are new, for reasons of sanitation, economy, uniformity, and convenience. European wineries sometimes sanitize and reuse discarded bottles; some crushed bottles are recycled in the United States.

Wine that is pasteurized or membrane-filtered is effectively sterile when it is bottled. Bottles are either capped with screw caps or, in the case of better wines, dated and sealed with natural corks. Wines destined for the store as fine table wines are binned or stacked in the winery's cellar. After a brief period of observation, they are shipped to market.

Becoming a Wine Connoisseur

Bottles

Four thousand years ago, a group of Phoenician traders were forced to beach their ship on a sandy Syrian shore. When they made their cooking fire on the beach, they couldn't find stones in the sand to support their kettle, so they used bricks of soda ash from the ship's hold. Exhausted from their day's adventures, they fell asleep right after dinner and didn't bother to put out their fire. In the morning, they saw a glittering substance where the fire had melted the soda ash into the sand. The glittering substance was glass.

It's a good story that Pliny tells, possibly even true. We do know that the Phoenicians knew glass, and soon the Egyptians were making ornaments and jewelry of it. By about 1500 B.C., glass was first being used for containers; Egyptian ruins have yielded a harvest of small brilliantly colored jars and bottles that were used for cosmetics and perfumes.

When glass-blowing and glass-molding were developed, it became possible to create larger and more uniform glass vessels, but it took the marriage of bottle and cork in the seventeenth century to make possible aged wine as we know it today. It was found that a tightly corked bottle of wine lasted much longer than wine kept in the barrel, and that wine aged in the bottle tasted different: It had acquired a bouquet.

The first wine bottles were shaped like carafes, with crude onion or lightbulb forms. These shapes proved impractical because the bottles could not be stored on their sides. The corks dried out, allowing air to enter the bottles and spoil the wine. The answer was cylindrical bottles: Now the wine could be stored horizontally, thus keeping the corks moist and expanded.

It was Louis Pasteur who, commissioned by Napoleon III, discovered the principle involved. Although a slight amount of oxygen helped the wine to mature, too much oxygen permitted the growth of bacteria that acted on the alcohol in the wine, turning it to vinegar. Wine stored in a barrel had a greater chance of overexposure to air and of picking up a taste from the wood, whereas wine stored in a glass bottle improved with time.

Over the years, different bottle shapes have become traditional for different wines. Chianti, which is not meant to age, is presented in rounded bottles that show little development from the early carafe shapes. Bordeaux bottles still show the shoulder of the carafe shape but have straight sides that permit easy storage of the wine on its side: You'll see Cabernet Sauvignon, Sauternes, and Zinfandel in similar feminine, high-shouldered bottles, tinted green. The whites and reds of Burgundy you'll find in bottles with sloping shoulders and a very short neck. European bottles of both Bordeaux and Burgundy show an indentation in the bottom, which serves for the accumulation of sediment. The characteristic shape of German wine bottles, both Moselle and Rhine wines, is slender and tall, with an elongated neck; Moselle wine bottles are green; Rhine wine bottles are brown.

The dark green Champagne bottle, with long neck and sloping shoulders, is one of the heaviest and thickest bottles made, and for good reason. Champagne bottles must be able to withstand a tre-

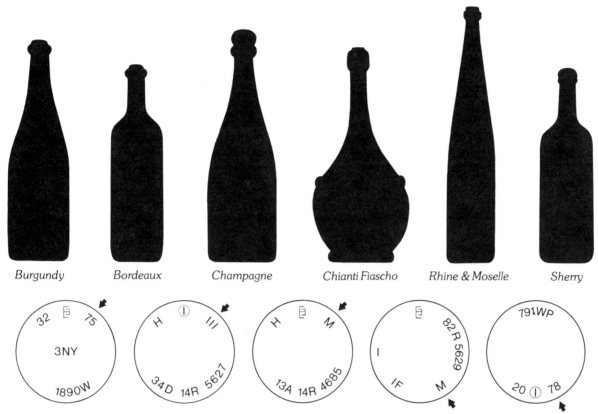

Burgundy   Bordeaux   Champagne   Chianti Fiascho   Rhine & Moselle   Sherry

mendous amount of pressure from the carbon dioxide in the wine. For the same reason, the cork is wired onto the bottle so that it will not be forced out by pressure. You'll also notice an indentation in the bottom of the bottle, which is another protection against pressure. If the bottom were flat, it could be blown out; the indentation serves to deflect the pressure.

Bottle sizes have always varied in wine-producing areas, although shapes have been legally restricted to specific areas. Starting in 1979, however, the only sizes of wine bottles permitted in the United States are the following:

3 liter size	101.6 fl. oz.	Jeroboam (four fifths)
1.5 liter size	50.8 fl. oz.	Magnum (two fifths)
1 liter size	33.9 fl. oz.	(Used in Europe)
750 millimeter size	25.4 fl. oz.	Standard (a fifth)
375 millimeter size	12.7 fl. oz.	Demi (half bottle)
187 millimeter size	6.3 fl. oz.	Split (quarter bottle)

Bottle size influences the aging capability of wine. The smaller the bottle, the faster the maturation; in a larger bottle, the wine will age more slowly and develop more subtle nuances. The traditional names of bottles, ranging from the smallest to the largest, are Demi, Magnum, Jeroboam, Rehoboam, Methuselah, Salmanazar, Balthasar, and Nebuchadnezzar. As of 1979, nothing larger than a Jeroboam is permitted into the United States.

A tip from the wine merchant: If you find yourself enjoying a wine that shows no vintage date on its label and wish to repeat the experience, check the bottom of the bottle. Bottlemakers use various codes that indicate the year the wine was made. Whether you see Roman numerals or letters of the alphabet, or both, look for the same combination on another bottle. That way, you'll know that the wine was made in the same year as the one you liked and will have the same characteristics.

Labels

There are three factors that indicate varying degrees of the quality and authenticity of a wine, and you can verify whether these are present by reading the wine label. The more clearly the three points are expressed on the label, the more obvious it is that you are getting a better wine. If they are not expressed on the label, you can be assured that you are not getting specified quality in that bottle of wine.

I could give you a number of step-by-step graphs that describe what to look for down to the tiniest detail. But common sense tells me you will not be carrying this book around with you every time you go shopping for wine. So first and foremost, learn to look for the three clues to quality, and think about them when you are making a purchase.

23

Here are the three points you should be aware of when buying wine:

1. Does the label tell you the variety of grape used to make the wine?
2. Does the label tell you where the grape was grown?
3. Does the label tell you anything about the weather conditions and the vintage year?

While wine laws in America are still undergoing certain changes, in Europe labels must give the geographic location where the wine's grape was grown. The European winemaking groups and regulating authorities have placed great emphasis on soil, believing it to be the single most important key to quality. As a result, they have established laws or *appellation contrôlées* to ensure that a producing area uses only specific grape varieties that have proven to be the best for that microclimate and soil. Government boards have been created to strictly police these laws, even to the point of determining how many gallons of grape juice is allowed to be produced per acre.

Controls have limited not only the production and quantity of wine but even the variety of grape that can be used. This is the result of hundreds of years of experience and decades of study of both climate and grape consistency. Specifically, it has been ascertained which grape will do best in a particular soil or area, and the winemaker or château owner must follow the rules of the district in producing his wine only from those grapes allowed to be grown in that district.

The European labels make it very easy for the consumer. To be assured of quality, all he has to do is look for the most precise and detailed appellation. It will not only give vintage date but information on both the geographic area and type of grape used.

The "Chevalier de Cadet" label is a *brand label*. You will notice that it does not give much information. Information omitted should immediately forewarn you as to the quality. For instance, it doesn't give you the grape variety name or the specific location where the grape comes from, and the only information you do get is the vintage date.

The label of "Mission Bell" shows a *precise appellation*. Indicated on the label are the exact location of the vineyard, its precise appellation, which informs you of the variety of grape grown, and vintage date. This label has provided the three important points you must consider when buying a wine of premium quality.

In the United States, the information required on a label is at present subject to change because of new rulings being decided upon by the Bureau of Alcohol, Tobacco, and Firearms. However, at this time, great stress is placed on the grape variety and the wine's manufacturer. The grape variety is stressed because in the United States, the grape is considered more important than the soil, and we do not as yet have regulatory laws pertaining to the method of production or to the yield per acre.

However, in order for a wine label to state that a wine was produced in Napa, Sonoma, or Mendocino counties, as of this writing, the label must state that 75 percent of the grapes came from that specific region. Very few estate-bottled wines exist in California. For a label to make this statement, the grapes must have been grown, and the wine bottled, at the same property.

A California wine label cannot, by law, use the word "produced" unless the winery has fermented and matured at least 75 percent of the wine in the bottle. "Made and bottled by" means that at least 10 percent of the wine in the bottle was vinified and aged at that particular winery. Anything that indicates that a wine was produced by someone other than the bottler would be suspect. The quality of the wine, then, would be dependent on an unnamed vintner who shipped the wine to the bottler. In order for a wine to have a vintage date, no less than 95 percent of the wine contained in that bottle must be fermented from grapes grown and harvested in the year stated.

In sum, if you can determine the precise location where the wine was produced and the weather conditions that prevailed, you will more readily be assured that you are buying a superior wine. If the label indicates the acre that produced the grapes used in the wine, you are probably buying a rare bottle.

Corks

In 1939, a number of vases dating from the third century were discovered in France. They had been stoppered with cork. Their contents was drinkable. In Java, corked bottles dating from the year A.D. 600 were found to contain excellent wine.

Cork is the perfect seal for wine, in my opinion surpassing any other material, natural or manmade. Metals corrode after a reasonably short time; plastics "breathe." Cork is the bark of *Quercus suber,* a species of oak tree that grows in the Mediterranean countries. Growing cork is a long-term investment; the bark is not stripped from a tree until it is twenty or twenty-five years old. In Portugal, the largest producer of cork, by law this harvesting can be repeated only every nine years. The properties of cork are admirably suited to the needs of wine: Cork is compressible, thus allowing perfect fit in the neck of the bottle; it is long lived without deterioration, thus able to protect bottle-aging wines for many years; it is impermeable to liquid and gases, thus protecting the wine from exposure to air, its most harmful enemy.

The cork will give you useful information about the bottle you're about to drink even before you remove it. But wait—you can't even see it yet. A corked bottle of wine is often topped with a capsule of lead or aluminum foil or plastic. Using the point of the corkscrew, neatly cut the capsule far enough below the lip of the bottle so that the wine will not come in contact with the edge of the cut capsule when it is poured.

But you're not ready to pour yet. Look at the level of the wine in the bottle. If there is more than half an inch of air space between the wine and the bottom of the cork, some of the contents has been lost after bottling by evaporation through a dry cork.

The appearance of mold or dry solids on the top of the cork does not necessarily mean that mold has reached the wine, and thus is of no consequence; however, this superficial mold should be wiped away with a damp cloth so that it will not contaminate the wine when it is poured. If mold has penetrated the cork, which fortunately rarely happens, the wine will have acquired an off-flavor and odor known, not surprisingly, as "corkiness."

Different sizes and qualities of cork are appropriately used for different qualities of wine. A lesser wine, meant to be drunk shortly after bottling, is satisfactorily stoppered with a short cork of cheaper quality. The standard cork for premium quality California wines is longer, one and three-quarter inches. Exceptional wines, which are meant to bottle-age for years, have corks at least two inches long. (But beware: Extremely long corks are sometimes evidence of nothing more than an attempt to impress you.)

Once you have withdrawn the cork, you won't allow your companions to see it if you are conducting a blind tasting, because the side of the cork in a good quality wine will be branded with the vintage, the name of the vintner, and other information that indicates the wine's origin. The branded cork in good wines is a sign of authenticity, which is important to you. But do not be alarmed if a very old vintage is stoppered with a new-appearing cork: Old wines are sometimes recorked after twenty or thirty years.

A quick sniff of the cork will tell you if the wine is faulty. If you smell moldiness or corkiness, the wine should not be served. Check the stains on the sides of the cork. Properly laid-down wine rests on its side, to keep the cork moist and thus expanded. By capillary action, wine is sucked up into the cork. If the wine has crept up further, a condition known as "weeping," either faulty corking created a tiny vertical pleat or groove in the side of the cork, providing a channel, or the larger pores of an inferior quality cork have merged through small cracks and imperfections, providing an irregular route by which the wine leaks. An imperfection on the side of the cork can be due to a bad quality cork or to faulty corking.

The shade of the color stain is a good indicator of the lightness or bigness of the wine. When a varietal wine that normally would stain the cork heavily leaves only a slight stain, this may be the result of excessive fining or filtration, which has caused the wine to lose depth and richness.

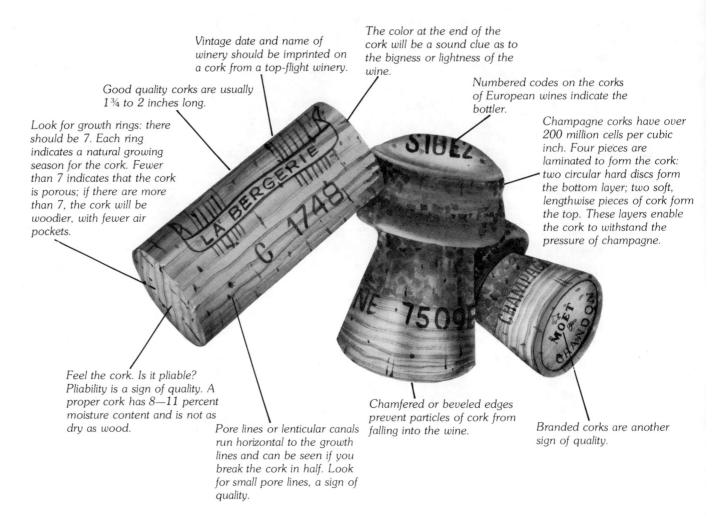

Vintage date and name of winery should be imprinted on a cork from a top-flight winery.

The color at the end of the cork will be a sound clue as to the bigness or lightness of the wine.

Good quality corks are usually 1¾ to 2 inches long.

Numbered codes on the corks of European wines indicate the bottler.

Look for growth rings: there should be 7. Each ring indicates a natural growing season for the cork. Fewer than 7 indicates that the cork is porous; if there are more than 7, the cork will be woodier, with fewer air pockets.

Champagne corks have over 200 million cells per cubic inch. Four pieces are laminated to form the cork: two circular hard discs form the bottom layer; two soft, lengthwise pieces of cork form the top. These layers enable the cork to withstand the pressure of champagne.

Feel the cork. Is it pliable? Pliability is a sign of quality. A proper cork has 8—11 percent moisture content and is not as dry as wood.

Pore lines or lenticular canals run horizontal to the growth lines and can be seen if you break the cork in half. Look for small pore lines, a sign of quality.

Chamfered or beveled edges prevent particles of cork from falling into the wine.

Branded corks are another sign of quality.

A deposit of cream of tartar crystals may be found on the bottom of the cork (if you're unsure about recognizing these crystals, rub the bottom of the cork; it will feel like sandpaper). This deposit is harmless, although the crystals in the wine are considered unattractive and may appear in old and in white wines. Its appearance indicates only that cold filtration has not been complete.

The cork material itself will show pronounced parallel lines, running from top to bottom. These are year rings, produced in the natural growth of the bark. In good years, the layers are large; in bad, dry years, the layers are thin, woodier, and with fewer air pockets. Finer cork should have seven large and fairly even layers.

When bottles are corked, the jaws of the corking machine compress the cork by about 25 percent of its diameter to permit insertion. If larger corks are used, more compression must be applied: This results in corks that lose their elasticity and become as hard as wooden pegs. If the cork has been forced into the bottle by an off-centered piston, the pressure is unequal, and the cork will be badly positioned and deformed.

To prevent cork dust and microorganisms from contaminating the wine, since the last century the ends of the cork have been hand cut. This is a thriving cottage industry in Spain and Portugal. Machines can do the job, although machine-cut corks look less elegant. To prevent bits of cork from falling into the bottle, many corks are chamfered, or beveled. The disadvantage of beveled corks is that the length of cork surface against the neck of the bottle is lessened.

Today's attitudes have raised a new problem: How to sterilize cork? The Germans were the first to solve the problem, followed by the Californians, who now also have sterilizing plants. Corks are dedusted and treated chemically. Proper moisture is restored after the cork is sterilized; to ensure further cleanliness, the corks are bagged in sterile polyethylene bags.

As the cork protects the wine, so the capsule protects the cork. (Or rather, it did; its function today is more to dress the bottle.) Originally the capsule was a wax seal meant to protect the cork from the activities of the cork-borer; today, the capsule's primary function is to protect the bottle lip from chipping, as well as provide insulation.

In the early nineteenth century, wax seals were succeeded by lead, which gave the bottles a more festive appearance and helped to hide uneven fills. The colors of the capsules became associated with the hues of their wines: green lead foil for white wines, red for Bordeaux and Burgundies, golden for Champagnes. The grades of the famous Johannisbergs of the Schloss Vollrads are indicated by the use of a variety of colors.

The holes in the tops of the capsules are made by the machine used in the process of putting the capsules on the bottles. They do serve a ventilation purpose and occur in both European and American bottles; there is no relationship between these holes and the quality of the wine.

Today, the use of plastic and aluminum foil capsules is increasing, replacing lead even for some better wines. I like the lead capsules, which are attractive and to me represent traditional quality. The connoisseur looks for the lead capsule because he's familiar with this kind of closure and its reputation. Plastic capsules still have cheap overtones and have for some time been associated with lesser-quality wines. But I'm sure similar feelings favored the wax seals when they were being replaced by lead a hundred years ago. Sentiment aside, lead capsules do present certain problems. The consumer protection movement will, I think, raise the issue of lead poisoning. And the fact is that lead doesn't protect the cork better than plastic; indeed, the plastic does a better job, ensuring proper moisture in the cork.

Good-quality wine doesn't mature fully in its barrels; only safely resting in its bottles will it achieve its fullness and greatness. Hermetically sealed and stoppered by cork, it maintains its natural color in perfect brightness, maturing and developing to perfection.

Faced with a bad cork, you can safely draw the conclusion that the winemaker didn't care enough about his wine to ensure its safety in the bottle, that the shipper didn't care enough about its transport to the retail market, that the wine merchant wasn't observant enough about what he bought and stored, and that the restaurateur didn't give enough concern to the wine he purchased to serve as a complement to his cuisine.

Enjoying the Art of Tasting

"Animal swallows; man drinks; man of wit tastes."

Tasting is a discipline based on time, a cultural endeavor that through the years brings you much pleasure, sharpening your awareness of all aspects of nature. Time is your teacher in this intuitive, yet methodical, study; you graduate only when you die.

Respect the pleasures of the table, whether fine food or fine wine. This is a sign of culture and refinement, not effete frivolity. Someone has taken painstaking care with the creation of the bottle of wine you are about to consume. You would do it—and yourself—a great injustice by rushing your appreciation of its qualities.

Your best evaluation will be made when you sample a wine several times, even at the same tasting. Expert or novice may overlook harmonies and tastes in a wine, which is like a symphony that must be listened to several times in order to capture its various nuances.

I'm reminded of a conversation I once had with Michael Broadbent, who is associated with Christie's of Great Britain and who is one of the men I most respect in the wine business. Broadbent is a wine auctioneer and author, a Master of Wine and one of the world's authentic wine authorities. He's also a fellow of enormous personal style and grace.

Along with the *crème de la crème* of European tasters, he had been invited by the prominent wine merchants of Germany to participate in a tasting of the various growths of the wines of the Médoc. Broadbent had had to rush to make his flight from London, and then risked life and limb on the Autobahn; he arrived at the tasting tired and flustered. More than twenty wines were opened, representing first, second, and third growths. The group began to sample the various wines in a blind tasting, and Broadbent immediately recognized Château Latour and Mouton-Rothschild. The other first growth in the tasting, Lafite-Rothschild, he did not identify, judging several lesser-growth wines as perhaps being the elusive Lafite.

After forty-five minutes, he again tasted the wines; this time he easily spotted the Lafite. Broadbent tells the story:

"It was absolutely amazing how the wine had, at that point, outshone the others, which had been so assertive and powerful when first tasted, with the Lafite so totally obscured. It made me acutely aware of the dangers of tasting wines of immense breeding with those of lesser quality. Second- or third-growth wines can make the immediate show. Yet, at this tasting, three-quarters of an hour later they showed a decline, while the great growths remained immensely powerful. More interestingly, the Lafite-Rothschild, which didn't at first make a distinct impression on me, fulfilled its feminine promise. It had developed with the brief aeration, showing its silkiness and perfumed beauty to perfection. It now left no doubt that it was a Lafite and a first growth."

If a professional like Broadbent can humbly declare that he can, on initial encounter, overlook a first-growth wine, imagine how important it is for the novice not to make superficial or quick assumptions.

Make your judgments after you've serenely, introspectively, and lengthily studied the wine, using your senses fully. Too often, we are swayed by a wine's initial impression or by the opinion of others. When this happens you may overlook some subtler beauties and retard your own progress in wine appreciation.

Taste in peaceful, quiet, and clean surroundings, and establish a state of stillness that will allow the wine to communicate with you. When you taste, it is as though you are meeting a wine as you would meet a new person. You're using your intellect and your senses to begin a conversation, an involvement with the wine before you. Be open to it, let yourself be affected by it. Let it tell you about itself as you look at it, smell it, taste it.

As does a new acquaintance, a wine makes its first impression through its appearance. Looking at a wine will give you clues about its age, its origin, its health, its character. The French speak of a wine's color as the "robe of experience," and a wine will be dressed appropriately to its age. Tilt the glass; hold it to the light or in front of a candle. A young red wine with three years of bottle age or less will have a purplish cast, which becomes browner with age. At three to six years of bottle age, it will begin to attain a ruby red color. At six to ten years, it will be red-brown; at ten to twenty, the wine will have developed a mahogany color, indicating mellowness and considerable maturity. Red wine over twenty years old will be tawny.

In a nobler grape variety, such as Cabernet Sauvignon or Pinot Noir, look for richness and texture in the color; in a lesser variety, such as Gamay Beaujolais, which is drunk young, look for brilliance. The wine may be clear and inviting or may present a hazy, murky appearance that is the sign of a troubled journey on which the robe has become dusty. But do not be too quick to judge: An old red wine that has been improperly decanted may show a tem-

porary cloudiness that will clear when the sediment settles in the glass.

White wines made from very ripe grapes contain more pigment than those produced from not fully ripened grapes of the same variety. Wine from grapes grown in cooler climates will generally have a greenish tint, while those from warmer regions will have a gold tinge rather than a yellow color. White wines, of course, are never pure white but range in color from greenish straw-yellow to dark amber. As you compare varieties and become familiar with their characteristic colors, you'll find shades of green-gold (Chenin Blanc and Vouvray), straw (Chardonnay and Chablis), gold (Sauvignon Blanc and Pouilly Fumé), and amber (Sauternes), topaz (late-picked Johannisberg Riesling). White wines tend to darken with age, unless they have been treated with excessive amounts of sulfur dioxide. In a young white wine, look for a gemlike brilliance of color; this indicates acidity, which will enable the wine to age and develop nuances.

A trick to verify your impression of a wine's age: Cover the glass with your hand and shake it, letting the wine froth. If the froth is white, with no pigment, the wine is old; younger wine will show color in the froth. Old or young, if the froth disappears rapidly, the wine is weak in alcohol and is light and thin.

Rosé wines, especially the better ones, have an orange tint; you'll see this particularly in rosés made from Grenache or Pinot Noir grapes. A pale, faded pink color may indicate that a combination of red and white wines was blended to produce a simulated rosé.

Holding the glass at the base of the stem, rotate it counterclockwise. As you swirl, the inner surface of the glass will become coated with a film. Within a few seconds, you will see the "teardrops" or "legs" of the wine accumulating on the sides of the glass. When plentiful and dense, they indicate a wine's richness; they are in large part created by the glycerin in wine.

About this business of swirling the glass; not only does it enable you to see the color and density of the wine more clearly, it releases the odor molecules. So learn how to do it without getting wine on your tie, or on your neighbor. Start with the glass flat on a table, holding the base of the stem. Imagine a circle smaller than the base of the glass and rotate the glass on the table in this circle. When you're used to the motion, describe the same small circle in the air. You'll soon develop a confident wrist action that will allow you to continue a conversation while sipping and swirling your glass. By the way, whether you're left-handed or right-handed, you'll find it easier to swirl your glass in a counterclockwise direction. Take a look at the water draining down your sink or bathtub. The natural motion of the whirlpool formed is counterclockwise. (Below the equator, of course, the direction is reversed, and when you drink wine in the Southern Hemisphere you will accordingly swirl clockwise.)

Your sense of smell will confirm and refine the impressions you gained by looking at the wine in your glass. The French historian Cloquet described a sixteenth-century ball at which the Duke of Anjou wiped his face with the discarded chemise of a young woman, and "from that moment on, conceived the most violent passion for her." The perfume of a fine wine can similarly excite you.

To open yourself to this possibility, you must develop an aggressive attitude toward the detection of aroma and bouquet. The first step is to recognize the difference between them, which will put you ahead of some wine experts who frequently confuse them.

Aroma is the lingering odor of the grape itself, and its strong presence indicates youth in a wine. Each variety has its own characteristic aroma; for example, you may be reminded of raw apples or melon (Chardonnay), mint (Pinot Noir), bell peppers (Cabernet Sauvignon), raspberry (Zinfandel), or some other fruit or vegetable.

Bouquet, however, is the fragrance of the wine as it matures and evolves in the bottle. Wine is a living thing, and as it ages, its chemical components and their odors are continually changing in character and proportion. The bouquet of a fine wine, properly aged, is to be enjoyed and savored. A premium wine of some years may have the bouquet of leather or tobacco (Bordeaux), toffee or caramel (Sauternes), or licorice (Barolo and Gattinara). Again, the bouquets are characteristic; as you taste different wines, you will become familiar with them and recognize them as friends.

Swirl the wine to release its volatile odor molecules. Prepare yourself to breathe properly, from the stomach, sniffing through the nostrils. Take in a gulp of air, breathe out, then take another; sniff all the way from the pit of your stomach. After the third inhalation, breathe out and quickly pass the wine across your nostrils as you inhale. The scent comes to you "as in a glass, darkly," giving you the wine's first clue about its essence. You will know immediately if the wine has faults: The off-odors of vinegar, moldiness, or sauerkraut tell you that undesirable chemical or bacterial changes have occurred in the wine.

Wait, patiently, fifteen seconds before you sniff

again. Don't fatigue your sense of smell.

The second time you smell, you should perceive additional volatile odors that were hidden from you during the first round but which are now rising quickly from the coated inner surface of the glass and filling its air space.

Allow thirty seconds to pass before you smell the wine again. Now sniff: You'll be confirming your previous impressions and storing them in your brain's remarkable memory bank. Be patient with older wines. It takes them a longer time to share their essences with you, but once they open up, they will outlast a lesser younger wine.

A way to detect a wine's bouquet if you are experiencing difficulty is to chambre the wine, a technique I call "popping" because it so quickly increases the release of the odor components and hence the potency of the scent. Hold the glass by the bottom of the bowl in one hand, covering it with the other. Now swirl. The heat of your hand releases additional odor molecules that are now concentrated in the enclosed air space. Breathe in, exhale; uncover the glass and sniff. Now the perfume will be intense.

Most of the flavor of wine comes through our sense of smell; but some of its qualities can be perceived only in the mouth, through taste and feel. Your first sip of wine should be chewed, allowing it to reach all parts of the tongue and mouth.

A strong, astringent taste that you can feel puckering and drying the roof of your mouth and the upper sides of your tongue is tannin. Found in grape skins, seeds, and stems, it is most noticeable in red wines, since they are fermented with their skins. Its quality as a preservative is what enables red wine to mature and acquire dimension; the harshness of its taste will fade as the wine ages in its bottle. Thus, the taste of tannin will be more prominent in a young red wine that in an old one. The crispness of acidity, too, is felt as well as tasted: You'll notice an astringent sensation in your cheeks. Sweetness is best perceived by the taste buds in the front of the tongue, and so you'll get your best hint of it if you lick your lips.

In your first taste, you're looking for the appropriate balance of these elements, which will be different in different wines, producing the crispness of a German Moselle or the richness of a Sauternes.

Taste again, refine and confirm your impressions. Hold the wine in the front of the mouth and gently suck in air. Swallow. Now your taste buds are stimulated and alert. You'll receive quick impressions of weight and texture, creaminess or sharpness, heaviness or lightness. You'll feel the alcohol's warmth under the tongue and on the cheeks. This will last only a second or two; then comes the mushrooming sensation in the mouth that the French call "the peacock's tail," leaving the lingering aftertaste.

None of this is a question of magic, innate ability, or scientific brilliance. Appreciation of wine is a hedonistic, sensual experience that is enhanced by continuous practice and observation. Taste the classic wines—Cabernet Sauvignon, Pinot Noir, and Riesling—and learn their characteristics. Taste with an interested friend and talk about your impressions. Make notes. Your increased experience of different wines, developing your palate and your sense memories, will give you confidence and discrimination— and a great deal of pleasure.

Storing and Serving Wine

Travel Fatigue

When imported wines arrive on the west coast of the United States via the Panama Canal, they have traveled almost halfway around the world. The journey from France to New York across the Atlantic, although shorter, is no less traumatic for delicate wines, and even wines bottled in the United States may travel hundreds or thousands of miles before they reach their destination. They may be exposed to the dangers of careless handling, extreme temperatures, changes in altitude and barometric pressure, humidity, and the physical motion of their means of transport. All these circumstances upset the balance of any fine wine, and it takes a few months for them to recover.

Knowledge of your wine merchant's buying and storing habits is important if you are a consistent and generous consumer of fine wine. Was the wine shipped direct from its place of origin? You'll be able to tell by the shipping labels. The more stops along the way, the greater the chance of improper storage or fraud.

If you are choosing between similar Montrachets, let the name of the shipper be the deciding factor: The firm of Louis Latour, for example, which has been in the wine trade for over 200 years, and the Latour name is an added guarantee that the wine has been properly stored and shipped. Shippers like Latour, Louis Jadot, and Joseph Drouhin, to mention three of the great Burgundy shippers, buy large quantities of estate-bottled wine from various Burgundy growers and store them in their own cellars. A wine kept at its point of production will generally be in its finest state throughout its life expectancy; a wine purchased and shipped on order and kept with the same merchant under ideal conditions should hold well throughout its life. If your merchant deals with reputable shippers (you'll find a list in the Appendix), he knows—and you will know—that the wine has been kept under optimum conditions since it was bottled.

Once you are satisfied that you are purchasing a first-class shipment, the responsibility for its care is yours. When you accept the merchandise, note that you have not yet inspected it—then inspect it as soon as possible and report to your merchant. No matter how carefully your wine merchant guards his stock, there is always the possibility that a bottle may be missing from the case. And regardless of how carefully the wine has been transported, there is always a chance that the case may contain a broken bottle. I regret to say that the occasional unscrupulous merchant may have sold you a case of wine that includes a bottle or two of a wine of lesser quality.

A wine that has experienced severe cold during its Atlantic crossing or while being transported over the Rockies, may have expanded, forcing the cork upward. Sample the wine. If it has not yet been damaged, recork the bottle with a good seal. The appearance of tartrate crystals at the bottom of the bottle or on the cork is also evidence of chilling. These crystals are, however, harmless and should not alarm you. If the lead foil capsule around the cork appears puffy, indicating an air pocket, the wine has been shipped under highly humid or warm conditions. If there has been wine seepage, return the bottle; if not, puncture the capsule and reseal with wax.

If the wine has been purchased with a view toward aging, taste one bottle now and keep notes of your tasting experience in a wine diary. This will give you a fairly accurate indication of how this wine will mature. Look for a balance of astringency, fruitiness, and acidity. A sherrylike off-aroma indicates that the wine was allowed to become too warm during shipping or was improperly stored; it will not recover.

Avoid transporting the wine you've bought if the temperature is over 80°F. The ideal storage temperature for all wines is 60°F.; freezing temperatures should be avoided.

If the wine has been shipped upside down in the cartons, sediment may have settled against the cork. Shake each bottle until the sediment is dislodged and is free to sink to the bottom of the bottle. Lay the wine in one area from which it will not be moved for at least two weeks to a month.

Some wines should be kept for years prior to their consumption; others can be drunk shortly after purchase. Remember that travel and warm climates hasten the bottle-aging of wine: A European wine in New York will be further along than the same vintage at home, and in the Sun Belt, it may have gained a full year of maturation.

Plan ahead. Hasty use of an important, rare vintage without preparing it for the occasion is a waste of good wine. You might take the precaution of storing a few bottles necks up at a 45-degree angle, rotating them monthly and making sure the corks are thoroughly wet (the wet cork expands and keeps air from leaking into the bottle). At this angle, the sediment will lie at the bottom rather than along the side of the bottle, and the wine will be acclimated to a position other than horizontal. Before serving, stand the bottles of a young wine upright for at least 24 hours, two weeks for a mature wine, one month for very old wine.

When is it absolutely the ideal time to drink a given wine? An important question, and one that could be answered, within a certain margin of safety, by the winemaker on his label (assuming, of course, proper handling by shipper, merchant, and consumer). Why isn't this done? Because you and I haven't demanded it. Many wine industry officials scoff at the idea of providing this information, using the excuse that "it's right when it tastes good to you." I think this is a cavalier way of treating a public whose increased enjoyment of wine we in the industry have an interest in promoting. This information would also be helpful to the retailer, especially in a supermarket or neighborhood liquor store, who sells under the handicap of lack of personal knowledge of wine and vintages.

At this stage of wine consciousness in America, probably your best bet is to follow the advice offered in *The Roar of the Greasepaint:* "Only buy claret from certified shippers." You may pay a little more, but the reassurance of consistency and quality will be worth the price.

Your Wine Cellar

One of the most fascinating aspects of my business are the personalities I meet, ranging from bankers and financiers to rock stars and actors. Some of my clients come from old-money families, others were working at a car wash until they struck it rich with a platinum record. What they all have in common is an overwhelming desire to start their own wine collection or cellar.

Perhaps for some a wine cellar is a status symbol. But most serious wine drinkers who finally decide to build a cellar do so for eminently practical reasons. It's a bother to keep running to the wine store, and the economy of buying in bulk, especially in these times of inflation, is very appealing. If you appreciate high-quality table wines, it's sensible to be able to bottle-age them in your own cellar, rather than incurring the extra cost of having them stored for you by the dealer. Having a good supply of wine ready at hand turns a family meal or impromptu gathering of friends into a special occasion. A wine collection is an attractive and interesting addition to a home as well as a focal point for an interchange among friends who enjoy tasting and evaluating wine.

Wherever the cellaring space is in your home or apartment, make sure it has a lock. My concern is not so much that you have thieving friends as with the vicissitudes of family life. We—my wife, daughter, and I—recently bought a new house, and I built a small, narrow cellar adjacent to the living room.

A housewarming party was planned, and I looked forward to the moment of showing off my carefully constructed cellar, and my wine. But my daughter, Tara, then six, had already inspected my cellar and judged it suitable for a personal playhouse, informing neither her mother nor me about her plans. When, with my friends assembled at my shoulder, I proudly opened the door, we were greeted by an array of Ken and Barbie dolls perched on top of my precious bottles. And for their nourishment, apparently, Tara had plugged her Betty Crocker toy oven into the electric system, and a variety of interestingly shaped mud pies was baking on top of a case of 1959 Château Lafite-Rothschild. There is now a lock on my cellar door. Despite my irrepressible Tara, I continue to be a firm believer in the joys of owning my own cellar.

Your wine cellar, of course, need not literally be constructed in the cellar—if so, half of Houston would be out of the running. And in fact, if your basement is also your laundry room, build carefully:

33

The vibrations of equipment like washing machines and dryers would keep your stock of wines in a constant state of travel fatigue. If you live in an earthquake-prone area, you should consider installing some type of panel or door immediately in front of your racks that will protect your precious bottles in case there is a sudden, strong tremor. Regardless of what kind of insurance coverage you may have, it will not replace a vintage that is no longer available. All that you really need is an enclosed area that can be modified to meet the fairly simple requirements of wine, which asks only to be allowed to rest quietly in a cool dark place at an even temperature. Strong light, especially sunlight, over long periods will be harmful to the color and keeping quality of your wines.

If your quarters are really cramped, don't forget your bathroom sink. You can build or buy a small cabinet, which will probably hold about three cases, to fit underneath; your wine will remain appropriately dark, damp and cool (less hot water is used in the bathroom than in the kitchen). The wine cellar, wherever it is, must be clean and protected from strong smells of paraffin, fuel oil, and grease, which would contaminate the wine.

Optimum temperature range is between 58° and 65°F., fluctuating not more than 2° in a twenty-four-hour period. An acceptable range is between 65° and 75°, fluctuating no more than 4° a day. Dangerous conditions exist if wine is stored at between 75° and 90° and the temperature fluctuates 10° in twenty-four hours. "Leakers" may be the warning signs of fluctuating temperatures, so check for discolored capsule tops. The most important factor in cellaring your wine, as with rearing a child, is consistency: No wine will stand alternating bouts of heat and cold. A steady warm temperature is better than radical changes in the environment. To keep the cork moist, your optimum humidity should be approximately 55 percent; more will not hurt your wines, but it could ruin your labels from damp and fungus.

To maintain these conditions you will probably need a cooling system. A friend who recently built a cellar prefers window air conditioning because it is economical and convenient, if the cellar is located where a unit can be (or already has been) installed. The thermostat will, of course, have to be modified. I personally prefer refrigeration, which affords more stable temperature control than does air conditioning. Some of my customers have objected that refrigeration is more expensive than air conditioning; they're wrong. Refrigeration can be run off a ¼-hp motor and a simple coil, and the equipment can be obtained at any home equipment store or through a Sears catalog. It should have the capacity to refrigerate an area of about 200 square feet, and cost no more than an air conditioner.

One disadvantage of air conditioning is that it has a tendency to draw moisture out of the air, drying out the corks and permitting air to enter the bottle; not only will this cause evaporation, the air will spoil the wine. Any bottle that shows ullage—extra air space between the level of the wine and the bottom of the cork—should be immediately consumed or used as a wine vinegar base. If air conditioning is what you have, set a bucket of water in the center of the room and place the end of a rag or towel in it. This "wick" will humidify the air. Another alternative would be to spread river bed sand or gravel on the floor and water it periodically.

Whether your cooling system is refrigeration or air conditioning, be sure to install insulation. If your cellar is in a room exposed to sun, especially if it has a southern exposure, I would recommend three inches of polyfoam. Even if power is interrupted, an insulated room will stay relatively cool for a period of time and the condition of your wine will not be affected. The temperature will go up gradually, say from 60° to 68°; it will take some time for a volume of cool wine to reach 70°, probably long enough to allow repairs and restore the system.

Bottles should always be stored horizontally to keep the corks moist. Your racks should be labeled so that it is not necessary to remove a bottle from its resting place to see what it is. Keep a cellar book, entering the name of each wine, where and when you purchased it, the name of the shipper, the vintage, when and with whom you shared it, and your comments on its taste. This sounds like a lot of work, but if you buy a substantial amount of wine, you'll find cellar notes are extremely useful.

The ideal cellar that provides a variety of stock for immediate consumption and sufficient storage for quantities of wine that you are aging requires space—about 200 square feet. This, I repeat, is the ideal and, depending on how elaborate it is, will require an investment of $5,000 to $30,000 for construction and climate control. It will have a capacity of 200 cases. You may think that's a lot. It is, but we're talking about a cellar that will serve your needs for a lifetime.

Needless to say, no matter what space you have available, the principles of good storage and a balanced variety of stock remains the same. In a small cellar, allot half your space for long-term storage of cases you are aging (keep them in their original cartons, lying on their sides) and the other half for individual bottles in pigeonhole racks.

For the larger cellar, I suggest using as well diamond-shaped bins that hold about 18 bottles, and vertical bins that hold 8 bottles in each row.

Whether you are in a position to build the ideal cellar or, through skill and imagination, have created good storage conditions for 50 to 100 bottles of wine, your buying patterns should be the same. I have developed a formula for building a wine collection that is just as practical for the young professional on a budget as it is for Mr. Rich. The difference is the amount of wine purchased, not the quality. It includes a variety of wines for immediate consumption and for aging, and has a built-in time factor. If you do it my way, the wine will see you through.

Phase I: For the first five years that you collect wine, you should buy one bottle of white wine to five bottles of Burgundian-type reds, to ten bottles of Bordeaux-type reds, to one bottle of dessert wine.

Phase II: During this next period of three years, you should buy an average of three white wines to four light reds, four Bordeaux-type reds, and two dessert wines.

Phase III: For the rest of your life, you will be adding interesting individual wines and replenishing your stock. The ratio will be two white wines, two light reds, two Bordeaux-type wines, one dessert wine. If these are good wines, they represent a sizable cash investment. Here are some tips that will help you to collect and maintain a fine wine stock.

If you are just learning about wines, buying a case of wine and following its particular life cycle is an invaluable experience. You should sample the same wine every four months if a white, and every eight months if it's a red. Record your observations and look at your notes occasionally. You will be amazed at how vividly that particular wine will begin to register in your mind. Signs that the wine is approaching its decline should prompt you to go ahead and drink it. Better you should drink your inventory with your friends than have it turn to vinegar without a party.

With your fine red wines, Bordeaux or Cabernet Sauvignons, this question arises: When will they be at their peak? With the help of a good vintage chart, here is a way of gauging the time of a wine's maturity that you'll find accurate and consistent:

If your vintage chart uses a 10-point scoring system, simply take the wine's rating and add 2 (representing the two years of barrel age), and add the sum to the vintage year. For example: You're considering a 1971 wine rated at 9 points.

$$9 + 2 = 11$$
$$1971 + 11 = 1982$$

Your wine will have reached its ideal of ripeness and maturity in 1982. If the chart you're using has a 20-point system, divide the rating by 2 before you proceed; if it's based on a 7-point top, multiply by 3.

You'll also be using your cellar for wines bought for everyday consumption. Here are some guidelines:

White wines should not be tasted until four months have elapsed from the date of bottling; that much time is necessary for reduction of the usually high initial sulfur dioxide content and for recovery from any temporary oxidation that may have occurred during the wine's preparation or bottling. (American wines, by law, must show the bottling date on the carton.)

Don't expect any improvement in generic whites, and consume white varietal wines in their first year if their price and appellation indicate an extensive use of a cheaper wine in the blend. This would apply particularly in the case of a low-priced California varietal wine.

Many white varietal wines will reach their maximum quality after their first year of age and generally don't hold up for longer than three years. Some types included in this group would be Chenin Blanc, French Colombard, Sylvaner, and others. Chardonnay, Sauvignon Blanc, and Johannisberg Riesling are white varietals from which you can expect longer life and improvement after three years.

A rule of thumb: When the white varietal wine is on the light, fresh, and fruity side with a lower alcohol content, generally it is best drunk in its first year. Heavier, higher alcohol wines (over 13 percent) may be pleasant to drink for four or five years. Not many white wines will improve after five years of total age (barrel age plus bottle age counted from the vintage date).

Rosé wines generally follow the same pattern of longevity as the white wines.

Generic wines, even if they were made with immediate consumption in mind, will benefit well from some waiting period between their bottling and date of consumption. One year is the most likely period, with an upper limit of three years.

Standard varietal wines improve remarkably with bottle age in their first year. During the second and third year, however, there is a slowing down in the maturation process. The life span for this type of wine is usually five years or less. If you've bought a case, it might be wise to observe the wine's progress, or decline, after the first year in the bottle. The wine should be good for about three to four years.

Although you should sample the wines you are aging from time to time, don't try to drink your first growths or other exceptionally fine wines before their time. A customer once asked me why Bordeaux wines couldn't be aged faster, at 65° or 70°F., thus greatly reducing his investment in maturing bottles of Margaux. The answer is simple—he could. He could keep his wines at 70° without ruining them. But, as with a beautiful girl who chews gum in public, something will be lost. The proper temperature of 58° means longer aging; it also means liquid perfection. Only when wine is properly stored, no matter how long the aging takes, will a great wine show the benefits of its breeding that make it a special experience.

If you are going to pay the current rate for a bottle of Margaux or another fine wine, don't deprive yourself of the ultimate of what it can offer you. Your perfect cellar and your ideal storage conditions make the investment worthwhile.

Decanting

One of the most frequently asked questions I receive is: "When should I decant my wine?" Decanting simply means pouring liquid from one container into another. Decanting wine has two purposes: to separate the clear wine from the sediment in the wine bottle and to allow the wine to "breathe," or gain exposure to air.

In some wine circles, a discussion about the "breathing controversy" is always heated and much like debating with a member of the Flat Earth Society: No matter what arguments you use to convince him, he will stubbornly remain convinced of the correctness of his own viewpoint. So it is with wine decanting and proponents for and against. From my vantage point, however, the question of whether to decant or not to decant depends on what you want to gain from the wine.

Although decanting generally improves the wine, it is unnecessary to decant wines under five years of age. As for older wines, I believe it won't hurt them. I've had Bordeaux that was over one hundred years of age that, despite two to three hours of airing, didn't fade at all. I've had younger wines from lesser vintages that when opened and poured, faded immediately. This same experience has also occurred with wines that were improperly stored.

Some people are purists about sediment, abhoring any of it in their wine, becoming absolutely livid if you pour past the area where sediment gathers in the bottle.

Then, there is the down-to-the-dregs school of thought, made up of funnel collectors who filter all of the wine, even catching the dregs to save every last drop of their precious wine.

The hedonist is the strangest of the lot, swallowing his wine down to its last drop, dregs and all, justifying his avarice by noting that the nuances of wine are lost if you don't drink every drop.

It all comes down to various taste preferences and the differences in personalities. There are some individuals who like to skyrocket on a wine's power and impact, while others prefer to be more patient, cool, and analytical, enjoying the "awakening" of the wine after it has had some air.

Remember that those little odor molecules become airborne at different temperatures. So a wine that gives you a "pow" feeling when first opened may be deader than a doornail within ten minutes. Conversely, a slower-opening wine may be a veritable rose in the same amount of time.

Regardless of your school of thought, here are some hard and fast rules to remember when tasting wine:

1. No Bordeaux or Cabernet Sauvignon should be tasted before it is five years of age.
2. Any wine under five years of bottle age doesn't have to be decanted. Just open and pour.
3. "Wine is a living thing" isn't just a cliché; it's the truth. When the bottle is opened, the wine absorbs oxygen from the air. Oxidation activates the development of a wine's aroma and bouquet.
4. White and rosé wine should be uncorked just before you serve it. These wines have a delicate fruity fragrance that will lose freshness when overly exposed to air.
5. Rosé, Champagne, or white table wines should not be served at room temperature. The refreshing, fruity qualities of these light wines are enhanced by being slightly—not overly—chilled.

Most wines consumed by wine buffs are already six, seven, or eight years of age. So the date of bottling is a mayor key as to whether you are going to decant or not.

If a wine is young, it is all snap, crackle, and pop. When you smell it, the wine explodes in your face. Give it a chance to breathe a few hours, and you may discover that the former refreshing liquid has become tight, raw, and full of astringency.

A premium wine that is more than five years of

age still explodes, but it holds something in reserve. There should be a dimension of sophistication that wasn't apparent earlier.

Wine has a cycle of life just like a person. So when a wine gets older, perhaps twenty or thirty years of age, you respect its maturity, giving it less time to breathe but enough to be great in its last run.

Ordinary wines are usually consumed before any deposit forms in the bottle, and standard stabilized wines may not form deposit for as long as five years. In high-quality red wines, however, it is inevitable that aging in the bottle for ten, twenty, or thirty years will cause the wine to deposit the same components it did when in the cask.

Now here are my suggestions for decanting the wine from the crust, or sediment:

Before you taste the wine, place it in an upright position and leave it this way for 48 hours to two weeks, depending upon the age and type of wine. Due to the law of gravity, most of the deposit will fall to the bottom of the bottle without any strain on your part. Just before tasting, decant the wine, leaving the crust in the bottle.

I'm not too keen on doing this ritual with filtering paper on top of the funnel. The wine, which has been sealed for many years, now is suddenly exposed to rapid oxidation. For that reason, the delicate bouquet components should be nurtured as much as possible. The filter paper, I believe, increases the chance that these bouquet components will be lost or diminished. Even when you pour the wine into the decanter, do it gently.

Baron Philippe de Rothschild, who in a startling innovation has set up a special decanting room at Mouton-Rothschild, gave me a tip on his favorite filtering method which I'd like to share with you. He has tried all kinds of filters and believes the cheapest material, nylon, is most adequate and works perfectly well. It is reusable and tasteless, the perfect strainer. Nylon can be used repeatedly as long as you rinse it in cold water immediately after each use.

It is difficult to serve from any bottle larger than a magnum, so I prefer to syphon the wine into a smaller container. Insert a narrow, flexible plastic tube into the larger bottle. You suck on one end of the tube to start the syphoning action. Once the wine is drawn into the tube, insert it into the decanter, which must be at a level lower than the bottle. This syphoning process allows the wine to be decanted without disturbing any sediment.

When a tasting is done on short notice, with no time for this elaborate process, the use of a wine cradle is fine. Take the wine from its place on the rack—still in a horizontal position—and without rolling or changing its angle, place it on the cradle.

Most of your ordinary wine won't be decanted and, in a wine that is less than five years of age, the appearance of sediment will indicate that something is wrong. But with expensive old wines or with wines that are unfiltered or unfined, decanting is a procedure that you should adopt for maximum pleasure.

Of particular importance, when it comes to decanting, is the handling of the red Médoc wines, which are not only distinctive, delicate, and highly tannic but also expensive.

Serving Médoc wines doesn't always follow strict rules. Everything depends on the year. A recent vintage will demand special attention; a venerable bottle, infinite care.

Alberic Michaut, president of the Hôtel Mutualité de France, and Jean Chauché, administrator of the Paris Sommeliers, both wrote to me on the delicate handling of the Médoc wines, which of course are not for everyday drinking but are instead reserved for special occasions.

Messrs. Michaut and Chauché wrote:

"The art of serving the Médoc wines doesn't follow strict rules. Everything depends on the date. A recent year always demands certain attention: a venerable bottle infinite care.

"If you want to open a bottle of Médoc on the spur of the moment, take a light and recent year. It must be rather cool. When selecting a great bottle, delicately remove it from the cellar and lay it to rest on its basket for some twenty hours. Then allow it to become acclimated to the room's temperature. One hour before serving it, the sediments will have stabilized. Now you can decant the wine into a glass carafe that is completely dry. This operation will eliminate the dregs and allow a slight aeration to develop the bouquet. The candle's light allows you to observe, through the transparency, the wine's luster, and to stop the decanting at the precise moment the dregs pass through the carafe.

"There is the Médocaine habit of fixing a silver chain to the cap in the neck of the carafe so that you can read the wine's title, stamped on the cap.

"And now we're ready to pour the contents of the carafe into the glass. Ah, how many great wines are spoiled by the wrong glasses. Ban from your table, at least in front of a noble wine, containers made out of crystal cut and colored in designs inspired by science fiction. For the Médoc wine, we recommend the tulip shape that promotes the development of the bouquet and keeps it in the impalpable walls.

"Now your glass is served. You hold it by the stem so that the light can freely play with the wine. You swirl your glass, allowing the precious ruby-colored liquid to dance, the color, more and more amber, as the wine ages. The legs or tears formed in the glass wall will indicate the fullness and body of the wine. And then you taste the developed bouquet, floral and fruity in a young wine, spiritual and powerful in an old wine.

"Médoc wines can remind you of truffles, violets, basil, and a lot of other delightful things. You find that the gustatory sensation of the Médoc wine is prolonged in your mouth, first full and tender, then tannic and perfumed, finally leaving in the palate a persistent and final impression."

The finest pleasure that anyone can have, no matter what his position or wealth, is a good conversation, which wine promotes. The fun part of drinking a great wine is the pleasure of talking about it. You can discuss anecdotes about the château of origin, the year or land in which it was cultivated, or give a detached scientific analysis of the wine, or lapse into poetic rapture. Whatever your temperament or inclination, the wine will reward your thoughtfulness and care with an even greater reward—a sublime gustatory experience.

Maintaining the wine at a stable, proper temperature is important after you've decanted wine. Some people decant a wine, then put it in a spot where it is either too warm or cold, making the wine "dumb" or lacking bouquet.

Keep in mind that the typical American room temperature is a good deal warmer than in Europe, where rooms are kept at colder temperatures. If you decant the wine and turn your thermostat to 80°F., you will be cooking the wine as if it were in a hot pot and the result will be "dumb" bouquet without any pizzazz. This is true for most wines, whether red or white, so keep the decanted wine at a stable 62°F. to ensure that it maintains its quality.

Temperature

My recommendations about temperature are quite simple. White wine should be served a few degrees lower than room temperature, and in hot weather the full-bodied whites can even be chilled to the point where they frost the glass. Red wines should be served at room temperature, and it will take about three hours to bring them up from cellar temperature. Remember, at extremely warm temperatures, the perfume of the finer qualities of a wine will disappear and the bouquet and aroma will become indistinguishable.

Simple enough. But I assure you that there are fashions in wine circles as anywhere else, and its

about time for temperature to become the subject of hot debate. You'll be seeing a lot of complex stuff in wine columns, so you might as well be aware of the various theories.

There's no question that temperature affects your perception of the flavor of a glass of wine. Odor molecules, carried in the volatile alcohols of wine, must be released into the air before you can sense them. As wine becomes warmer, the odor molecules diffuse from the surface of the wine to the air space in the glass, where the converging sides of the glass force them to accumulate. The different alcohols evaporate at different rates; as the wine continues to warm, more and different components will be released. Old-time winemakers open the bottle at cellar temperature, warming the wine in the glass with the hands, following its awakening with frequent sniffings.

Now for the Martin Ray position on Cabernets. Ray, the late and controversial owner of Villa Mt. Eden winery in Napa Valley, was a fellow of colorful and decisive personality whose wines were either stupendous or terrible. He believed that a great unblended Cabernet Sauvignon must, because of its high tannin content, be given an aging of ten years. One hundred percent Cabernets should be warmed to 80°F., a temperature not uncommonly warm on the tongue. Cabernets treated in this manner, he believed, would smooth out, glorifying their tannic qualities and releasing their magnificent flavor. Similarly, great Pinot Noirs, he advised, should be "chambred" (literally, brought to room, or *chambre,* temperature) in a warm place to about 75°F., long before serving.

Ray's tutor was Paul Masson, who presented this theory to the young Ray by demonstration. According to Ray: "It was most impressive. He decanted two bottles of Cabernet Sauvignon into two pitchers, set one in a pan of very warm water and had me stir it with a silver spoon as it warmed. I tested the temperature with a thermometer and tasted the wine frequently. The other wine was left unwarmed. The difference was astonishing. As the wine warmed, it began to improve rapidly, becoming delightfully smooth, its fragrancy expanding. Since that time, I have demonstrated this old-world technique to guests here at Mt. Eden, and astonished them. Always, the ideal temperature is proclaimed by one and all to be somewhere around 80°F. Naturally, young Cabernet Sauvignon wines demand more warming than well-aged ones. But even those of venerable years reach perfection only when amply warmed."

The question of temperature is made more

complex by M. C. Folonneau, who pointed out the effect of other elements in the environment on tasting: light, sound, and interfering smells. Distracting odors and sounds will distort our perception; the reduced light on a cloudy day will produce more agreeable odors in both white and red wines. If optimum environmental conditions are met, Folonneau prefers reds at 78.8° to 80.6°F., whites at 57.2° to 59°.

Maynard A. Amerine and Edward B. Roessler of the University of California presented their views on temperature in *Wines: Their Sensory Evaluation.* They point out that wines retain carbon dioxide at lower temperatures, which is positive for Champagne and other sparkling wines. Lower temperatures also reduce the volatility of sulfur dioxide, so its taste in white wines will be less noticeable if the wine is colder.

Amerine and Roessler report that temperature affects the palate as well as the wine; this may be a conditioned response, but it nonetheless influences the tasting experience. At higher temperatures, about 95°, we are more sensitive to sweetness and sourness; at lower temperatures, bitterness becomes more apparent. That is why, at higher temperatures, white and dessert wines will seem more cloying and sweet, and why red wine if tasted cold will taste bitter. Their serving recommendations: Red table wines should be served at 68°. White wines should be served at 60°. Sparking wines should be served at 55°. Dessert wines should be served at 65°—at higher temperatures, they will appear too alcoholic and give the taster a heady feeling.

The fashion of tomorrow may be Champagne on the rocks because someone read somewhere that the carbon dioxide bubbles are retained at lower temperatures and got carried away. Drop in an ice cube; you'll keep the bubbles but lose the bouquet—anything can be carried to extreme.

Accessories

Having purchased your first case of wine or started your personal cellar, you might be inclined to buy every gadget proposed to you by a clever salesman. What you will really need are corkscrews, port tongs, a funnel, decanters, and glasses.

The corkscrew is an invention of the seventeenth century. It probably originated in the *worm* or the *endless screw,* either single or double, which was used to clean firearms. At first the tool was encased in a gold barrel and was nicknamed "the little engine." How it evolved from being a muzzle-cleaner to a handy household tool isn't exactly known, but by the beginning of the eighteenth century, it was a necessity in every middle-class household where wine was consumed.

All devices for extracting cork, whether traditional or modern, are constructed of a metal spiral affixed to a handle. Most important in shopping for your corkscrew is the worm, or screw, itself. The best tip should be blunt, not pointed, and have an edge that will bite into the cork, but these are hard to come by. Most corkscrews have sharp, pointed tips. Also, a good corkscrew will be fashioned so that the tip of the worm, or *mèche,* is not centered in the spiral.

For fine wines with longer-than-average corks, look for a spiral that is between 2¼ and 2¾ inches in length—long enough to get a good grip throughout all of the cork. The best corkscrew will be tapered into an open spiral that has rounded rather than sharp edges that could shred the cork as you're pulling it out of the bottle.

My first recommendation in the way of corkscrews is the *Ah-so* brand, which has blades that compress inside the bottle neck so you can easily extract the cork.

Other types of corkscrew that are available include the *Waiter's single lever,* which is a portable, fold-up tool. Its basic flaw is that it has a solid-core worm called a *gimlet,* which is not as efficient as the open spiral.

Another corkscrew is the *bell cap.* With this type, you twist the worm down into the cork, and the cork will raise up into the bell as you continue to turn the handle. To remove the cork from the bottle, first you rock the handle, then give a pull to release the cork.

A design that gives fine leverage and is easy for the ladies to use is the *twin lever opener.* Once the worm is inserted down into the cork, you simply push down on the two arms, or wings, to draw up the cork.

The *Zig-Zag* originated in France and derives its name from a latticelike gear-reduction system that demands less hand-and-arm leverage than would be required to open a pop-top can. The worm of this type is a long hollow-center helix of the finest design, and even the stubbornest cork can be removed without exerting even the slightest bit of strain.

The *Maxram* corkscrew has a double steel worm that allows both spirals to sink firmly into the cork and turn as a single unit in the bottle neck while you're gently withdrawing the cork.

The *bistro* or *French wooden corkscrew* has a spiral gear and a hollow-core worm. The worm is

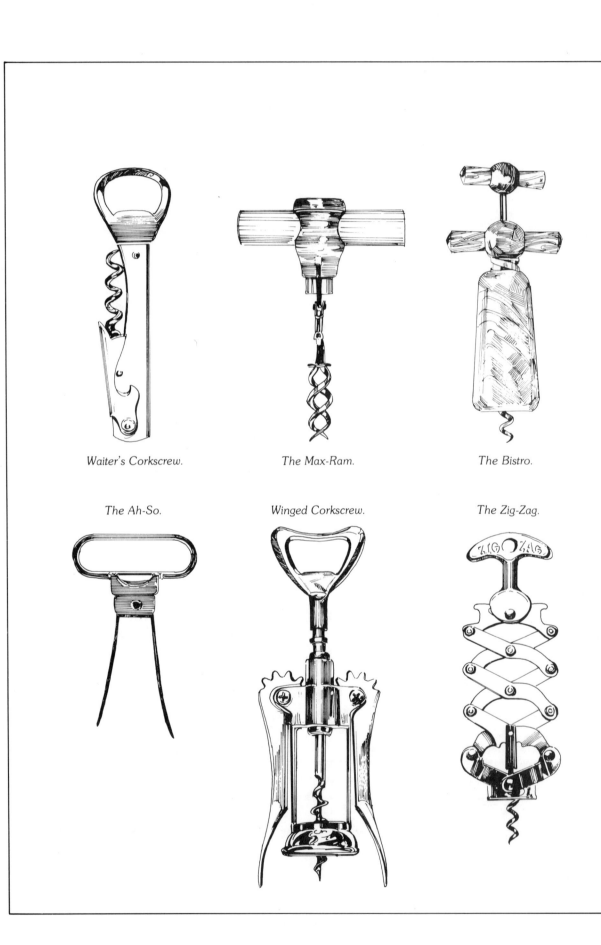

Waiter's Corkscrew.

The Max-Ram.

The Bistro.

The Ah-So.

Winged Corkscrew.

The Zig-Zag.

worked into the cork with the top crossbar and unscrewed with the lower one.

Special corkscrews have been designed for particular needs. For example, there is an old corkscrew called *Apollonaris,* which was used for the tall stoneware containers of German mineral water. Another German type, the *Gambrinus,* was made for beer and was named for the mythical Flemish king who supposedly invented the foamy liquid. The *Champagne tap* was designed to pierce the cork and supply small quantities of the bubbly wine to recuperating invalids. The latter was a uniquely French invention.

Another cork-extractor, peculiar to Champagne, is the *Champagne pliers or tweezers,* a blunt-toothed instrument designed for the purpose. When tweezers are used, the procedure should be the following:

1. Make sure that a glass is handy just in case you botch the extraction and wine spurts out of the bottle.
2. Remove the gold foil from the neck and cut or twist off the wire muzzle.
3. Stand the bottle on a flat surface; then grip its neck with the left hand, leaving the forefinger free to curl itself over the cork to hold it down firmly.
4. Hold the tweezers in the right hand as you grip the cork with them and ease it upwards.
5. As soon as the pressure of the gas on the bottom of the cork is felt by the left forefinger, put down the tweezers and gradually change the position of the left hand so that the cork pressure is taken by the palm and all five fingers, pointing downward, are gripping the bottle neck.
6. Finally, tilt the bottle to the side, in a 45° angle away from you—but not toward someone else—and, while the palm of the left hand takes the pressure, gently ease the cork out with the thumb and forefinger of the right hand.

The *cork lift* or *needle cork-extractor* operates by means of air pumped through a hollow needle. If all goes well, air pressure builds up and pushes the cork out of the bottle. If the cork doesn't rise after pumping, it may be stuck. If so, go back to the familiar corkscrew you normally use to finish the job. Pumps have been known to explode weak bottles. At the very least, wrap a towel tightly around the bottle to prevent flying bits of shattered glass in the event of a mishap.

Should any cork accidentally slip into the bottle,

use a *cork rescuer.* This wooden-handled three-pronged utensil contracts and expands inside the bottle, allowing you to fish out the cork.

While *port tongs* are difficult to obtain, the search is worth it. The purpose of *port tongs* is to remove the neck of the bottle where the old cork is lodged. The tongs are first heated to glowing red and are then positioned to grip the neck of the bottle just under the lip. Twist the tong a quarter-turn and grip for thirty seconds longer. Then remove them and use a wet rag to cool down the ring burned in by the tongs. The neck will break cleanly at the ring and will separate from the bottle.

A flamboyant way of removing old corks is to chop the neck of the bottle off. This is done as follows: First, insert a corkscrew into the cork and wrap a cloth around the bottle for safety's sake. Then, with the back of a large knife, give a sharp upward blow below the ridge at the mouth of the bottle. It will result in a clean break and allow the cork and top of the bottle to be removed together.

You may need to recork a fine wine from time to time, and you'll need a recorker. This handy tool is available for about $5 and up at almost any wine hobby shop or better wine store. Here are some guidelines about recorking:

1. Any bottle of wine more than twenty-five years of age must be recorked.
2. You will need sealing wax, corks, and glass marbles—all of which, except for the marbles, is available at any winemaking supply store.
3. You simply remove the old cork and, if the level has dropped more than a half-inch, put in the necessary number of marbles to bring the fill back up, and recork.
4. If you open the bottle and the wine smells oxidized, don't bother going any further. When a wine is dead, it's dead. Recorking certainly won't restore it to life.
5. Once you have decided that the wine is sound, insert the new cork and seal the top with wax. Now you have recorked your wine.

For those of you who are interested in collections either for display in your cellar or for financial investment, here are a few items that you may consider purchasing.

The shape and style of drinking glassware is not only varied, but a collection of several pieces would be a worthwhile investment, especially if you find antique opaque-white twist stems, or drawn trumpet liqueur glasses (known as mercurials), or facet-cut glasses with gilded decorations. Don't plan on using them, however. Consider them a precious investment.

The clear, lustrous, and heavy lead glass that set England ahead of the Continent in the manufacture of high-quality crystal was developed because The Worshipful Company of Glass Sellers was dissatisfied with the previous kinds of materials used to make glass, namely sand, potash, and soda lime. An early example of this kind of glassware would be extremely valuable and a sound investment.

Other items of mechanical art that you should consider investing in would be antique decanters, bottles, coasters, wine labels, bin labels, silver and gold funnels, punch bowl and ladle, toddy lifters, mortar and pestle, wine coolers, and corkscrews.

One parting word of caution: Make sure that you authenticate and obtain verification before you purchase any antique. Don't buy imitations. The genuine articles will not only give you practical and visual enjoyment but will increase in value and prove to be a sound investment.

Wine
at the
Top

Classifications: 1824, 1827, 1855 . . . ?

There are glamour lists for stamp collectors, coin devotees, and every other hobbyist. Wine buffs are no exception. Their citadels of excellence, the most desirable and expensive, are those venerable sixty-one wines listed as the *crème de la crème* of the Médoc: The classified growths.

The classification of what was the best in Bordeaux wines was started a number of times, historically recorded as early as 1775, but did not become fossilized until 1855, when the Exposition Universelle de Paris, the World's Fair of the day, was celebrated.

Bordeaux brokers and shippers had already set up an informal system of ranking based on the quality of the wines, and a first classification had already been made in 1824, and another in 1827.

Here are the wines that rose to the top of the classification in 1824, 1827, and 1855:

1824

First Growths

Château Margaux, Margaux
Château Laffite, Pauillac
Château Latour, St.-Lambert

Second Growths

Brane-Mouton, Pauillac
Lascombes, Margaux
Durfort-(Viviens), Margaux
Gorse, Cantenac
Léoville, St.-Julien
Gruaud-La Rose, St.-Julien

Third Growths

Pichon-Longueville, St. Lambert
Cos-d'Estournel, St.-Estèphe
Bergeron (Ducru), St.-Julien

1827

First Growths

Château Margaux, Margaux
Château Laffite, Pauillac
Château Latour, St.-Lambert

Second Growths

Brane-Mouton, Pauillac
Rauzan, Margaux
Léoville, St.-Julien
Gruaud-La Rose, St.-Julien

Third Growths

Gorse, Cantenac
Pichon-Longueville, Pauillac
Cos-d'Estournel, St.-Estèphe

1855

First Growths

Château Laffite, Pauillac
Château Margaux, Margaux
Château Latour, Pauillac
Château Haut-Brion, Pessac

Second Growths

Château Mouton-Rothschild, Pauillac
Château Rausan-Ségla, Margaux
Château Rauzan-Gassies, Margaux
Château Léoville-Las-Cases, St.-Julien
Château Léoville-Poyferré, St.-Julien
Château Léoville-Barton, St.-Julien
Château Durfort-Vivens, Margaux
Château Gruaud-Larose, St.-Julien
Château Lascombes, Margaux
Château Brane-Cantenac, Cantenac-Margaux
Château Pichon-Longueville, Pauillac
Château Pichon-Longueville-Lalande, Pauillac
Château Ducru-Beaucaillou, St.-Julien
Château Cos-d'Estournel, St.-Estèphe
Château Montrose, St.-Estèphe

Third Growths

Château Kirwan, Cantenac-Margaux
Château d'Issan, Cantenac-Margaux
Château Lagrange, St.-Julien

Brane-Arbonet (Cabarrur), St.-Julien
Pontet-Langlois (Bartero), St.-Julien
Kirwan, Cantenac
Le Chateaude Candale, Cantenac
Malescot-Pierlot, Margaux
Loyac, Margaux

Calon, St.-Estèphe
Lascombes, Margaux
Bergeron, St.-Julien
Brane-Arbonet, St.-Julien
Pontet-Langlois, St.-Julien

Château Langoa, St.-Julien
Château Giscours, Labarde-Margaux
Château Malescot-St.-Exupéry, Margaux
Château Cantenac-Brown, Cantenac-Margaux
Château Boyd-Cantenac, Contenac-Margaux
Château Palmer, Cantenac-Margaux
Château La Lagune, Ludon
Château Desmirail, Margaux
Château Calon-Ségur, St.-Estèphe
Château Ferrière, Margaux
Château Marquis-d'Alesme-Becker, Margaux

Fourth Growths

Giscours, Labarde
St.-Pierre, St.-Julien
Duluc, St.-Julien
Mondavit (Milon), Pauillac
Canet (Pontet), Pauillac
Dinac, St.-Guirons, Pauillac
Lacolonie, Margaux
Ferrière, Margaux
Tronqueoy, St.-Estèphe
Ducasse, Pauillac
Poujet, Cantenac
Determe, Cantenac
Boyd, Cantenac

Fourth Growths

Kirwan, Cantenac
Le Château de Candale, Cantenac
Giscours, Labarde
St.-Pierre, St.-Julien
Duluc, St.-Julien
Durfort, Margaux
Malescot, Margaux
Loyac, Margaux
Mondavit (Milon), Pauillac
Canet, Pauillac
Dinac, St.-Guirons, Pauillac
Lacolonie, Margaux
Ferrière, Margaux
Tronqueoy, St.-Estèphe
Ducasse, Pauillac
Poujet, Cantenac
Determe, Cantenac
Boyd, Cantenac

Fourth Growths

Château St.-Pierre, St.-Julien
Château Talbot, St.-Julien
Château Branaire-Ducru, St.-Julien
Château Duhart-Milon, Pauillac
Château Pouget, Cantenac-Margaux
Château La Tour-Carnet, St.-Laurent
Château Lafon-Rochet, St.-Estèphe
Château Beychevelle, St.-Julien
Château Prieuré-Lichine, Cantenac-Margaux
Château Marquis-de-Terme, Margaux

The 1824 and 1827 classifications did not go to a fifth level. Only in 1855 were fifth growths classified:

Château Pontet-Canet, Pauillac
Château Batailley, Pauillac
Château Haut-Batailley, Pauillac
Château Grand-Puy-Lacoste, Pauillac
Château Grand-Puy-Ducasse, Pauillac
Château Lynch-Bages, Pauillac
Château Lynch-Moussas, Pauillac
Château Dauzac, Labarde
Château Mouton d'Armailhacq, Pauillac
    (in 1956, became Château Mouton-Baron Philippe; in
    1979 it was renamed Mouton-Baronne Pauline)
Château du Tertre, Arsac
Château Haut-Bages-Libéral, Pauillac
Château Pédesclaux, Pauillac
Château Belgrave, Saint-Laurent
Château Camensac, Saint-Laurent
Château Cos Labory, Saint-Estèphe
Château Clerc-Milon-Mondon, Pauillac
Château Croizet-Bages, Pauillac
Château Cantemerle, Macau

As can be seen, certain vineyards do always rise to the top as was the case with Châteaux Margaux, Lafite, and Latour, all three of which were at the head of the class in all rankings. You may notice that in the 1824 and 1827 classifications only the first growths are given the honor of a "Château" prefix. But what is meant by the two f's in Laffite? It has nothing to do with the Rue Lafitte in Paris where the Rothschild Bank is located. Actually, the name is de-rived from the Médocain word, *lahite,* which is a cor-ruption of *la hauteur* (the height), but the changes in spelling have no concrete explanation.

As happens with all things, including vineyards, transitions have occurred through the years altering the original list. Some châteaux have vanished in-cluding Gorse, Brane-Arbonet, and Loyac, while others have changed names including Brane-Mou-ton, now Mouton-Rothschild; Pontet-Langlois, now Langoa; Duluc, now Branaire-Ducru; Dinac, now Grand-Puy-Lacoste; and Determe, now Marquis-de-Terme.

Prices of the first, second, third, and fourth *crus* did not fluctuate within the three years between the first two classifications, and a difference of only three hundred francs was the normal average between each *cru.*

The 1824 and 1827 classifications are indeed interesting—more so because of the number of wines that were left out of the groupings. Only 32 and 34 respectively, were included in the first classi-fications—rather small numbers when compared to the 58 wines of the 1855 classification.

Some châteaux like Dugnon, also known as Dugnon-Talbot, no longer exist. Some wines, such as Durfort, the second wine of Château Margaux, are now rarely sold to the trade. Others have been

45

split in two parts as in the case of Batailley, now known as Batailley and Haut-Batailley.

The 1855 classification's importance is not derived from the fact that the event was so well thought out or that it was so important to trade insiders. In fact, it took the manager of Château Latour an entire year to inform his boss that the wine had received a top ranking. What it did require, however, was the prestige and importance of the Exposition Universelle de Paris and the power and drive of a leader like Napoleon III to make the ranking more public and permanent in nature. It was he who insisted that the city fathers of Bordeaux provide a list of the best vineyards to mark that auspicious moment in his reign. Napoleon's directive was not met with overwhelming enthusiasm by those concerned. It was a hot potato. The Chamber of Commerce turned to the brokers of the Bordeaux Stock Exchange to make the choices since they had been the creators of the previous, more informal classifications. They were the most logical choice since they were the ones who negotiated between the owner and shipper and were familiar with Bordeaux exchange procedures and wines being traded and sold.

Some châteaux were choosing to withhold their casks for sale, allowing the wines to age an additional year so that they could move up in classification and eventually be sold at a higher price. But this matter of the 1855 classification was, in effect, going to freeze positions, and it was a distinct tactical problem for the parties involved to agree on the event's outcome.

In order that no Chamber member be accused of prejudice, it was decided to present the wines in an order fondé sur le temps et sur l'expérience, which translates to "based on time and experience." Clearly no personal bias or injection of personal taste was to prevail. Judgments were to be based on the past performance of each château, not only in the quality of wine produced but in the prices the product had fetched in the marketplace.

The special commission of members of the Chamber of Commerce and the Bordeaux Syndicate of Brokers met on April 18, 1855. This meeting was fairly official since the brokers were appointed through the Chamber by governmental decree.

As with most human-directed functions, some petty jealousies and rivalries existed. Questions still arise over the omission of the districts of St.-Émilion and Pomerol. Was it because the wines from these areas had descended from their former popularity of the Middle Ages, or was it that the Bordeaux Syndicate of Brokers was interested solely in promoting the wines they knew were top-sellers in the international wine market?

Obviously, Château Haut Brion of Graves, a powerhouse on the market, couldn't be ignored. But St.-Émilion and Pomerol, separated from the center of Bordeaux trade by the Dordogne and Garonne rivers, were as distant as the moon to the Bordelais, and scant attention was paid to the wines of those areas. On a nineteenth-century shipper's wine list, wines such as Cheval Blanc, Figeac, Pape Clement or La Mission-Haut-Brion were not considered worthy of even a third- or fourth-growth rating.

Whatever the reasons for the omission, whether lack of quality in the wine or regional elitism, the fact remains that the exact wording used in the decree sent by Napoleon was that the organizing committee was to set up "Une representation complète et satisfaisante des vins du department."

Wines of the department were to be exhibited by communes, except for the classified growths, which were to be shown under neutral labels giving the name of the vineyard and owner, along with the year. Communal wines were presented under the name of the label, that of the Chamber of Commerce, with the name of the commune as additional information.

Even this simple directive didn't go without controversy. Emile Goudal, the director-general of Château Lafite, an arrogant exhibitionist, demanded that his bottles of Lafite be displayed separately from the others, going directly against instructions of the Chamber of Commerce. He appealed straight to the top, to Napoleon himself. Goudal used the excuse that the Chamber, composed largely of shippers, wished to put difficulties in the way of those wishing to buy directly from the estate.

The wine must have been overwhelmingly good because Goudal not only got his own way with Napoleon, but he even got his own name put on the label along that of the proprietor of Lafite, Samuel Scott.

Another aspect of this 1855 affair that is still being argued is whether or not the position of each château within the different classifications was done by order of excellence or by chance. Proof that the growths within each of the various classes were considered to have equal merit is furnished in a letter from the Syndicat des Courtiers to the Chamber of Commerce, dated September 15, 1855, in which this point is emphasized. The first growths aren't placed in alphabetical order, either by the name of the property, owner, or commune. So if it isn't alphabetical, then what is it?

In 1862, another Universal Exhibition was held,

this time in London; an official catalogue entry, signed by officials of the Jury Département de la Gironde, stated that the *crus classés* were ranked within each category according to merit.

The rankings remained the same until 1973, when Mouton-Rothschild, the first of the second *crus*, was elevated to first-growth ranking. I wonder if the change would have occurred if the person goading those in charge had been any other than the redoubtable charmer, Baron Philippe de Rothschild.

Recently I asked Baron Philippe if he was surprised at the 1973 elevation. His answer: "You can never call a surprise what takes twenty years to be accomplished. It should have happened in September 1972, but the naughty people who were against me, by jealousy, greed, envy, and all sorts of negative emotions, made the last delaying action which, in fact, infuriated the authorities. From then on, they really tried to push the reclassification, a move which was a long time overdue. For fifty years Mouton-Rothschild had deserved to be a first rate growth—and indeed was considered such by the whole world."

I asked him why Mouton-Rothschild was not made a first growth in 1855. Baron Philippe replied, "I think there was no chance for Mouton-Rothschild to be reclassified in 1855 for three reasons. The first was that my great-grandfather Nathaniel bought Brane-Mouton, which soon everyone called Mouton-Rothschild, in 1853, only two years before the classification. He was a newcomer and people thought of him as a neophyte. They felt time was needed to see how he was going to run the show. Secondly, the place was in a shambles—there were no living quarters, cows and oxen were going in and out around a manure pit. It was still in those conditions when I came to it in 1918.

"Another factor was the pattern of ownership in the Médoc. Until the early eighteenth century, estates were far from being what they are today. They were huge, and Mouton was part of Lafite. Throughout the eighteenth century the estates were being split into smaller parcels; Mouton became an independent vineyard, Brane-Mouton. In 1853, when it became Mouton-Rothschild, it had been an independent winemaking estate for a little over a hundred years. For a vineyard this corresponds to an individual's tenth year, and it would be considered a baby vineyard."

According to Baron Philippe, the struggle he undertook to gain Mouton-Rothschild's position among the first growths was not so much an effort to place his own estate in a more favorable situation as to initiate a new first-growth classification. He hoped

all the châteaux would be listed in alphabetical order, thus putting them in equal position. Mouton-Rothschild was elevated to first-growth status after many long battles that lasted for years.

The first of these began in 1960, when a proposal for reclassification was put to the Institut National des Appellations d'Origine. That organization came up with a new classification that apparently had all the undertones of a Watergate plumbers' operation. Baron Philippe told me there was a secret conclave among INAO members in which 17 of the 1855 ranked estates were struck off the list and 10 new châteaux were added. The Baron got news of the proposed reclassification on the evening of November 4, when he received a call at his home from Jack Prevost, a reporter for the local newspaper, *Sud Ouest*. Prevost asked Baron Philippe to read his column the next morning; it would carry the news that Mouton-Rothschild had been elevated to first-growth status.

The Baron's reaction? "Nothing done in secrecy is valid," he told me. "France is a democracy, and the legal situation is such that the title *cru classé,* first or fifth, belongs to the land and therefore to the owner of the land. No change can be made without, if not the approval, at least the cooperation of the landowner. I was outraged by the INAO's act. It was a disturbing blunder not to have consulted the owners. The INAO was wrong to think it could impose this classification without wide and open discussion with the châteaux owners. It is exactly like a horse race. The owners have to enlist their horses in the race."

He continued the story: "Following the press scoop I wrote a registered letter to the INAO saying, 'The classification you intend to implement goes against law and, still worse, against all normal acts of decency. Therefore I wish to inform you that in spite of the fact that you elevate Mouton-Rothschild to a first growth, if you ever publish this classification I will carry on with a lawsuit to make it null and void.' "

A couple of weeks later, said Baron Philippe, many of the other châteaux owners also sent angry letters to the INAO. As a result of the furore, the classification conceived by the INAO was never implemented, and any leaks to the general public about who were in or out of this exclusive list were merely "fancy gossip or conjecture."

The INAO scandal impelled Baron Philippe to contact the Minister of Agriculture, with whom he discussed reform of the INAO. Shortly thereafter the Minister told the Baron that he had organized a working committee to study the wine problems of

France, and that he would like the Baron to make proposals for INAO reformation. "I made up a draft of my ideas for reforming the INAO structure and suggested that the INAO leading committee should be changed. This was put into action, but it took eight years, until 1969, for the reforms of the INAO to come through."

"It was only in 1969 that a new INAO group was convened," Baron Philippe told me. "After many meetings they came with me to the study of the classification problem. The idea then came to them to entrust the Bordeaux Chamber of Commerce with the task. This body having accepted, it soon had to admit that it saw no other solution than a revision of the entire 1855 classification—a hopeless task." Then Baron Philippe came up with a new and important suggestion: "Instead of reclassifying in one bulk, I suggested making the process class by class. The proposal was adopted, thus permitting consideration of the first growths separately." Since there were only five competitors, the procedure was expected to move smoothly, but enlisting the cooperation of the four first-growth château owners proved more difficult than anticipated. The conflict lasted three years. Finally, under pressure of the authorities, they agreed. In June 1973 the new classification was published, with the châteaux in alphabetical order, and at last Mouton-Rothschild was classified a first growth.

The Chamber of Commerce made efforts to continue with the other classes but, Baron Philippe explained, the second-growth owners flatly refused to participate. The reclassification could go no further.

Not everyone agrees with Baron Philippe's conclusions. Alexis Lichine told me, "Now that Philippe de Rothschild has gained first-class status for Mouton, he has let go completely. When upgrading took place, it should have been reflected in the entire region and not just one vineyard." When I asked Baron Philippe, he pointed out that the matter of following up the classification was "no more up to him," but totally in the hands of the Bordeaux Chamber of Commerce.

Lichine remains in favor of new classification, but is totally pessimistic about the possibility of further such action. He has drawn up his own list, which avoids numbers, substituting five other categories ranging from *cru hors classe*—the nonpareils "beyond classification"—through *cru exceptionnel, grand cru, cru superieur,* down to *bon cru.*

Classification serves an extremely important purpose: to give the consumer a way of gauging how the different châteaux and their wines are rated by the experts. To be a second, third, fourth, of fifth *cru* is not a bad thing, particularly when we consider that only 61 among approximately 3,000 vineyards are regarded as excellent enough to be part of this exalted group. Keep in mind, especially if you are a label buyer, that only on the *average* are the first growths the best wines; in some years, others equal or even surpass them. Life can be very tame and safe if one buys only first growths from great vintage years, but an expensive price is paid for this security and prestige. Exceptional growths, bourgeois or artisan class wines are more modestly priced, sometimes delightful, and certainly able to suit you admirably on most occasions.

Classifications should, I believe, be reviewed approximately every 25 years; waiting 125 years to reevaluate a list of wines is far too long a time. In 1867, just twelve years after the 1855 classification, Charles Cocks commented, "Like all human institutions, this one is subject to the laws of time and must at certain times be rejuvenated and kept abreast of progress. The vineyards themselves, in changing ownership, may often be modified. A certain vine site neglected by a careless owner or by one who has fallen into debt, may fall into the hands of a rich, active, and intelligent man, and because of this may give a better product."

His point, of course, is still valid today. Soil and subsoil do not whimsically change, true, but vineyards are at the mercy of the attention (or lack of it) given to them by the proprietor. Improved technology, methods of vinification, awareness of popular taste, and successful promotion have done much to raise the prestige of some vineyards, and indifference to these factors has caused the decline of others. Dedicated owners should be rewarded for their dedication to quality and the effort they expend.

But as Jean-Eugène Borie pointed out, "Always there is some injustice in a classification as in a court of justice. The sentence obtained for killing your wife in Paris may not be as bad as you would get in Versailles. In my opinion, the market makes the difference and a classification may be too severe or rigid, leaving too many quality first growths out while allowing too many new ones to be entered. It is difficult to draw the line. Why at ten and not eleven? That is why there is not too much interest in a classification—because justice is too difficult."

Another fellow who views a new classification with a jaundiced eye is Christian Moueix, now manager of Pétrus: "I'll give you my personal opinion. We don't wish a new classification for Pomerol. We are not afraid for Petrus. It will be at the top of the eight with no problem. But in classifying one wine better than another, jealousies are created, and this makes it difficult for all concerned."

I brought up the question of price and classification with Baron Philippe; he dismissed it airily, telling me, "Everyone knows that Beychevelle was a fourth and is now a second growth; and that Mouton-Baronne Pauline was a fifth and now is a second growth. Nobody bothers with the classification, really. I bothered because I had a fight with my cousins, that's all."

Since the Baron is a man of immense intelligence, vigor, and principle, spiced with a substantial dose of the theatrical, I doubt any real or imagined family rivalry would be the only, or primary, reason for his desire for an elevation of status for Mouton-Rothschild. The rivalry between the châteaux antedates any Rothschild rivalry, real or imagined, and could be compared to competition for the spotlight between Tiffany and Van Cleef and Arpels.

As of this writing it is clear to me that whatever Baron Philippe's motivation he did much to revive the dialogue on this issue and provided the first change in status since that splendid summer of 1855. Perhaps it will require the power, prestige, and interest of another Napoleon III for another review to take place. We know why it happened in 1855. The future is only conjecture.

Although I am tempted to become embroiled in a discussion of the merits of such a classification of California wines, a scenario similar to that which existed in 1855 will probably lead to the same results in this country. The marketplace, in my opinion, is the true arbiter of quality, and wines able to sustain a high price tag for a consistent period of time usually have something more than hype in their corner. Another way of testing quality publicly is through the many wine festivals and county fairs throughout the country where many wines are tasted and judged. All that is needed to formalize the results of these semi-official evaluations are the energies of another strong personality like Napoleon III, or another momentous event like the 1976 Bicentennial tasting conducted by Stephen Spurrier, in which two then unknown California wineries, Stag's Leap and Château Montelena, garnered the highest ratings.

I believe that wines that are not classified growths certainly should test their mettle against those that are ranked. Vineyards do undergo changes, and new wineries with enterprising owners might be worthy of a higher rank in the classification of the year 2000. Fundamentally, I believe that the current classified growths represent the best Bordeaux wines, and they have earned their place within fair and sound guidelines. But no procedure created by man is infallible. And while sipping a glass of Château Gloria or Château de Pez, I am sometimes reminded that wines not included in the prestigious list can sometimes be equal to those that are.

The Masters of Wine

Titles abound in the wine and spirits industry. You may be the top salesman of your district or have joined a prestigious wine society and worked your way through the ranks. Some groups, or titles, of course, have more clout than others. Two of the most interesting processes of honoring tasting expertise belong to the French and English, who have surrounded the pomp and circumstance of becoming renowned in the field with a lot of colorful ritual and enjoyable camaraderie.

The most prestigious company of tasters emanates from England and is called the Institute of Masters of Wine. One doesn't become a Master of Wine by bribing someone or by selling more Château Lafite-Rothschild than any other salesman. You have to be a lot more knowledgeable about wines than practically anyone in the world, and because of this pursuit of excellence, the field of winners is terribly, terribly exclusive: 104 members, with 4 women in the group.

The road to becoming a Master of Wine is rather long and rocky, and there is no caste system prohibiting anyone from becoming a member. You must, however, be endowed with the endurance of a camel, and you must take numerous courses prior to the great day when you pass the final examination that publicly honors you as one of the best in the field.

The first person you might meet on your way to becoming a superman (or woman) of wines is a cherubic-faced, genial gentleman by the name of Arthur G. R. Bone. He is the director of studies of the Wine & Spirit Education Trust Limited, which is the school of learning that trains all prospective candidates for the title of Master of Wine. Their program is approved by the Department of Education and Science, and the school is governed by a body of eight Trustees, three of whom are appointed by the Worshipful Company of Vintners, three by the Wine & Spirit Association of Great Britain, one by the Worshipful Company of Distillers, and one by the Institute of Masters of Wine.

Now let me back up a minute. When I speak of the "Worshipful" this or that, I'm referring to guild companies that have been in existence since the Middle Ages, with close ties to the Royal Family and a lot of power within the wine and spirit trade of the United Kingdom.

To give you an idea of the prestige attached to being a member of the Company of Vintners, it is presently composed of 326 members, and there is a waiting list time of seven or eight years for those who want to join. The Company enjoys tremendous prestige as a trade association and is conferred many traditional honors by Her Majesty, including the unique one of being the only group, other than the Dyers Company, that is allowed to eat a swan once a year.

Wine merchants enjoy a professional regard in the United Kingdom, and part of this respect comes from the education, established by the Trust, of all those associated with the wine and spirit trade, among whom include wine waiters and assistant shop attendants as well as highly paid executives.

Situated next door to the famed Vintners Hall, the Education Trust Limited building's backside faces the Thames river, where one hundred years ago, casks of wine were brought in from foreign places. Today, Five Kings House, as the building is called, is filled with a host of people, including lecturers, teachers, staff aides, and many, many students.

On the day I visited the classroom, a young woman was giving a lengthy and fascinating account of the influence of Eleanor of Aquitaine, and her French dowry of Guienne, on the English taste for red Bordeaux (in England referred to as claret).

Most individuals who are sponsored to become a Master of Wine have already undergone the Education Trust's courses and exams and must have obtained their Diploma. Browsing through the informational booklet on the various courses given, one can see how varied and academic most of the topics are.

A *Certificate Course* is the most common one given, usually to those in the physical side of service, such as those employed as wine waiters or clerks, but it is a starter course for all those interested in any facet of the wine and spirit industry.

The *Higher Certificate Course and Examination* is intended for those who have already attained a *Certificate* standard or for those who have equivalent knowledge and wish to go further in their training. Examination for this course takes the form of a two-hour multiple-choice paper of 100 questions that emphasize wine culture in various parts of the world and the production and character of various wines and spirits.

Final exhaustive study is required before taking the highest test, the *Diploma Course and Examination,* ordinarily given to students who have passed the other courses and are ready to complete two to three years of further study.

During this period, students not only perfect their knowledge of wine, but they also learn management principles and techniques as well as the national and international restrictions governing the wine industry. The number of students is limited to fifty per course, and in addition to lectures, a wide selection of reading material is assigned, requiring at least 150 hours of private study. Subjects include United Kingdom Custom Procedure, Importation and Exportation Procedures, Legal Aspects of the United Kingdom Wine and Spirit Trade, Modern Cellar Management, Security, and other strictly wine-related topics.

Candidates for the Master of Wine exam must have five years' work experience in the British wine trade, three of which must have been spent in England, the other two spent elsewhere in the wine trade. Candidates are generally sponsored by the firm for whom they work, and many of them are directors of wine companies or quality controllers buyers in their companies. Fees for the training are paid by the individual's employer, as part of the company's compliance with the Industrial Training Act. Started in 1964, this act places the burden of responsibility for training on the employer, thereby hopefully enhancing the education of personnel in the commercial and industrial sectors, enabling them to more effectively fulfill their duties.

The four-day test to become a Master of Wine includes identification of more than 30 wines served to the prospective Masters in neutral bottles. In addition, candidates must pass both written and practical exams, and in the practical examination not only must they be able to identify the country of origin, the region, and the district of various wines, but they must also describe the wines, their quality, and state their reasons for these conclusions.

"We don't want people who are just good tasters with excellent knowledge," said John Boys, current chairman of the Institute of Masters of Wine. "We also want them to be able to write something, if necessary, that others may want or have to read. And to read it with pleasure."

Boys is proud of the organization because it is not commercial in nature and because theirs is the only examination imposed by a trade upon its members that is the equivalent, academically, of an examination required of someone going into a professional field.

Little wine trade education was available in United Kingdom apart from some lectures arranged by the old wine trade, sports club and the wine and

THE WORSHIPFUL COMPANY OF VINTNERS
and
THE WINE & SPIRIT ASSOCIATION OF GREAT BRITAIN [INCORPORATED]
MASTER OF WINE EXAMINATION 1978
PAPER 1A
CULTIVATION OF THE VINE

16th May, 1978 ... . 2¼ hours 10.00 a.m. - 12.30 p.m

THREE questions ONLY to be answered.
The first question MUST be answered, and carries 400 marks.
Any two of the remaining four may be chosen, and carry 300 marks each.

1. The character and quality of wines made from vines cultivated in a particular area depend on certain influences. Discuss this statement and illustrate your answer by contrasting the vineyards of Rioja and the Médoc.
2. Describe the factors that have led to the introduction of mechanical aids in vine cultivation and harvesting. Discuss the advantages and disadvantages of these methods.
3. What steps are the authorities taking to reduce over-production of inferior wines within the E.E.C.
4. Describe the principal pests and maladies of the vine which the vineyard owner can expect to encounter in the course of the viticultural year and the steps he takes to combat them.
5. Compare the training and pruning of vines in England, the Mosel Valley, Minho, Madeira and the Coté d'Or and explain why these methods are used in each case.

PAPER 1B
PRODUCTION OF WINE

16th May, 1978 ... . 2¼ hours 2.00 p.m. - 4.30 p.m.

THREE questions ONLY to be answered.
The first question MUST be answered, and carries 400 marks.
Any two of the remaining four may be chosen, and carry 300 marks each.

1. Describe the processes by which grape must is converted into red table wine ready for bottling. (The expression 'table wine' in this question implies the conventional and not the E.E.C. definition).
2. What preservatives in wine are permitted by E.E.C. regulations? To what limits are they permitted? Describe their uses and effectiveness.
3. Compare and contrast the methods of making Port, Sherry, and Vins de Liqueur from southern France.
4. Write a few lines about each of the following:—

   (a) membrane filters
   (b) DEPC
   (c) sorbic acid
   (d) protein stability

   (e) transvasage
   (f) centrifuging
   (g) chaptalisation
   (h) thermo-vinification

5. Describe in detail the methode champenoise.

PRACTICAL EXAMINATION No. 1

17th May, 1978 ... . 2 hours 10.30 a.m. - 12.30 p.m

1. All questions are to be answered.
2. All wines are in bottles of neutral shape and colour.
3. Candidates are asked to ensure that:—

   (a) They write their examination number and the words "Practical Examination No. 1" at the top of EVERY sheet.
   (b) They show clearly to which number wine their answer refers.
   (c) Theih answers are brief, concise and definite.

1. Wines 1 to 3 come from the same region.
   (a) Identify the country of origin, the region and district, giving your reasons briefly.
   (b) Describe the wines and place them in order of quality, stating your reasons.
2. Wines 4 to 6 come from the same region.
   (a) Identify the country of origin, the region and district, giving your reasons briefly.
   (b) Describe briefly the qualitative and stylistic differences between the wines.
3. Wines 7 to 12.
   (a) Give the country of origin of each wine.
   (b) Identify the region and district where appropriate.
   (c) Identify the grape variety and assess the quality of each wine, giving your reasons briefly.

PAPER II
TECHNIQUES AND GENERAL PROCEDURE OF
HANDLING WINES IN GREAT BRITAIN

17th May, 1978 ... . 2¼ hours 2.00 p.m. - 4.30 p.m.

THREE questions ONLY to be answered.
The first question MUST be answered, and carries 400 marks.
Any two of the remaining four may be chosen, and carry 300 marks each.

1. How does a Wine Standards Board inspector trace the authenticity of:—
   (a) Beaujolais bottled in the U.K.?
   (b) Chianti Classico bottled at source?
   (c) Hungarian red wine shipped in bulk?
2. What are the methods available to a bottler in the United Kingdom for ensuring that the contents of bottles filled will conform to the quantity stated on the label?
3. What are the causes of:—
   (a) Tartrate deposit in a white Burgundy in bottle?
   (b) High volatile acidity in a red Bordeaux imported in a 2,400-litre container?
   (c) Protein instability in a Spanish sweet white wine imported in a ship's tank?
   What treatment would you consider in each instance?
4. You are starting a small wholesale wine business operating from a single warehouse. Describe the system you would install to control stocks so as to ensure that these are maintained at an appropriate level.
5. You are asked by your company to draw up plans for the construction of a bulk storage installation with a capacity of up to 50,000 hl for the receipt and storage of wine. What factors would you consider? Outline your plan.

PRACTICAL EXAMINATION No. 2

18th May, 1978 ... . 2 hours 10.30 a.m. - 12.30 p.m.

1. All questions are to be answered.
2. All wines are in bottles of neutral shape and colour.
3. Candidates are asked to ensure that:—

   (a) They write their examination number and the words "Practical Examination No. II" at the top of EVERY sheet.
   (b) They show clearly to which number wine their answer refers.
   (c) Their answers are brief, concise and definite.

1. Wines 1 to 3 come from the same region.
   (a) Identify the country of origin, the region and district, giving your reasons briefly.
   (b) Describe the wines and place them in order of quality, stating your reasons.
2. Wines 4 and 5 come from the same district.
   (a) Identify the country of origin, the region and district, giving your reasons briefly.
   (b) Assess the quality of the wines.
3. Wines 6 and 7 come from different districts in the same region.
   (a) Identify the country of origin, the region and district, giving your reasons briefly.
   (b) Assess the quality of the wines.
4. Wines 8 to 12.
   (a) Give the country of origin of each wine.
   (b) Identify the region where appropriate.
   (c) Assess the quality of each wine, giving your reasons briefly.

spirits association of London and two or three provincial towns. In 1963 the Industrial Training Act was passed and Arthur Bone was made the training officer by this association.

Only six people passed the first test, held in 1953. However, the examinations continued to be given each year. At times, not one single person passed the rigorous test; occasionally only one new member was added, sometimes more.

Boys explained that the written examination is divided into three sections. The first tests knowledge about the cultivation of the vine and the production of wine. Next is a two-part practical examination that involves the tasting of wine. The student is expected to answer specific questions about each wine in a well-written and articulate essay. The last section tests knowledge of the techniques and general procedures of handling wines in Great Britain.

After an individual has become a Master of Wine, he adds the initials M.W. to his name. This implies a certain degree of excellence in and out of the British wine trade, considering the drastic numbers who fail the test. It may seem rather absurd to the uninitiated that such intensive training is given, with so much prestige inherent in the final honor. But like tea tasters or perfume sniffers, wine tasters are a breed apart, maintaining a standard of quality that in an age of six-week courses in everything from sky diving to bar tending denotes a certain pursuit of excellence that is formidable, unique, and very refreshing.

Britain, an island that for centuries has been the mainstream of trade for goods from all over the world, enjoys the opportunity of tasting and appreciating wines from almost every wine-producing area in the world. Boys, typical of his very select group of wine connoisseurs, is rather democratic in his judgments about the various contemporary wines offered on the marketplace. He, along with other Masters of Wine, tasted a number of California wines at an American embassy tasting in which California wines were featured. He thoroughly enjoyed the tasting, and along with American wines, has been impressed with those he's tasted from Australia, Spain, and South Africa.

Since the Masters of Wine are highly regarded among wine connoisseurs, it seemed strange to me that no effort had been made to expand the M.W. certificate program beyond the United Kingdom. Boys explained that this would be difficult because the program, conceived by the Worshipful Company of Vintners and the Wine & Spirit Association, was primarily designed for the English trade. Since membership requires five years of service in the Brit-

ish trade, the Masters cannot see how they can bend the rules for those from other countries. "There's nothing to stop an American, Greek, or Japanese from taking the M.W. exam, if he can pass," Boys said, "but he must comply with the regulations."

Another problem with expansion is that of paper work and personnel. The group is small in number, and about 50 percent of the membership is involved in the affairs of the Institute, either in preparing exams, correcting papers, or some other task.

"How would we cope with a vast influx of people from America or other countries who would want to take the exam? It would be quite a problem," said Boys. Therefore he's more interested in seeing the idea of the Master of Wine incorporated into the laws and customs of other countries rather than expanding the organization from its British base.

Boys pointed to the many advantages in the United Kingdom for those who hold the title of Master of Wine. "If a big company is advertising for a manager and they narrow the field down to three or four people, and one of them is an M.W., unless his personality is rather brazen, he's going to have an edge on the others. It is a qualification."

In France, two of the most well-known, fascinating wine organizations are La Confrèrie des Chevaliers du Tastevin of Burgundy and La Commanderie du Bontemps du Médoc et de Graves of Bordeaux.

La Confrèrie des Chevaliers du Tastevin was founded in 1933 by a group of Burgundian gourmets and winemen to rescue their beloved Burgundy from a period of slump and despair by promoting its inimitable products. It was headed by Camille Rodier and Georges Faiveley.

Within the fraternity there are four honorary ranks—*chevalier, commandeur, commandeur-major, and grand officier* being the highest. The honor of each rank is based upon a member's standing in the world of wine and his knowledge of wine, particularly Burgundy.

The brotherhood was named after the traditional Burgundian tasting cup, which is made of irregularly fluted and dimpled silver to show the color and clarity of the wine being tasted. It is slung on a moiré ribbon with beautifully finished ends of scarlet and gold.

It was this organization that acquired the Cistercian Château Clos de Vougeot and restored it to its former splendor.

In addition to its regular series of banquets, La Confrèrie occasionally holds huge banquets at which postulants are made members or enthroned as *chevaliers*. Festivities begin with the halberdiers and trumpeters of La Confrèrie, in red and gold uniforms, preceding the chapter. Then come the members in their long scarlet robes and high doctoral hats. Four men in hunting costume then play a fanfare on horns, and the first of the countless allocutions are given.

Postulants are called up to have their qualifications for the society cited. Each in turn must take an oath of fidelity to Burgundy and be dubbed on the shoulder with a vine root while the Grand Chancellier addresses him in ancient French. The candidate is then kissed on both cheeks by the Grand Master and is given his ribbon with the silver tastevin and is invited to sign the book of honor with a quill pen.

This ceremony is followed by an elaborate six-course dinner and several servings of six different wines interspersed with the *grivois* songs of the Cadets de Bourgogne, a very fine singing group made up of locals.

The greatest sessions of La Confrèrie take place each year during the third weekend of November and are known as Les Trois Glorieuses, named after the three historic but disappointing days of 1830 that saw the change of dynasty in Paris.

The first dinner is held on Saturday at Clos de Vougeot; the next, on Sunday at Côte de Beaune after the auction of the Hospices wines takes place. Burgundy boasts of the well-known Hospices de Beaune, the hospital that was built and endowed with vineyards for its major source of income. The hospital tends to the sick of Beaune without charge, on the sale of its wine each year. This banquet aims to re-create the ancient festivals of the Dukes of Burgundy. Finally, on Monday, the Chevaliers and members of the wine trade gather for a picnic that lasts all afternoon in celebration of the Paulée à Meursault. (Paulée means the midday pause of the vineyard workers.)

I remember well my initiation into the other well-known French wine society, La Commanderie du Bontemps du Médoc et de Graves. I recall this event as one of the highlights of my life, not only because of the honor bestowed but because of the warmth of the hospitable people of Bordeaux. It took place at a picturesque wine château named Maucaillou (vineyard of bad stones and good wine) in the heart of the Médoc. It was very impressive to see the château owners dressed in their traditional robes of ermine-lined wine velvet, with the white *bontemps* caps on their heads.

I was accompanied by one of my original "angels," Dick Martin, the actor-comedian. He was being initiated as a fledgling member, while I was being advanced to the position of Grand Master.

With trepidation and apprehension, Dick and I accepted the challenge before us, ready to accept our linkship with a past dating back to the Knights Templar of Malta, founded in Benon-St.-Laurent (Médoc) in 1155.

La Commanderie suffered a decline in ranks in the fifteenth century, languishing until 1950, when it was revived by Henri Martin and other château owners, with headquarters at Château Grand Puy-Ducasse.

Although each of us was being considered for a different position, both of us faced the difficult task of passing a wine-tasting test. It consisted mainly of identifying a specific wine's vintage, château, and region, and only a perfect mark would do.

Passing the wine-tasting test is essential for membership, whether you are a native of the Médoc or a foreigner. No hints or advance information on the wine is given, yet you must identify the wine offered, and there are no chances for retakes.

All persons being considered for this society must have a sponsor. My godfather was Jean-Eugène Borie, owner of Ducru-Beaucaillou, a noted château of the Saint-Julien region. Leading the proceedings, Henri Martin, owner of Château Gloria and also Dick Martin's sponsor, explained in rapid French why we were being considered for this honor. He said that we not only possessed unusually good palates but that we also had exceptional knowledge of French wines.

In addition, I was being honored because I had become a Professeur du Vin (professor of wine) in 1976, an honor accorded me by the French government's commercial consulate.

"You are going to be presented with a glass of wine," Henri Martin said to me when the ceremony began. "Please identify it as completely as possible."

The group immediately quieted, and a sealed, unlabeled bottle of wine was brought out on a silver tray. Samples were poured into my goblet. I smelled the wine, twirled it, smelled it again, identifying it as a 1970 vintage of Château Maucaillou.

I was then asked to place my left hand on a *ponte* (bowl), a symbol of the past, and to hold the goblet with my right. When La Commanderie raised their glasses in approval, the colorful robe was placed on my shoulders, and a medallion of gold, initialed with the order's insignia, was pinned on my chest. Since I don't understand French, this was my first realization that I had, indeed, been correct.

The ceremony concluded when a heavy wooden mallet was slammed against a filled wine cask twelve times. Like a 12-gun salute, the dull thud reverberated through the wine cellar.

During my stay in France, each time I visited a château in Médoc or Graves, sporting my La Commanderie pin, I would be ceremoniously ushered into the wine cellar. There I would sample the family's wine, with the thump-thump of the mallet still sounding in my ears.

Wine in Official Households

The heads of official houses can include monarchy, publicly elected officials, or religious figures, but all of their households operate on an entirely different premise than do those of most private families. They entertain more, being required to fulfill official social duties, and all their activities, whether mundane or momentous, are observed by the entire world.

It doesn't matter whether we refer to the presidents or kings and queens of nations, or even to the Pope; each of these public personalities is advised by a specialist, whether in protocol or in wine. I decided to find out how these connoisseurs advise their employers on the subject of wine, and I started with Buckingham Palace.

Justerini & Brooks, the site of my first interview, is a distinguished wine firm that has been in existence for many years. It is a dignified and conservative establishment, with mementos decorating the walls attesting to the firm's long-time favor with the Royal Household of Great Britain.

Jeffrey Jameson, the Queen's wine advisor, agreed to speak to me on this most delicate of subjects. A strong handshake and a congenial smile from Jameson dispelled trepidation I felt about asking what the Queen likes to serve her guests for dinner. As the official who supervises wine-acquisition for the Royal Household, Jameson is known as Clerk of the Royal Cellars and is in a prime position to divulge oenophilistic secrets. He is, after all, responsible for inventory of wines stored at the various castles and state homes like Balmoral Castle, Windsor Castle, and Buckingham Palace. Aside from inventorial duties, he and other members of the Royal Household Wine Committee purchase all wines and spirits for Her Majesty the Queen.

British monarchy is not lacking when it comes to the cellaring of wine. Actually, their system of wine selection is practical, efficient, and effective, both in maintaining the right type of inventory and making sure that expenses are kept within bounds.

Housewives who are kept on a strict domestic budget need not feel jealous. The Queen of England is allotted a fixed amount to spend for her household needs. In her case, however, she has a fellow known

Queen Elizabeth II

as Keeper of the Privy Purse who manages all of her expenditures. He too is a member of the Wine Committee.

Another member of the Wine Committee, of which Jameson is secretary, is the Master of the Royal Household. This gentleman supervises all individuals who are employed by the Queen. They, and four other senior members of the English wine trade, act as tasters when there is a decision to be made about wines to be purchased for the royal cellars. Jameson doesn't himself taste the wine because he is the one who requests samples from various firms and blind-bags the wines to be evaluated by the Committee.

Samples of wine are requested only from those individuals holding Royal Warrants. The warrant always is assigned to an individual, not a firm, and is granted to an establishment that is located within a prescribed boundary of London. Men who, as of this writing, have been granted Royal Warrants, include executives from the firms of Berry Brothers & Rudd Ltd., Christopher & Co. Ltd., Findlater, Mackie, Todd & Co. Ltd., John Harvey & Sons Ltd., Corney & Barrow, and Justerini & Brooks Ltd.

"It is really amazing how this group of individuals will generally agree," said Jameson about the Wine Committee. "The selections are absolutely fairly made, and no one except myself knows what is contained in each of the blind-bags. But I'm limited in being allowed to solicit samples only from people with Royal Warrants," he said.

When asked how someone obtains a Royal Warrant, Jameson chuckled and remarked, "It is a case of what comes first, the chicken or the egg? People are chosen to hold these warrants because they own firms, or are employed by firms, within a near proximity to the Palace. They have to be knowledgeable about wines and, on the whole, persons approved by the Committee."

Interestingly enough, if an individual who has been granted a warrant dies or leaves the wine firm where he was employed, the Royal Warrant does not go with him, either to the tomb or to his next job, but is instead reissued to someone else or taken back by the Royal Household.

Jameson said that Her Majesty and Prince Philip are rather conservative in their wine tastes: "On the whole, I think they prefer white wines, especially German types, along with Burgundies, clarets, vintage port, and Champagne. That's about it."

Pressure from other merchants soliciting their services, or other types of impositions, does not disturb Jameson or the rest of the Committee. Although the Committee will, of course, recognize the various types of wines they are tasting, they have no idea which of the Royal Warrant wine firms supplied any of the samples and therefore can judge each of the prospective wines dispassionately and objectively.

"There is no way that I can put anything into those cellars without being found out," Jameson said. "The only way that someone could get a Royal Warrant would be if the Queen or Prince Philip specifically requested this be the case or wanted something special sold by a different supplier. They could then ask that the individual be given a warrant."

Annually, the Committee meets to discuss names that have been put forth by Jameson from a list of people who would like to cater to the Royal Household. The Committee, including the Master of the Household, and the Chairman decide on whether to recommend any or none of the applicants to Her Majesty. The Queen then has the right to approve or disapprove the submission.

It is Jameson, however, who chooses the wines to be served at different state dinners, and he does the wine selection in accordance with a menu submitted to him prior to the event.

A former Secretary of the Royal Household Wine Committee, Jack Rutherford, enlarged upon this meticulous planning, which is part of the orderly precision of the social service of a huge household like that of the Queen of England. He explained to me, "The Master of the Household knows a year in advance what the social program will be and, there-fore, what will be needed. It is only a question of budgeting well the money allotted for the purchase of wine.

"A lot of wine is consumed because, although the Queen and Prince Philip drink a modest amount, there is much entertaining, including big dinner parties, diplomatic receptions, and so on. Naturally, when people come to dine at Buckingham Palace, they expect to be served the best, whether in food or wine, and that is what is attempted through this procedure."

Flying to Rome to meet my next interviewee, Bishop Jacques Martin, I envisioned the Vatican as a somber and solemn religious center and wondered what type of social activities might call for the use of wine within its cloistered setting.

I was in for a rude surprise. The Vatican is as busy as a honeycomb full of bees darting in and out of its many chambers. The outside of the building is filled with tourists from all over the world, and the ambiance is definitely not one of meditative silence

Pope John Paul II

but rather that of an ecclesiastical version of Grand Central Terminal.

Bishop Jacques Martin of France, then the head of the pontifical household, had been quite obliging when I spoke to him on the phone (via an Italian interpreter) and had casually asked me "to drop by when I arrived in Rome."

In person, however, I was told that within Vatican City, there were no official banquets given by the Pope and that each of the Cardinals, within his own apartment, could entertain as he personally chose.

The Vatican supermarket is run by a civil agency and is open to all people living inside this ecclesiastical enclave within the city of Rome, and inhabitants of Vatican City benefit in a manner similar to GIs getting cheaper prices at the PX.

"Some Cardinals," he said to me through an interpreter, "drink no wine. Others drink ordinary Italian table wines; and still others are connoisseurs. It is all a matter of personal taste.

"We don't give information on who buys what because we don't want it to appear as if the various Cardinals were giving personal endorsements of products, especially the wines they prefer to drink."

Having no further luck in obtaining information, I sought out the Vatican library to research the canon regarding sacramental wine. The most interesting discovery for me was that the wine used in the Eucharist may be either red or white and that since the sixteenth century, when use of the purificator became common, white wine has more often been used because it leaves fewer traces on this linen cloth, which is used to wipe the chalice and to dry the celebrant's fingers.

Another requirement of the law is that "the wine be a natural wine of the grape and not corrupted," and where fresh grapes are unobtainable, "altar wine may be made from dried grapes or raisins but not from other fruit."

Wine is also used in the consecration of Roman churches and during the most holy part of the Mass, when the celebrant sprinkles the altar and the interior of the church with specially prepared water known as Gregorian water. It contains salt, ashes, and wine. In the Greek Church, wine replaces the water in this mixture, which is used along with holy chrism and holy water to consecrate the portable altar used by the Greeks.

I chuckled, not out of irreverence, but remembering a conversation I had with Reverend Bernard Hrico regarding his first parochial duty as the junior priest. It seems that at this particular parish, the presiding cleric liked to buy wine in a barrel.

The wine, having been kept too long in the barrel without being properly sealed, had turned to vinegar. Father Hrico couldn't bring himself to throw it out, so the thrifty priest had to drink this bitter liquid every day for months at morning Mass.

Father Hrico told me also that the amount of wine consumed during Mass can vary according to the personal tastes of the presiding priest. The most popular size bought for Mass purposes is the gallon-jug size.

Altar wine that has begun to turn to vinegar or to which other substances have been added cannot be used during Mass unless in an emergency. However, in production of altar wine, especially the sweet variety, the Holy Office has permitted the addition of alcohol only if it is distilled from grape wine and if it is added before completion of fermentation.

Spain, a predominantly Catholic country, was my next destination in search of information on royal tastes. I was to visit two individuals, Doña Mercedes Soriano, the charming lady who is the Royal Housekeeper to King Juan Carlos and Queen Sophia, and Señor Fernando Fuertes de Villavicencio, who is in charge of official banquets for the Royal Family.

I was to meet Doña Mercedes at the Palacio de la Zarzuela, where she lives, and this represented a long cab journey because the official home is a fair distance from Madrid. A couple of stops at various security checkpoints preceded my arrival at the palace itself. The drive was quite pleasant, since the forestlike area is surrounded by wild game of all types and is quite pastoral and peaceful.

King Juan Carlos

The home was unpretentious but elegantly appointed, and much more of a family residence than a national monument. Doña Mercedes, a slight, pretty woman, spoke English with a decided British lilt, and I learned that this was the influence of her Anglo-Saxon nanny.

The Royal Housekeeper said that the attractive young couple are very devoted to their children and home, and although they have an extensive cellar filled exclusively with Spanish wines, their own personal tastes are extremely simple.

"They always drink and serve Spanish wines at home, whether it is red Rioja wine with a meat dish, sherry for aperitif, or white wine with fish," said Doña Mercedes. She was discreet, although agitated, due to the impending visit to the palace of the King and Queen of Belgium and asked me to contact Señor Fuertes de Villavicencio to ask him the questions regarding wines served for formal gatherings.

Señor Villavicencio confirmed that in all public and private occasions concerning their Majesties, only Spanish wines were served, ranging from dry sherries for aperitifs; dry white Rioja wine with fish courses; red Rioja wines with a meat dish; and with desserts, sparkling wines that are made in northern Spain. Good cigars and coffee are topped with Spanish brandy.

"Is a wine from any other country ever served?" I asked Señor Villavicencio. "Normally, no," he replied.

The impending visit of the monarchs of Belgium reminded me that in 1955 the wine produced in the Château Saint-Pierre-Sevaistre was the one served at the marriage celebration of King Baudouin of Belgium and Princess Fabiola of Spain.

But what about our own American version of royalty, the Presidents and other important personalities? The White House was rather tight-lipped on the subject of wine, turning down my request for an interview with their wine steward of many years.

I had other sources, however, and recalled an informal dinner at the San Clemente Inn, during which Mr. Nixon, who was President at the time, was asked to choose the wine. He turned to one of his two dinner companions and asked him to select the wine. This individual, who knew nothing about wine, passed the buck on to the President's good friend, Bebe Rebozo.

Mr. Rebozo, who isn't a wine connoisseur, handed the list back to the President, saying: "Mr. President, you select the wine." The President studied the list very carefully, then handed it to the maitre'd and said: "We'll have a bottle of number 47." The maitre'd walked away most likely stunned, because number 47 on that wine list was a dessert wine. The President, who was pleased with his decision, made the comment, "That number 47 is great. I had 47 at the Sans Souci in Washington."

It is a delightful story because we've all struggled through wine lists, and I'm sure some of us have expected the numbers on wine lists to always correspond throughout the country. Wouldn't it be great if this were the case? Just think of all the hassle both customer and waiter could be spared if universal coding were applied to wine, sparing us the ordeal of pronouncing those French and German names on the labels. Anyway, I hope the threesome enjoyed the dessert wine that was served with their prime rib dinner!

A valuable source of information on Presidential wine taste is that crusty and witty Eastern wine merchant, Sam Aaron. He's been selling wine to different American Presidents since the thirties. According to Aaron, Mamie Eisenhower liked Perrier-Jouët Champagne, and President Eisenhower enjoyed Dubonnet. On the Democratic side, the Kennedy clan were enthusiastic boosters of Château Pétrus, Stolichnaya Vodka, and Dom Pérignon Champagne. The latter is now rarer and more expensive than morphine. That says something about public figures and their influence on our tastes. The late President Harry S Truman, according to Aaron, was enamored with pre-Prohibition bourbon dating prior to World War I. Another Democratic President, Lyndon B. Johnson, liked Cutty Sark Scotch whisky.

Aaron had another amusing Nixon story about the time he was paged in a California restaurant by the White House Office of Protocol during the Nixon tenure and asked for advice on the wine service for a state dinner.

"I recommended Château Margaux of the 1959 vintage and later found out that this is the wine Nixon has been drinking ever since. In the book *The Final Days,* it is recounted how President Nixon would wrap it in a white napkin, while serving everyone else who was dining with him Mondavi, a California wine."

Aaron went on to say that Lyndon Baines Johnson was the President who really promoted California wines, adding that "a lot of Robert Mondavi wine was consumed at State dinners during his administration."

Aaron said that American wines are now more the norm, with Freemark Abbey Chardonnay and Robert Mondavi and Heitz's Cellars Cabernets among those served. "They continue to drink European wines," observed Aaron, "but the main wines consumed are the American ones, especially those from small wineries."

A staple among the *haut monde,* especially those cloaked in purple, is Champagne. Seven Champagne firms have British Royal Warrants, and these same firms are favorably used when it comes to any soirée of majestic proportion. I sought out Frederick de Chandon, Killian Hennessy, and Bertrand Mure, all *Champenois* of the first water, for more information.

It was while visiting Mure at Ruinart that I was

amused to learn that he also had a preoccupation with royal taste, especially those of Margrethe II, the Queen of Denmark.

"Dennis," he asked conspiratorially, "do you know what Queen Margrethe drinks? She is visiting us next week, and I don't know what to serve her."

I thought to myself that Champagne would do nicely . . . but how was I to respond? After all, I was the fellow doing the snooping on European royal families and what they consume, but when did I become the expert?

Luckily, I remembered reading that Queen Margrethe liked Quincy, a crisp white wine, and gave him this piece of information. This made the very serious and charming Mr. Mure's face break into a delighted smile, vastly increasing his *bonhomie* and my credibility as a relentless investigator.

Mure should have asked the author Patrick Forbes for this type of information, since Forbes is really an expert on royal palates, especially when it comes to Champagne. In his book *Champagne,* Forbes writes about Pol Roger, supposedly Winston Churchill's favorite Champagne, which he preferred bottled in imperial pints.

Churchill was known to have great fondness also for the beautiful Madame Jacques Pol Roger, whom he met for the first time at a luncheon party given by Lady Diana Cooper at the British Embassy in Paris in November 1944. After the war, Sir Winston named one of his fillies after the lady, and Odette Pol Roger won four races during her racing career.

When Sir Winston died, a black border was added to the labels of Pol Roger Champagne in memory of the statesman.

I also learned from Forbes that King Albert of Belgium drank Champagne for breakfast with two poached eggs. The Belgians are known for their superlative taste when it comes to food and wine, so this doesn't surprise me. What is even more interesting, however, are Forbes's notes on wine and food entertainment both at the Élysée Palace of France and the Royal Palace of Brussels. According to Forbes, Champagne is almost always served as an aperitif at both places because no other wine so effectively sharpens the appetite and stimulates the flow of gastric juices.

Another interesting story told by Forbes recalls the evening in Potsdam, Germany, when Wilhelm II served ex-Chancellor Bismarck a "champagne" from his country known as Sekt. Bismarck tasted the wine, then put it down. The Kaiser looked at him inquiringly. "Your Majesty," said Bismarck, "I cannot drink German champagne." Wilhelm tried to explain his choice on the grounds that Sekt, rather than the Iron Chancellor's beloved Heidsieck, represented not only patriotism but frugality on the part of the Royal Household.

"Your Majesty," said Bismarck, in reply, "I am extremely sorry, but my patriotism stops short of my stomach."

Another Champagne of Reims, Pommery & Greno, also has been widely served at important parties by virtue not only of its excellence but of the nobility of the Polignacs, owners of the firm through the marriage of Louise Pommery to Comte Guy de Polignac in 1879.

This Champagne, specially labeled for the occasion, was served at the April 1956 wedding of Prince Rainier of Monaco to Miss Grace Kelly; in March 1957, for the baptism of Princess Caroline; and in March 1958, for the baptism of Prince Albert. Reports tell it was served also at Princess Caroline's wedding.

In 1959, the Prince and Princess Guy de Polignac gave a luncheon for Prince Rainier and Princess Grace at the family's château des Crayères, with a special note added to the occasion. In front of each guest's plate stood a crystal pipe, about six inches high, with two small taps that, when opened by the guest, produced a supply of either white still wine of Avize or sparkling Pommery. This method of serving Champagne was devised by Prince Melchior de Polignac in 1914 and has been used at luncheons given by Polignac for distinguished guests including Queen Juliana of the Netherlands, President John F. Kennedy, Anastas Mikoyan, Pope John XXIII, and Queen Marie of Rumania.

The Moët & Chandon group, represented by Frederick de Chandon and Ghislain de Vogüé, have not been slouches when it comes to entertaining royalty, commencing with Jean-Remy Moët and his friendship with the Emperor Napoleon I.

Moët had two homes built for the emperor and was often afforded a visit by Napoleon as he went back and forth from and to the eastern front on one of his many battles. Indeed, Moët's guest book for the summer of 1814 reads like a veritable *Who's Who,* as leaders from all countries gathered in 1814 for the Congress of Vienna. Among those who attended were Emperor Alexander I of Russia; Emperor Francis II of Austria; King Frederick William III of Prussia; and the Duke of Wellington of Great Britain. In more recent history, the firm's famous Dom Pérignon was served to President Kennedy on the night before he was assassinated.

Both Ghislain de Vogüé and Frederick de Chandon spoke proudly of the family tradition of sprinkling infants with a few drops of Champagne when they are baptized—and thus inducted into "Champagne aristocracy" at a very early age.

Former chairman of Moët & Chandon, Killian Hennessy, has great hopes for a return to increased consumption in the Orient of Hennessy Cognac, a long-time favorite of the Chinese mainlanders. "If you attend an official Chinese dinner," said Hennessy, "it is Cognac and soda, or Cognac and water. They even have Cognac for nightcaps. In fact, the Chinese were not *just* faithful customers; they drank our most expensive Cognac. Now that trade with Red China is opening up again, I'm hopeful that they'll again start purchasing fine Cognac."

According to some members of the Cognac trade, it was the might of the British Navy and its inroads into the Orient that created this Asiatic interest in brandy (derived from the Dutch phrase for burnt wine). English sailors who were devotees of brandy not only popularized the distilled product in Great Britain but carried French brandy to the Far East.

Closer to home, our third President, Thomas Jefferson, was probably the most knowledgeable we've ever had on the subject of wine, having become acquainted with French cuisine and wines while serving as trade commissioner to France from 1785 to 1789. He was one of the first to mix White House business with pleasure with menus designed specifically to please certain guests as social weapons in the already intricate politics of the newly established nation.

Jefferson was not ashamed to shop in the markets with his staff, selecting fresh items for each evening's meal, preferring vegetables to meats and having a particular fondness for French pastries and soufflés. He enjoyed wine as a necessity of life and had plenty to say regarding the subject when Congress considered reducing the wine import tax: "I rejoice as a moralist, at the prospect of a reduction of the duties on wine by our national legislature. It is an error to view a tax on that liquor as merely a tax on the rich. It is the prohibition of its use to the middling class by our citizens and a condemnation of them to the poison of whiskey which is desolating their houses. No nation is drunk where wine is cheap; and none sober where the dearness of wine substitutes harder spirits as common beverage."

No one surpassed Jefferson when it came to spending on wine or on lavish entertaining. His first-year expenses as President came to $4,504.84 in provisions—and $2,787.28 of that money was spent on wines. His wine bill for his two-term tenure was $10,855.90, which was certainly a huge sum in his day and one that I would view with respect were he my customer!

In 1804, Jefferson wrote: "The consumption has been 207 bottles, which on 651 persons dined is a bottle to 3 and one-seventh persons." His bill that year for Champagne, Madeira, and Sauternes was almost $3,000.

So ardent was Jefferson's interest in viticulture and other aspects of wine that he even imported vines from Burgundy and Bordeaux to be cultivated in his native Virginia. Unfortunately, the phylloxera plant louse dashed his visionary hopes for the cultivation of that wine in his beloved America.

Conversations with the Greats

Jean-Eugène Borie

Château Ducru-Beaucaillou

Monsieur Jean-Eugène Borie was my godfather when I was made a member of La Commanderie du Bontemps de Médoc et des Graves, and I've always been impressed by his quiet competence and gentle demeanor.

Jean-Eugène Borie

Monsieur Borie's home, palatial even by the standards of an Arab sheik, is a majestic square building flanked by two massive Victorian towers that crown the top of a hill rising above the Gironde River. The view of the river is quite breathtaking as is the hospitality of Monsieur Borie and his beautiful wife, Monique, something not often experienced in this day of brusque, hasty politeness.

A consummate perfectionist, Borie has secured the second-growth status of Ducru-Beaucaillou after his father, François Borie, bought the vineyard in 1942. Its fine reputation is ample testimony to Borie's talents as administrator and proprietor of one of the loveliest châteaux and wines of the entire world. We met in his salon in the late morning and, over a glass of Champagne, discussed his philosophy and the essence of Ducru-Beaucaillou. Borie has had years to think about it, since his grandfather was both a wine producer and shipper, as was his wife's family too.

Evidently, the now immaculate château wasn't quite so impeccable during the war, because Borie recalls that in his youth, there were no electric lights nor furniture, and even the bathrooms were in a bad state.

As a young man, Borie wanted to study medicine, but his father asked him to help with the first harvest, and after one year away at school, he returned to St.-Julien and the estate of the "beautiful pebbles."

Ducru-Beaucaillou is known as a very stable label, exemplifying the quintessence of what constitutes a classic St.-Julien. Borie, a meticulous winemaker, must be given large credit for this fact, although he defines his philosophy modestly.

"I always try to make the best wine, and we prefer to sell to many people. They'll buy only if the quality and reputation is good. In St.-Julien, we really make very good wine. There is only one château whose status is in question—Gloria, where the wine is better than its classification. The market knows it, and you can find more Gloria throughout the world than you can find many classified growths. It would be justice for Château Gloria to be elevated."

On the question of whether a palate for wine is inherited or acquired, Borie said that "it is always a question of education. Like art, wine is something for which one must develop appreciation. Someone tasting wine for the first time will appreciate just white and sweet wines. After a while, they will enjoy red wine, but perhaps only sweet. After more education, they will appreciate more difficult red wine with tannin, which is the noblest of wines.

"But I think that when you begin, you must start slowly and with pleasure, because tasting is a pleasure. It isn't a business. I'm often asked how long someone should wait before they taste their bottle of Ducru-Beaucaillou. In Bordeaux, generally, people wait for five years, and sometimes more, but the rule is your personal satisfaction."

Monsieur Borie doesn't worry about lack of cellar space in this modern age and continues to make a wine that requires a lengthy aging period. "In terms of the world, ours is not a large production, and we want to maintain the old standards." Part of the old standards includes a family gathering after the harvest with his wife, children, and the Ducru-Beaucaillou staff for a tasting of the new wine. "The best palate in the family," he said with a smile, "is my wife's, Monique. Of course," he added, "she tastes only twice a year."

Michael Broadbent

Christie's

John Michael Broadbent, better known as Michael, is the fellow whom I've always viewed as the Fred

Astaire to my Gene Kelly. He is elegant, witty, urbane, and one of the most knowledgeable wine men I've ever had the pleasure to meet.

He was born in May, 1927. His *curriculum vitae* notes this was a bad vintage for Bordeaux and a good one for Porto. Well, it may be so, but Broadbent has been a valuable addition to the world of wine. Currently responsible for an average of 33 annual wine auctions for Christie's, he is the head of their wine department and was recently appointed chairman of the South Kensington branch. He lectures regularly on the techniques of tasting at the Universities of Oxford, Cambridge, and Exeter, and at universities in many other parts of the world. He has been a Master of Wine since 1960. He is a member of numerous wine societies and a recipient of many honors, both for his extraordinary tasting expertise and his literary talents.

Michael Broadbent

Having given you such an elaborate prologue to this charming gentleman, let me hasten to add that he is also refreshingly modest and lacking in affectation. His office sits high above a busy London street, and Broadbent, a slim and elegant man, never sits long in his fashionably appointed office. He is surrounded by wine memorabilia—books, magazines, glassware—and very expensive wines, but a host of activities keeps him in a perpetual state of motion, with his eyeglasses askew on his head.

On the day I visited him, another guest was there, a lovely woman who was hired to take on the herculean task of introducing fine wines to the Tokyo marketplace and of translating Mr. Broadbent's books into Japanese.

Another unusual visitor was Mrs. Tiny Roberts, who has the great distinction of having been the first woman wine merchant in London. She is now retired but remains imbued with vigor and many colorful anecdotes of her years as the only woman al-

lowed into the conservative Vintners Hall, where, she said, "I kept quiet for years until I got to be *their* girl."

We sat grouped around Broadbent's desk, talking about characters in the trade, while we sipped some excellent Champagne. Broadbent commented that he found that the attitudes of wine buffs throughout the world are most often similar but that the Americans are far more enthusiastic than anyone else.

"The English are half-way between the Americans and the French," he said. "They are more blasé about wine and think that they know more about it than most people. I think to a certain extent this is true, because we've known about fine wines for two hundred years, since Edward III actually, and the London wine market has been active for at least two hundred fifty years.

"Wines reflect the tastes of each time," he added, noting that the popular taste of the 1820s and 1830s was in the sweet wines of Portugal, Canary Islands, Malaga, and Sicily."

Broadbent added that Christie's, which was started in 1766, sold wines reflecting the times, with Madeira and Bordeaux being the first wines that they auctioned.

"The taste of the English in those days was for rather rich, heavy, alcoholic, and sweet wines. At the same time, there was a refined aristocratic taste. For example, up until the nineteenth century, very dry wines and still dry Champagnes such as Sillery or Ay were high class and fashionable.

"Another wine popular then that is now out of fashion was Old Hock. Old Hock was similar to sherry. In fact, it was a dry German white wine that was kept in casks anywhere from twenty-five to a hundred years."

Commenting that Old Hock is unavailable, Broadbent told me that in the town of Bremen, specifically the town hall, there is Old Hock going back to the seventeenth century.

"If you have an introduction to the director, which I could give you, you could have a taste. It is rather like old Madeira. Very rich, with a high level of acidity. Very tangy and interesting."

Champagne, he continued to explain, was more the rage in the nineteenth century, principally because of the popularity of the 1874 vintage and the influence of the Prince of Wales and his social set. It is perplexing to the Champenois but part of British peculiarity, I suppose, that old Champagne is treasured by the English connoisseur as if it were a priceless jewel. Broadbent had no explanation for this phenomenon but pointed out that the Russians have always preferred sweet Champagne, while the British drink it dry. He said there is a "goût Americain" and that Champagne with more dosage—is additional sugar syrup—prepared especially for the Yankee taste. "Now, of course, the American market is highly sophisticated and their taste is as catholic as that of the English aristocracy."

Broadbent was emphatic when he advised that, regardless of where a wine conoisseur lives, buying wines from the right shipper is most important. "Shippers from established firms have reputations to lose, and thus are forced to maintain high standards. Generally speaking, their wines are well worth the price. It is extremely expensive and complicated to find individual growers of high quality. If you live in Paris and you drive down the motorway frequently, and you make the contacts, that's fine. But for large quantities, you must go to a firm like Drouhin or Latour and you must rely on their judgment.

"After all, anything that arrives at your dinner table is a distillation of other people's choices, whether it is the grower, shipper, or principal supplier. Choices are made all the way down the line. So, happily what a good wine merchant finally selects is the best wine that his shipper selected and the best that the shipper, in his turn, had selected from his principals."

Frederick de Chandon and Ghislain de Vogüé

Moët & Chandon

The two wine faces of France can allegorically be linked to the lusty, rich nature of Burgundian wines and the intellectual, subtle nuances of the Bordeaux. But a third face exists. This is the face of France that strangers remember when they are back in their homeland, far away from the joie de vivre of the district of Champagne.

The Bordelais come closest to achieving the aristocratic life style of the Champenois, while the Burgundians suspiciously murmur that the former two are full of foppery and delusions of grandeur.

Be this as it may, the châteaux and villas of the Champagne aristocracy of Reims and Épernay are more wonderful than any writer's description and truly typify the glory that is Champagne.

The oldest of the Champagne firms, the house of Ruinart, is typical of the firms of Champagne. Nicolas Ruinart, an Épernay textile merchant, was the founder. His skills as a Champagne-maker, it is said,

lay in the fact that his uncle, Dom Thierry Ruinart, a priest of Reims, was a well-known scholar and contemporary of Dom Pérignon.

The family was full of colorful characters, such as Irenée Ruinart, who sold Champagne to the great names of the empire, including Josephine Bonaparte, who after her divorce, declined to pay her Champagne bill. Irenée's son, Edmond, visited America in 1832, and his description of the journey attests to the spirit of adventure required of wine merchants who desired to expand their trade beyond the borders of France. Ruinart spent three weeks in New York and then visited Philadelphia, Baltimore, and Washington, where he was received by President Andrew Jackson. "Entering the drawing room, I perceived an old man with tousled white hair, tall and slender, smoking a pipe. Seated next to him were several people speaking with him," wrote Edmond to his family. The President addressed several questions to Ruinart concerning affairs in France and expressed hope that the United States would soon be able to establish diplomatic representation in France without difficulty.

Frederick de Chandon   Ghislain de Vogüé

"As can be imagined, I was overwhelmed with my visit, and although I was flattered and satisfied with my reception, I was astonished by the simplicity of this President, the Head of State of this immense republic, who was quietly smoking his pipe like an old veteran.

"Upon leaving him, I examined the living quarters and I found all around me an overriding simplicity."

Ruinart was curious and intrigued by the American form of government, the patriotic pride each countryman felt because he had an active part in even the smallest happening, speaking with fervor about their Constitution and liberty. Ruinart recalled one incident in particular: "I remember speaking to a worker near the Capitol to whom I addressed several questions about the city. He pointed out the house of the President. I told him that I had been presented to President Jackson and that he had received me cordially but without much ado." The individual didn't seem to be surprised, responding that 'it must have been easy. We brought him to where he is now and he is no better than any of us.' "

Edmond was astonished not only by the patriotism of Americans but by their prodigious consumption of alcohol. He went further to write that with such a problem, a campaign of temperance among the upper classes should be instituted. He wrote to his family that in addition to Madeiras and sherries, wines from France, especially those of Bordeaux and Champagne, were very popular. Typical of a Champagne magnate, Edmond returned home in time for the vintage in early October, satisfied with his Champagne promotion in the raw new country called America.

Edmond's son, Edgar, was as intrepid as his father, leaving for Russia in 1850. In his diary, he recorded every detail of the 4,000 mile journey adding that he had "never been so miserable in my whole life—after one stretch of 18 hours in the train without going out or moving my arms or my legs, not even eating a piece of bread, or drinking a glass of water."

It was because of these kinds of men that exports of Champagne rose from a mere 5 million bottles in 1850 to 10 million in 1865 and 21 million in 1890.

The present prototype of the intrepid Ruinarts is Moët & Chandon. This is by far the biggest of the Champagne houses and was until 1962 one of the larger businesses in France entirely owned and run by one family.

A Moët was present when Joan of Arc assisted in the crowning of Charles VII in Reims Cathedral in 1429. And Jean-Remy Moët became mayor of Épernay in 1802 and was an extremely close friend of the Emperor Napoleon Bonaparte. In 1815, Jean-Remy Moët resigned as mayor of Épernay, and the following year, his daughter, Adelaide, married Pierre-Gabriel Chandon de Briailles. A sophisticated descendant of this son-in-law is now chairman of the board of Moët & Chandon, Frederick de Chandon-Briailles. Chandon was brought into the firm by the then president, Count Robert-Jean de Vogüé, whose son, Ghislain, is now president of the firm.

Comte de Vogüé, who died in 1976 at eighty, was a remarkable man, true to the spirit of earlier Champenois. He was known as a very progressive employer, being the leading light in organizing the Comité Interprofessionnel du Vin de Champagne. Much credit must be given to the present prosperity of the current Champagne trade because of the C.I.V.C. Organized in the dark days of 1941, they tried to achieve a fair and organized balance between the *négociants* and *vignerons*, with representatives from both sides, management and labor, meeting to resolve common problems. He was not only the late chairman of the board of Moët-Hennessy but was awarded the Commandeur de la Légion d'Honneur. This honor was given to de Vogüé for his resistance against the Nazi occupation of Champagne and the appointment of Herr Klaebisch, a member of a Rhineland wine family, as *Führer* of Champagne.

One day late in 1942, Comte de Vogüé, then chief delegate of the C.I.V.C. Champagne-makers, drove to Reims to attend a meeting at the *Führer*'s office. Before the meeting began, the *Führer* was called to the telephone. When he returned, he said: "I'm sorry, gentlemen, that was the Gestapo on the phone. You are under arrest." He referred not only to de Vogüé, but Claude-Fourmon and René Sabée, two other Champenois in attendance.

News of the arrests was received with great indignation, especially when it became known that de Vogüé had been condemned to death for obstructing the Germans' demands. Protests poured into the *Führer*'s office, among these a joint one from 16 firms. Subsequently, these firms were fined 1 million francs for their troubles. The death sentence was never carried out but neither was it revoked. Both Comte de Vogüé and M. Claude-Fourmon spent the rest of the war in concentration camps; M. René Sabée was imprisoned and eventually freed.

Reminiscing about Comte de Vogüé in the plush corporate dining room of Moët & Chandon, in a penthouse suite overlooking the Avenue Hoche in Paris, Frederick de Chandon recalls the count with great affection, his strong, aquiline features softening as he spoke of his late mentor:

"I always respected him because he was the cleverest man in this business. He was a man with fantastic intuition. He hadn't seen me since I was five years old, and yet when he met me again as an adult, he immediately asked me to join the firm because he knew, or he thought, I would do something for the business.

"I always agreed with him, and we worked together twenty years. He was a leader. And that's why I respected him. When you're forty-five or fifty years old, you don't always think of who will be your successor. You see the present and the near future, but with a family business, if you have the opportunity, you try to select a person who can be important to the future of the business. He chose me as a bridge to the future, and that's the way it was."

Our other companion at this relaxed luncheon, Ghislain de Vogüé, the count's son, is a medium-built, slender and outgoing man. De Vogüé seduced Chandon away from the soap business, but his own son, Ghislain, had planned on becoming a banker. "My father told me I must join the company. I said no and for a year, I continued to say no," he said laughing. "Finally, it was Fred who convinced me to become part of the company."

Both men are aware of their dominant position in the Champagne trade. To what do they attribute their success?

"Because we are cleverer than the others," Chandon said mischieviously, his broad and thin mouth settling into a sardonic smile. "This didn't happen overnight. It happened because Ghislain's father developed the business before the war and became more efficient than his competitors. It doesn't mean that the wine is much better than that of the other fifteen houses."

He continued by citing the example of the house of Krug, which was founded by Joseph Krug in 1843. "A long time ago, between the First and Second World Wars, Krug was the most prestigious Champagne in the world. People would give twenty-four, perhaps forty-eight, bottles of Moét & Chandon in order to get six bottles of Krug. The mentality of Krug was—'We are the best and we don't want to produce too much Champagne.' It was a *grand cru*. Now, Krug makes perhaps 500,000 bottles and nobody knows about it. Only a few people who are seventy or eighty years old still know about it. The wine in its time had exactly the same reputation as Moët & Chandon. Now they have no reputation because no one knows about the wine."

The two agree that de Vogüé played a pivotal role in the ascendancy of Moët & Chandon, and before him, the Clicquot and the Polignac families. The most interesting relative they can remember was Blanche Chandon, who liked to associate with artists and other interesting people and once gave a party to which she invited an entire circus, complete with horses and elephants.

Dom Ruinart was recently acquired by Moët & Chandon and the family tree shows much intermarriage between the Brimonts and Hennessys. The Ruinart house is now one of the brightest ornaments of the Moët-Hennessy group and continues to blend its own *cuvées* in the cellars at 4 Rue des Crayères.

Dom Ruinart, explained Chandon, was an assistant of Dom Pérignon and lived part of the year at the College of Saint Germaine in Paris. "Dom Pérignon has the image of being the man who invented Champagne," but, he explains, "this is not true. He invented blending. Prior to Pérignon's time, Champagne was almost a mono grape and the secret to good modern Champagne is in the blending.

"It was he who realized that there could be a secondary fermentation in the bottle and that this could be controlled. At that time, they didn't chemically understand what was taking place. Dom Pérignon only realized that after the first fermentation, when the weather in Champagne was becoming cool, the fermentation stopped. Then he realized that the fermentation started again when the weather became warmer in March. He came to the conclusion that the first fermentation was stopped because winter arrives earlier in Champagne than it does in Bordeaux or Burgundy. The residual sugar left in the wine precipitated the secondary fermentation in the bottle." Champenois continue to revere Dom Pérignon, both Chandon and De Vogüé said, and a statue of the cellar master today graces the courtyard of Moët & Chandon.

Both claim that Champagne is right for almost any occasion and of the two, Chandon is the more prodigious drinker. "I drink one bottle very easily in a half hour and if I rush just a little, I can do it in fifteen minutes," he said, in mock seriousness.

In a more serious vein, de Vogüé said that neither of them are technicians because "we employ the best technicians, whether working in the Champagne district or at our other operation in California. We give our opinion on the more than forty different types of wine in this area, but our opinions are not the final determining factor."

Chandon added that they do try to have identical *cuvées* and if they are aiming to have a vintage wine, they try to capture the characteristics of that vintage. "We sell a lot of nonvintage wine because this is what the consumer demands. Our aim is always to have great consistency in what we are doing. In a good year, for instance, we will put aside some wine from that stock, and if the following year isn't as good, we use some of this wine to enhance that year's stock. We must obtain a consistent wine because when the consumer buys a bottle, he wants to obtain the same quality in that bottle as he did in the wine he bought three months or a year previously."

Aside from the Domaine Chandon winery in Napa, California, a dream of Robert-Jean de Vogüé, the company has also expanded its interests in Brazil. Said Chandon, "In Brazil we produce sparkling wines and the fruit is good. It's impossible to export French Champagne to Brazil because the custom tax is too expensive. The bottle would cost $100 in Brazil, so we produce our own wine there. It's comparable to our Champagne and that of Domaine Chandon. Domaine Chandon is not a French Champagne, but it's very, very good."

Jack Davies

Schramsberg Vineyards

A heavily wooded road leads to Jack Davies's property, and the only indication that one is heading towards the home of one of California's finest champagne producers is a discreetly placed sign informing the impromptu visitor that visits are "by appointment only." Traversing the steeply narrow, winding road, walled on both sides by trees, it is obvious that in spite of the sign, guests would be hard pressed to find their way to Schramsberg, whether by invitation or simply pushing their luck.

Jack Davies, owner of this pioneering champagne-making site, can be crusty or extremely cordial—depending upon the situation or the company—but he is, first, last, and always a professional. He started in the business world as a vice president of Ducommun, Inc., where he was responsible for diversification and acquisition, and, as he puts it, "was in the business of making things, not providing services." Davies, the businessman, loved Cham-

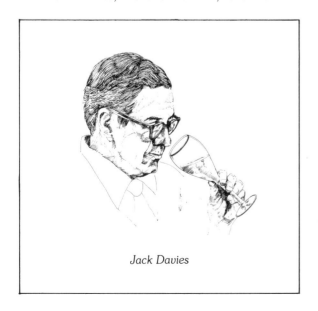

Jack Davies

pagne, and became interested in wine generally. He even served an apprenticeship with Martin Ray. After this experience, he decided to turn his hobby into a profitable profession, seizing upon the idea of making great California champagne.

Fortunately for Davies, his attractive wife, Jamie, a gourmet cook, shared in his goals and dreams and was a firm supporter in his decision to go into the wine business. Davies told me, "All of these tributaries were coming together and we decided to make a search for a winery. We felt it should be in the Napa Valley because it was a proven environment. I wasn't going to pioneer in any area that hadn't been tested."

Also of importance, said Davies, were the friends and associates that were of help when he was beginning his business, especially Jerome Draper, Sr., who helped him discover the Catherine Sebrian estate, his future home and winery. "I'll never forget the day we came here with Jerry," Davies reminisced. "It was raining and the entire place looked rundown and desolate. However, in the back of our minds was the champagne-making idea. When we saw the old cellars, now ruined and desolate, that clinched it.

"We came back another day with Jerome Draper's foreman, Joe Torres, and it was raining. Torres was a philosophical man and after looking over the entire property, his comment was: 'You'll ask advice from many, many people and they'll tell you do this or do that. You'll read books and they'll tell you to do something else. But in the final analysis, you'll have to decide for yourself, and what makes sense to you. The only advice I can give you is that once you make up your mind, go ahead, and don't continually reevaluate your judgment.'

"I think that was good advice and we've tried to follow a certain line of reasoning. I don't have layers and layers of human walls between myself and those that do the work. I have help, of course, but my wife and I have stayed very much involved."

In August 1965, the Davies became owners of the Sebrian estate, formerly Jacob Schram's old home, and they single-mindedly decided to make champagne the only wine they would produce. "We'd made the decision before we acquired the property," said Davies. "I believe in becoming a specialist. I picked champagne because Jamie and I felt it wasn't getting the attention it deserved. I didn't want to produce a commodity like salt—where is the difference from one salt to another detected? Wine is a product upon which the producer can place his mark. It might all be good or poor, but certainly not the same. Champagne is a specialty that wasn't getting the attention that it deserved in the American wine market. Because of the hand manipulation required in the *méthode champenoise,* it was a business in which smallness was not a detriment."

Schramsberg's name was kept on the property because it was a bona fide name, said Davies, along with being a historical one. Davies takes pride in the evolution of his estate, perched high on a hill above Calistoga, and believes his previous training as a businessman was invaluable in the winemaking venture. "Anyone planning on starting his own winery has to be mindful of the various aspects involved and financial planning is indispensable," he said.

The turn in the road for Davies came when President Richard Nixon took his champagne to China on the first eventful gesture of rapprochement between the two countries. Davies, however, is unsure how the entire episode evolved. "I've heard a number of people claim credit for the event," he said smilingly, "but the first inkling we had was when someone called us from the State Department and asked us to take some champagne over to Travis Air Force Base in order to have the champagne available for a dinner in New York City two weeks from the date of the call."

Davies took the wine to the military base and two days later received a call from Maxine Cheshire of the Washington *Post* asking him how he felt now that his champagne was going to China with the President.

"I said, 'I don't know anything about it,' " Davies told me. The winemaker, a believer in small price escalations, suddenly was flooded with requests for his already popular champagne. "The demand was already strong and then became impossible," said Davies. Although he has been told that the decision to take Schramsberg Champagne was made because it was the President's favorite and because it is a California champagne, Davies, still baffled, is only grateful that it happened.

The only apparent regret expressed by the businessman-turned-winemaker is that he didn't start in the business with more capital; he would then have been able to make progress more satisfactorily at a faster rate. "But that's a little bit of hindsight because in the beginning I'd never have made wine, let alone champagne," he said ruefully. "I wanted to find my niche, a place with which I could be identified. Fortunately for me, Jamie went along with my plans. We've tried to follow the advice of Joe Torres and kept this a hands-off place where we don't have layers and layers of people between me and what goes on, and we try to do as much of it ourselves as we can."

François and Françoise Dewavrin

Château La Mission-Haut-Brion

On first glance through the high, vaulted heavy wooden door, your eyes are drawn to the curved iron-railed staircase and the walls on each side that are covered with hundreds upon hundreds of holy water stoups and a splendid collection of Delft dishes. Everywhere there are holy artifacts and impish porcelain babes from whose phalluses wine can be dispensed.

It is a museum that is a home, or vice versa, but the effect is quite appealing. As châtelaine of La Mission-Haut-Brion, Madame Françoise Dewavrin is at home in this formal living room with an adjacent museum-chapel, but her chic Parisian *couturière* suit and sophisticated manner attest to her wider experience in the world outside of Bordeaux.

She is not unlike a Rosalyn Carter in her magnolia softness, but the hint of steel is enveloped in warm smiles and a lovely lilting laugh and an outwardly polite deference to her husband, François.

François and Françoise Dewavrin

François is a brown-haired, bespectacled wire-haired terrier of a man. He is energetic, opinionated, and an unabashed chauvinist. Yet he is charming in his assumption that his own opinions are correct and that the rest of the world, particularly his French compatriots, is slightly wacko—especially when it comes to wine.

"We wear a lot of caps, but Françoise is a very smart woman. She knows that the best manager of her business is her husband, and so we have to wear two caps," said Dewavrin emphatically.

The two caps involve responsibility over La Mission-Haut-Brion, which Françoise inherited from her father, Fernand Woltner, and the wine warehouses, started by François, who in 1974 became outraged because of the low price at which some French wines were being sold.

"We were in New York, Françoise and I," the volatile François said, "and it was a crazy situation. We were meeting with the people of Austin-Nichols and they were trying to get rid of wine at ridiculous prices, like $25.00 for a case of Château Figeac and $100 for a case of Château Petrus.

"So when we saw this wine being sold for nothing . . . peanuts . . . we decided that it was stupid to see a Bordeaux château selling cheaper than Beaujolais. There was something wrong. And that's how we got into the wine business."

We had been sitting in the charmingly appointed living room, adjacent to the chapel, filled with dainty satin furniture and pictures of various members of the family on the walls, when dinner was announced. Madame Henri Woltner joined us. She is the widow of Françoise's uncle, the well-respected winemaker and accomplished manager of La Mission until his death in October 1974.

François is enthusiastic about the wine warehouses, explaining that the couple went into business with 2,000 cases, advertising "classified growths at the price of Beaujolais." "We sold the stuff like hot dogs," our host said jubilantly. "So in two year's time, we opened a second warehouse and bought 200,000 cases from Austin-Nichols."

The couple divide their responsibilities, with Françoise manager of La Mission-Haut-Brion and François in charge of the warehouses. When it comes to winemaking, however, the Dewavrins defer to the expertise of their winemaker, Henri Lagardère, who learned under the fabled Henri Woltner.

"Henri Woltner was a fabulous winemaker and he was so dedicated that he knew the quality of the wine in the *chai* after the first pressing. Never was he wrong about his prognosis," said François vehemently. "You might read that he wanted to recheck his notes in six months, but he was *never* wrong.

"He knew his grapes, and he was a hard worker who would get up early in the morning, almost at dawn, to see what the grapes were doing. His judgment was based on knowledge, not instinct. I don't believe in instinct when it comes to winemaking. It can mean you make a lot of bad and costly mistakes. Good soil and hard work produce fine wine, and this requires discipline and knowledge."

Henri Lagardère and his son, Michel, are the La Mission winemakers and the couple agree that non-interference with the winemaker is the best way of producing fine wine. "They've been doing this for years and years. I would not presume to tell them when to pick the grapes," Françoise said. "They are here the year round and Mr. Lagardère has been here since 1944 and made his first wine in 1954."

"Our job," François explained, "is to supply what he requests in order to make fine wine, and that's our primary objective. There is more money in the land than there is in the wine, so if we wanted to simply make more money, we would visit Mayor Chaban-Delmas and ask him if the city of Bordeaux would like to buy the property."

The Château residence, although not as large or majestic as some, is totally charming, reflecting its religious history as the seventeenth-century home of the Congregation of the Mission of the Lazarites in the cross of St. Vincent adorning the entrance gate to the small ornamental garden sheltering both wings of the property. One wing is occasionally occupied by the Dewavrins, who have homes also in Belgium and in Paris, while the other section includes part of the cellars, winemaking areas, and comfortable guest apartments.

"The Château is not the best . . . but it belongs to us," said François, enjoying an exploratory sip of Champagne, "and the sun is God's work.

"Very few people are winemakers, you know, and very few people like good wine. Those who really know about wine are even a fewer number. That's good, of course, because if too many people liked wine, then we wouldn't have any left. We're always in the happy state of being in short supply," he said rather smugly, taking another sip of his Pol Roger Champagne.

The Élysée Palace is one of the biggest customers for La Mission-Haut-Brion and, said Dewavrin, both Giscard d'Estaing and Charles de Gaulle have been fans of La Mission-Haut-Brion. Normally, the Château produces between 8,000 and 10,000 cases of wine, so the output to their worldwide network of collectors is limited, and neither one is sure of whether the premium-wine business will still be feasible 50 years down the road, or whether premium wines will be able to maintain their quality.

"People want to work a forty-hour week and no more," said François. "Sure, the wine tested and coming out of a laboratory will be perfect in its predictability. But I hate tasting wine that's always the same," he said with relish.

An outspoken and opinionated man, François was quick to say he finds a lot of modern methods of viniculture absurd, and added, "There already is enough Beaujolais in the world. Why make more? Do you realize that over six million bottles of wine are produced in France, that *only* two million bottles are classified growths, and that these, grouped with lesser growths, number only 30 million bottles for the entire world?"

Not leaving time for a response, François plunged on: "To drink the same wine every day means you might as well drink Coca-Cola. You always expect it to taste the same way. Where is the pleasure?"

Dewavrin isn't impressed by the amount of a customer's consumption but by the quality of what he drinks. "I'm not interested in a five-and-dime type of business . . . or a man who considers his wine that casually." "We are living in a country where wine is consumed like Coca-Cola by the average Frenchman, but that's not my customer. The average Frenchman doesn't know anything about wine. Our good wines are going to Scandinavia, Belgium, England, the United States, and to people who appreciate our product. The five percent of premium wine that stays in the country ends up at Le Tour Argent or at all the other five-star restaurants. Who drinks our wine in France? One percent . . . maybe two percent. They can't afford it. Belgium is our best customer, and they buy not so much in volume but in quality."

He's particularly rankled about the upsurge of talk about Bordeaux Nouveau, since aping Beaujolais, to him, is foolish. "The Beaujolais make that kind of wine, and good for them. But this is Bordeaux, and we're not that. We should, in my opinion, be making Bordeaux wine—not a copy of someone else's."

Comparing fine wine to fine music, François is of the opinion that the "symphony orchestra of Bordeaux is appreciated by Germans and other Europeans more than it is in its own country," citing the fact that on some occasions he and Françoise have been invited to the home of wealthy compatriots who, knowing that the Dewavrins are in the wine business, will proudly present them with a bottle of Mouton-Cadet, mistaking it for Mouton-Rothschild. "Can you imagine an educated person who makes over $50,000 a year making that kind of mistake," he said, eyes peering heavenward. "They don't know the difference!"

Frenchmen assume that they are connoisseurs, he said, because they've been drinking wine since they were toddlers. "They have no idea of what they *want* to drink, and it isn't uncommon for them to tell you that they want a fine, everyday table wine for under $2. They'll say, 'I want something modest, medium, or expensive.' No, they won't say I want a Médoc, a Pomerol, or even give a château name. They don't know how."

Aside from the *Sud-Ouest,* the Bordeaux paper, Dewavrin said that the national ignorance about wine can be seen from the lack of journalistic coverage of wine and the fact that *Revue du Vin de France,* the world's most respected wine journal, has over 2,000 mostly industry and foreign subscribers, while the average French person barely knows or is concerned about the subject.

Reinforcing his argument, François pointed out that the bulk of visitors coming to Bordeaux are not the native French but foreigners from all over the world. "There are two kinds of wine trades. There is the Coca-Cola crowd, and then there are those of us who deal with people who have the most discriminating drinking habits in the world. Those are *my* customers. What possible satisfaction would I have in dealing with the others?" he asked rhetorically.

Françoise decided to switch the subject, and we spoke about her childhood in Bordeaux. She remembered that all of the young girls were in love with Daniel Lawton, the handsomest of the Chartronnais, the oldest family of wine merchants in Bordeaux, and that her parents were insistent that she learn about wine at 12 years of age. "When my father and mother asked me to taste at the table, they'd ask me for an opinion and expect some response. It was always a very sophisticated dinner and a sort of game, but after a while I learned a lot about wine."

Françoise has the best palate in the family, as her husband acknowledges, and the ability is now apparent in their nine-year-old daughter. "She likes to taste wine, and if she knows it is a very old bottle, she's very impressed. She embarrasses me sometimes," Françoise said, "because we'll go to someone else's home for dinner, and she'll taste the wine and perhaps remark that it's not as nice as the wine at home. But we appreciate and respect her comments, and little by little, she will learn to develop her palate and appreciate the wine for what it is."

Douglas Dillon

Château Haut-Brion

Comfortably ensconced in a sofa that is part of Douglas Dillon's plush office decor, high above the New York landscape in the General Motors Building, it seems highly unreal to be discussing the beauties and labors of managing the pastoral and elegant Château Haut-Brion, thousands of miles away.

Douglas Dillon, former United States Ambassador and Secretary of Finance under the late President John F. Kennedy, was voluble on the subject

Douglas Dillon

and jovially discussed both his family's acquisition of a classified *cru* of Graves and the novelty of being the first American family to own and operate the number one *cru* of the Graves classification.

I asked him about the amusing story connected with his father's acquisition of Château Haut-Brion. The way it usually is related, it seems that Clarence Dillon went into St.-Émilion during a pouring rain, wanting to take a look at Château Cheval Blanc, the estate he hoped to buy. He got so disgusted at tramping around in the rain with no sign of the elusive estate, that in a state of pique, he bought Château Haut-Brion instead.

"That's about ninety percent poppycock," said Dillon. "He wasn't planning on buying any particular wine estate at the time. It just happened that the investment banking business here was absolutely flat in the early 1930s, and he had an apartment in Paris, where he'd go each year for two to three months.

"While he was there, he'd visit different businessmen, bankers and such," continued Dillon, "but after a while it got a little boring. One of his friends, I think it was one of the Rothschilds, suggested that he buy a vineyard as a couple of them were for sale.

"A cousin of mine lived on the Continent and kept up with these things, and found that three of the top vineyards were available: Châteaux Margaux, Cheval Blanc, and Haut-Brion. Haut-Brion wasn't totally on the market because the owner at that time wanted to give the estate to the city of Bordeaux.

"So my father looked at all of these places, and Haut-Brion was the most attractive to him because it was the closest to the city of Bordeaux. At that very same time, the city turned down the gift because there was a condition attached to the gift: that the vineyard be preserved as such forever. Forever is too long, so they demurred. I don't think the environmental movement had started then, but the owner came to my father and asked if he still wanted to buy it. And that's how the deal was concluded."

Clarence Dillon, his son explained, wasn't so much an avid wine buff as he was curious about the interesting and fun aspects of owning a vineyard. He was intrigued because most of his friends knew and talked about wine. During the following 25 years, particularly when the Germans occupied France, little was done with the vineyard, and "it was no great shakes," Dillon said.

Dillon had offered the Château to the French government to be used as a convalescent home, but when the Germans arrived on the scene, they decided to house a long-range bomber reconnaissance squad on the premise, and the group smashed the place up rather badly.

After the war, business didn't become profitable until the early 1960s, and although Douglas Dillon went to the estate on a regular basis after the war, it is presently run by his daughter, Princess Joan of Luxembourg—now Duchess of Mouchy. She was named president of Haut-Brion in 1975.

"She's lived in Europe for the past 23 years," Dillon explained, "was married over there, and then her first husband died. She recently remarried a Frenchman, and although she lives outside Paris, it is easy for them to go to the Château and make sure everything is in proper order."

He spoke highly of the Château manager, Jean-Bernard Delmas, but said that the Duchess of Mouchy supervises primarily the marketing and selling of the wine, which is an enormous responsibility, and that she's assisted in this effort by her husband who owns over 4,000 acres in farmland and is knowledgeable about the managing and cultivating of agricultural properties.

"One thing we've tried to do over the years," he added, "is to restore and maintain the buildings in the best possible shape. We've come close to the end, and there's not much more to restore, but that's been another of her responsibilities."

Dillon confessed that neither he nor his daughter is particularly expert in winemaking techniques, although they know more about the Bordelais style of winemaking than any other, and he added, that aside from Frenchmen in the wine business, the natives treat wine in a nonchalant fashion, and it isn't as faddish or great news as it is in America.

He is proud of the Dillon ownership of Haut-Brion because "it has a great tradition and is the oldest of the list of first growths to be recognized. Its history actually dates back further than that of the Médoc—the area was producing wine when the Médoc was still a swamp. It's a nice place to live on and a wonderfully fortunate geographic area with deep soil and beds of gravel. So we just try to make it as big and powerful a wine as it used to be.

"When my father bought it, the wine wasn't quite as good," Dillon said, explaining that the previous owner had not been cooperative with the Bordeaux wine trade, preferring to make more money by selling everything direct and not going through the local wine establishment.

As a result, odd coincidences began to occur, explained Dillon, and "they rapidly discovered there were bugs in the wine. It was really awful. So when my father was looking at the place, he asked about this and no one seemed to have an answer. He reassured the Bordeaux establishment, most of them friends of his, that he would be dealing with them. Then they said, 'Oh, then it will be no problem.' So he took over the property and had a wine tasting about six months later. Then they said: 'Hmm, that funny taste formerly in the wine seems to have disappeared.'"

Dillon, being a shrewd businessman, makes sure that his firm deals exclusively with the Bordeaux wine trade but admits that a lot of the first growths have drawn away from this practice, preferring to set up their own companies. "Mainly, because we were Americans and because of the absenteeism factor, we felt we should deal more tightly with the Bordeaux wine trade than not."

National Distillers was prevented from purchasing the Château Margaux by Charles de Gaulle's government, primarily because of chauvinistic feelings, and I asked Dillon whether this type of nationalism every played a negative role in his family's ownership of Château Haut-Brion. He told me, "My father purchased the land years before that particular incident. As you may know, I was Ambassador to France for four years in the fifties, and ownership of Haut-Brion was the greatest boon to me. Everywhere I went, people would say: 'Oh, you own a piece of French land. If you are a French landowner, you must understand and love us. And we like you.' They gave me an entree far beyond any other, and in my duties, I found this factor very helpful. I don't know if the feeling would have been the same if we'd transferred the property to a corporate entity. I don't think they would have liked it. But we've been in Bordeaux for so many years, they've become accustomed to us."

Within the Bordeaux wine structure, Dillon most admires Daniel Lawton, Sr., the man who ne-gotiated the sale of Château Haut-Brion, along with Seymour Weller. "He was the absolute king of Bordeaux, old man Daniel Lawton was, and a good friend to my father. I admired him because he had great style and knowledge of wine," said Dillon.

Asked whether he made subliminal judgments about people based on their love or knowledge of wine, Dillon thought a minute, then replied, "I don't think so, but if someone drinks good wine, it is an area of compatibility. It would be the same as if you were interested in tennis or polo and met someone with a similar interest. It's more a plus than a minus."

Dillon said that he's been spoiled by drinking so much excellent wine, particularly having consumed "properly aged wine, which is very expensive but a fabulous experience. The great majority of first-growth wines that come to this country are consumed before they are drinkable. That's just a total waste."

Dillon drinks smaller wines when they are young, claiming that a quicker-maturing wine is much pleasanter at that early stage than a first growth. "Some of the good growths mature quicker than others, but the really fine first growths take forever. As an example, the Château Haut-Brion that is at its peak now [1978] is the 1959. You have to go back that far. The 1964, 1965, and 1966 all will have to wait two, three, and possibly five more years from now. 1971, on the other hand, is a quick-maturing wine and won't last as long."

In evaluating wines, Dillon said that among the first growths, Château Latour will immediately assert itself as the heaviest, while Châteaux Haut-Brion, Lafite, and Margaux will display a delicacy of character that the Latour and the St.-Émilion wines do not have.

Like a proud Boy Scout who has received good marks in marksmanship, Dillon closed the interview by showing me a result of a recent tasting by fourteen wine experts, Harry Waugh included, in which Haut-Brion had scored at the top. He sent me on my way, tasting notes in hand, a combination Yankee-Bordelais at heart.

Louis Latour

Maison Louis Latour

Louis Latour VI parked the Peugeot by the door of the cellar. Once out of the car, his large portly 47-year-old frame lumbered ahead in a dignified fashion, irreverently resembling that of a seal with its nose sniffing upward as if there were a secret scent in the wind to be ferreted or discovered. His workers ignored our intrusion into their business as they processed the newly picked grapes.

Latour is a man, one suspects, of kindliness and humor, but only when he's had a chance to get your bearings and consider your character. Otherwise, he is businesslike, with a moon-shaped face that is serious and prominent Spaniel-brown eyes that are a bit sad, aloof, and tentatively friendly. His voice, nasal and fog-bound, reminds you of Brando's characterization of the Godfather, and he continued to speak about wine as we made our way down the circuitous and narrow, iron-railed stair leading to the caves, with the head of Maison Louis Latour, *négociants*, leading the way, candle in hand.

We became part of the dampish, musty darkness, and finally arrived at a mossy grotto, covered with funguslike plants, where the gentle host was going to give me a taste of some of his wines.

I discovered that as a child he used to play among these narrow corridors, and it isn't surprising, because he is a man in love with his own heritage.

Latour is the sixth to bear the name Louis and the sixth Latour to control the family business; he was born in Château Grancey, in Corton, near Beaune, as were his forebears, and is as much a part of this mysterious, mossy chamber as his ancestors.

"The important thing is the fruit itself; the proper vine; the proper pruning; and the winemaker's restraint in not trying to get too high a degree of yield. You cannot change the quality of wine just by a trick of vinification. I think this is an error that people often make when they are mentioning the problems of new vinification," said Latour. "It doesn't change any of the quality of the wine. You can lose it, but you cannot improve it. I am always laughing when I hear about poor vintages.

"We are producing individual lots of wine, just as in the old days craftsmen made motor cars by hand. Each vintage is different from another, and in an excellent year, the distinctions between sections are not noticeable. For example, in an excellent year, like 1978, the wines produced at Chassagne-Montrachet can rival those of Montrachet itself. So it is dangerous to oversimplify."

Latour explained that in picking grapes, it is most important not to bruise the grapes, because when the grapes are damaged, oxidation can start immediately, killing the wine. "Air is our worst enemy," he said. "So, you must place the grapes gently into the basket, immediately bringing them into the winery. You will then have grapes that are free of oxidation."

Because of the concern for this aspect of winemaking, the baskets used by the pickers are made of wicker, resembling two large oval containers held together by a central wicker handle, and Latour said that these are far safer than plastic pails.

Comparing attempts to make good Pinot Noir in California with that of the Burgundy region is fruitless, he believes, because California Pinot Noir is totally different from the Burgundy Pinot Noir, and the latter is only produced excellently in Burgundy.

Latour said that his father visited California 17 years ago, and "he came back and told me what they called Pinot Noir in California is not our Pinot Noir. There is no doubt that it is different. I think that Pinot Noir is perfectly adapted to a climate where it doesn't overly ripen. You have to have adversities with Pinot Noir; a shower here and there; a little cold

Louis Latour

at a certain stage. Finally, it comes out, always with effort. This struggle adds quality to the wine because we *need* acidity in our wines. The California Pinot Noir has no acidity."

He has very definite theories on the vintage question: "I do not equate a good vintage to a long-lasting vintage. You know, the public's mind is shaped by the Bordeaux idea of what is a good vintage. They tend to say that if it is 1865, it is still a good vintage today. But that's not the truth here in Burgundy. The 1947s have been one of the most pleasant vintages we've seen, and it lasted 12 years. Explain to me what is the use of having vintages that last forever when you have only one percent or a half of one percent of the wines harvested that year still available.

"If you have pleasure in drinking wines which are six, seven, eight years of age, and you can drink them under the best possible circumstances, I think these are definitely good vintages. If they last longer, even better. But if they don't last, they are still good vintages. Some of the vintages which have lasted forever were not good vintages. For instance, 1926 has been good all of its life, but it is no better than the '27s, which have been dead for ages.''

Latour then remarked that he doesn't want to see Burgundy become a northern version of Bordeaux. "When I started in the wine business twenty years ago, the best vintages still were considered those of the pre-war vintages. There still were '34s, '28s, and '29s available, and they couldn't be compared with the '45s and the '47s and the '49s, which existed in bigger quantities. Everybody was warning that since the war Burgundy has not been making good vintages.

"And we continue to see articles, telling how in the past twenty years, the Burgundy winegrowers have gone down the drain; we're not making as good a wine as before, and to substantiate these statements, they say that the taste of the '64s and '66s is much better than the '71s and the '72s.

"Well, this is obvious. In the same way, we can compare the '34s and the '29s and say that they are better than the '49s or the '47s or the '45s. Now the '64s and '66s are better than the '71s and the '72s. But in ten years' time, they will say the '71s and '72s are so much better than the '81s and '83s. And the story will again repeat itself.

"We are not Champagne people. We are not jet setters. Our wines are grown by serious people, and we want our wines to be consumed by people who are like us. People who come here are truly interested in Burgundy wines rather than just sightseeing the countryside.''

The Latour family has its own forest property and supply of oak, and has been using wood from their domain to make barrels for over 70 years. In fact, they are the only Burgundy wine shippers who make their own barrels. When I asked Latour what type of wood or, more specifically, oak he considered important, he looked a bit puzzled by the question and finally responded: "Good oak. The idea that different types of woods are going to chemically influence the wine, in my opinion, isn't very valid.''

Latour has just bought a German press that he believes is far more sophisticated and useful to the pressing of the Pinot Noir grape than most he's tried, especially powerful presses with small surfaces and excessive pressure, which he believes are not desirable for Pinot Noir production. He admires much of the German technology of winemaking and said that "they are masters at using sulphur. They use just enough to give a nice nose and a fresh taste.''

Latour is not adverse to modern technology but is cautious about the types of technological improvements he introduces to his own winemaking process. For instance, he is cautious about filtering.

"Filtering is something that has to be done very gently. The origin and idea of filtering is racking, and racking means that after six months in the cask you have sediment. You pump the wine; you have sediment. In the old days, there was no filtering at all. Again, this is something which modern technology has put at our disposal. So now we have filtering processes. But we don't allow this to take away from time. Patience is the word. We cannot do anything before fifteen or eighteen months. And it is very important that it is done at the end of the process, *never* in between.''

When asked what someone should look for in a good Burgundy wine, Latour responded that there should be a combination of finesse and strength. "The Pinot is always fine. Even in the worst vintages, there is fineness in the Pinot. In good vintages, this is enhanced by power. This is a very rare combination, because a wine may be powerful but not necessarily fine. Or it may be fine but not powerful.

"I think that in Burgundy, this Pinot Noir ripening under adverse circumstances produces the right combination.'' He questioned the use of the word "fruity" to describe the Burgundian Pinot Noir and said, "I wrote a few weeks ago to some people because one of our seventy-two wines had been judged by an expert panel as lacking in fruit. 'I asked them: 'What is a fruit for Burgundy? Fruit exists in Beaujolais but not in Burgundy. It is not Burgundian in character. It may be true of the California Pinot Noir but not our Pinot Noir.'

"The fact is, we have vintages just as they are. There is a maximum of one hundred points for Burgundy vintages, which when reached may be like the vintage of '71. After that, we had a descending scale, rating the vintages from one hundred to zero. But when a vintage is eighty or seventy, it is fine. You just cannot change it. We do not try to make marvelous wine every year. If the '72s are considered by Mr. So-and-So as being a little too this and a little too that, well, what can we say?'' he asked, his sad brown eyes looking quizzically at me through the gray gloom of the cavern.

"The wine is just as we got it from the hill of Corton, and this we just cannot change. People will have to adapt themselves to this idea, that there is not an established perfection; erase the notion that every year we must produce something which is at the top; that it should be this or that. They have to adapt their taste to what is produced every year. Because it is changing every year, and every year we have a surprise. We are now comparing the '78s and the '79s because the analysis is the same. But the analysis is a very poor approach to the problem.

There are many characteristics of these wines which have established '78 as being something different from everything we have known in the past. Because in a lifetime, you never exhaust all the versatilities of the Burgundy Pinot Noir, and there is always an element in one vintage that doesn't exist in another."

Latour has been called the most reputable wine producer and shipper in Burgundy, but Louis Latour VI does not seem anxious to boast about this fact. It isn't easy to even find his office in Beaune. You must make your way down a thirteenth-century cobblestoned Rue de Tonneliers and look for a sign indicating the whereabouts of the firm. You are very likely to pass number 18. And when you find it, you find a glass plate simply engraved *L. Latour*. Beyond the door, there is a courtyard and building that look more like a home than a thriving business. And, in a sense, this is the attitude of Latour about his own shipping business and about the wine business of Burgundy.

"We have been here for two hundred years," he said. "And the first Louis Latour was born in 1780. I'm the sixth, and my son is the seventh. It seems strange to have been around so long, when considered from the standpoint of the United States, but in Burgundy it is quite common. Many shipper families have been very ancient on this land. Burgundy has never been invaded and has always been a very quiet place. So the families have been here for a long time. This is not extraordinary. We have towns here that were already in existence in the fifteenth century, and no one leaves."

Asked when he became aware of the fact that he was going to inherit the family business, Louis Latour VI said that it was a consciousness that grew with him since he was a child. "I don't remember at any stage being told something, which for me, was quite ordinary. I just had my family name and my first name, and that was all. Especially in Beaune, since many young children are connected with the wine trade, it isn't considered unusual. My son is the same. He is in a class of children of his own age, and the sons of other brokers attend his class. They don't see each other as competitors. They are just schoolchildren playing together."

Is there huge competition? I asked. "No, there's not huge competition, and it is not due to our own virtue. Basically, there is a shortage of Burgundy wine. So there is no big problem in selling it. We don't have to fight among ourselves to obtain the wine, which is quite different from Bordeaux.

"We are much smaller an area and city. Our backgrounds are all the same. We are all the same.

We are all bourgeois families that have emerged from peasant origins. We were all peasants—three, four, five generations ago. And my forefathers were winegrowers."

Do you intend to intermarry within the families? "No," he said. "Usually the wives come from other parts of France, and intermarriage isn't that common. It's a very limited tank," he says, chuckling. "The shipper families are no more than maybe a hundred or something like that. It's not large."

Would he object if his daughter married the son of Robert Drouhin or another shipper? Would there be a feud? "No, no, no," he protested. "There are not these problems with Protestants against Catholics. There are no problems here in Burgundy. We don't consider ourselves the center of the world. We are, as I was telling you, humble as winegrowers and modest as far as we are concerned. There are very rich people in Beaune, with a lot of money. But they don't flaunt it. They lead a peasant life, where none is boss. We are, I think, very simple people. It is reflected in the conflicts which are inevitable between our workers and ourselves—we don't cling to the ruling class and try to be above everyone else. We in Burgundy have an easier time and are much more easily accepted."

Comparing Burgundy to Bordeaux, Latour said, "I think in the Bordeaux scandal, there was resentment of many people against the Chartronnais family because they considered themselves so important. This was only partially true, because in Bordeaux, even at the height of their power, they were very small by economic standards. We are a small family firm, but we are big by Burgundy standards. But it is not the end of the world to build a wine trade, and considering that, we never have had social conflicts of large amplitude with our workers."

Latour employs about 100 people, and although the Burgundy firms are becoming larger and his own firm has increased in size in the past 15 years, he said that not much has changed in the way of attitudes. "We know everybody, and we are in touch with everyone. And the attitude is that we are one family. That is not to say that the boss is having a fun life. But we've grown up together. We have gone to school together. And so our attitude toward one another is different."

He scoffs at, in his opinion, the inflated reputation of Domaine Romanée-Conti. "Romanée-Conti of fifty years ago was considered a very, very good vineyard, very well placed, and producing very good wine. This played a large part in its reputation, but in another way, it also is a creation of publicity. Romanée-Conti is just a good wine, a *grand cru* among many others. You will never meet anyone among us who will say that Romanée-Conti isn't a good wine. Everyone knows that they are able to sell their wine at high prices, but economically speaking, they don't play a large part because they have a very limited production.''

When asked what wine, in his opinion, has been the best, consistently year after year, he spoke about Corton-Charlemagne, and his great-grandfather's involvement in its creation.

"He was the one who was instrumental in growing white vines on top of the hill. Before him, no white wines existed north of Meursault. And so we are extremely proud of Corton-Charlemagne. We have made its reputation, and we are the biggest growers of Corton-Charlemagne even now. Ours is the best place in the southern side of the hillside, and so for us, Corton-Charlemagne is a matter of pride. It is something that we like to talk about. It has a very unusual quality, this wine—an earthiness and yet at the same time a finesse, which makes it very, very special. My grandfather always taught us that this special character is due to the fact that the hill and the vines are facing south, which is a rare exposure, because Burgundy usually faces southeast, not south. But here we have an enormous amount of sunshine, and so the ripening of the grape is extremely well done.''

What wisdom did he learn from his father and grandfather, and what advice would he give to his own son, Louis Latour VII, when he takes over the firm? Latour pondered the question a minute, then said: "Well, I would tell him what I have learned from my own experience and from my family's background—from my father and my grandfather. We have never changed, and we will never change. There are adaptations which have to be made, but that doesn't change what is valid and which, in my view, has been established as a truism forever.''

Lalou Leroy-Bize and Aubert de Villaine

Romanée-Conti

Romanée-Conti is an amazing four and one-half acres nestled in the gentle hills of Burgundy, producing the finest, rarest, and most expensive wine of the world, averaging approximately 8,500 bottles of wine per year. The stewards of this priceless piece of earth are two middle-aged French people: Aubert de Villaine and Lalou Leroy-Bize.

Romanée-Conti has been a source of vinicul-

tural wonder since its earliest times, and even since the time when the Abbey of St.-Vivant sold it to the Cronenbourg family in 1750, it has never varied in size by so much as a square meter. In 1760, the Cronenbourgs put it up for sale, and a great battle for ownership flared between Madame de Pompadour and the Prince of Conti.

When you walk up to the gates of this domaine, it is difficult to imagine this unpretentious dwelling as the contested property desired by both Madame de Pompadour and the Prince of Conti. The Prince

Lalou Leroy-Bize

won the battle at a price of 80,000 livres during the eighteenth century. It must have been worth the hefty price to the Prince because he kept all the wine for his private cellars.

"The more you take care of this place, the more you realize that the soil is the important thing. We are part of a chain of people who have been responsible for this vineyard, and our personalities aren't as important as Romanée-Conti,'' said Aubert de Villaine. He is a serious, reflective, and rather shy man, with black slicked-back hair and dark-rimmed glasses, whose father owned the property until 1942. Monsieur de Villaine was a bank manager in Moulins and a leading pioneer of domaine-bottling, which revolutionized the wine industry of the area and set a standard for all great Burgundies.

His son, Aubert, still retains a portion of the estate, along with another portion held by Henri Leroy and his daughter, Lalou Leroy-Bize. At Romanée-Conti, the de Villaine family deal mostly with the growing of the grapes and the sales, while the quality control is Madame Leroy-Bize's responsibility.

"In California, the winemakers think they are more important than the soil,'' added de Villaine, "but this isn't the case in either Burgundy or Bordeaux. Aside from the Rothschilds, who knows anything about the owners of the first growths? It is the château itself that is important, not the owner."

Our chat is interrupted by the entrance of Madame Leroy-Bize and her father, Henri Leroy, and the rambuctious family pet, a mastiff named Babette. Monsieur Leroy speaks no English, so Madame Leroy-Bize and de Villaine do the translating honors as we speak of this prized vineyard, halfway down the Côte de Nuits, often referred to as the central pearl of the Burgundian necklace.

Although Madame Leroy-Bize is a taut, birdlike woman with obvious energy, she doesn't appear, even in broken English, to be a sentimentalist. But when she, her father, or de Villaine speak of Romanée-Conti, it is as though they were curators of the Louvre or some other center of great art. "We've become very strict about who we allow to visit," said de Villaine, "because we've discovered people taking away parts of the soil, and even grafting. One man in the wine trade even kept a box with a bit of Romanée-Conti soil in his office."

De Villaine studied economics and lived in New York for some years while his father ran the business. When his father, Henri de Villaine, died, Aubert took his place in the business. The two families have worked together since 1942, when Henri Leroy became a partner of de Villaine's grandfather, a man Leroy described as "one of the last great gentlemen of Burgundy."

Madame Leroy-Bize, who obviously adores her father, said that she became interested in wine when she was very young, perhaps three years old, and would take secret nips of the leftover wine from her parents' supper parties. Her first serious evaluation, however, came when she was 14 and tasted a 1914 vintage of Romanée-Conti that was not yet a good wine. "My father gave me a few bottles as gifts to some friends. Now we have a few bottles, and it is a fine wine," she said, shooing Babette away from the office with a push of her hand.

The partners lack any false modesty about their own contributions to the reputation of Romanée-Conti because, as Monsieur Leroy explained to me through de Villaine's translation: "This property has been the best of its type since the fourteenth century, and we continue to maintain that level of quality. The better the wines are made, the more jealous people become. But we continue to do our best, as have all the people before us that have owned Romanée-Conti."

He is a potbellied and solemn man, given to terse comments, and after he placed both his hands on top of his cane, through his daughter, he explained his primary advice to others on winemaking: "You must wait until the grapes are ripe before you harvest." That seems simple, but de Villaine added "It is not. It's very difficult."

The limited output of Romanée-Conti, coupled with the unceasing demand among the wealthy and notable of the world, has led to the strictly held policy of "conditional selling" for its red wines. Cases are sold, to the original buyers, in the combination of one bottle of Romanée-Conti, three of La Tâche, and two each of Richebourg, Grands-Echézaux, and Romanée-St.-Vivant, all owned by the Leroy–de Villaine duo.

"Very often, we cannot supply the demand, and instead of Romanée-Conti, we must give people La Tâche, and this includes the President of France. He asks for wine often, but doesn't always get it. We just don't have enough," said Madame Leroy-Bize.

Madame Leroy-Bize has been said to be able to taste from 50 to 100 wines a day, and is considered the "best palate in Burgundy" by her father, whose other daughter, Pauline, is married to a businessman in the prefabricated-construction enterprise and who is not involved in winemaking. Thus, the wine tasting and evaluating mantle fell on Lalou, and will probably be inherited by her only child, sixteen-year-old Perrine.

Madame Leroy-Bize's husband, Marcel, is a Swiss-born, former typographer and ski champion who now runs their own 900 acres of land stocked with a fine herd of Charolais and famous for its game and mushrooms. "He had never touched a drop of wine when I met him," she said, laughing. "So I conquered him with La Tâche and now he enjoys it."

Madame Leroy-Bize starts her day at six in the morning, exercises, eats a huge breakfast, and then sets off for her office at Auxey Duresses, where she takes care of her correspondence and "drinks an average of fifty wines a day."

"When I taste a wine, I do not like to know its identity. When one is tasting, you need a lot of practice, like playing the piano. My sense of smell and taste have developed as a result of all this work, and now I have a very good memory. I don't normally forget a wine, and I refer to my memory bank of wines when I'm judging the quality of a wine."

Romanée-Conti, until 1945, still had pre-phylloxera roots, but due to the lack of fertilizers during World War II, they had to be replaced after the war by grafts of the Pinot Noir on American stocks. Thus there was no Romanée-Conti between 1945 and 1952.

When asked about a comparison of Burgundy and California Pinot Noirs, the three responded quite differently. Aubert de Villaine referred a response to Monsieur Leroy, while Madame Leroy-

75

Bize simply chuckled. The old man came to the point: "The soil and climate are different, and the Pinot Noir of California reflects that difference." End of subject.

Madame Leroy-Bize added that her daughter had recently spent the summer with Don Chappellet and his wife, Molly, in California, where they own the Chappellet Vineyards in Napa Valley, and that "we were immediately brothers and sisters. They are very good winemakers, and we love them very much. They have the same love for the wine that we do, and this is important. Wine is life, after all. And good winemakers are a big fraternity."

Since Romanée-Conti is part of France's national heritage and has changed hands only nine times in the last 700 years, the present owners are not inclined to take their responsibilities lightly. "The soil is the most important thing," said the old man, "and this land will always be the same. Romanée-Conti is a legend."

"That's true," agreed Madame Leroy-Bize. "We are simply good workers."

There was a pause in the sparse, quiet room, and de Villaine broke the silence with an odd remark. "We have this office, the caves, and the vineyard. We are humbled by the fact that we've been placed in the position of maintaining this treasure."

Alexis Lichine

Alexis Lichine et Cie.

If you are a devotee of pool, the name "Minnesota Fats" means the best there is when it comes to playing the game. In wine, there are a handful of men who have captured the public's imagination, conveying the message of wine in an effective colorful way.

Alexis Lichine was promoting wine when times were rough and when American knowledge and consumption of the beverage was at its lowest ebb. He and Frank Schoonmaker did more to popularize wine in this country than any two people before and after their time.

I was never fortunate enough to meet Schoonmaker, the best in this field, but luckily, I've had the pleasure of meeting Lichine a couple of times. He can, one suspects, be abrasive, arrogant, and aloof, all negative qualities. Yet, there is about the man a candor and a robust intelligence coupled with a sense of ennui that is compelling. You don't skate over conversations with Lichine, chatting breezily about hectares or Brix levels. Conversations become opportunities to challenge your mind (with

Alexis Lichine

Lichine dominating the conversation), but somehow you don't mind. It is like having lunch with a tidal wave: wet but enervating. He must have landed in Bordeaux much in the same way, ruffling feathers without a bat of his heavy-lidded eyes.

Now in his sixties, Lichine has experienced most of the pleasures of a Russian gourmet, including the best wines; marriage three times (once to actress Arlene Dahl); and two children, Sacha and Sandra, the products of his first union to Belgium-born Gisele Edenbourgh.

His center of operations is Château Prieuré-Lichine, a sixteenth-century priory nestled behind the Church of Cantenac, near the village of Margaux, but the promotion of his wines, distributed through Somerset Imports, takes him all over the globe.

I asked Lichine about the chances of reclassification of the major growths of Bordeaux because I know he's deeply interested in having an overall review of the 1855 classification: "I'm the only person that I know in France who has tried to remedy this situation, a classification which I believe to be obsolete. But these people in Bordeaux won't change anything. They are too smug and cowardly and set in their ways. There is a lack of men who have the courage to speak forcibly against this injustice.

"I'm fighting the best way I know of, however, through my letters, books, and published thoughts."

Lichine doesn't regard his promotion of wine as hucksterism (though he's viewed in that light by some), saying that "I don't consider being a promoter—or being labeled as such—a form of insult. I look upon the promotion of wine as a noble pursuit. Many people who sell wines don't know how to promote them, and they can't be as impartial as I have been. Not just with wines of France but with all wines, generally.''

He currently acts as a consultant and corporate officer for Somerset Imports along with buying and selecting wines for the firm. "Standardizing wines,'' he admitted, "is quite difficult, since the beverage has highs and lows and is subject to the microclimate of the year of its creation.''

Lichine considers comparisons between California and European wines, especially those of France, fruitless, because "in a blind tasting, the wine which is more powerful and rough when young shows up. It has happened to me with some of the best tasters of Bordeaux. That's why a wine like Lynch-Bages, for example, will often show better than the first growths in a blind tasting, when these wines are still unbalanced and immature.

"Of course, the first growths of Bordeaux have a certain finesse, depth and longevity which isn't apparent when they are first bottled. So in a blind tasting, the wine giving the greatest impact will gain the highest rating. I've seen it happen over and over again. This doesn't mean, of course, that the wine will ultimately have the greatest finesse or the longest life.''

California winemakers, he says, tend to be faddish as with the current obsession with botrytized wines. "They are still experimenting," he said, "and they haven't decided what mode to follow, so they switch positions every couple of years.''

Since I'm well aware that the society of Bordeaux is rather clannish, I asked him how he had succeeded in becoming part of the city's wine clique, or if he had. "I've never worried much about it because many of the things I've done have been revolutionary to their way of thinking and subject to misunderstanding.

"For instance, I've started a state botany, and I've sold wines differently. So my main concern never has been winning applause from my competitors. I'd rather be criticized for whatever errors I might have committed than go through life unnoticed as some people in the Bordeaux wine industry. They've been born, defeated, and died without making a ripple in the vat. They cannot stand in their own shadow because they haven't created one.''

Ines and Liliane Mayol de Lupé

Château-Gris

A husky, booming voice over the telephone welcomed me to Burgundy in excellent English, a language for which I had been thirsting after weeks of

traveling through France encumbered by my atrocious French. We made a date for dinner that evening, in a restaurant near her home in Nuits-St.-Georges, but Mlle. de Lupé had insisted we meet at her home, and due to her excellent navigational instructions, I made my way through the dark countryside to the rendevouz.

Ines and Liliane Mayol de Lupé

Nuit-St.-Georges is a small French town that looks much as it did in the seventeenth century. At night, it doesn't look very hospitable and is as closed to the outside world as a *bouchon,* or cork, closes wine to the air.

Ines and Liliane Mayol de Lupé, the *grandes dames* of the town, have their feet squarely placed between the world of the past and that of the present. They greeted me with warm hospitality in their kitchen, the nearest room to the great gate that leads to the ancient gray house where the two women live. They introduced their cat, Minette, before we went out into the night, the light from the ancient Château in the distance warming the darkness.

"We must hurry," admonished Ines, the lady with the booming voice, as we made our way in the dark to the restaurant, "because of the crazy people that drive by here. There's a lot of theft going on.''

It was reassuring to know that the Countesses Ines and Liliane were taking me in hand, and despite their fluttery counterpoint conversation, they are the kind of older, sage, and totally charming women that could grace a Kaufman play or poison old men in total innocence as did the two in *Arsenic and Old Lace.* Charming *and* very, very sharp and formidable in the wine business.

Fortunately, these two adorable vixens do not poison people but happen to make good *premier cru* Burgundian wine as the owners of Château-Gris, the premier vineyard, and the Burgundy shipping firm of Lupé-Cholet.

In Nuits-St.-Georges, they are called *La Grosse* for the stouter, more aggressive Ines, and *La Maigre* for the thinner, quieter, Liliane. But known to wine lovers throughout the world, no one labels them foolish old women. Ines and Liliane have been doing their thing in Burgundy for the past 28 years, and their small, highly respected shipping firm is probably the only such establishment in France owned and operated by women.

At the restaurant, over glasses of their rich red wine and roast boar, we spoke about their advent into the wine business, the result of the death of their elder brother, Count Jacques de Mayol de Lupé, in an accident in 1953, when Ines was busily working as a translator at the United Nations.

"Our education in a convent didn't exactly prepare us to run a wine business," said Ines, smiling as she lighted a small cigar, her dark flamboyance in sharp contrast with Liliane's dainty and demure demeanor. "There's been a de Mayol de Lupé in Nuits-St.-Georges since 1700, and although we were frightened at the prospects of running the business, our competitors helped us."

"Tell them what Monsieur l'Église said about you," Liliane prompted her elder sister. "Mais non." "Mais oui," Liliane replied. "All right," said Ines, pretending she'd been coaxed. "Monsieur l'Église is the head oenologist in Beaune. When people asked him recently who was the best judge of wine in the area, he said, 'I know only one after me, and that's Ines de Lupé.'"

The ladies believe that the fact that their father was French, their mother, Spanish, and their fraternal grandmother, Italian, has given them a "continental flair, which makes a difference in dealing with so many people, and helps a lot," said Ines.

Business is better than ever at Château-Gris with a hectare of third growth, established at 1 million francs in 1977, that escalated to 18 million francs in 1978.

The De Lupé sisters have to pay 4.5 percent to the bank in interest because of the taxes (averaging 6 percent) that have to be paid on the property, and while the land is expensive and rare in Burgundy, if sold, the money can't be taken out of France.

Neither of the two forgets that they are selling a luxury commodity, and Ines said that "there will always be a clientele for quality products such as mine—at luxury prices."

"Business is very complicated," piped in Liliane, as Ines explained that "business is getting worse every day. People are suggesting changes in the

laws, and they know nothing about the trade, absolutely nothing."

Liliane switched the subject by prodding her sister to go into the story about the port, and Ines picked up the cue and launched into her story with gusto. "Well, I ordered a pipe of port because Liliane and I do like our port—especially in winter here. I like white and Liliane likes red. When it arrived, the customs inspector called us up and said, 'I didn't know you ladies were in the port business.' I told him it was for our personal use and that of our friends. He thought I was fibbing, I suspect, because he said it was far too much port for two old ladies and their friends. So I went down to the warehouse—Château-Gris—and gave them some. Then he understood."

Having arrived in Nuits-St.-Georges in late October, I couldn't tour the entire house as the ladies had already closed off the larger rooms of their townhouse, retiring to a back wing, where they hibernate in winter with the cat, Minette, as company, while Ines translates for Monsieur l'Église and reads in foreign languages to her sister.

The night was freezing cold as we walked back to the Lupé-Cholet townhouse through the dark, cobblestoned streets. The sisters opened the great gate and we walked into the huge courtyard making our way to a far door. We walked inside a beautifully appointed room and my eyes were immediately attracted to a high stone wall on which portraits of the various Mayol ancestors had been hung. One regal lady is the sisters' Spanish aunt, whom Ines strongly resembles, and another is their father, a handsome man, impeccably dressed, with a mustache and white gloves. Another woman, dressed in blue velvet, is another relative, I was told, who was shot during the Revolution—the original French Revolution, no less.

The paintings swept up the stairs as if the models were momentarily to come alive and speak to us. It was a decidely eery moment, but the sisters, who have lived with a prayer book of Maria Leszczyńska, the wife of Louis XV, and the *bibelots* and possessions of their ancestors who date back to Saint Mayol, who died in A.D. 950, take it all in their stride.

Although Liliane is the aristocrat who stays home by the fire after the harvest, Ines is never still, wandering anywhere in the world, attending a wine function, promoting her wine, or visiting friends.

"I'm so glad we had all of those English nannies," Ines said with a wicked smile. "It prepared us for *everything.*" Then, with immense relish, she told us about her visit to Australia and an appearance on a television show there. Her host, she said, turned out to be a teetotaler. Since she'd been asked to talk about wine, she asked him: "What am I doing here?" To which, he replied: "My dear, I put the question to you. What are you doing in the wine trade? Why aren't you in show business?"

Robert Mondavi

Robert Mondavi Winery

Robert Mondavi walked rapidly toward the high-arched entryway to his winery, a trim, compact and sturdy figure, not as tall as his photographs suggest but nevertheless imposing. We shook hands, and he led me into the tasting room adjoining the tourist center, which is now calm and silent on the Napa Valley sabbath rest from tourists and staff.

Mondavi spoke in a gravelly, low tone about things that he believes in, principally the importance of leaving something of value to future generations. This was part of his motivation in establishing the Robert Mondavi Winery in 1966 with his son, Michael. "I didn't have the money to compete with the large conglomerates who could do many things with money to get their wines placed here and there. We had to have something that would compete. It had to be something of character and distinctive style that would lead people to have faith in us," he said.

Robert Mondavi

Mondavi's rugged, raw-boned face almost glowed as he spoke of a timeframe encompassing a number of generations and decades and his desires to pursue a winemaking career. "It was a way of life. I felt it could be a beautiful way of life for my family if they chose to follow me. This business has an affinity for families."

Mondavi spoke enthusiastically about his travels in search of wine perfection, and it was obvious to me that he is a man who is totally obsessed with his life's work and enchanted with what it offers him. He avidly searches for the nuances of the finest wines and the search takes him all over the world. "If you want to know the wine business, you've got to travel the world. You have to understand the philosophy of wine, and it doesn't matter whether it is Italy, France, Switzerland, Germany, Austria, or Australia. Once you begin to grasp the philosophy, then you begin to realize your place in the overall perspective. I'm one of those that has to see . . . I have to feel it." He laughed wryly, adding that he is not "so strong an individual as he is 'determined.' "

Determination is etched on his face from the firm mouth to the aristocratic nose, and it is obvious that love of winemaking has consumed this man much more than the profit motive. "I knew that the natural elements were here and that if I dedicated myself to the product, I'd eventually make a profit. I felt that outstanding effort would be rewarded, whether sooner or later. I wasn't being egotistical but practical." He is awed by the mystery of wine and its production and said that "we haven't even scratched the surface . . . even with as much as we have done in California. Nobody makes their Pinot Noirs, Cabernets, or Burgundies differently. They are generally made under the same conditions."

California, Mondavi in particular, was among the first to experiment in treating the various grapes differently, whether placing them in different barrels, fermenting them at different temperatures, or prolonging or shortening the period of contact with the grape skins. "Now you have everybody and his brother doing it and I think it is wonderful," Mondavi told me. "In my opinion, that's what's building up the great name of California wines. Not only in California, but in Washington, Oregon, and other places. We're coming out with wines that have something interesting and are full of character. Before, we would strip all our wines and filter the heck out of them. Now even the big companies are changing their attitude about doing these things. So you see, we've gone a long, long way in a very short period of time. But we're still babes in the woods."

Mondavi stepped into the wine business because Cesare Mondavi, his father, belonged to an Italian club in Minnesota and was sent to California to buy grapes. Cesare Mondavi liked the place so well that he decided to bring the family to the Coast and to settle in the Lodi region. He bought grapes from the North Coast and from Lodi, Fresno, and Modesto. Then Prohibition was repealed.

Mondavi recalled that he was a junior at Stanford when his father asked him what he wanted to do for a living. "I told him that I liked business and law and he told me that he thought there was a future in the wine business. At the time, eighty percent of the wine sold was Muscatel. He believed that public taste would change and that the Napa Valley would prove to be the most outstanding wine region in America. In those days, you didn't argue with your parents. Everything Papa said was as if God had said it. But to be very honest with you, usually he was right. And in this instance, he was a hundred percent correct.''

Actually, while the elder Mondavi was sure about the future of table wines, he wasn't so sure that he wanted to expand into the business in a big-time way, and it was only by a circuitous route that Mondavi persuaded his father to expand.

Mondavi's father had, between 1937 and 1940, become a partner in the Sunny St. Helena Winery. The son continued to press him on the fact that the future depended upon fine table wines and that eventually the cheaper wines from San Martin would force the Mondavi group out of business. "Mr. Alexander, who was president of the Bank of America, realized that I wanted to go into the fine wine business. He told me about the Charles Krug Winery and that it was going up for sale. This was in 1943. He came to me and said, 'Bob, I've accepted the place from Charles Krug' and added, 'You're going to have to work very fast because we know that Mr. Moffatt has gone to Los Angeles and already has an offer on the property. You have to wrap it up this weekend.' The conversation took place on Thursday and at the time wine was selling at eighteen cents a gallon," recalled Mondavi.

The elder Mondavi wasn't overjoyed at the possibility of buying the property, saying, "I'm happy. We don't have to be so big." Robert, totally frustrated by this reply, went to his mother. "She was listening in the kitchen, and I told her that she had to do something. I have complete faith in the power of a woman. The next day my father came down to breakfast, and the first thing he said was, 'When are we going to St. Helena?' I looked at him, flabbergasted, and said, 'Now!' And that's truly how it all began."

Christian Moueix

Châteaux Petrus and Cheval-Blanc

Libourne is a small sleepy town and the drive from the railroad to the offices of the Moueix family doesn't pass by imposing avenues and aristocratic ancient buildings as is the case if one drives through the heart of Bordeaux.

The people of Libourne, once considered a bit déclassé by their more cosmopolitan neighbors, now have reason to crow and boast. Their wines, most particularly Châteaux Petrus and Cheval-Blanc, have placed them on equal footing with the best of Pauillac and Bordeaux. If this is the case, then the Moueix family and the remarkable Madame Loubat, now deceased, have something to do with this increased prestige.

Christian Moueix, manager of all the Moueix properties, is the man I met, and the rendevouz spot was the immaculate offices of the firm, situated by the river Dordogne.

Christian Moueix is a bookish-looking young man, with a warm smile and a tall pencil-slim body and aristocratic bearing. He seems much too young to be responsible for the operation of such bastions of excellence as Châteaux Petrus and Magdelaine, but he has obviously been a careful student under the shrewd tutelage of his father, Jean-Pierre Moueix.

The family, explained Moueix in fluid English, came from the area of Correze, a spectacularly beautiful but poor department in the Massif Central Mountains, hundreds of miles east of the Gironde. In *The Winemasters,* Nicholas Faith wrote of these people and how in their search for a better life, they placed all of their worldly possessions into a tiny boat and made their way down the Dordogne River, connecting them with the town of Libourne.

The Moueix family came in such a manner, and Antoine, the patriarch of the family, arrived in 1906 and bought a small business that his heirs—his grandson Armand and his nephew Bernard—have continued to run. Another member of the family is Jean-Pierre Moueix, the father of Christian, and the most successful Moueix of all.

A crackerjack salesman, Jean-Pierre started selling wine during the Depression, when his father bought Château Fonrôque in St.-Émilion, and at eighteen was what the French call an *agent multicarte,* who on his first assignment to Belgium sold all of his father's wine within a few days.

"We were very poor and a large family," explained Moueix, "and we weren't received in Bordeaux, so we came to Libourne, where my people became small wine merchants. My family were very hard workers, and little by little, they became, if not important, at least wealthy.

"My grandfather and my great-uncle came in 1931, and they bought two vineyards in St.-Émilion, and since it was during the Depression, they bought these for practically nothing."

Christian's father, Jean-Pierre, was such a good

salesman that he was able to become a wine merchant and open his own business in 1946, just after World War II. Then he decided that eventually he would buy a château and produce his own wine, and the first such acquisition was Château Magdelaine in 1952. He continued by buying Château Trotanoy, one of the three or four best in Pomerol, and eventually became, in a very real sense, a one-man classification system.

The control over Château Petrus was another story altogether, initiated not only by the fact that Moueix was selling Petrus as part of his work as a wine merchant, but because of his friendship with Mme. Loubat, then the owner, who herself came from a well-known winemaking family.

Christian Moueix

"Madame Loubat had a lot of personality, and was accustomed to wearing big hats. My own memory of her as a small boy was that she was very kind and that she was driving a sports car when she was sixty years of age. She was a very sympathetic person, and as owner of the Hôtel Loubat, in Libourne, she would invite people to visit Château Petrus and to taste the wine," Moueix reminisced.

Moueix said that through word of mouth, the fame of Mme. Loubat's Petrus began to spread, with the advantage that the wine's composition is 95 percent Merlot, which means that it matures faster than other wines. "That's a great advantage, today," explained Moueix, "when people want to drink their wines younger and younger."

Jean-Pierre and Mme. Loubat were firm friends, said his son, and as the female winemaker aged, she feared for her wine. There's a great story about the frost of February 15, 1956, when, related Moueix, "there was a temperature approximately fifteen degrees below Fahrenheit, which is critical for us. Everything was covered with snow, and the

ground was frozen. The trunks of the vines were frozen. So what were we to do? In 1956, most of these vines were twenty-two years of age, and Madame Loubat was seventy-five years old."

Should she uproot the vines or take additional risks by doing something more radical? Mme. Loubat knew that if she uprooted all of her vines, she would never in her lifetime produce another bottle of good Petrus because it takes the vine ten years to produce good wine.

So she risked that although the trunks were frozen, the deep roots were still sound. She either regrafted the vines or took suckers from the old roots and grafted them onto the trunks. "Thanks to this process, Petrus was producing very good wine in the sixties," Moueix said with a smile, and "some of the vines have been replanted—but not much. The average age of Petrus is forty-five years. So there is something to Madame Loubat's dedication to quality. That was her foremost concern. That's why she and my father understood and appreciated each other so much."

When Madame Loubat died in 1961, she gave her niece and nephew each half of the shares of Château Petrus, but because they didn't get on together and because she appreciated what Jean-Pierre had done to commercialize Petrus, she gave him one share out of every seven, thus neutralizing any squabbles among her kin.

In the end, that did not resolve the problem, and Moueix, Sr., bought out the nephew's shares, which means that today, the niece, Mme. Lacoste, at age seventy, is half-owner with Moueix.

Moueix claims that his father could walk through the delicate waters of family disputes due to his own extraordinary sense of patience and prudence, and as Moueix explained: "He always sees things from a very high point of view. He once told me that there was always time for doing things and that we should do them carefully. 'Everything will one day be sold,' he said. 'So take your time in making decisions. It would be nice to have everything you want in a year . . . but sometimes it takes a lifetime . . . and sometimes it doesn't happen for you but for your children. So take your time, and don't hurry things.' "

Moueix, a graduate in mechanical engineering, has studied also at the University of California at Davis and obtained his master's in winemaking at that prestigious school.

"I learned a lot there because the studies were practical. In Bordeaux, I've never been served a wine from Burgundy, and at home, I drink one-third domestic wine to those from abroad. Many owners will say, 'My wine is marvelous!' But that's because they have become accustomed to their own wines. In California, I tasted all kinds of wines and made many friends among the winemakers. You have improved a lot in California, and you are making very good wines. Some of them could compete with, if not with our best, at least our good wines."

What about the success of Petrus? Moueix synthesized his answer into three words: quality, soil, and adherence to proven methods. "We think of quality, never of quantity. Being in charge of Petrus means we try to do the best all year long; no chemicals, just manure and good plowing. We have to be careful in plowing because it is clay soil, and the spraying has to be done precisely. We have to pick at the perfect time, and I check the weather forecast very carefully, making sure that our big team of 170 pickers goes to the fields at exactly the right time. On principle, picking is done at Petrus in the afternoon, preferably on sunny, dry days; this is to prevent morning dew and rain from affecting the must.

"We sell Petrus *en primeur* or at the same price as the younger crop," explained Moueix, "and this is important, because when you see auctions, such as Christie's, or when you see the retail prices in New York for Petrus, they are always higher than the others. Which means that someone besides us is making a profit from Petrus. This is part of the wine's success.

"Petrus is something very special. I think because, for at least the last ten years, there is no possibility that the wine will be bad. And Petrus will always be ranked among the top three of Bordeaux. We make the best possible wine for any vintage, and people know that this is the case. We receive a lot of Americans (prime market for Petrus), and they see the difference in quality. If you are going to spend twenty-five dollars for a bottle of wine, then you don't want to risk quality."

When should we consume Petrus? Moueix repeated that the current desire for younger and younger wines is a plus factor for Petrus but that normal vintages of the wine should not be consumed before it has five years of bottle age; great vintages can be consumed after ten years.

Since Petrus is in short supply, other Pomerol wines that he would classify as good would be listed in the following order: First, Petrus; second, Château L'Évangile; third, Château Trotanoy; and fourth, La Conseillante. Vieux Certan would be fifth. Château La-Fleur would be sixth, and Château Lafleur-Petrus would be seventh.

Moueix takes a very modest point of view when it comes to his own prowess as a winemaker, stating that "soil is eighty percent of the quality. You will meet many owners, and this is very silly, I think, who will assume they are making top wine because they are important people. This is absolutely wrong. We are owners only by luck. The soil makes good wine.

"I agree with Philippe de Rothschild on the question of soil," he added. "Then you look at the age of the vines, which on an average should be about thirty years. Then you look at the yearly variables and choices made by each owner. The human factor is the fourth. Of course, if there is no human factor, you can miss the first three points."

On the question of the human factor, Moueix ranks the vineyard manager, winemaker, and *maître de chai* on an equal basis. No one can be good at all three jobs, and specialization is most important.

Since the Petrus crop is small, Mouiex doesn't keep a great stock of the wine and generally has no more than a few cases. In his opinion, the best vintages were 1929, 1947, and 1949, describing 1947 as the "most eccentric."

He likes old Médoc wines along with Margaux wines and doesn't personally drink much Petrus. "We are quiet people, and that is part of the success of our wine. This is a wine for which we never give parties. We say that the best advertisement is *quality* So we receive few people; we never see tourists, and we don't have ceremonies. I think the mysterious, secret quality of Petrus . . . its hidden character . . . that's its charm."

Professor Emile Peynaud

Bordeaux Oenological Station

I made rather halting and basic conversation with the Frenchman on the telephone, and our mutual inability to communicate beyond the most rudimentary fashion was a definite obstacle that I felt had to be overcome by the following morning's 9 A.M. appointment. Professor Emile Peynaud was someone I'd been anxious to encounter, both because of his knowledge of the subject of oenology and viticulture and because for years he was the director of Bordeaux's Oenological Station and as such represents the academic vinicultural community. He is now retired and acts as consultant.

He and I hadn't met previously, so I asked him for a description of himself. He said that he was large in build and that I'd probably recognize his "potbelly." Or at least, that's what I *think* he said.

I waited for him in the restaurant and the minute a tall, barrel-chested man with round sloping shoulders came into the room, I thought it might be my

Professor Emile Peynaud

man. When the hotel manager rushed up to him with a bright smile and a cheerfully enunciated, "Bonjour, professeur," I knew he was. Up to that point, the manager of the hotel had exhibited the personality of Buster Keaton in mourning. Definitely an indrawn personality.

I'd been a bit perplexed about how I was going to conduct this conversation—my French was so poor, I could barely communicate hello. As luck would have it, I cornered a young staffer of the hotel who spoke English and volunteered to act as interpreter. But I needn't have worried. The *bonhommie* of Peynaud's persona is contagious and the professor makes you relax easily. He doesn't act the least bit professorial in manner, explaining that a fraternity of ideas exists between the scientists of America and those of France, although differences exist between them and himself.

"They are theorists," he explained, "and I'm a practical viticulturist working in the field." He hastened to add that frequent correspondence took place and that in the scientific community, there were agreements on essential theories.

The person he learned the most from was another eminent oenologist, Dr. Ribereau-Gayon, also of Bordeaux, with whom he had worked for a number of years. "I started working with him when I was fifteen and he was twenty-two," he recalled. "The relationship was a good one. Gayon provided the theory and I the intuition."

Since there's been a surge of interest in wine among women, especially Americans, I asked him if this was occurring also in France. He replied that about one-quarter of the oenological students of the University were women, but that most went into laboratory work. "They aren't strong enough to work in the caves," he added.

His own daughters are in science; one a doctor

and the other a chemist, but neither is interested in wine other than as a social beverage. Peynaud, however, is enthralled with the idea of providing better-quality wines to more of the world's population. No longer burdened by professorial duties at Bordeaux's Oenological Station, he's still a consultant to the world's wineries, traveling to South America, South Africa, and other parts of Europe in an attempt to improve the wines of each region.

"I have high hopes for the white wines of South Africa and the red wines of Australia," he explained to the interpreter in rapid French, while she, rather huffy at such an affront to La Belle France, translated the message to me. He attributes this optimism to the wealth of sunshine in both regions and said that these wines are *beaucoup bien* and more to the taste of the Americans and the English rather than the French, who have more of a Latin taste.

Since I was not acquainted with what this phenomenon would be, I asked for an explanation. He defined the Latin taste as one typical of people who have wine with their meals as opposed to those who drink wine by itself. French white wines have less acidity than other white wines, and the French reds have less tannin than those of other countries. The French wines are ideal for the cuisine of that country, he explained, just as the Italian hearty reds are good with the heavily tomato-based food of that country.

Professor Peynaud was now more relaxed over his *café au lait* and hot croissants, and he became more philosophical with each bite and sip. He said that the major obstacle to superior winemaking throughout the world is an inability to control temperature. This is particularly the case in climates where grapes mature well but suffer from too much heat. An example he cited is Spain, where he's worked for the Marquis de Riscal, trying to improve their product. "Better equipment would do much to improve the Spanish wines," he said, "but the economy is too poor for this modernization to be set in motion. Money may be the root of all evil, but it is essential to the development of superior wine production"—that was an intriguing statement to come out of the good professor.

Like bio-rhythm, countries go through peaks of prosperity and decline. In each case, when the state is at its apex, that's when the wine becomes superior to all others. Backing up this theory, he cited Spain in the fifteenth century and France in the eighteenth century as examples of periods in history when the wines of the country matched the rise of prosperity. America, especially North America, is next to enjoy this Golden Age, because in the twenty-first century, it could support quality wine production. Economically unstable Chile could have been the next giant, but as a dollar-poor country, they couldn't do it. Napa Valley, California, is especially choice territory, and Professor Peynaud is of the opinion that in limited quantities it is producing wine as good as that of France.

I asked Professor Peynaud if he had any comments about the current elaborate production measures taken to ensure that wines come to the market without any sediment, and was this obsession with squeaky-clean wines valid. "Any sediment that is in the bottle before it is five years old is not normal," he replied. "But after five or ten years, it is completely normal, and the wine makes the sediment and continues to do so."

It was time to go, and the interpreter, still slightly ruffled at all the treacherous talk about wines of other countries, told me that Professor Peynaud wanted to say one last thing. "Just remember that wines are like books or memories. My one hope is that people remember me for what I added to their library of wines. That's what I want to make my contribution."

Baron Elie de Rothschild

Château Lafite-Rothschild

I think Baron Elie de Rothschild explained the position of Lafite (the best there is) with sardonic good humor and elegant posturing. He is tall, hawk-nosed, slim, and totally sophisticated, and—unlike his cousin Philippe, who will speak at length about his opinions, decisions, and projects—is a master of brevity and "no comment." In typical Rothschild fashion, however, he is rapier fast in wit and intelligence, with, one suspects, a streak of softness hidden under the thorny exterior.

Baron Elie de Rothschild

"Our wine has been the best since the days of the Romans," Baron Elie said with an aristocratic English accent. "We even own a poster which says: 'Up for sale is Château Lafite, the first of the first of all the wines of Bordeaux.' "

The outstanding vintages of the estate, he said, are 1870, 1895, and approximately 50 years later, 1926 and 1928 were very big years. "Since the war, the best bottle has been 1945," he added for the sake of those unable to get older vintages.

Since I adored the Carruades de Lafite 1966, I asked him whether there were any plans afoot to start this secondary label for Lafite. He replied negatively, explaining his reason with a simile about a forest: "When you are operating a forest, you cut so many trees every year. Then, every twenty-five years, you renew the whole thing. It's the same thing with wines. You keep them for thirty to thirty-five years, and then you tear them up and allow the earth to rest for about three years. Then you replant and wait and wait for a number of more years before it produces really good wine.

"After the Second World War, we had to tear up a lot of vines, and we had a greater proportion of young vines over older ones. So I made Carruades de Lafite, which was pure Lafite but not what I call top outstanding quality. I allowed the production of Carruades until I could return to my normal revolution of tearing up every thirty-five years and going on properly. So I don't need Carruades anymore."

I brought up the suggestion that he had ceased producing Carruades because it was nearly as good as Lafite and could easily compete with it. His response was, "The Carruades was slightly inferior in quality, but the more it caught up with the quality of the Lafite, the more it was finished. I wouldn't be stupid enough to undercut myself."

Baron Elie also becomes irritated at talk about wine as an investment, because wine, in his opinion, is something one drinks, and it isn't meant to be put into a safe for future profit. "I remember someone to whom I'd given a case of 1859," he recalled, "and one day, the man came up to me and said that he couldn't drink the wine. I asked him why not, and he said that it was worth too much money. 'Well', I said, 'I didn't give it to you as a way for you to make a profit. I gave it to you to drink.' The proof of the pudding is in the eating. The proof of Lafite is in the drinking."

When asked to describe the essence of Lafite, he responded that it is very subtle, with a fragrance of violets, and that this unique blend of taste and fragrance comes from the way the Château's land is composed. "The Pauillacs can be very hard," he explained. "The difference is that Mouton is completely on a plateau and gets sun all the time. Latour has very, very strong earth and thus produces very strong wine. Lafite has very poor earth, purely gravel.

"Philippe decided in the years between the two wars to make a wine that resembled a Burgundy rather than a Bordeaux. In those days, Burgundy was the more popular of the two. And so he made wines with a higher proportion of Cabernet Sauvignon in the blend. Lafite is a blend of a smaller proportion of Cabernet Sauvignon, Petit Verdot, Merlot, and Cabernet Franc."

Baron Elie hates banquets, comparing them to American conventions, but he remembered the best party at Lafite as being when the former *maître de chai*, Georges Revelle, was appointed to La Légion d'Honneur in 1959, for his services to wine.

"We threw a little party for Monsieur Revelle, who got the Legion of Honor for having produced the best wine of France for so many years, and he gave an extraordinarily moving speech," the Baron remarked.

He had "no comment" on the 1855 classification or the rumored rivalries between himself and his cousin Philippe. And as far as foreign involvement and investments in the first growths of the Gironde are concerned, he isn't overly worried. "Are they going to change the earth? Bring in American soil?" he asked.

Like most of the men of the Gironde, Baron Elie believes that the earth is more important than anything else. "Tractors? We've got them. Sprays? We use them. The dramatic changes have happened with mechanization. There are no bad years anymore. The wine will always be good, healthy. So there'll always be a harvest. It's a very delicate thing," he added, "very *fingerspich,* as they say in German."

"What is *fingerspich?*" I asked.

"*Fingerspich* is the tip of your fingers. You've got to play it by ear very often."

Baron Philippe de Rothschild

Château Mouton-Rothschild

What a sight! There he sits, in his regal splendor, books and papers and other paraphernalia scattered about his swirl-posted bed—Baron Philippe de Rothschild in residence. So much is he like a Cheshire cat, complete with padded black slipper paws and round jolly face, that it is hard to resist a chuckle to view such a delicious creature. Except that like a cat,

he's so intelligent and quick that you don't dare, because he will strike you dead with one slashing paw.

Baron Philippe has earned his high profile by howling about his first-growth status, by making the excellent Château Mouton-Rothschild wines, and by living a spectacular life.

I'm convinced that wines sell better when their producers have personality. Even if Baron Philippe's wines were less fine, the author, translator, curator, and jet-setting personality would still be able to promote them. He is, without a doubt, one of the most original men in the entire world and certainly the most colorful of conservative and conventional Bordeaux.

Baron Philippe de Rothschild

Baron Philippe gives audiences in his private bedroom, but only to a select few. When he is not entertaining, he is traveling or working. The man's energy is boundless.

"What's happened since you became a first growth," I asked, hoping for an audacious reply—which, indeed, I got.

"I remained a first growth. . . . I *remained* a first growth," he declared proudly. "I have always been . . . except on paper."

He talked about the classification itself, explaining that unless all the owners of the various châteaux agree, it is no good to impose a set of rules on them. "You can't impose a classification without agreement, because each growth belongs to the earth. It's part of the property. Each owner has to say: 'Yes, I agree,' or it can't be done."

As suddenly as a chameleon he changed moods, recalling an anecdote about Raoul Blondin, his winemaker: "I asked him what he thought of the 1975 vintage," confided Rothschild. "Raoul looked at me with tears in his eyes, saying he could not believe that God had blessed him in one lifetime with two unbelievable vintages—1945 and 1975—and he told me that he knew the 1975 was the best of his lifetime.''

Rothschild's involvement with Mouton-Rothschild began in 1918, when he visited the Château on his summer vacation.

"The place was in shambles, and I began fixing it up,'' he said, explaining that this rusticity was an inheritance of the absentee landlords of the nineteenth century. "The place was a desert,'' he recalled. "It took nine hours to get here by train from Paris. Then I had to take another train in Bordeaux for another hour and one-half. Then a horse cart picked me up, and that was another half-hour ride to the Château.

"Aside from that inconvenience, there was no one to talk to,'' he reminisced. "There were only the workers, and they were very charming and endearing people, but poor company. So what was the purpose of coming here? Absentee landlords were putting money into these estates, but they weren't reaping great profits.''

The nineteenth-century Bordeaux *négociants* and shippers were quite flashy, explained the Baron, traveling throughout the world selling the wines of the region—and with splendid results. "I'm the one who has moved the activity away from Bordeaux—the first to start the great activities in the land and not in Bordeaux. Life is moving away from Bordeaux because there is no more work there, and it is too crowded. Also, communications are easier now.''

People were very charming in the old days, he said, and many witty conversationalists existed. "But those days are disintegrating. Those elegant men with their tails and the lavish parties—all that is a thing of the past.'' Of present-day personalities in wine, he likes Alexis Lichine very much. He believes the man has done much to open the market for Bordeaux wines, of which Baron Philippe's Mouton-Cadet is the top seller. "I'm number one in Bordeaux wines. I've amazed myself, you see. But it's a good wine.''

Baron Philippe has been a commercial pioneer since his first days as manager of Mouton-Rothschild. For better or worse, he has changed the ways of Bordeaux by château-bottling and -labeling, and by promoting a blended wine (his trademarked Mouton-Cadet). He began bottling the harvest at Château Mouton-Rothschild soon after his arrival as a young man of twenty-one. He was concerned about the loss of control if Mouton-Rothschild was shipped to Bordeaux merchants and even abroad in barrels, and thus the bottles labeled in his absence. The practice of château-bottling was revolutionary,

and changed the face of the business; it is still a matter of discussion. "I didn't want to attach my personal label if I couldn't be sure it was being done correctly. I immediately called the owners of the other first growths and said, 'My dear friends, this is what I would like to do.' Everyone thought it was a good idea, and only one was against—Lafite. They said, 'Well, little boy, we are doing very well. Why oblige us to do things that are complicated? The shippers will get mad, and they won't buy from us,' and so on, and so on. It took them a year to make up their minds, but when they saw the other châteaux working with me and that we had a gentleman's agreement to be a united group when dealing with the Bordeaux merchants . . . then they decided to join in. But until then, they thought I was mad. We worked very well together, until 1940. That's when the new generation came in after the war. Then the whole thing blew up again.''

Currently, the Rothschild cousins are speaking, and Baron Philippe continues his magical mystery tour of life, attributing his enormous energy to strong healthy ancestors; quoting his late wife, Pauline, he said: "I owe my energy to all my ailments; they are so many.''

Peter Sichel

Château Palmer

In his ample, airy office high above the Quai de Bacalan sits the sandy-haired, youngish Peter Sichel, wine merchant, author, and authority on Bordeaux and the wine trade. He is immensely respected in Bordeaux and was the first foreigner to become president of the Bordeaux Syndicate of Growers.

Sichel exhibits the dry wit of his late father, Allan Sichel, a man of letters who not only was a great wine merchant but did much for the renaissance of quality at Château Palmer. Sichel went on to explain his intricate relationship both to Peter Max Sichel, who is active in New York selling mainly Blue Nun Liebfraumilch, and to Walter Sichel, who has a wine brokerage firm operating out of London.

"They are on the German side of the family,'' he explained. "It all started in the 1850s with a man named Herz Sichel, who was quite prosperous as a wine broker. My great-grandfather, who was Danish, married into the family, came into the business, and changed his name to Sichel.''

Peter Sichel is the first person in his family to live in Bordeaux on a permanent basis, and he and his family reside at the Château Angludet in Can-

Clusters are small- to medium-sized and weigh 1/6 to 1/4 of a pound; yield is 3 to 6 tons per acre.

Berry is pale yellow with a greenish tint.

Berries are medium-sized and weigh 1.5 gr.

Berry skin is thick and tough.

Tip is felty.

3 seeds.

Leaf is large, green with rust spots.

Cluster is winged and conical.

Teeth are convex and concave.

Orbicular leaf has lyre-shaped edges. The underside is cobwebbed.

PINOT BLANC makes Tokay d'Alsace; primarily used as a blending wine
Aroma: Tart green apples
Bouquet: Vanilla
Taste: Dry, rich, with tannic qualities
At best: Austere, rich, firm wine
Aging potential: 1—5 years
Climate Regions: 1, 2

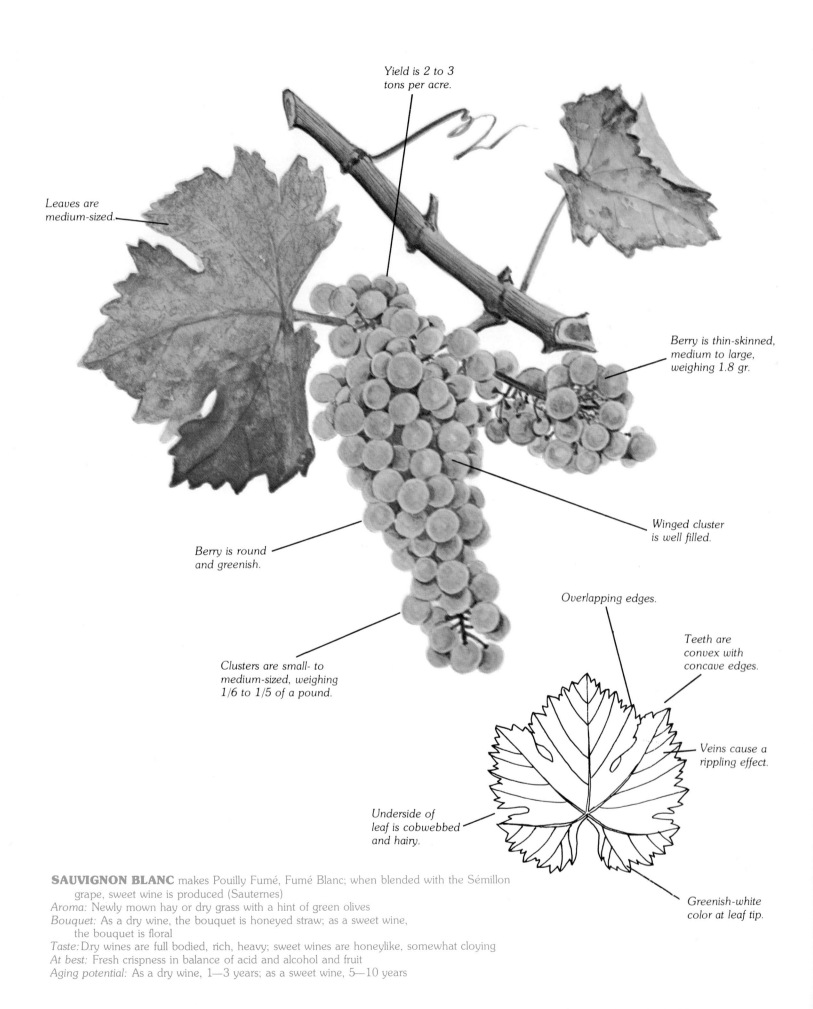

Yield is 2 to 3 tons per acre.

Leaves are medium-sized.

Berry is thin-skinned, medium to large, weighing 1.8 gr.

Winged cluster is well filled.

Berry is round and greenish.

Overlapping edges.

Teeth are convex with concave edges.

Veins cause a rippling effect.

Clusters are small- to medium-sized, weighing 1/6 to 1/5 of a pound.

Underside of leaf is cobwebbed and hairy.

Greenish-white color at leaf tip.

SAUVIGNON BLANC makes Pouilly Fumé, Fumé Blanc; when blended with the Sémillon grape, sweet wine is produced (Sauternes)

Aroma: Newly mown hay or dry grass with a hint of green olives

Bouquet: As a dry wine, the bouquet is honeyed straw; as a sweet wine, the bouquet is floral

Taste: Dry wines are full bodied, rich, heavy; sweet wines are honeylike, somewhat cloying

At best: Fresh crispness in balance of acid and alcohol and fruit

Aging potential: As a dry wine, 1—3 years; as a sweet wine, 5—10 years

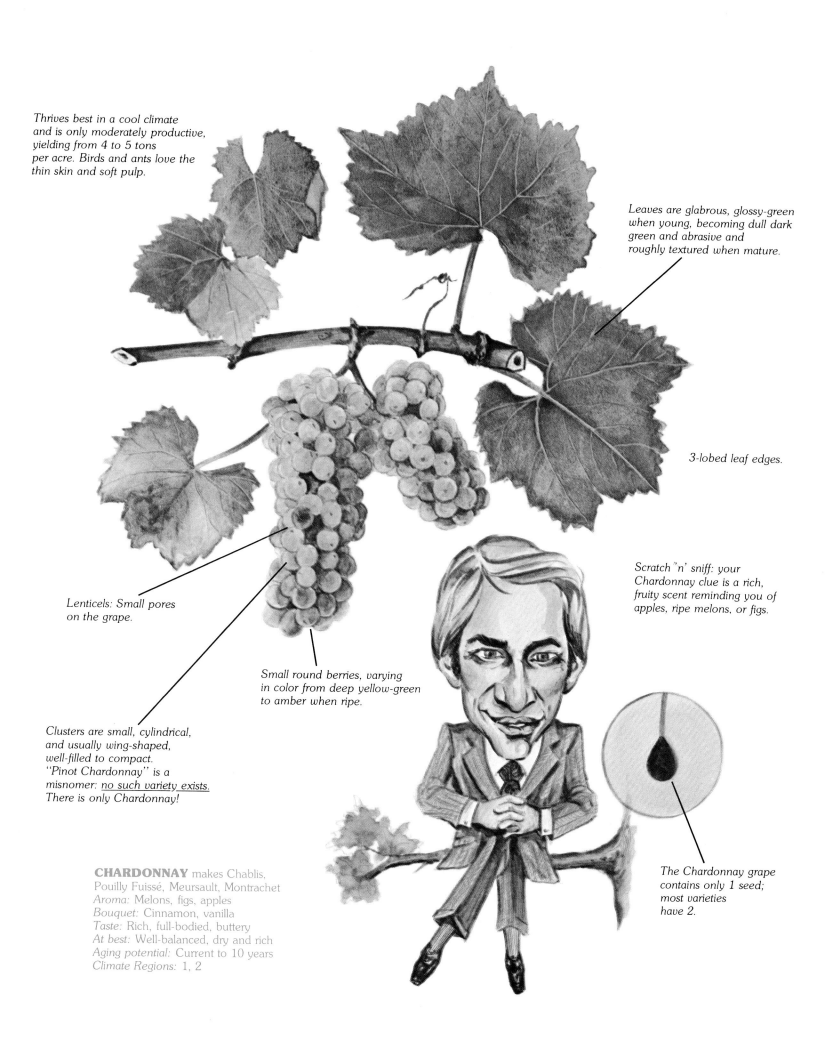

Thrives best in a cool climate and is only moderately productive, yielding from 4 to 5 tons per acre. Birds and ants love the thin skin and soft pulp.

Leaves are glabrous, glossy-green when young, becoming dull dark green and abrasive and roughly textured when mature.

3-lobed leaf edges.

Lenticels: Small pores on the grape.

Scratch "n' sniff: your Chardonnay clue is a rich, fruity scent reminding you of apples, ripe melons, or figs.

Small round berries, varying in color from deep yellow-green to amber when ripe.

Clusters are small, cylindrical, and usually wing-shaped, well-filled to compact. "Pinot Chardonnay" is a misnomer: <u>no such variety exists.</u> There is only Chardonnay!

The Chardonnay grape contains only 1 seed; most varieties have 2.

CHARDONNAY makes Chablis, Pouilly Fuissé, Meursault, Montrachet
Aroma: Melons, figs, apples
Bouquet: Cinnamon, vanilla
Taste: Rich, full-bodied, buttery
At best: Well-balanced, dry and rich
Aging potential: Current to 10 years
Climate Regions: 1, 2

Sparse leaf cover.
Leaf is a dark
russet green.

Cluster is winged
and heavily shouldered;
weighs 1/3 to 1/2 of a pound.

Berry is ellipsoidal,
medium to large with
a soft, thin skin.
Color is black
with a silver bloom.

Clusters are
compact and
cylindrical.

5-lobed leaf
with deeply
indented sinuses.

PETITE SIRAH makes Rhône Valley wines
Aroma: Black pepper, raisins, currants, violets
Bouquet: Wood, tar, tobacco
Taste: Solid body, slightly harsh in youth and smoother in maturity
At best: Vigorous, full-bodied richness with acidity
Aging potential: 5—10 years
Climate Regions: 2, 3, 4

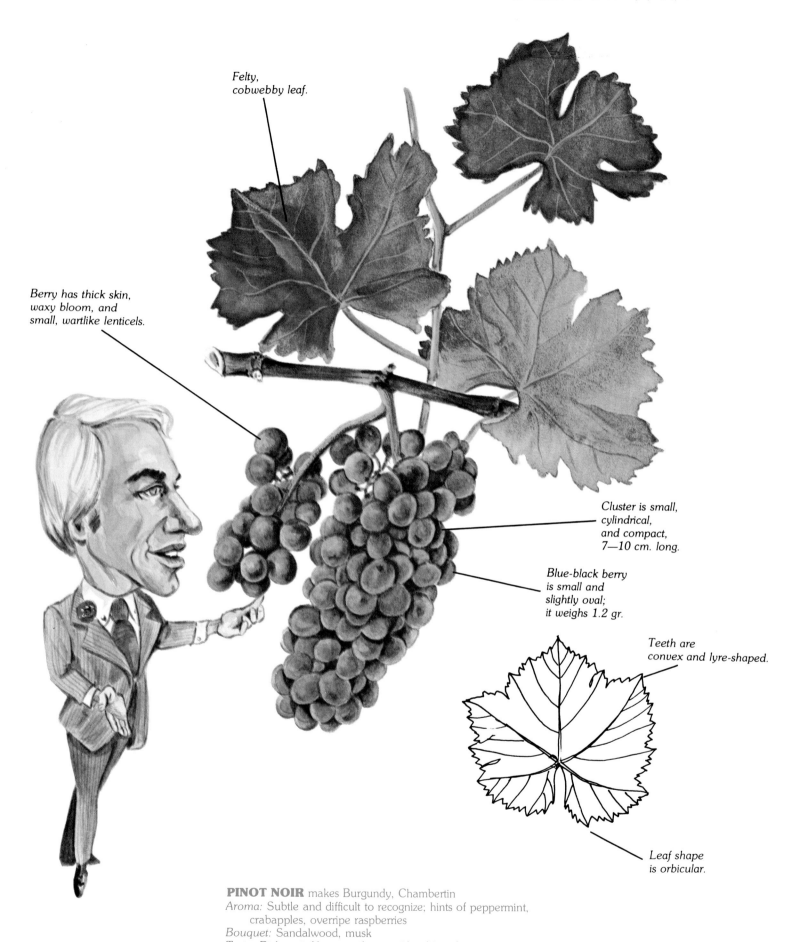

Felty, cobwebby leaf.

Berry has thick skin, waxy bloom, and small, wartlike lenticels.

Cluster is small, cylindrical, and compact, 7—10 cm. long.

Blue-black berry is small and slightly oval; it weighs 1.2 gr.

Teeth are convex and lyre-shaped.

Leaf shape is orbicular.

PINOT NOIR makes Burgundy, Chambertin
Aroma: Subtle and difficult to recognize; hints of peppermint, crabapples, overripe raspberries
Bouquet: Sandalwood, musk
Taste: Rich, satinlike smoothness with a hint of sweetness
At best: Rich, fruity acids, good dark crimson red color
Aging potential: 5—7 years; can continue development for much longer
Climate Regions: 1, 2

Leaves are dark-green.

Deep sinuses are typical.

Leaves have 5 to 7 lobes with fuzzy undersides.

Cluster stem is woody.

Berry is thin-skinned and medium-sized, weighing 2.0 gr.

Compact clusters are medium to large in size, and weigh 1/3 to 1/2 of a pound. Yield is 4 to 10 tons per acre.

Cluster is cylindrical and heavy-winged.

Rust-colored dots at apex.

ZINFANDEL grown only in California
Aroma: Raspberries, strawberries, roses
Bouquet: Faded roses with overtones of woodiness
Taste: Tangy spicelike dryness
At best: Fresh acid and fruit in balance
Aging potential: 3—8 years
Climate Regions: 2, 3

Greenish-white leaf.

Leaf is orbicular in shape.

Teeth are convex.

Clusters are compact and yield 5 to 10 tons per acre.

Clusters are heavily shouldered and slightly conical, weighing 1/5 to 1/3 of a pound.

GREY RIESLING primarily used as a blending wine in Blanc de Blancs
Aroma: Melons
Bouquet: Dried fruit; raisinlike, honeylike
Taste: Grapey wine with a certain tart quality
At best: Dry, with fresh acidity
Aging potential: Current to 3 years
Climate Regions: 2, 3

Berry is long, oval, and medium to small. Color is reddish tan and greenish.

Oval-shaped berry weighs 2.0 gr.

Cane is a pale pink-brown color.

Cylindrical, slightly winged cluster is compact; yield is 5 to 8 tons per acre.

Leaf is shiny with copper patches.

Berry is black with white bloom and thick skin.

3-lobed leaves, appearing cobwebby.

Growing tip is white.

GAMAY makes Beaujolais
Aroma: Fresh raspberries, roses
Bouquet: Best drunk young; will not develop much bottle bouquet
Taste: Fruity and tart with crisp freshness
At best: Bright red color and tart acid and fruity character
Aging potential: Current to 3 years
Climate Regions: 2, 3

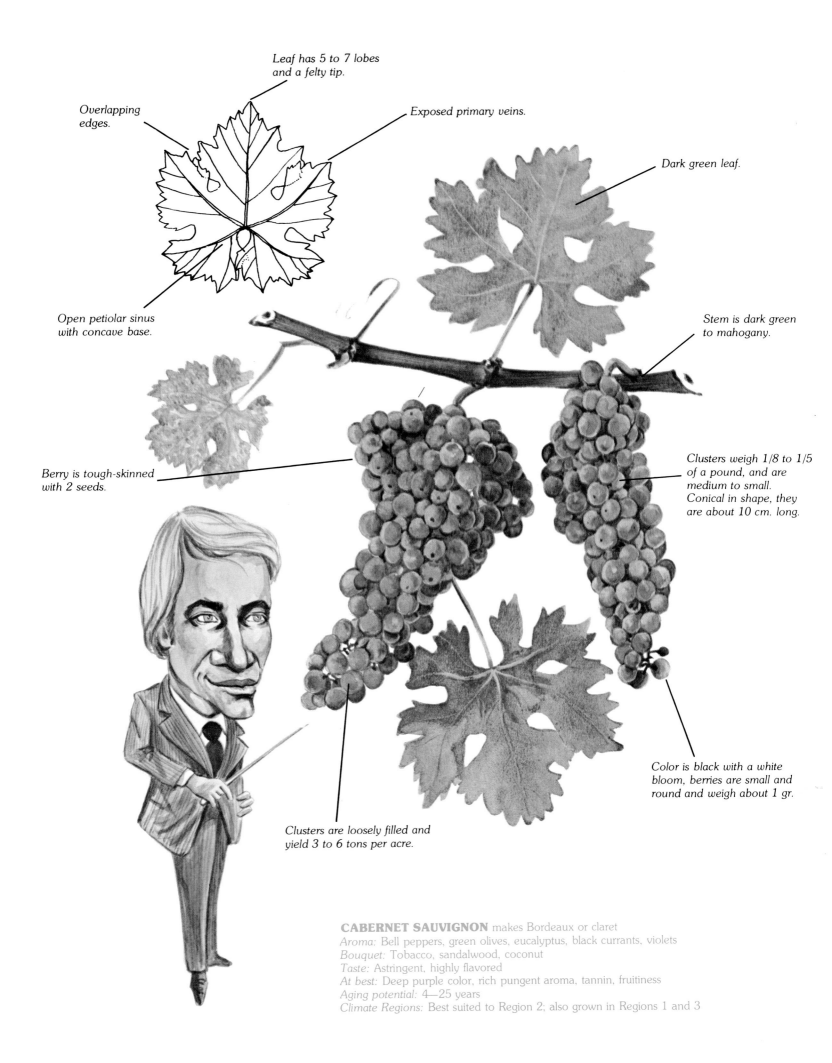

Leaf has 5 to 7 lobes and a felty tip.

Overlapping edges.

Exposed primary veins.

Dark green leaf.

Open petiolar sinus with concave base.

Stem is dark green to mahogany.

Berry is tough-skinned with 2 seeds.

Clusters weigh 1/8 to 1/5 of a pound, and are medium to small. Conical in shape, they are about 10 cm. long.

Color is black with a white bloom, berries are small and round and weigh about 1 gr.

Clusters are loosely filled and yield 3 to 6 tons per acre.

CABERNET SAUVIGNON makes Bordeaux or claret
Aroma: Bell peppers, green olives, eucalyptus, black currants, violets
Bouquet: Tobacco, sandalwood, coconut
Taste: Astringent, highly flavored
At best: Deep purple color, rich pungent aroma, tannin, fruitiness
Aging potential: 4—25 years
Climate Regions: Best suited to Region 2; also grown in Regions 1 and 3

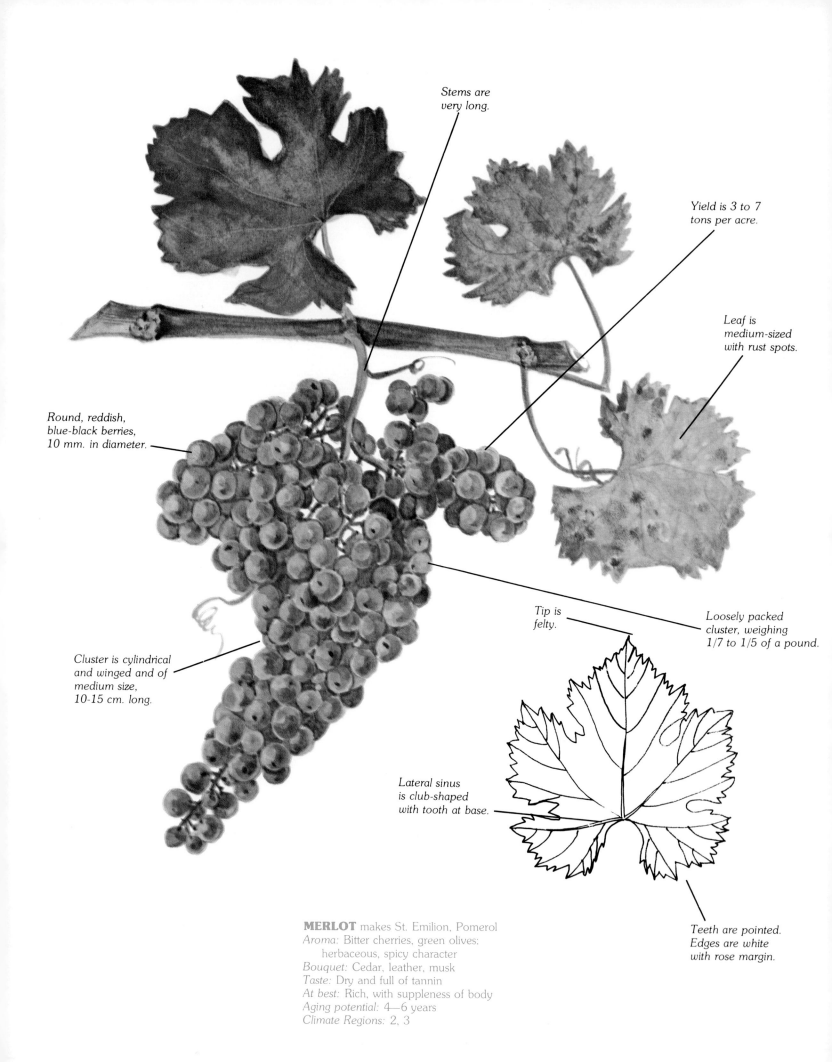

Stems are
very long.

Yield is 3 to 7
tons per acre.

Leaf is
medium-sized
with rust spots.

Round, reddish,
blue-black berries,
10 mm. in diameter.

Cluster is cylindrical
and winged and of
medium size,
10-15 cm. long.

Tip is
felty.

Loosely packed
cluster, weighing
1/7 to 1/5 of a pound.

Lateral sinus
is club-shaped
with tooth at base.

Teeth are pointed.
Edges are white
with rose margin.

MERLOT makes St. Emilion, Pomerol
Aroma: Bitter cherries, green olives;
    herbaceous, spicy character
Bouquet: Cedar, leather, musk
Taste: Dry and full of tannin
At best: Rich, with suppleness of body
Aging potential: 4—6 years
Climate Regions: 2, 3

Cane is beige
with dark streaks.

Leaves are dark green
with brown patches.

Yield is 4 to 10
tons per acre.

Clusters are compact
and weigh about
1/3 of a pound.

Clusters are winged
and conical,
15-20 cm. long.

Tip is felty.

Berry is oval,
weighs 1.6 gr.
and is firm and
golden yellow.

Surface veins are red.

Edges tend to overlap.

Teeth are convex.

Lyre-shaped leaf
has 3 to 5 lobes.

CHENIN BLANC makes Vouvray, Saumur
Aroma: Fruity ripe melons
Bouquet: Best drunk young; will not develop much bottle bouquet
Taste: Light, delicate, slightly acid with a touch of sweetness
At best: Fresh crisp acid-and-sugar balance creates a lively wine
Aging potential: 1—3 years
Climate Regions: 2, 3, 4

Cluster is small to medium, weighing 1/5 to 1/6 of a pound.

Thick-skinned berry is medium to small, weighs 1.4 gr., and is greenish-yellow.

Cluster is cylindrical and winged, well-filled and compact. It yields 4 to 7 tons per acre.

Subject to botrytis cinerea.

Overlapping edges.

Leaf shape is orbicular.

Convex teeth.

Closed, club-shaped.

WHITE RIESLING makes Moselle, Rhinegau
Aroma: Apricots, peaches, honeylike ripe fruit
Bouquet: Dried fruit; raisinlike, honeylike
Taste: Distinct, rich, slightly sweet wine with much acidity
At best: Good acidity, golden color, delicate aroma
Aging potential: 2—4 years; extremely late-picked berries continue
    developing up to 20 years
Climate Region: 1

tenac-Margaux, not far from Château Palmer, which is still in his family. He loves the way of life in Bordeaux but claims that it is far removed from the way it is described in the books of Mauriac or even in Nicholas Faith's recent book, *The Winemasters: The Story Behind the Glory & the Scandal of Bordeaux.* He said, "Bordeaux is fairly isolated geographically from the main run of traffic running north and south through France. But Faith's book was a bit exaggerated in my personal point of view."

Sichel admitted that the *négociant*'s role in the Bordeaux wine trade is changing, as are the necessities of a middleman between the grower and the importer. "In the old days the *négociant* had to buy wine in a very raw state, storing it because the growers were incapable of looking after the wine themselves. *Négociants* were bringing wine into cellars, bottling it and then shipping it to all parts of the world. The whole economics of producing wine was so poor that even up to 1959 the top châteaux were selling a bulk of their wine prior to the vintage in order to pay for it. Now the entire apparatus has changed. Fewer and fewer growers are making wine, and very small producers are selling their land to the larger growers or taking their wines to cooperatives. So the aspect of business that was ours before has changed. Still, it is only on a different scale."

Peter Sichel

No company in France, Sichel explained, covers all the various aspects of the wine business. Ten years ago, his company decided to build their own winery. Instead of buying wines from the growers, they could buy the grapes and make the wine themselves, an important step in their plans for future expansion.

The second part of the Sichel business is still entirely exporting, and Sichel maintains that it isn't feasible for growers individually to look after their own markets, since traveling throughout the world would be financially prohibitive. The advantage in using a *négociant* in today's market, he said, is that the grower is afforded both an efficient method of worldwide distribution and the benefits of a company that is in contact with the individual cooperatives and wineries. In other markets, the firm does the classic job of a *négociant,* guaranteeing prices for a year, offering the advantages of dealing with an established firm with a guaranteed continuity of price and quality. Although the buying of wine in the raw state has diminished, the commercial side is even more necessary because many more countries are buying wine now than have at any other time in history.

Sichel pointed out that château-bottling is only a guarantee that the wine has come from the legitimate point of origin. It is not a guarantee of quality. He said that "there is a lot of bad château-bottled wine, and from the many we taste, we select one in fifty."

Sichel is not afraid of changes when it comes to winemaking methods and is quite curious about macerobic fermentation, or *macération carbonique* (fermentation without oxygen, using instead the enzymes in the grape to convert the sugar into alcohol) and believes that this process will have considerable impact on the way people make wines.

Surrounded by a host of competitors, each vying to be the most successful and manipulating a commodity that can be volatile, I asked Sichel if he believed Bordeaux would experience wine booms and busts as it had during the period of 1971. "There's been speculation in Bordeaux since the twelfth century," he said, "and the city lends itself to it. Previously, it had been done by people with funds that were sound but not unlimited. Then, in the period of the middle sixties, we had an influx of corporate money into Bordeaux. The amount of money these companies expended to chase after the same amount of goods multiplied by ten. So consequently, the whole group mentality of speculation was accelerated and accentuated. The big corporations took a hell of a beating, and they're not going to start again. But in another ten years, it might be forgotten and could reoccur. It won't be for some time. . . . too much money was lost."

As I left Peter Sichel's office, I was reminded of the fact that while some things change, others remain the same. Sichel, a transplanted Englishman, has become a true Bordelais who is devoted to his new home and who is able to transcend all the changes that economies or corporate speculation may inject into the Bordeaux wine trade.

André Trichot

Guide Michelin

André Trichot, a staff member of the Guide Michelin, blends into the military-gray drabness of the office in which we speak as easily as he must fade in and out of the gastronomical centers of France. He would make a terrific C.I.A. agent because his manner is polite and unobtrusive; his physical appearance, singularly nondescript.

Hidden deep within the labyrinth of rooms that are the Guide Michelin, we spoke about restaurant service, particularly when it comes to wine, and how inspectors from the Guide Michelin rate this aspect of the restaurant business. Through an interpreter, Trichot spoke slowly and carefully, telling me that the quality of the restaurant dictates how strictly it will be rated on wine service. Citadels of French gastronomy like La Tour d'Argent, Taillevent, Lasserre, or L'Archestrate would be more rigorously judged since they are the best dining spots in the world.

Rules prevail, especially if a restaurant has a sommelier who is aware of the faults of the various wines and is capable of identifying complaints voiced by a customer. A restaurant with a sommelier is rated more strictly than one without because it is assumed that a wine specialist knows what is in his cellar and what wine to recommend with your meal. If you ask him to take back a wine you've ordered, tell him specifically what you don't like about the wine and ask him to taste it.

A wine waiter, Trichot said, should know enough to pour from the left of the person he is serving, pouring the glass three-quarters full, and never, never waiting until it is empty before he refills the glass.

You can safely wager that Monsieur Trichot doesn't easily give three-star ratings, but he also said that a certain amount of tolerance must be exercised because good waiters, in France, like in most other places, are very hard to find.

It is also fair pricing, explained Trichot, to expect to pay more for your wine in a restaurant as you do from a retail outlet, and the special expertise of the sommelier merits a generous tip.

Trichot lamented the dwindling ranks of sommeliers, though he optimistically hoped the reviving interest in the trade among young people might fatten the ranks and elevate the professional standards. When asked if a restaurant could receive a lesser rating because of poor wine service, Trichot replied in the affirmative, saying, "A good sommelier must have a sense of enthusiasm about discovering new wines and relaying this information to his customers, recommending imaginative selections to the people he is serving. If we go to a new restaurant, and the wine service doesn't come to the standards of the food, then we will underrate the restaurant accordingly."

Restaurateurs would be better served if they learned how to buy wines for the establishments they own, especially if they can purchase wines from different regions, added Trichot, noting that three-star restaurants are judged both for their food and wines along with fair prices for services and goods rendered.

The Guide Michelin will not be duplicated in America, at least not by the original French company, because the attempt to evaluate the restaurants of the United States wasn't a resounding success, Trichot said. "We are more old-fashioned in France," he remarked. "You have many chain restaurants in America, while in France, it still is more predominant to see a chef and his family operating the establishment."

Curiously, for a man who appears as precise as a Swiss clock, Trichot displayed an unsuspected streak of romanticism when I asked him what the worst faux pas would be regarding wine in a restaurant. With one grayish eyebrow raised eloquently, he quietly said, "You must never shake a bottle . . . never. With a bottle you must be as delicate as if you were with an infant."

Your Very Own Vineyard

Whether we wine buffs are millionaires or just getting by financially, most of us in our heart of hearts want to buy a vineyard and own a winery. But while you're seeing yourself as the next Robert Mondavi or Madame Leroy-Bize, keep in mind that this is a long-term investment and your financial return will not come in the immediate future. Here are some points to remember:

1. A new vineyard will not reach maturity for seven years.
2. Agriculture is a gamble with nature. You can limit your risks to some extent, but you won't always be able to control disease or bad weather.
3. Unless you are better than Nostradamus, you will find it difficult to anticipate public favorites ten or twenty years down the line. Your best bet in deciding which grapes to grow is to plant what is right for the land you buy.
4. Developing a winery is even more of a headache and one that requires, in California, a financial investment of about $1,000,000—and that is a conservative figure based on today's inflationary dollar.

On the other hand:

1. Wine is the most glamorous agricultural byproduct there is. You will need money, creativity, management skills, and a knowledge of wine. But if Professor Peynaud is right and Napa Valley becomes the next Golden Slope of Wine, your investment in California should eventually make you a nice profit and bring you prestige—unless, of course, there's an earthquake or you find yourself being taken over by a giant condominium, in which case all bets are off.
2. If you have to get out, it's reassuring to remember that real estate always increases in value in prime areas and accelerates faster than other properties.

This said, let me admit that I too have been bitten by the bug. I've been trying to find my Napa Valley dream spot for many years, but bringing together the right investors and the right property at the right time is not easy.

A friend in real estate who specializes in vineyard properties has a sixth sense about what's likely to come up on the market, and every time his sixth sense vibrates, he faithfully calls me, certain that I and my group will eventually be able to purchase a truly great vineyard. Having spent a good deal of time trudging through rows of Cabernet Sauvignon with José, I've become something of an expert on inspecting vineyards.

A recent phone call from José advised me of a "beautiful piece of property you've got to see. This could be the one." Ever optimistic (you have to be—you never know), I drove north with him to the Napa fields to look at still another property. This one was a totally rundown piece of land, with poor, shallow soil. The ancient barn and ranch house were falling apart, the fence was crumbling, and the farm equipment, totally rusted, was circa 1900.

But it would have been a big mistake to shrug and turn away. The woebegone appearance of the site didn't fool me. The location on a hillside provided excellent drainage, and there was a nearby river and a man-made lake on the property. The slope had good afternoon exposure to the sun. When you're looking to purchase a vineyard, forget about amenities such as indoor plumbing: you're looking at the soil, water, and sun. Tall weeds are a telltale sign that the soil is retaining excess water that can rot the vine roots. Water sources are very important, especially in drought-prone California, where water reservoirs are built not only to irrigate but to protect the delicate vines from frost. Look at the contours of the land: a site with many hills and slopes will have a variety of microclimates and sun exposures. Examine the soil: while fertile soil will produce heavier crops, lighter complex soil with layers of gravel and sand will give forth quality grapes.

Is the soil heavy clay? Is it poorly drained? Does it have a high concentration of alkali salts or other toxic materials? In California at least, a yes answer to any of these questions should make you reconsider. Incidentally, discussing these points with the real estate man and the owner will let them know you're not a greenhorn.

The desolate-looking parcel we saw that day met all the qualifications. José was right—this could have been the one. Unfortunately, the owner's heir decided not to sell. So I couldn't yet report to my potential investors that I'd found El Dorado. My group, incidentally, comes from the music industry. Music personalities are making huge sums of money and can make the sizable financial investment required without depending on immediate return. They're looking for an investment that makes a statement about quality and gives prestige. Ownership of a first-class California winery certainly fits that bill. Many of these people have curiosity about and love for good wines—I know, because some of them are my customers—and their names are capable of generating interest in wines and a new winery. I had many meetings with rock stars and moguls of the industry and learned the first lesson: Someone in your group has to know something about the business and must be ready—tactfully—to help those who don't. I recall a meeting about what types of

SAMPLE COSTS TO PRODUCE
CANE-PRUNED, TRELLISED WINE GRAPES
NORTH COAST COUNTIES—1978

Yield: 4 tons per acre

Operation	Hours per acre	Labor	Fuel and repairs	Cash and labor cost per acre Materials Kind and quantity Dollars	Cost	Total
Cultural Costs						
Pruning—413 vines/acre	26.0	124.00				124.00
Brush disposal (chopper)	.5	2.65	2.35			5.00
Tying canes	4.0	19.00				19.00
Sulfuring 4X	1.2	5.70	4.30	Sulfur 50# @ 5¢	3.00	13.00
Insect control				Application 300 gal. @ 3½¢	10.50	
				Materials	23.50	34.00
Fertilize	.5	2.40	2.10	Nitrogen 30# @ 25¢	7.50	12.00
Suckering	5.0	24.00				24.00
Vine row spray to control				Materials	11.00	
annual weeds				Application	4.00	15.00
Cultivate 4X	3.0	15.75	8.25			24.00
Irrigation 2X	1.0	4.75	17.25	Pumping 6"	16.00	38.00
Frost protection	1.0	4.75	17.25	Pumping 6"	16.00	38.00
Misc. labor supplies, etc.		10.00	5.00		17.00	32.00
Interest on operating capital 9%					17.00	17.00
TOTAL CULTURAL COSTS		213.00	56.50		125.50	395.00
Harvest Costs						
Picking—4 tons @ $55/ton		220.00				220.00
Supervision	4.0	21.00				21.00
Move gondolas, misc.	2.0	12.00	3.00			15.00
Haul to winery				4 tons @ $10/ton	40.00	40.00
TOTAL HARVEST COSTS		253.00	3.00		40.00	296.00
Cash Overhead						
Misc., office, etc.					40.00	
Taxes					172.00	
TOTAL CASH OVERHEAD						212.00
TOTAL CASH COST		466.00	59.50		377.50	903.00
Management						120.00

Investment Cost	Per acre	Annual cost Depreciation	Interest @ 8%	
Land	$ 4,000		$320	
Vineyard	5,680	$189	227	
Irrigation system	1,800	90	72	
Buildings	250	12	10	
Equipment	1,000	100	40	
Site conversion	900		72	
	$13,630.	$391	$741	1,132.00
TOTAL COST PER ACRE				2,155.00
Cost per ton @ 4 ton yield				538.75

COST PER TON AT VARYING YIELDS
CANE-PRUNED, TRELLISED WINE GRAPES

Tons	Picking cost Per ton	Per acre	Haul Per acre	Other costs Per acre	Total cost Per acre	Per ton
2	$100	$200	$20	$1,895	$2,115	$1,058
3	60	180	30	1,895	2,105	702
4	55	220	40	1,895	2,155	539
5	45	225	50	1,895	2,170	434
6	45	270	60	1,895	2,225	371

grapes should be grown on a proposed property. One very famous rock star, $500,000 check in hand, declared that his only concern was that he be able to see the Cabernet Sauvignon *trees* from his condominium window.

While I could, gently, straighten him out on that one, there were still many things I too had to learn. As the wine man in our group, I was asked to supply facts and figures. I found the Federal Land Bank most helpful. In California, excellent sources of information are California State University at Fresno and the University of California at Davis, whose department of viticulture and oenology is world famous and has done much to establish the excellence of California's wine-producing regions. From them I received detailed data about climatic conditions, soils, microclimates, and the ripening patterns of grapes. The University of California Cooperative Extension provided me with sample first-, second-, and third-year costs for establishing a vineyard as well as sample costs for grape production. To put you in the picture right away, before you plant a single vine, your initial investment on a 40-acre plot—including land purchase, site conversion (tree or vine removal), soil ripping and fumigation, irrigation and frost control, buildings and equipment—is estimated (in 1978) at $7,950 per acre.

Having acquired your site, you'll find your first year of ownership filled with activity as you prepare the land to sustain a healthy vineyard. Very little open land is available in California, and most vineyards are planted on old orchard and vineyard sites. So beginning right after the rainy season, you'll be clearing up access roads and fencing your land. The soil will be ripped to a depth of four feet by a plowlike device shaped like a large tooth that is dragged through the soil by a heavy tractor. Ripping aerates the soil, allowing the next winter's rains to penetrate and break up the hard pan layers of soil that would prevent root development of the young wines. The soil must be analyzed and appropriately fertilized, as well as fumigated to eliminate disease-causing pests.

The vine will have to be protected from frost damage by wind machines, heaters, or sprinklers. Heaters are rarely used today because of the cost of petroleum. The obvious advantage of the sprinkler system, despite its expense, is that it will also provide irrigation in dry seasons. Its usefulness against frost damage relies on the 32°F. freezing point of water and the fact that when water freezes, this physical change produces heat. If the air temperature is 30°, the umbrella of water spraying over the vineyard is much warmer. If the air temperature falls to 26° or 24°, the spraying water will begin to coat the vines

with ice. These mid-20° temperatures are the lowest you're likely to get, and these periods of cold usually last only a few hours before dawn. Because heat is produced in the process of freezing, the ice will, for a time, actually protect the vines, which will be warmer than the surrounding air. A sprinkler system is expensive because it requires a reservoir of water, powerful pumps, and a network of pipes to carry the water throughout the vineyard without interfering with plowing or drainage.

To make sure the vine roots will be dry and not subject to rot, low areas are dug up and gravel is run into tile drainage pipes. The soil is harrowed to a fine powder, and the vineyard is graded to trim off high spots and fill in the lower areas. The land is surveyed so that the rows of the vines will be straight and evenly spaced, thus allowing them to have maximum exposure to the sun. The spot where each vine is to be planted is marked with chalk, and a vine-supporting stake is firmly driven into the ground. Trenches are dug, and the piping is laid for the sprinkler system. The pipes in the ground are connected at regular intervals with six-foot-high vertical pipes with sprinkler head attachments.

When you're ready to plant in the spring, you'll purchase vines from a nursery that specializes in these plants, which should be one or two years of age, of the proper clonal type, and certified to be disease resistant and virus free.

You may need temporary fencing to protect your vineyard from rabbits for the first two or three years, and in some locations you may have to install permanent fencing to keep off deer. These costs vary depending on the individual location, but they generally range from $3 to $4 per foot of installed fence, with an annual overhead and maintenance cost of $35 to $50 per acre. And don't forget gopher control.

You will need a tractor, a pick-up truck, disc harrow, chopper, duster, and a couple of gondolas, as well as small shop tools. Of course, you may be able to reduce your investment here by buying used equipment or renting equipment that you use only occasionally.

Your personnel costs are a very important consideration. Vital to your organization is a knowledgeable vineyard manager. He's the fellow who must have intimate knowledge not only of the land but literally of each vine in the vineyard. He must be aware of the low spots in the land, where drainage may be improper. He knows the cycles of each particular plot of land and what it has the potential to produce.

In your vineyard's second year, you'll be cultivating, irrigating, waging war on gophers, fertilizing, and spring pruning.

In the third year—known as the third leaf—you'll have your first crop for harvest. In the fourth year, income from the vineyard should pay for operating expenses; the cycle of maintenance will re-main essentially the same. It will be in the seventh year that the seventh leaf will flower and the vine-yard will come into its maturity, fulfilling its produc-tion potential. You are now a grapegrower. And I promise you: Most people who start by growing wine grapes are soon crushing them into wine.

Touring the Wine Regions of the World

Before You Go . . .

Adopt the Boy Scout motto "Be Prepared" when planning a trip to your favorite winery, whether at home or abroad. Not only will you enjoy the trip more heartily, you'll also be a more appreciated guest. The owners of wineries producing first-class wines are like matinee idols. They are lionized, besieged, and assaulted as if all the fan clubs of the world had turned into the hordes of Atilla the Hun. I will never forget a luncheon at Mouton-Rothschild, before the new visitors' center and tasting area were built. Tourists were tapping and peering through the windows of the Baron's private quarters like a mob of groupies.

Regardless of a château's fame for its fabulous wine, it is still someone's private home. When you visit, therefore, even though you may be highly enthusiastic, maintain the same polite sense of decorum you would have entering someone's living room as a dinner guest.

You will bestow enormous flattery on a winery owner when it is obvious that you've taken the time to learn about him and his wines; he will respond to your informed interest and will regard you as someone special. And if you do your homework, you won't be caught asking Louis Latour of Burgundy about Cabernet produced in the Médoc, or Peter Sichel of Bordeaux about his expertise in producing a terrific Gevrey-Chambertin. You don't have to be afraid to ask questions, but make them intelligent and relevant to the person you're talking to.

Become familiar with the grapes that grow in a particular region, the local methods of vinification, and the history of the area. Then, while on your trip and listening to your guide or a winemaker, you'll be better able to appreciate what he has to say. Write to the winery or wineries that you are planning to tour, giving the dates you'd like to visit. Don't be bashful about expressing your feelings about their product, if you are sincere. Say how impressed you've been by the winery's history and its magnificent wines. Make it clear that you are a fan and that you plan to let others know about this wonderful winery.

If you have a regular wine merchant, ask him to write a letter of introduction for you. If you shop at a large chain store or supermarket, prepare a letter for the liquor manager's signature; even offer to mail it for him. As your visit approaches, send a telegram confirming your arrival on a particular day at a set time.

On behalf of the wine merchants and liquor-store owners of the world, I'd now like to make a personal plea. If your wine merchant goes to the trouble of arranging an appointment, try to be polite and on time. Failure to appear may mean a staff member will be kept waiting for you, wasting an afternoon that could be used for other business duties. Also, rudeness on your part will reflect unpleasantly on your wine merchant, who probably has had to contact the shipper with whom he deals, requiring a middleman to make further arrangements for you. In August, when almost all of the Bordeaux wine cellars are closed for the entire month, with only a skeleton staff on duty, this increases the inconvenience to your prospective host or hostess.

If for emergency reasons you must cancel your

appointment, make sure you are courteous enough to call or send a telegram. If your French, Spanish, German, or Portuguese isn't good enough, have the hotel staff call for you.

Most shippers will try to accommodate their retail clients. But it is up to you, as the individual being extended the courtesy, to make sure you don't become one more horror story for their files. Every shipper can tell you Ugly Tourist stories about people who come at noon, hoping for a free meal, or cause a lot of waste and inconvenience at an estate by wanting to taste a number of wines, or who try to cart off souvenirs beyond postcards and brochures.

One more word about your wine merchant: Send him a note of thanks, or better yet, bring him a souvenir of your trip. I've sent many people abroad with letters of introduction and many hours of secretarial time were spent in paper work and communiqués, but very few have taken the time to thank me for the effort expended. One man brought me back an old corkscrew, and that made him a very special individual in my eyes. Now, when there is a rarity or limited amount of stock in a particular wine, he's one of the first individuals I call. Why? Because he was thoughtful and polite. That's the way you want to be remembered by everyone who plans your trip.

I have traveled all over Europe visiting many wineries. Winemakers and proprietors are always impressed with my gift of a cowboy hat or a "Wine Merchant" T-shirt, no matter how wealthy or important they are. It is a case of making the unexpected gesture, showing someone that you were thoughtful enough to appreciate the time they are giving you.

To capture the moment, snap a photograph of you and your host, who may be wearing your gift. Send him a copy of the photograph later, further reminding him of you and your visit. Believe me, even if you are Mr. Average American (whatever that means) you'll be a Very Important Person with this approach.

The following are some general pointers that I'd like to give you about traveling through the wine country of France. Each wine region of the country has its own government office (Comité Interprofessionnel du Vin) that will supply information to tourists wishing to visit the various châteaux (addresses in the Appendix). Many have maps and booklets that detail which proprietors welcome tourists and have tasting facilities or offer tours.

For detailed information about each wine-producing district in France, write to the French Government Tourist Office and ask them to send you *Wine Regions/The Traveler in France.* They will also send free maps, brochures, and guidebooks, but be sure to ask. Their offices are at the following addresses:

> *Room 840*
> *9401 Wilshire Blvd.*
> *Beverly Hills 90212*
> *(213) 272-2661*

> *810 Fifth Ave.*
> *New York 10020*
> *(212) 757-1125*

> *Suite 430*
> *645 North Michigan Ave.*
> *Chicago 60611*
> *(312) 337-6301*

> *Room 417*
> *323 Geary St.*
> *San Francisco 94102*
> *(415) 986-4161*

> *1840 Ouest, Rue Sherbrooke*
> *Montreal, Canada*

> *Suite 610*
> *372 Bay Street*
> *Toronto, Canada*

For gastronomical tips on eating your way through France (what a wonderful experience) write to:

> *Traditions et Qualité*
> *15 Rue Lamennais*
> *75008 Paris*
> *France*

Ask for their *Traditions et Qualité Passeport Gastronomique,* a pictorial booklet of 70 top restaurants with a list of their specialties.

Also, write to:

> *Pierre Alexandre*
> *30800 Garons*
> *France*

Ask M. Alexandre to send you *Entente Nationale des Restaurateurs Cuisiniers and Hotelliers de Metier.* This guidebook with English text describing 75 restaurants and hotels, including some in the moderate price range, can be yours for $1.00 and a self-addressed envelope.

Hotels in France must be chosen carefully because you can run into tacky accommodations, including saggy uncomfortable beds and communal bathrooms. In order to be ahead of the game, book yourself in the Relais et Châteaux hotels, which are by far the most reliable. These can range from actual castles to simple inns, but they will all offer high standards of quality and service, and very fine cuisine. A pictorial catalog and rate list of the Relais et Châteaux is available from Air France and from the

French Government Tourist Offices, or write to them directly at: Relais et Châteaux, 17 Place Vendome, 75001 Paris, France.

Hotels and Motels in France and *Guide des Hôtels/Paris, Île de France* are the names of two additional catalogs that you may wish to request from the Tourist Offices in France.

Michelin's red guide to hotels and restaurants of France is another must purchase that is available in bookstores for about $7.00. It is written in French but contains explanatory sections in English. It will give you information on the wine districts and where to find the small bistros and out-of-the-way inns that will appeal to the adventurous traveler.

The Michelin guide has a rating for each restaurant and hotel, giving the price range, number of rooms, map location, address, phone number, and even details like decor, ambiance, and setting. Michelin's inexpensive road maps also are excellent. You can purchase the red map of France for general reference and the more detailed yellow maps for specific regions.

If you feel up to hoofing your way through Paris, there is *Paris, Île de France,* which gives you a street map of Paris and the surrounding areas.

A final note to all travelers: In Europe, don't depend on the telephone. Telex is much safer.

California

Unless you are a seasoned traveler, I suggest that your first foray into the wine country be a domestic one—to the winemaking areas of California—rather than a more complex tour of the European wine scene. But while traveling through California's vineyards, be aware that you are traveling very much in the here and now. This is definitely the fast lane of traffic. California is modern technology and year-to-year innovation.

The advantages in making the home tour first are numerous: People speak the same language you do, comfortable hotels and motels abound, and the California Historical Society (2090 Jackson St., San Francisco 94108) and The Wine Institute (165 Post St., San Francisco 94108) offer much background information on what is available to see and how it is historically relevant. (A list of California wineries appears in the Appendix.)

Most of you will start your tour of the California wine scene from San Francisco. You might enjoy getting into the mood of your wine trip by taking a

tour of the Wine Museum of San Francisco, where wine-related art and objects are centered around viticultural themes such as the grape, harvest, wine mythology, and other subjects.

Most of you are familiar with the Napa Valley, California's most glamorous winemaking area. Many interesting Napa Valley wineries are open to the public, but the three choices I suggest would be the following:

The first would be a visit to the Robert Mondavi winery. Certainly it is one, if not the most, modern winery in the world. Mondavi's curious attitude and habit of listening, copying, and viewing no limitations is reflected in the way the winery is operated. Nothing is sacred, and everything is tried. If something doesn't work, it is thrown out. Computers, high technology, and constant change—that's the Mondavi style. You are quite likely to be pleasantly surprised in the tasting room, where you may get a chance to sip one of the winery's new wines.

The next winery I would visit is again embarked on a path toward high technology and the twenty-first century. No matter how many times you visit, you always learn something. I'm speaking about the French investment in California, Domaine Chandon, the brain child of Robert de Vogüé, former chairman of the board of Moët & Chandon.

This is the place where you learn everything you've ever wanted to know about California champagne and where you get to see the French operation do a bit of experimentation, free of the restrictive union and bureaucratic French laws. You may see mechanical riddling, new yeast-cell experimentation, and even new crushing methods.

The large-scale facility, open to tourists every day but Tuesday and Wednesday, not only teaches you how the *méthode champenoise* has been adapted to California sparkling-wine production but offers a splendid restaurant as an added attraction. Be sure to make advance reservations because the luncheon and dinners are limited to sixty people, and it is very popular with both natives and visitors.

The third stop on our visit to the winemaking methods of the twenty-first century would be a stop at Sterling Vineyards. This mountain-high operation, with its funicular that leads to the top and to the stark-white winery, is straight out of Disneyland. You have the feeling of walking through a hospital (suffering from a lobotomy, perhaps) as visual images and soft voices tell of winemaking, past, present, and future.

This brings up another point I'd like to discuss with you. In my opinion, as the California wine industry's pace has become more hectic, leaving behind the placid pace of the forties and fifties, it is more and more difficult to plan a leisurely visit with the various winemakers. They simply don't have the time to spend an afternoon sipping wine with their out-of-town visitors, and if they do, it is the exception, not the rule.

This doesn't mean that California's wine industry has lessened its lure to a string of educated, free-spirited, and independent people who want to get away from it all. Rewards of the rigorous but emotionally satisfying life of a winemaker has captured the heart of many.

If you want to find this independent loner, it might be worth your while to stray from the beaten path and follow the fellow with the John Deere hat you see shopping in Napa. You are likely to discover he's patriotic, pioneering, and totally intense about making not just good wine but the best. It may be a bumpy, dusty ride to his place but certainly an exhilarating experience for the traveler who wants to have a genuine Napa encounter and not just a casual walking tour.

And visiting the endless number of cellars is only exciting to the wine cognoscente or a person in the industry itself. As Spiro Agnew so cynically put it: "If you've seen one ghetto, you've seen them all." While multimillion-dollar wineries aren't anything like Harlem, there is a certain similarity in the rows of stainless steel tanks you find everywhere, as are the oak casks of aging wine. No matter how beautiful and modern the facility, the scenario is rather similar.

California's wine history isn't old by European standards, and tradition doesn't play a strong role in this area of the world. The theme that should run through your tour, in my opinion, is the architectural and sensory one. In all five regions of California's viticulture, you'll find a diversity of structures, from Cliff May's mission style winery for Robert Mondavi to Beringer's Rheinhaus and to Souverain's hop-kiln style, a Sonoma County landmark.

Venture away from the beaten path. I realize that Napa Valley is the most well-known area to the European or Eastern traveler, but out of more than 400 wineries, only a fraction are located in that county. Poking behind a caravan of cars cautiously making their way through Napa Valley isn't my idea of a terrific holiday. And you can hardly expect a personalized and intimate welcome when the overworked staff has to cater to 50 or 100 people besides yourself.

If you are going to visit Napa, try to drive through the Silverado Trail, especially in the early spring before tourists abound and plowers take over the mustard flowers forming a brilliant yellow carpet that decorates this area. Be sure to stop at Taplin Road, near St. Helena, one of the original 60 or 70 stone bridges that was the reason this valley was called County of Bridges in 1900.

Robert Louis Stevenson spent his honeymoon in the Napa Valley area from 1879 to 1880. The exact location where the Scottish writer and his American bride stayed was an abandoned bunkhouse on the Silverado Trail on Mount St. Helena.

Silver and quicksilver mining in the mountains north and east of Napa Valley inspired the name Silverado, and recollecting his romantic stay in this part of the world, Stevenson wrote *Silverado Squatters.* He is kindly remembered by the citizens of St. Helena, who have treasured Stevenson memorabilia and artifacts in the Silverado Museum.

Each county in California has its own personal history and places of interest. If you are going to link technology, history, and wine together, then my suggestion for a sensible trip would be to select one or two wineries within each of the five climatic regions of California (the only place in the world where this is the case) and visit on a selective basis. This way, you will gain a more graphic example of the best of California's winemaking technology.

Let me give you an example: In Region 1, you could visit Santa Cruz instead of Napa Valley; in Region 2, you might venture into Sonoma or Monterey; in Region 3, you could stop at a few of the Livermore wineries; and in Region 4, you could go to Ukiah or Lodi; or even visit the Eli Callaway winery in Rancho California, which has a Region 5 climate all the way south in San Diego County.

One county, for instance, that offers many viticultural and historical delights is Sonoma County, where on June 14, 1846, the first Bear Flag of the Republic of California was raised. You will see many historical points of interest as you drive or walk through the Old Plaza of Sonoma. The town has many refurbished nineteenth-century buildings, giving you the sensation that at any moment, California's last Mexican Governor, General Mariano Guadalupe Vallejo, will make an appearance.

California's wine history is liberally sprinkled with aggressive characters. General Vallejo, an early California wine pioneer, is certainly among this group. His home, named after a nearby foothill with a flowing stream, is a historical monument, impeccably maintained. It is fascinating not only because you see the General's awards for being a great winemaker (he bottled a bold red wine named Lachryma Montis) but because it gives you a glimpse into what Victorian life was like in California in 1858.

Not too far away, in Glen Ellen, is the 1,400-

acre domain of another romantic, Jack London. This historical state park, the last home of the writer, contains fascinating memorabilia about the author, including London's handwritten diary.

Some of the fine wineries you can visit in this area include Sebastiani (without an appointment) and Grand Cru, Kenwood, and Hanzell Vineyards (where you must give advance notice). Others include Buena Vista and Hacienda Wine Cellars. Sebastiani's tour is extremely informative because you learn old winemaking methods, seeing the contrast with stainless steel and centrifuge technology. At the conclusion, you can taste some of the wine in a charming room that is filled with the family's storehouse of memories.

Sonoma's other principal wine region, the Russian River group, is another area that, if you have adequate time, you should explore. Information can be obtained by writing to Russian River Wine Road, P.O. Box 127, Geyserville 95441. While in this area you can also visit the Korbel Champagne Cellars and one of California's most striking contemporary wineries, Sonoma Vineyards. Souverain Cellars overlooks the Mayacama Mountains, and the winery offers an excellently presented tour.

For those of you who like to combine your vino with a look at the Pacific Ocean, try the Bay Area and Central Coast Counties, where you will find wineries like Wente Brothers, Concannon Vineyards, and Weibel Champagne Vineyards. Just below San Jose is Mirassou Vineyards, one of California's oldest continuing wineries, and the Paul Masson Winery in Saratoga.

If you want to head south towards Los Angeles, travel via the dramatic coastal route of Highway 1. At Paso Robles you can visit Hoffman Mountain Ranch Winery, and near Santa Barbara, in the Santa Ynez Valley, is the Firestone Vineyard and Winery.

If you start your wine tour from Los Angeles, be sure to stop at my shop and browse through our block of underground cellars. You'll also enjoy seeing one of the world's most expensive bottles of wine, a 1929 Jeroboam of Mouton-Rothschild, turned over to me by Baron Philippe de Rothschild. It sits on its own pedestal in my wine shop at 9701 Santa Monica Blvd., Beverly Hills. We are open from 9:30 to 6:30 P.M., Monday through Saturday, and it's definitely worth a visit for any wine lover.

Having dipped your feet in domestic waters, you are now most likely ready to taste the delights of Burgundy and Bordeaux, the serious wine bastions of the French Republic, along with an overview of the German, Italian, Spanish, and Portuguese wine regions.

Bordeaux

A wine buff looks forward to Bordeaux as a Moslem must revere Mecca. It is the holy of holy when it comes to wine, not simply because the wine from this area is considered the world's finest but because tradition, world history, and the wine industry weave a particularly interesting tapestry in this corner of southwestern France.

Bordeaux and its first growths have established themselves as the wine aristocrats of the world. While we may sniff and grumble that Château Lafite isn't quite up to par this year, its name still has impact in Tokyo, Brussels, or in any other cosmopolitan city. The great Bordeaux wines, aside from their quality and variety, have an indefinable glamour. This favorable situation isn't totally unrelated to the history of the area, full of fascinating men and women that left a colorful thread within the weave— long before any current movers created the majestic wine estates.

So prior to reading brochures on hotels, car rentals, and guided tours, step into a time machine and go back, through this chapter, into the life of Bordeaux as it was in the Middle Ages, when this part of the world was isolated from Paris and far closer to London in spirit and trade.

It all started with a woman. Doesn't it always? But this woman was one of the most exciting in history, the beautiful, intelligent, and bewitching Eleanor of Aquitaine. This glamorous heiress to all that she surveyed was the granddaughter of Duke William IX of Aquitaine, the first of the troubadors and a composer of love songs.

She exhibited a distinct sense of style (due, perhaps, to her immense wealth as the heiress to the Duchy of Guienne, Perigord, Limousin, and a half-dozen other pieces of real estate), and was the Jackie Kennedy of her day. Naturally, in keeping with a royal dowry, Eleanor wed two kings. Unfortunately, neither marriage was a smashing success.

The first ceremony occurred in 1137, when she married Prince Louis VII, the son of King Louis VI of France, in the cathedral of Bordeaux. He was a bit of a prig (known as the crowned monk), and in 1152, when he returned from the Second Crusade, Louis decided Eleanor was too light-minded and promptly divorced her. She didn't seem brokenhearted, declaring that "I had thought I'd married a man, not a monk."

Two months later, she married another prospective monarch, Henry Plantagenet, Comte d'Anjou, who also ruled Maine, Touraine, and Normandy, or most of the western part of northwestern France. Henry was all of 19 and Eleanor an older woman of 30. Whether it was a marriage of love or convenience, it certainly was a coupling of two head-strong people. Eleanor's dowry was the southwestern part of Europe, and two years later, when King Stephen of England died, she and Henry II became the monarchs of England, continuing the Plantagenet line.

Two of her sons, Richard the Lion-Hearted and John, inherited the throne after their father's death, but only after Henry and Eleanor had squabbled over his infidelities with the "fair Rosamond" and Eleanor had aided her sons in an unsuccessful plot against Henry's own throne.

Despite their mutual antagonism (Henry had Eleanor kept confined for many years), Eleanor established her own Court of Love at Poitiers and helped her son Richard to secure the throne of England. The battling couple today lie in their eternal rest, side by side, in the great church of Fontevrault near Saumur.

Eleanor's influence over the history of Aquitaine, and Bordeaux, cannot be underestimated. Ten English kings ruled that land as a result of her marriage to Henry II, and free land was granted to the natives as long as they tilled the land and planted vines.

The trade of wine between the port of Bordeaux and England was brisk despite wars and insurrection, and the natives were so pro English that Philip III, son of Louis IX of France, occupied Bordeaux from 1285 until peace resided in 1303. Philip III and Edward II met in Paris to sign a makeshift peace that wasn't to last a very long time. Marriages were arranged to keep peace in the area, with the English hoping to consolidate the dowry for the Crown.

The people of Bordeaux were inclined to favor English rule because they were profiting from the arrangement by selling enormous amounts of wine, and they had gained many privileges, both in business and government. In fact, when Edward II married, he ordered a thousand *tonneau* of wine, equaling 1,152,000 gallons today. In 1442, however, Charles VII of France wanted to be rid of the English and was assisted by Joan of Arc, while Henry VI of England was busy contending with the Wars of Roses.

The French Crown, under Charles VII, eventually regained possession of Bordeaux and negotiated a peace with the clever strategist, Archbishop Peay Berland. Taxes were paid to the French Crown for approximately ten years, but the burghers of Bor-

deaux soon tired of their French brothers and refused to pay taxes, begging Henry VI to send troops to Bordeaux to be rid of their oppressors.

In 1452, Sir John Talbot, Earl of Shrewsbury and head of the English fleet was again sent to do battle in France. Sir John had come out of retirement, but he still had immense dignity in his suit of armor, plumed helmet, jerkin worked with fleur-de-lis, and ermine mantle as part of his costume.

Château Talbot, a *quatrième cru* of St.-Julien, is rumored to have been his headquarters during this final chapter of the Hundred Years' War, and in October 1452, when the citizens of Bordeaux welcomed him as their savior, it probably saw one of the most elaborate receptions the city had ever given. "Le Roi Talbot," he was called. In accord with his rank, a small fortune was given to him by the grateful French. Through the centuries, there has been much speculation about Sir John's fortune, with some rumors being circulated that the treasure was hidden in his headquarters, Château Talbot.

The complete French Army of Charles VII was pitted against Sir John and his small band of men, so on July 15, 1453, Sir John decided to launch a surprise attack against the enemy. Talbot managed to surprise Charles VII and won the day's round. Not waiting for his back-up troops, however, Sir John made a fatal mistake in pressing onward with the fight. The French rallied and won the Battle of Castillon as it became known.

Sir John had, in previous years of fighting, promised the French king when captured, that he would not personally bear arms against his Gallic neighbors. This promise, kept by the honorable gentleman, proved his downfall on July 17, because venturing into battle unarmed, he was fatally wounded. The final scene of Talbot's life is described by William Shakespeare in *Henry VI, Part One,* in which the old man, distraught because his son has just fallen in battle, himself dying, speaks to his troops: "Soldiers, adieu. I have what I would have. Now my old arms are young Talbot's grave."

We may never know whether Sir John buried his treasure at Château Talbot or not, but it is certain that his memory is kindly held by the Bordelais and that the wine bearing his name keeps its promise of excellence. Just as Sir John kept his promise, so do the wines.

Approximately a decade ago, underground caverns crisscrossing the estate were discovered, but digging them thoroughly would have meant destroying the vines. Thus, Sir John's fortune remains speculation.

Another St.-Julien estate, Château Gruaud-Larose, a *deuxième cru,* had an influential owner of a different character. Monsieur Gruaud bought the property in 1757 and was such a perfectionist and disciplinarian that he would observe his workers from the Château tower, where he had a perfect vantage point of the entire property. Anyone caught tippling or slacking on the job would be in serious trouble, especially during the harvest. After the harvest, he would indicate what type of wine had been made by means of a flag. The German flag meant the wine would be supple; the British, that it would be assertive; and the Dutch, that it would be something in between the first two.

It was M. Larose, a descendant of this formidable man, who actively promoted the wine, launching an effective promotion with the slogan: "Le roi des vins, le vin des rois!" This motto—"King of wines, wine of kings"—is still used on the label.

Glamour and magic go hand in hand with the classified growths of Bordeaux, and some châteaux have been greatly influenced by the daring and particular style of one or of many owners.

Château Lagrange, a *troisième cru* of the Médoc is such a place, resembling a haunted fairy-tale palace with its vast park, overgrown lake, and endless barns and stables emanating a strange haunting loneliness. No one has lived there since 1919, and forty bedrooms await the return of human life to the once glorious mansion.

Many Médocains insist it is a malaise of the heart and that spirits of the dead still haunt the spacious rooms and grounds. If so, then one ghost in particular is said to dominate the Château's dim corridors. Her name is Thérésa de Cabarrús, the daughter of Conde de Cabarrús, who governed Spain for Napoleon in 1790. Her beauty was already legendary when she became the mistress and then wife of the French revolutionist Jean Lambert Tallien. She was no ordinary demimondaine but a noblewoman who became the Princesse de Caraman-Chimay and a leader of French society after the Reign of Terror, the bloody culmination to the French Revolution. Madame de la Tour du Pin describes her as a woman with the height of Diana the Huntress of Greek mythology, with ebony tresses that shimmered with silky beauty, and movements described as "those filled with matchless grace."

It was her husband, Jean Tallien, who along with other revolutionaries overthrew Robespierre on the eleventh month of the French Revolutionary Calendar, marked as the *coup d'etat* of 9 Thermidor (July 27, 1794), signaling the end of Robespierre and the great Terror.

Although he was a Thermidorian leader, Tallien had taken part in the Terror and was a butcher, wrote Madame de la Tour du Pin, noting that "it was painful to remember that all of this youth, beauty and grace of Thérésa de Cabarrus are abandoned to a man who every morning signed the death warrants of so many innocent people."

Divine intervention might have played a role in the strange life of Thérésa, for it was through her hold on the fanatic Tallien that she saved the lives of many aristocrats (including Madame de la Tour du Pin), earning the *sobriquet,* or nickname, "Notre Dame de Thermidor."

During the Reign of Terror, the couple lived in Bordeaux at the Hôtel d'Angleterre. History doesn't record whether Mme. Tallien went to Lagrange at vintage time, escaping the crazed times by viewing the peaceful scene of park and vineyard. She was a friend of the painter Goya. Did they go there together?

The estate was sold around 1817, long after her divorce from Tallien, but the passing influence of a Mr. Brown, who briefly owned Lagrange, did not lessen Thérésa's spell on the property. (It might have been Mr. Brown who added the tower, an imitation Italian campanile, simply because it bears no relation to the estate's neoclassic dimensions, more closely resembling the Victorian towers of England, built as viewing perches for the rich.)

Another majestic and haunting figure of Lagrange was the Comte Duchâtel, Finance Minister to King Louis Philippe, who bought the estate in 1842, reigning over a series of hunting parties in the park during his 40 years of ownership. He had been a jovial man, fond of musicals, who had planted giant exotic trees throughout the estate. It was after Duchâtel's death that the estate went into its decline, and the furniture, which might have been of his choosing, is now shabby and worn. Only empty palm pots, vast threadbare pouffs, an abandoned billiard table, and old wicker chairs testify to a more glorious age.

Another Spanish family, the Cendoyas of San Sebastian, have owned Lagrange since 1919. But they don't live there, and the estate manager resides in a cottage near the property. In 1950, the oldest part of the estate was being remodeled, when it was burnt down mysteriously. Was it Thérésa or Comte Duchâtel giving a sign of their presence? The Château remains silent, brooking no intruders, melancholy in the back country of St.-Julien, the shadows of night betraying a feminine profile in the dusk.

Cos-d'Estournel is a château full of life, despite its long history, and is chronicled in an anecdote about a famous taster. It seems this gentleman had a carriage accident that resulted in a serious skull fracture for the gourmand. The man was carried unceremoniously into the nearest home. The doctor treating him decided to bathe the wound with old wine, and as the patient lay there, with some of the liquid trickling down the corner of his mouth, he began to move his lips. Everyone in the room strained to hear what the stricken man was trying to say. Gasping for his final gulp of air, the man uttered these final whispered words: "Cos-d'Estournel. . . 1848 . . ." With that, the epicurean died, correctly identifying the name and vintage, a true connoisseur to the end.

Cos-d'Estournel, a *deuxième cru,* is located in a commune or suburb of St.-Estèphe, and the village of the same name was established on the old capital of the Gallo-Romans. It also is the home of another ancient and noble château, Calon-Ségur, a *troisième cru.* In olden times, *calon* meant "woods," and small medieval boats transported soldiers away in boats called *calones.* The Château became the most favored property of the Marquis Alexandre de Ségur, then president of the Parlement of Bordeaux and owner of the famous Châteaux, Lafite, Latour, and Mouton. Still, Calon-Ségur was the one most beloved by the Marquis, who said: "I make wine at Lafite and Latour, but my heart is at Calon."

St.-Estèphe is a parish known for producing assertive wines that mature with great beauty. Certainly, one of its most famous châteaux with an interesting history is Château Montrose, a *deuxième cru,* also at one time owned by Marquis de Ségur.

In the center of the estate is a small mound of heather that turns pink when it blooms. For this reason, at its inception, the estate became known as Mont-Rose. The Château structure looks a bit like a Swiss chalet, a tribute perhaps to its most influential owner, a Monsieur Mathieu Dollfus from Alsace. Monsieur Dollfus was a progressive employer who added the present *chais,* introduced profit sharing, paid sickness costs for his employees, and even aided expectant mothers.

Dollfus never recovered from nostalgia for his native land, even going to the extent of naming the small streets of the estate Rue d'Alsace, Rue Mulhouse, and so on, trying to recapture the flavor of his former home. Unfortunately, the man's desire to return to his native Alsace wasn't alleviated, and he remained at Montrose long enough to witness the destruction of his vineyard by phylloxera. He became despondent and finally left Bordeaux on his way back to Alsace. His journey was shortened by a heart attack in Paris, and Dollfus never again saw his homeland. Perhaps this is why occasionally when you visit Montrose, heard, late at night, is an echo that is a sound almost like a lost sigh.

Château Carbonnieux, a classified growth of Graves, is another fascinating château that began its history as a place of refuge for General Épernon during the *Fronde* Wars, a series of outbreaks in France during the minority of Louis XIV caused by dissension between the Parlement of Paris and Royal authority along with excessive taxation of the people.

In 1741, the Château passed into the hands of the Benedictines of Sainte Croix de Bordeaux, from which stems the cross emblem of the label. These enterprising monks were interested in research and development and came up with a novel marketing program. Their lovely white wine was immensely popular with the Europeans, but their biggest customers were the Turks. However, since Turkey was a Moslem country where alcoholic beverages were forbidden, the casks arrived in Constantinople with the following phrase stamped on the casks: "Mineral Water from Carbonnieux."

Invitation to the Sistine Chapel and meditation—that's what another classified *cru* of Graves, Château Pape-Clement, is all about. The venerable roots of this Château go back 700 years in time. What secrets does this wine awaken? To me, it is an invitation to meditate—a Palace of Silence. The wine's color is not the normal purple of the Médoc— and not one normally found in Cabernet Sauvignon. Purple has always held a connotation of or a link with wealth, power, and majesty. But this purple isn't a royal or imperial hue. It is the Papal purple of the Church.

The Château once belonged to a prince of the Roman Catholic Church, Bertrand de Got, who inherited the place from his brother, Gaillard. De Got must have been a bit of a puzzle to his neighbors. Evidently he was considered quite eccentric or mad by some, because of his habit of praying in the vineyards. I personally suspect he was trying to exorcise the pests by praying for their quick ascent to another estate of consciousness, but Bertrand never left word on why he conducted himself in such a bizarre manner. He was a very religious man, or at least a highly politicized cleric, and became the Pope in 1305. He took the name Clement V at the time of his consecration at Avignon.

De Got's advance to becoming Pope was greatly assisted by a good friend, Philip the Fair, one of the most powerful dukes of Burgundy. Philip's name was a misnomer because he was anything but fair. He was, however, a devoted pal to de Got. In fact, he had the distinction of being the first person to imprison a Pope. Object: to have the next head of the Church be a Frenchman, namely de Got.

Whatever his qualifications may or may not have been for Pope, Bertrand genuinely enjoyed producing a fine vineyard and built the estate to its greatest success, continuing to read to the vines until he was named Pope. De Got died in 1314, and one of his instructions for burial was that he be laid to rest in his native village of Uzeste by the ports of Bordeaux. He is the only Pope in history not interred in the Vatican. In honor of Pope Clement V, the Château Pape-Clement label reproduces the emblems of the Papal arms; a tiara, keys, and the coat of arms with the three papal girdles.

Men of the Church have continued to praise this noble Château, from the Duc de Richelieu, who wore quartz stones from the vineyard on his vests, to Rabelais, who loved the wine and created the character Clementin in his writings.

The most curious mystery about this place, today owned by Leon Montaigne, is that if you get permission to go into the fields of the estate late at night, it is said that you can hear the singing of a choir of angels. Is it myth or the wind . . . or Pope Clement singing to his vines? No one really knows.

The spirit of Rabelais, Eleanor, and all of the others is close to the ambiance of today's Bordeaux. Eleanor's face is reproduced in the Cathedral of St.-André's north wall column, west of the pulpit. But it won't mean much to you if you don't know what she represents to Bordeaux's rise to fame. And Rabelais and Montaigne capture the heart and spirit of the Bordelais. But how will you know if you don't check out their works? Bordeaux is much more than touring numerous caves or sipping wine. It represents an important part of Western history, and to be truly enjoyed, it must be viewed from that angle prior to your departure.

The current influx of visitors to Bordeaux is 20,000 to 30,000 annually, and Château Mouton-Rothschild is possibly the most popular stop for tourists in the area. The charming ensemble of *chais*, cellars, buildings, and park is the only one mentioned with two stars by the Guide Michelin, and part of the reason may be the glorious museum created by the Baron Philippe de Rothschild and his late wife, Pauline. The museum is exquisitely appointed with many unique works of art, all connected with wine. It is a far-ranging collection featuring Persian goblets, tapestries from around the world, and eating and drinking utensils from many civilizations. While the cellars and the newly opened decanting room behind the vat room are open to the general public, access to the museum is available only to those who are sponsored or made known to the staff through a

third party. The estate is open to the public Monday through Friday from 9 A.M. to noon and 2 P.M. to 5 P.M. Huge new parking facilities and a tourist center accommodate the casual visitor arriving by car.

In today's Bordeaux a car is essential, so rent one or hire a chauffeur. The roads are good but the area is large and complex, and five to eight days are necessary for a good tour. Long-distance autobuses and provincial trains are available, but to visit wine estates like Mouton-Rothschild it is easier with your own vehicle. Bordeaux, despite its medieval glories, is a modern city in at least one respect: peak hour traffic is a killer.

Try to use your credit card whenever possible. You could be overcharged at a restaurant or find your hotel bill padded. With a credit card, you can allow American Express or Visa the privilege of arguing with the management. Make all your long distance calls collect, and use a Telex machine when possible. You then have physical proof of delivery and the telephone operator can't lose or forget an oral message.

Make sure you have a decent map of the city and surrounding parishes and have sound directions prior to leaving your hotel. Many of the wine estates are situated off the highway and on side roads. You'll miss them and the local historical points of interest I previously mentioned unless you are savvy on road directions to and from your lodging.

Now here are my general suggestions on the procedures you should follow in order to enhance your Bordeaux touring experience:

If you can't arrange for a wine merchant to open doors in Bordeaux, then contact the Comité International du Vin de Bordeaux, 3 Cours du Juillet. If given a reasonable amount of time, and if you are part of a group, club, or trade association, they will arrange for your group to see various properties.

If you are traveling alone, or with your family, contact the Comité or one of the local *syndicats* in the various districts. The Syndicat d'Initiative in Bordeaux is located at the corner of the allées de Tourney and Cours du Juillet. Eilher group will give you information on visiting hours for the various estates and which ones are open to visitors. Through your hotel, you should be able to contact a tour operator who may include visits to certain properties on his itinerary, and the larger hotels generally have information on when certain estates are open.

If your wine merchant has made travel arrangements for you, confirm all your appointments the minute you arrive at your hotel. Contact the individuals, whether château owners, *négociants,* winery owners, or shippers. If you've contacted the winery yourself and have a written confirmation, contact the château via your hotel telephone, or go to the Maison du Vin (C.I.V.B.) and ask them to confirm your appointment. The telephone is (56) 44 37 82.

Letters addressed to the nearest village within a particular district will reach the estate in that manner. Coordinate your trip with the château's best time for visitors, and in most cases, you will find that this is in June, July, and early September.

Certain modes of etiquette will be required from you in Bordeaux (it is a traditional and conservative city), and even more so when you visit the wine estates. Here are your cues to avoid any faux pas in your behavior:

1. These estates are viewed as the family treasures, and the soil and vines are revered. You may innocently come home with a jar of soil or a cutting, thinking it is something of little importance to the property owner. He or she, however, may not view this as a compliment to their land but misunderstand it as an insult.

2. Don't be misled by signs indicating that "Visitors Are Welcome." In some estates, they don't encourage visitors. (Château Petrus is one), and in others, they'd rather have prior notice of your arrival.

3. You may or may not be offered a sample of the château's wine, and if you are offered bottled wine, it will be served in the reception room. Not surprisingly, sometimes even the dregs of a glass will be carefully poured into a cask or in the second year *chai* and blended with the principal wine.

4. The French take their lunch hour seriously. It is an hourly repast starting at noon or 1 P.M. Call ahead, and make sure someone is ready to give you a tour if you are visiting a wine estate near midday.

5. Thank your host when you leave the château but unless otherwise indicated, don't tip. The exception might be a guide on a formal tour.

Diplomacy becomes even more important when comparing the wines of your host with those of a rival estate or family, especially if you are tasting at a dinner party or luncheon. Bordeaux wine trade people all know each other, have gone to school together, and have intermarried. Like any small, closed society, they gossip and have occasional feuds. Extravagant praise of one wine over another, even that of your host, will make the grapevine quicker than you can believe.

You may have an interest in purchasing wine.

At the bigger properties, you certainly will not be able to buy wine directly, because it will already have been purchased by shippers, merchants, and brokers. However, at smaller properties without an export market, or which can arrange sales of single cases, it may be possible to buy a dozen bottles for yourself.

Be informed before you embark upon a wine-buying spree, and don't necessarily believe information given to you by your wine merchant or your buddy at the local wine appreciation tastings. To receive the direct and correct information on what you can and cannot do, call or write your nearest State Alcoholic Beverage Control Board. The federal government doesn't care what you bring into the country in the way of wine, asking you to pay only a small duty for the privilege.

The state is another story. State laws can be as varied in rules and regulations as a Cantonese bazaar. Even transporting wine across state lines is prohibited, and purchasing wine in California that is going to be shipped to Texas has proved more than one man's undoing.

A whole battery of lawyers, therefore, may not be able to assist you in bringing three cases of that wonderful little French château wine into your state, much less your cellar. Californians, as an example, cannot bring more than two fifths per person into the state. So finding out where you stand with your state's regulating board will save you more than a migraine; it may save you some money.

Many French people like to buy their wine directly from small properties. The question may be asked, however, why, if a wine is such a good bargain, it isn't sold through regular channels? The best course for a nonresident, in my opinion, is to ask the shipper or property representative who their agent is in your homeland. If they sell to various firms, ask if they will give you the names, so that you can make a personal selection from the list. The local *syndicats* can be helpful in obtaining information on the vineyards in their districts and securing appointments for tours.

Burgundy

Burgundy is as different from Bordeaux as Salem, Massachusetts, is from Los Angeles. You won't find the cosmopolitan rush of Paris or the provincial aspiration of Bordeaux. Burgundian towns and hamlets instead slither through your hands like a series of pearls held together by a strand, each possessing its own luster and dimension and tied together by the common denominator, wine.

There are four modern *départements* that produce Burgundy wine: Yonne for Chablis, the Côte d'Or for the wines of that region, Saône-et-Loire for Chalonnais and Maconnais, and Rhône for Beaujolais. The Burgundy region, comprised of about 75,000 acres of vineyards, centers about the Côte d'Or, a strip of land that runs immediately south of Dijon and extends southwest to just beyond Santenay. Its northwest border is Côte de Nuits (famous for its great Burgundy reds) and to the southeast, Côte de Beaune (best known for its Burgundy whites).

Everything in Burgundy seems smaller in dimension than in Bordeaux with its wide flat land, imposing châteaux, and 600,000 vineyard acres. But the Burgundian villages with their mossy, black-slate roofs and tucked-away restaurants with sensational food offer much interest to you. The ancient remains from Roman times, gorgeous Romanesque and Gothic architecture, fine castles and elegant châteaux, even the vast forest of the Morvan, provide an immense feast of delights for the traveler willing to "ease on down the road" of Burgundy.

Many people can be owners of one parcel of prestigious soil in Burgundy, and there is a sense of pride in owning even a tiny portion of something great. Here, properties have smaller walled areas within, with neat plaques bearing the owner's name. But since the land within the enclosed vineyards all looks alike, it can be *très difficile* to tell which is the most superior.

A typical wealthy Burgundian will possibly wear flannel suits, drive a BMW or a Citroën, yet speak of himself in terms that are more than modest. He is as laid back as the $200,000 Beverly Hills lawyer wearing the sanded jeans, open shirt, gold chain, and Gucci bag, claiming he's one of the people. But it sits better on the Burgundian, who uses the word *humble* frequently in his conversation, dropping references to his ancestral origins from humble French peasants.

Knowing that the price of land in Burgundy now goes for about $250,000 an acre, it is difficult to picture a Burgundian shipper or château owner in such a humble fashion. But each will, on different occasions, describe himself in that way, sniffing at the Bordelais for their preoccupation with lineage, affectation, and high-toned ways. This sets the stage for an explanation of Burgundy methods of viniculture, which can be characterized as simply "cooperating with Nature."

If a number of Burgundians see themselves as role models for Millet's *Angelus,* so much the better.

Whether local posturing or fact, their brand of modesty has produced fabulous wines. Regard for the luscious wine has produced a number of admirers who have either shown it public respect or extolled its merits in architecture. French Revolutionist Colonel Bisson, who is known to have been extremely fond of the *grand cru* Clos de Vougeot, ordered his soldiers to "present arms," while the regimental band blazed away in front of the vineyard; and Pope Gregory made a cardinal of another man, clever enough to send him thirty barrels of the same notable wine.

Erasmus, a fifteenth-century Dutch Catholic priest and humanist, said that the only sound reason he could think of for going to France was to drink Burgundy where it was made. He even received a note from the Pope, chastising him for drinking too much Pommard, to which Erasmus replied, "Only my heart is Catholic, Your Eminence. My stomach is Protestant."

Another priest of the day, the Bishop of Lyon, also received a disciplinary note for using too expensive a sacramental wine in celebrating the Mass. His classic response was: "Your Eminence, I cannot afford to be making faces when I'm confronting our Lord."

Burgundy's many faces, reflected in its widely varying wines, should for true enjoyment of the region, become familiar to you before your trip. Then you'll truly appreciate Erasmus's fascination with this rich wine region. The first wine town that is officially part of Burgundy is Chablis, known for its flinty, clean wine of a pale yellow color with a green tinge. It is a peaceful, quiet country town with an excellent restaurant at the Hôtel d'Étoile. The finest *grand cru* Chablis comes from a single slope with 125 acres of vines. Seven vineyards, quite small, comprise the whole: Vaudesir, Clos, Grenouilles, Valmur, Blanchots, Preuses, and Bougros.

Then comes Côte de Nuits, still in the north, producing three quarters of all the great red wines of Burgundy. The southern area, known as the Côte de Beaune, makes all the spectacular white wines and the rest of the reds. These are followed by the Côtes Chalonnaise, Maconnaise, and Beaujolais, offering sound wines but not of the grandeur of the first three regions.

In medieval times, a fourth region existed, called the Côte de Dijon. The only remnant of this time in history is "Big Maggie," or officially, "The Duke's wine press," the world's largest.

Marguerite, lusty Duchess of Burgundy and mother of Philip the Bold (Philip III) was the person for whom the wine press is nicknamed. The Duchess, a generous-hearted person, was noted for her active participation in the annual *bacchanale* or harvest festival. She was discriminating enough, however, to bestow her favor only on the fastest harvester and the best vintner.

Côte de Nuits begins near the village of Fixin, just above the vineyards of Gevrey-Chambertin, Napoleon's daily wine during his days of power. It is said that some Parisian merchants took commercial advantage of this after the retreat from the ill-fated Russian campaign in 1812, offering "Chambertin Retour de Moscou" to Napoleonic admirers as a souvenir of the disastrous campaign.

This is the beginning of the road called the Route des Grands Crus, or Route of the Great Growths. Physical appearance will not give credence to this fact, and no outward appearance marks your entrance into the best wine area of Burgundy. It is a narrow dirty road that has been rutted by carts and can be bypassed completely unless you know where you are going.

A citizen of Fixin, a certain Captain Noisot of the Imperial Guard, was so overcome by the emotional departure of Napoleon from Fontainebleau in 1815 that he purchased the land in 1846 and created a park. He commissioned a statue to be made of Napoleon. It shows the Corsican just about to open his eyes, a dead eagle at his feet. Noisot evidently wanted the statue to depict the legend that Napoleon would someday be momentarily renewed to life. The statue stands in a wooded glade behind Fixin in the Parc Noisot. A grand avenue of pine trees leads to a museum honoring Napoleon. The building is a replica, two thirds the size of Napoleon's final residence in St.-Helena.

The road to Gevrey-Chambertin, or "Le Grand Seigneur," continues on to Morey-Saint-Denis, Chambolle, Musigny, and finally, Vougeot and its Clos.

Vougeot's most well-known wine, a great growth, is Clos de Vougeot, a vineyard that is one of France's most revered treasures. It was started by St. Bernard of Clairvaux's Cistercian monks and he was the first to plant vines where Clos de Vougeot stands today. The vineyards, located on the slopes of their monastery, stayed in the clergy's hands until the French Revolution, when the State confiscated Church property. The monks left Clos de Vougeot and resettled in Germany, where they again became famous for their winemaking skills, founding a vineyard called Steinberg.

Prior to it confiscation by the State, the Clos de Vougeot vineyard was so big, it was decided that a house for the wine press should be added to the building inside the wall. Drawing of the plans was entrusted to a young monk, who was so empassioned with the assignment he made the fatal error of signing the completed blueprint with his own name. The abbot informed him he had committed the deadly sin of pride and ordered that the plans be given to other monks for completion. These new people botched the job completely.

The abbot called in the architect, showed him the plans, and ordered that the castle be built as shown, with all the flaws and errors intact, as a reminder of the sinful pride of the now disfavored monk. Not finished until the fifteenth century, the building is all that's left of the ancient monastery and has been repaired constantly ever since. Millions of francs have been spent in repairing the building, which had been used during World War II as a billet by the Germans during the occupation and later as a prison camp by the Americans.

At one point, the disgruntled German prisoners tried to burn up the centuries-old presses, claiming they needed the wood for fires. The caretaker rushed to the American commander, who slapped up a barbed-wire barricade around the massive machines.

Money for restoration has come through contributions made by Chevaliers du Tastevin, Burgundy's promotional organization made up of growers, shippers, and private citizens in love with Burgundian wine. They bought the castle for their meetings, and every other month, they have a big dinner for themselves, dressed up in red robes and square black hats, with silver *tastevins* dangling from a red-and-orange ribbon looped around their necks.

The wall around the Clos is between eight and ten feet high and is built of split stone. Along the rear section on the inside are espaliered fruit trees, and along the short, terraced drive to the castle itself is the tombstone of one Leonce Boquet, who united the vineyard into a single domain in the nineteenth century. Today the Clos is split among 60 owners.

The great room used by the 500 members of the Chevaliers du Tastevin was formerly a storage shed for casks. Pillars of the giant hall are stone monoliths, tapering up some 20 feet to enormous beams, and hanging on the pillars are the leather baskets formerly used for gathering grapes. The baskets are decorated with a painted coat of arms and with dates of the most famous vintages, the oldest being 1108. (Clos de Vougeot is open to the public and sells colorful souvenirs to take home as mementos.)

The vineyard road crosses the boundary of Vosne-Romanée, scarcely 100 yards from the wall surrounding Clos de Vougeot. This commune produces more great wines than any other, and the fewest small ones. Yet, the best vineyards, among them Romanée-Conti, Richebourg, La Tâche, and Romanée-St.-Vivant total less than 150 acres. Their wines are among the most expensive on earth, and wine lovers revel in the moments they can taste these rare wines.

Epitomizing more of France's grandeur is Romanée-Conti, scarcely four and one-half acres in size, which has changed hands only nine times since the thirteenth century. Contrary to the usual Burgundy practice, all wine from Romanée-Conti is estate-bottled, and every bottle carries, on its label and cork, the seal of the Société Civile de la Romanée-Conti, owners of this vineyard and the renowned La Tâche, as well as parts of others.

The principal city of this area is Nuits-St.-Georges, which lies on both sides of the highway and is the home of many shipping firms. There is an excellent restaurant in the city, the Hôtel de la Côte d'Or, which I recommend you try. The wild boar I tasted there is one of the gastronomic delights in which chef, Jean Crôtet, seems to specialize.

Vineyards of the Côte de Beaune begin the limestone quarry where the Côte de Nuits breaks off, continuing on below Santenay, a distance of approximately 15 miles. Beaune, the barrel and wine capital of the Côte d'Or, is an ancient, walled city, full of shippers and their cellars, and the homes of proprietors of the many surrounding vineyards. The entire town is a historical monument, encompassed by ramparts, with every street, square, and courtyard offering something of interest to the adventurous tourist.

One of the best wine museums of the world, the Musée du Vin de Bourgogne, is housed in a hotel formerly owned by the Dukes of Burgundy. Burgundian wine history from ancient times is illustrated through many beautiful and interesting objects, each placed appropriately in a continuing theme as the visitor follows the story from room to room.

Check with the Office de Tourisme of Beaune. They have both names and addresses of cellars, including Le Marché aux Vins, where you can taste local wines in the ambiance of a cellar.

The sight you must see while in Beaune is the Hôtel-Dieu, or the Hospices de Beaune, in the heart of the city, just off the main square. The Hospice, or hospital, is crowded among other old buildings and is a four-story structure faced with an archway that leads through the buildings into the main court. Above the entrance is an ornate ninety-foot steeple projecting out over the sidewalk and unsupported by a tower. The building is of medieval Flemish style,

and the steeple was the model for the Sainte-Chapelle in Paris.

The world's most famous wine auction is held in Beaune, usually on the third Sunday in November, with the money going to support the sick and the poor. Buyers come from all over the globe, and although the Hospice owns vineyards only in the Côte de Beaune, the wines and prices are a basis for judging all those of the Côte d'Or. The hospital was founded 50 years before Columbus discovered America by a tax collector under Louis XI, Nicolas Rollin. Rollin, it has been said, could easily afford to build a charitable institution for the poor, because he'd made so many of them poor.

Operating money for the Hospices is derived from the sale of its wines, which have been auctioned annually for a century. I would not advise you to go during this season, however, because the town is crowded with wine merchants and others of the trade. Guided tours are conducted, and you should allow about an hour for the expedition. You will appreciate the remarkably patterned roof, the Salle des Pauvres, with the curtained bunk-type beds arranged so that patients can share in the celebration of Mass at the end of the huge room. There is also the pharmacy, the enormous kitchen, and a fabulous work of art, Roger van der Weiden's *Last Judgment*.

The number of people coming to this fascinating town seems to increase every year. New hotels have sprung up, including the Hôtel de Bourgogne and the casual Samôtel, and others, like Le Cep. My favorite (and that of almost everyone I know) is still the Hôtel de la Poste. It has comfort and charm, along with delightful food.

I'd strongly advise you, however, to avoid the motor hotels outside the city. A sudden trip to Burgundy forced me to stay at one of these horrors. It was an experience I would not care to repeat. For starters, the motor hotel I stayed in spans both sides of a freeway, which turns pitch black at night. No lights of any kind show where you are going. The hotel's all-night restaurant is situated in the middle of a bridge interconnecting the accommodations, and dual registration centers are placed on each side of the expanse. While I was there, the only person who spoke English and sent Telex messages conversed with difficulty and took coffee breaks every 15 minutes. She was also in the registration center on the opposite side of the road from me, so it was a hike of some distance if I needed her services.

Even worse was driving to the place, especially at night. If you were driving along the right side of the freeway, you would have to park in the lot built on that side of the freeway. For those unfortunates like me staying on the left-hand side, this meant a long walk to my room in the damp, cold, nocturnal Burgundian air.

The only other alternative was to drive 30 miles farther on the freeway to the next turn-around. Making a U-turn, as Louis Latour pointed out to me, could mean a stiff fine or a night in the Beaune city jail. (At that point, the jail didn't seem such a bad idea.) But don't risk your health, life, or pocketbook. Make sure your hotel reservation is made far in advance in one of the nice hotels in the middle of Beaune. At least you can get a taxi, find someone who can send a Telex in English, or drive yourself out of the city without crashing.

This brings up another problem: transportation. Beaune has one car-rental service, Avis, and it rents only cars with stick shifts. It can also be booked solid during the tourist season. Make sure to arrange to have a car in advance of your trip, or better yet, get a car and chauffeur. An agency that can arrange for both is Bernard Durand Car Rental Agency, located at 2 Rue l'Église, Paris. You also can organize an excursion through the vineyards by contacting the Office de Tourisme and Syndicat d'Initiative.

South of Beaune, you will arrive at Pommard, a town full of sunlight, greenery, mossy stone, and the sound of flowing water from the Dheune River. The wine was the favorite of Victor Hugo, the French novelist. One of the handsomest buildings in Burgundy is seen just before you reach Pommard itself. It is the Château de Pommard, a single enclosed vineyard, a rarity in Burgundy. Built in 1098, it is owned by M. La Planche.

Volnay, a hillside town, is a few miles south of Pommard and has interesting vineyards dating from the Gallo-Roman period, where relics often are found.

Continuing on the Route des Grands Crus, you will come to Meursault, an old and wealthy town, formerly a Roman garrison. In the square is the country hotel and inn, Le Chevreuil, where you can taste some of the local wines with such specialities as *lapins* and *escargots*.

Just below Meursault lies the village of Puligny, home of the greatest dry white table wine, Montrachet. Its fame dates back to the time of Rabelais, who called it "divine," and Alexander Dumas, who declared it should "be drunk kneeling, with one's head bared."

Having gone beyond Puligny, you will find the vineyard road cuts across the main Paris-Riviera highway, a few yards from Montrachet, and you immediately enter the town of Chassagne. Below Chassagne is the last wine town of the Côte d'Or, Santenay, where light red wines are produced. It is at this point that you will note the transition from the Côte d'Or Burgundies to those of the Côte Chalonnaise.

While in this area of Burgundy, try the food at the Hôtel Lameloise, in Chagny, about fifteen kilometers to the south of Beaune. Decorated in the style of a sophisticated country inn, it has old furniture, a fireplace in the bar, and a dining area composed of many tiny vaulted rooms.

From Chagny, you can take a pleasant drive through the vineyards of Rully, Mercurey, and Givry, to Tournus. The eighteenth-century painter Jean Baptiste Greuze was born in Tournus, and the hometown boy is remembered with a small museum collection of his work. Jean Ducloux's Restaurant Greuze is named after him. This rustic restaurant is worth a visit when you are in Tournus.

At this point, you are in Maconnais and Beaujolais country and have opportunities to taste the wines of these regions at the various Maison Maconnaise des Vins. One is located at the northern approach to Mâcon, and another is near Belleville. At both, owned by the growers, you can taste wines of the regions.

Mâcon is prosperous with some attractive sights that include the Montrevel mansion on the quai, now the town hall, and a seventeenth-century pharmacy in the Hôtel-Dieu. A great restaurant to visit while in Mâcon is Auberge Bressane, owned by a M. Duret.

Traveling south from Mâcon, you will head straight into Beaujolais. There are *caveau de degustation* at Willie-Morgon and at Juliénas. The former is under an old château that now is a town hall, and at Juliénas, in a deconsecrated church. An excellent restaurant, the Auberge Salesienne-La-Benoite, is located in the village of Salles-Arbuissonnas-en-Beaujolais. The specialty of the house is wild boar. Walking off your meal, stop at the twelfth-century abbey of the village and take special note of the Romanesque cloister.

Burgundy is known for its wine and its food, and one of its famous personalities of the past was the cunning Nicolas Rolin. At Autun, you can visit the Rolin home, now open to the public and called the Le Musée Rolin. While you are in Autun, visit the Cathedral of Saint-Lazare, a classic example of bold Roman architecture.

Having eaten the robust delights of the Burgundian table and partaken of its wines, you can now say *adieu*. You have shared in the warming friendship of Beaujolais; the integrity of Maconnais; the sensualism of the Côte de Beaune, and my favorite, the Côte de Nuits, where magic rules the land through the enchanted soil. Romanée-Conti, Romanée-St.-Vivant, La Tâche, Richebourg. We find ourselves humbled by their majesty and by the venerable soil. Indeed, perhaps there is a reason why even the most aristocratic Burgundian shrugs his shoulder and says, "I am only a servant of Nature."

Germany

One of the most picturesque wine regions in the world is in Germany, where the Rhine and Moselle scenery vie with each other as to which is the more beautiful. For serious wine lovers, especially those who are fond of German wines and want to learn more about them, the German Wine Academy conducts several five-day seminars each year. Lectures in English for novices and advanced students are given at Kloster Eberbach. Students taste and evaluate about 150 different wines: They will also attend professional tastings and visit regions such as the Moselle and Rheingau to observe wines being processed and aged. The Academy takes care of all arrangements, including meals, lodging, and transportation, leaving you to concentrate solely on wine. Information is available by writing to the German Wine Information Bureau, 99 Park Avenue, New York 10016 (212) 599–6900.

German wine estates have three types of visiting policies: Some accept no visitors, some accept members of the trade, and some welcome everyone. If you are planning to visit a particular estate, you should call, or have your *concierge* call, to make an appointment. The estate personnel will want to know in which language you speak, the number of guests in your party, and whether a tasting is desired. If you are a member of the wine industry, whether in production, marketing, or education and research, be sure to mention this. Be specific about the things you want to see, especially if it is a subject of great personal interest.

Drinking and driving in Europe as in any civilized area of the world can mean a stiff fine or a stay in jail. In Germany, this violation of the law, whether you are a native or tourist, can certainly bring you legal problems. Traveling through the highways of the country, you will find that people go at speeds considerably higher than our own national 55-m.p.h. speed limit. In fact, German drivers go faster than anyone else in Europe, with an extremely high accident statistic to prove it.

For this reason, if you are planning to visit several estates and are driving alone, go easy on the amount you drink. If there are several people in your party, try to rotate the driving assignment. Reward whoever has been chauffeur for the day with something special at evening time, maybe a free meal or a bottle of his favorite German wine.

You had better rent a car if you want to see the wine estates, because many of them are in rather remote areas. Driving there is the easiest way. German roads are well marked, and established routes on existing roads lead through the most interesting vineyards of a region.

The German Wine Road (Deutsche Weinstrasse), for instance, is a route running northsouth through the Rheinpfalz region, along the Hardt Mountains from Grünstadt through Bad Dürkheim and Neustadt to Schweigen. It was established in 1932 and is marked with signposts showing a bunch of grapes.

The Baden Wine Road (Badische Weinstrasse) leads from Weinheim, past the Kaiserstuhl and through the Markgräflerland to the Swiss border. It is marked with signposts showing grapes and the Baden coat of arms.

The Nahe Wine Road (Nahe Weinstrasse) is a circle that starts and ends in Bad Kreuznach and is marked with signposts showing a Römer wine glass and a large letter N.

Wandering through the Rheingau from Lorch to Hochheim, the Rheingau Riesling Route has been marked since 1973 with signs showing a wine glass with a crown.

In Franken there is the Bocksbeutel Road (Bocksbeutelstrasse), but it is unofficial and unmarked. It isn't necessary to have marked wine roads along the river, as in the Moselle Valley, where the vineyards are adjacent the river, but in flat areas such as Württemberg, the wine-producing area is harder to find.

You may want to visit Germany during one of the many wine festivals. With the exception of January, there is a wine *fest* taking place in some part of Germany at almost any time of the year. During August and September, there are so many festivals that you can find at least one of these events in any wine region. Festivals will vary, some being formal events with bands and entertainment, while others allow you to generate your own amusement. You will, however, have an excellent chance to taste wine of the region and meet the local citizens.

Plan your wine trip to Germany for between April and October, making a point of attending at least one *fest* during your visit. You can obtain further information by writing to:

Deutsche Wein Information
6500 Main, Fuststrasse 4
West Germany

Lufthansa German Airlines
Public Relations Department
1640 Hempstead Turnpike
East Meadow 11554
(516) 794–2020

German National Tourist Offices:

104 South Michigan Ave.
Chicago 60603
(312) 263–2958

700 Flower St.
Los Angeles 90017
(213) 688–7332

630 Fifth Ave.
New York 10020
(212) 757–8570

The Mediterranean

Wine was being produced in Italy, Spain, and Portugal long before the renaissance of winemaking in most northern regions of Europe. Touring the wine estates of these countries can prove a fascinating experience, and one that I would recommend to the knowledgeable wine connoisseur who is already familiar with the methods used in America, Burgundy, and Bordeaux.

Italy

Italy's wine production stems the length and breadth of the country, from vineyards nestled close to the Alps to those stretching within sight of the African coast. It is a land of many types of climate and soil, producing more varieties of wine than any other country in the world, with a wine production averaging more than 2 billion gallons per year, of which more than 16 million dollars' worth is exported.

I think it is always fun to attend a fair or festival related to wine, and in the towns of Siena, Verona, Asti, and Florence, these generally take place in early October. Those of you who dabbled in medieval history and wept through *Romeo and Juliet* may remember that the Italian city-states of Siena and Florence enjoyed a fierce rivalry during those times. Seeds of controversy sprouted as a result of their mutual desire for control of Chianti, situated between both cities, and home of Italy's most fa-

mous wine. This area is in the province of Tuscany, home of some of Italy's greatest minds, including Leonardo da Vinci, Michelangelo, Machiavelli, and Galileo, and one of Italy's fabulous red wines, Brunello di Montalcino.

This unspoiled northern region is situated on the Western coast of Italy and is blessed with beautiful beaches, rolling inland hills, and quaint hamlets as well as extremely sophisticated cities.

At present, Tuscany has 14 DOC—Denominazione di Origine Controllata—wines (that is, recognized wines of controlled origin, whose production is regulated by Italy's federal government) and nearly 100 additional local varieties.

Main red grapes of the region are the Sangiovese, Brunello, Canaiolo, Raspinossa, and Mammolo, while the most important white grapes include the Trebbiano, Toscano, Malvasia, and Canaiolo Bianco. North of Tuscany is Piedmont, also known for such red wines as Barolo, Barbaresco, Gattinara and Ghemme.

In the capital city, Turin, all of Italy was united in 1861 under the House of Savoy. The political architect of this unity was Conte Camillo Benso di Cavour, who before he became the first prime minister of a united Italy, was also an amateur viniculturist. Anxious to expand on the local reputation of Barolo wine, native to the area, he even invited an eminent French oenologist, Louis Oudard, to stay in Turin and explore the possibilities of improving the production of this wine. Oudard's tests, which took years to complete, resulted in the refinement of the wine, which became known as "the king of wines and the wine of kings." Meals at court were planned around this robust red liquid, and it became the favorite wine of Victor Emmanuel II, Italy's first king.

An ideal city in which to stay while visiting this part of Italy would be Alba, the center of the Langhe. It is an elegant, ancient city, full of hospitable people and interesting structures straight out of the 1800s. The *trattorie* are full of delicious dishes including, in autumn, a local specialty, *tartufo*, or white truffle. It is the color of burnished gold and is called locally "diamond of Alba." Traveling around the area you will see undulating hills and striking castles and farms. Delicate mists, known as the *nebbioline* (hence, the name Nebbiolo), add to the region's poetic spirit. The castle of Grinzane has a wonderful treasure of wines, and at Abbazia dell'Annunziata below La Morra is a small but interesting wine museum. In addition to the excellent wine, the Langhe is a gourmet's paradise and some of the dishes I would recommend include *taglierini col tartufo*, (slender noodles dressed with butter and shaved truffles) or *lasagne al sangue* (a pasta dish flavored with a rich gravy made out of pig's blood) or *agnolotti*, literally "fat little lambs," or rolls of pasta with a meat stuffing.

Near the Langhe district are the Monferrato hills, whose capital is Asti, home of the famous Spumante. If you stop here, see the town's cathedral with its columns adorned in reliefs depicting vine shoots and grape clusters.

Veneto, another northern area is situated between Lake Garda and the Po and Piave rivers. It is best known for a trio of Veronese wines: Valpolicella, Bardolino, and Soave. Soave is the only white wine out of the three and the most popular white wine to come out of Italy.

A lesser-known treasure of the area is the still dry red Amarone of Valpolicella, made only from the *recie* (ears) of each cluster of grapes, or those berries thrusting themselves at the top of the bunch to receive most sunlight.

Emilia-Romagna and Bologna are two other Italian areas that should not be overlooked by the wine enthusiast. Emilia-Romagna is the center of Italy's most avid wine production, resting its laurels on such wines as Sangiovese (red) and Albana and Trebbiano (both white), while Bologna, of course, is one of Italy's most food-conscious regions with Lambrusco (a dry semisparkling red wine) one of the four wines it produces as partners to its rich cuisine. Romagna, flat in its northern border, becomes hill and mountain to the south, where it borders Tuscany, the Marches, and Europe's oldest republic, San Marino.

Wine is grown principally in the mountainous region and the zone is crisscrossed with official wine roads that traverse vineyards south of the autostrada and the Via Emilia, the Roman road linking Bologna, Romagna, and Rimini. Romagna includes the provinces of Ravenna and Forli, parts of Bologna and Ferrara, and small portions of the Montefeltro mountain range. Its wine roads are among the most extensive and best organized of the peninsula, with clearly marked signs ushering the tourist through each zone.

Wine fraternities have been behind this movement to encourage tourism, chief among them the Societa del Passatore, a society composed of producers, restaurateurs, and wine buffs who have banded together under the nickname of the famed Romagnian version of Robin Hood, whose wide-brimmed hat is also the symbol of the consortium for the three DOC wines. You are able to taste the wines of this area at the tasting houses along the wine roads. These are known as *ca' de be'* and the most

famous is at Bertinoro. In the charming inn, you can sip wine by the classic country fireplace, musing over the no less classic Latin description: "*Bibe hospe abibis laetior.*" (Drink guest and you will go in joy.)

Umbria squats in the center of the boot, to the left of the Marches, with Latium on its southern border. Although it is one of the smaller Italian regions, it produces a great white wine, Orvieto. Center of production for this dessert wine is a city, bearing the same name, perched on a massive rock out of which are carved the cellars where the wine matures. Orvieto is produced both dry and *abboccato* (semisweet) and the latter is the area's pride.

Latium, its neighbor, is famous for its strong, fragrant white Frascati, which is made only in dry and *abboccato* style. However, Frascati is only one of the many Castelli Romani wines made among the Roman castles in the Alban hills southeast of Rome. Another enticing wine of the region, Est Est Est, comes from the slopes around Lake Bolsena. It is clear, dry, and somewhat lighter than Frascati. The story behind this wine originates in the twelfth century, when, it is said, a steward of a German bishop traveling to Rome was sent ahead of his master in order to scout and mark the inns according to the quality of their wines. If satisfied he was to write "*Est*" (It is) on the wall; if not, his comment was to be "*Non est.*" At Montefiascone he became so enthusiastic about the wine that he chalked "*Est! Est!! Est!!!*" on the door of the inn. And thus the local wine received its name.

Marches faces the Adriatic Sea, and the gently rolling hills undulating toward the ocean and the area's seafood cuisine reflect this dependence on agriculture and marine life. The Verdicchio grape and the amphora-shaped bottle in which the dry white wine is shipped have added to Marches' fame wherever Italian food is served.

The best-known Verdicchio comes from the Castelli di Iesi area, inland from Ancona, but many good Verdicchios are made in other districts of the province. The wine, it is said, was brought into Italy by Alaric, king of the Visigoths, on his way to conquering Rome in A.D. 410, because he was convinced that it would give his soldiers increased courage to conquer the natives.

Further to the south, Campania, in southern Italy, is attractive to the tourist not only because of its luxurious resorts but because of the wines of the island of Ischia, especially Lachryma Christi, or "tears of Christ." The wine is grown on the slopes of the volcano Vesuvius, and it is distinguished by the added phrase, *del Vesuvio*, whether it is produced as a red, white, or rosé type.

In the southernmost parts of Italy, while visiting Calabria, Sardinia, or Sicily, you can taste the wines, gaining perceptions about the culture and civilization of each of the three areas. Calabria is the "toe" of the Peninsula, and in Ciro, one of its cities, the inhabitants claim that the big, robust red wine is the direct descendant of the wine brought in by the ancient Greek settlers of the area.

The island of Sicily has been in the quality wine business for two centuries and is known for its fortified wine, Marsala, which not only achieved fame as a superior dessert wine but as an indispensable touch to fine cooking. The spicy cuisine of the area is complemented by the wine produced on the slopes of Mount Etna, both in Etna Red and White, and from southern Sicily, Draceno, Drepano, and Saturno, dry red and white table wines supposedly named after the ancient Greek city of Segesta.

Sardinia also produces some interesting wines, including the dry, appetizingly bitter aperitif wine, Vernaccia di Oristano, produced from the grape of the same name. Sardinians drink it after and before meals.

For further information about the wine-growing regions of Italy and traveling tips for each area, write to the following:

Italian Wine Promotion Center
One World Trade Center
Suite 2057, New York 10048

Italian Embassy
Commercial Office
1601 Fuller Street
Washington, D.C. 20009

Spain is a country of high mountains and arid dry plains where fine wines can be tasted and pleasant adventures enjoyed by the intrepid oenophile. Spain's table wines, along with its foods, divide quite naturally into five areas: the Mediterranean center; those regions south and east; and those from the Atlantic climate of the north and west.

Speaking from a culinary point of view, the country will likewise place regional emphasis on five zones: the north and west for sauces; the center for roasts; the south for fried dishes; and the east, for rice-based entrees. Also typical of the eastern region is an Iberian red sauce with the curious title of *chilindron*. This spicy pungent sauce is made from a base of tomatoes, onions, red peppers, garlic, parsley, toasted saffron, cayenne, paprika, and small green peppers known as *ají picante*.

Spanish wines coincide with the gastronomical zones, and northern wines are known as *vinhos verdes* (green wines) in the Basque and Galician regions; hill and La Mancha wines are produced in two sub-zones of the center of Spain separated by the Guadarrama mountains; aromatic wines are typical of the south; and to the east are produced the sparkling wines of Catalonia and the relatively sweet red wine of Tarragona. To the northeast, in the Basque province of Rioja, are produced wines that go with the region's *chilindron* sauce, with the best of the three Riojas coming from Rioja Alta.

Although Spain is the world's third largest wine producer, many of its wines never make it out of the country and are consumed with their lengthy meals and heavy regional dishes. As an example, there are more than fifty different ways that the Spaniards cook potatoes; they have created at least thirty classical gazpacho dishes (the latter is very ancient, descending to the contemporary Spanish kitchen from the Alboránian soup of the Andalusian Moors) and many other regional foods that go well with certain wines.

The most prodigious wine produced in Spain, for instance, is the La Mancha wine known in the wine markets as Valdepeñas, taking the name of a major Spanish wine town about 140 miles south of Madrid. This town has no less than fifty bodegas, or roughly one for every thousand inhabitants. The wine is generally light and dry, and comparable to a budding Beaujolais, and the most popular red carafe wine available in Spanish restaurants. A wine buff anxious to learn more about Spanish wines on his tour of Spain would be better served, I believe, if he would taste the local wines at each of his stops, preferably with the local specialty. Remember that the table wines of Navarra, Aragón, and Murcia, or the heavyweight wines of Jumilla, Cariñena, and Yecla, or the famed sherries of Jerez, will all be ideal with a dish from that region.

Spanish cooking, like the people, is essentially sober and conservative. Paella is the only Spanish concession to overstatement, and while there are unlimited number of dishes for each province, you should learn to recognize the big four: *cocido*, *fabada*, *paella*, and *gazpacho*.

Whether you are supping in an open-air restaurant in Madrid's Plaza de San Miguel or dining in a Galician inn, you will start any Spanish meal with an *entremés*. This is not a plateful of hors d'oeuvres but rather a Spanish-style antipasto, including anything from shellfish, Spanish ham, sausage, crayfish and a variety of olives. With the shellfish you would be wise to choose a "green wine" such as Chacoli or a

111

white Galician Ribeiro or a sparkling Agullo.

Soups are as common to Spanish cuisine as cabbage and corn beef are to the Irish, and while some Spaniards will not go as far as the native writer Valle-Inclán, who claimed that any well-dressed table should have tablecloths of real linen complete with well-marked creases, they do agree that the steaming broth dilates the stomach and prepares it to accept other nourishment.

One of the most important dishes is a *cocido*, which is a stew. It is also called a *puchero* after the pot in which it is boiled. Again, there are a number of variations of this dish, including some to which chickpeas are added; others are enhanced by potato and cabbage, meat, *tocino* or salt sowbelly, or spiced sausage and dumplings.

Some of the finest *cocido* is found in Pedraza de la Sierra, in Segovia, where the *cocido*, true to its Jewish origin, is a modified form of the Hebraic *adafina*, left simmering on Friday nights for Saturday. The date of its birth can be set at about 1493 and the transition from Jewish to Christian is seen in the omission of the traditional boiled eggs of the *adafina* and the addition of pork. With any type of *cocido*, a strong "black" or dark red wine is recommended.

Spain's most well-known culinary export is the *paella* and this dish is at its most glorious along the Valencia coast. A delicious medley of ingredients can be added to this dish and a dry Utiel or Requena wine is its best partner.

Fabada, another Spanish classic, is not to be confused with the *cassoulet* of France but should include the best Asturian beans cooked with well-cured ham and kiln-cured sausage. This is a marvelous dish, but not for those of you with delicate stomachs. My suggestion is that you enjoy this hearty dish with a "green" Basque wine.

Mussels, hake, eel, dried cod, and trout are Spanish specialties along with shrimp and other fresh fish. A slightly sweet wine is ideal with the hake, and a white wine is perfect with the dried cod, trout, or any other fish.

Chicken a la Chilindron is found in southern Navarra, the Rioja, and Aragón, but the *chilindron* capital is Saragoza, where you can find lamb, rabbit, pigeon, suckling lamb, and chicken prepared in this fashion. The best place to taste dishes cooked in this style is the Saragozan district known as El Tubo, and the ideal wine is a "black" Aragónese varietal.

The ancient kingdoms of León and Castile are best known for the roast lamb or suckling pig roasts, and for many centuries the cities of Arevalo and Segovia have debated over which was the roasting pig capital. The trick is to find out how the lamb or suckling pig are cooked. The best way is in a baker's oven, and the wine that complements both dishes is a La Mancha red wine.

Undoubtedly one of the two most interesting wine regions to the oenophile on a sabbatical would be Jerez and the Rioja region. The latter has been reknown for its wines since the time of King Alphonso X, who in his *Crónica General* described the Rioja region as "fertile and abundant land." Carlos III, the Bourbon king, encouraged cultivation of the wine in this region and these were the favorites of his table.

La Rioja includes part of the provinces of Logroño, Navarra, and Álava. It is divided into Rioja Alta, on the right side of the Ebro River; Rioja Alavesa, on the opposite side; Rioja Baja, south of the others; and La Riojilla, which lies between the provinces of Logroño and Burgos. For the wine buff, Rioja Alta offers the best opportunity to taste fine red wine.

You may travel 500 miles of the main road, passing through Seville, the Roman town of Mérida, the university city of Salamanca and on through Valladolid and Burgos. At the pass of Pancorbo, you will turn off a quiet country lane leading through the first of the Rioja towns, Haro. Two rivers, the Ebro and Oja, now join, flowing beside the road running through the 75-mile strip of land divided into three districts.

This is a country of nightingales, with small individual plots of land rather than large wine estates. The soil is ideal for fine wine and the Pyrenees Mountains, protective against cold winds, allow the southern slope to thrive with a lot of sun.

This land is 200 miles south of Bordeaux, and although the region gained its official recognition for making fine wine in 1102, it wasn't until the late nineteenth century, when the phylloxera plague struck the wines of Europe, that Rioja came into its own.

Many French vineyardists, bankrupted by the plague, made their way south where a climate and soil were similar to their own. This was a great period for Rioja wines, and French expertise along with Spanish money and industry produced some fine wines. Unfortunately for Rioja, by the turn of the century, the French wine trade returned to normalcy and the wines of this northern Spanish region lost much of their international appeal.

The name of this province is Logroño, and here you see the Rioja at its most striking. Logroño is not so much a Castilian capital as it is a town on the Ebro—with two bridges spanning the river—and one of these, the stone one, marking the route of the faithful to Santiago.

You will immediately notice that in this province, the kitchen is the dominant feature of the home and that traditionally it has a big smoke funnel surrounded by wooden benches. Behind the center of gastronomy is a small alcove called the *cantarera*, where large kegs of wine are aged and preserved.

Festivals abound in this rugged and mountainous land, and many of them are centered around food and wine. There is the Fiesta of St. Barnabas on June 11th, which has as its main feature the distribution of bread, fish, and wine, commemorating the siege of Logroño by the French in 1521. In that siege, fish, bread, and wine were the only foods the people had to eat. Also very popular is the Celebration of Bread and Cheese, dating from the fifteenth century, which takes place in the village of Quel on August 6th of each year. Also of interest is the Wine Harvest Festival, which is held during the second fortnight in September.

Many magnificent castles and monasteries abound in this land, including the castle at Clavijo, now a national monument, and three monasteries, all national monuments, which also deserve to be visited. Two, San Millan de Suso and San Millan de Yuso, are at San Millan de la Cogolla.

The first, a Mozarabic structure of the tenth century, contains the sepulchres of the legendary Seven Princes of Lara. The second, called the Escorial of La Rioja, was one of the most prominent monasteries of the Middle Ages; it has an inspiring Gothic cloister and an interesting collection of eleventh-century ivory.

Other sightseeing points of interest that you will enjoy viewing in this area is Santa María la Real, the Pantheon of the Kings of Navarra, and the town of Santo Domingo de la Calzada with its cathedral of Romanesque-Gothic style and the remains of the saint of the same name. The baroque tower and Renaissance choir of this cathedral are outstanding as are its collection of Flemish tryptichs.

There are many more sites to see in this historic area of Spain, but following the Ruta del Vino—the wine route—through Haro, Cenicero, Fuenmayor, Logroño, Calahorra, San Adrian, Quel, Arnedo, Laguardia, Elciego, and the other small hamlets of La Rioja, will afford the wine connoisseur his biggest pleasure.

At the other end of Spain, close to the Mediterranean Sea, lies a land that wine writer Julian Jeffs once described in the following manner: "When a traveler stops in Jerez, he finds himself in Lotus Land. It is a city of light and joy." This opinion is happily shared by a host of tourists, including myself, and this sherry-producing area of the world, along with Puerto de Santa María and Sanlúcar de Barrameda, two other sherry-producing towns, are a must for the wine buff in Spain.

Jerez de la Frontera is the largest and most imposing, and located a scant ten kilometers from the sea, it enjoys lush and beautiful weather. Flying down from Madrid with its familiar L.A. smog, it is particularly refreshing. You can spend endless days touring the numerous wine cellars, totaling more than 500,000 casks in capacity.

You will never tire of the beautiful Coast of Light, which marks this part of southern Spain. All of the Costa de la Luz is washed by the waters of the Atlantic, and the entire coastline, the Atlantic side of Andalusia, is bathed by an ever-present sun shining from a deep blue sky. The horizon is marked by shadowy outlines of scattered pine forests, and the great sandy white beaches offer their own blend of glistening gold and glittering steel color.

The towns in this area are particularly delightful, especially during one of the many festivals, when you can see the girls riding in back of the gorgeous Carthusian horses, while the gentlemen *caballeros* sit proudly in the saddle, holding their glass of sherry steadily in hand.

For the wine buff, the ideal time to visit this lovely area of Spain is during the middle of September, when the vintage is celebrated in Jerez de la Frontera and other cities. During May, Cádiz is the scene of a Folklore Festival with a colorful Battle of the Flowers, and of course, there are the spring festivals of Puerto de Santa María and Jerez de la Frontera, particularly the latter's famed Horse Fair.

Wine, bulls, and horses—these are the three passions of these colorful people. Vineyards are everywhere in Cádiz and Huelva, climbing the slopes or running down to the edge of the sea. The cuisine of this area, aside from the gazpacho, stews, mountain hams, and other stylized Spanish dishes, is rich in all types of sea foods, particularly the excellent shellfish.

Another interesting wine town is Puerto de Santa María. The town has many valuable artistic monuments, such as the church of Nuestra Señora de los Milagros, the Baroque temple of San Francisco, the Capuchino Convent, and the ancient monastery of Nuestra Señora de la Victoria. Natural beauties include the beaches of Valdelagrana, Vista Hermosa, and Fuentebravía, and a tour of the famous wine vaults. The town contains numerous vestiges of its Greek colonization, and magnificent palaces compete with a landscape of pines, beaches,

113

and salt-marshes surrounding the town.

Manzanilla, a fine, very pale wine, light to the taste and very crisp is the special sherry of Sanlucar de Barrameda, starting point of Columbus's third voyage to America. In the taste of Manzanilla, there is a hint of the Atlantic sea breezes that are so much a part of the Bajo de Guia and the Guadalquivir River. Across the river from the city is the fabulous Donana National Park, the only wildlife sanctuary in Europe totally devoted to migratory birds who fly here for sanctuary before winter begins.

Other areas of interest to the wine lover would be Moguer, home of the Nobel Prize-winning poet, Juan Ramon Jimenez, whose home has become a museum; Palma del Condado; and Chiclana de la Frontera, famous for its white wines known as *pastos*—wines that can be drunk with food.

Last but not least for this neck of the world is Cádiz, which sits at the tip of a long finger of land that closes the lovely bay. It is the oldest inhabited city in Spain, and it was here that Julius Caesar dreamed his dreams of empire and the Phoenicians ruled the seas. The Puertas de Tierra divide the city into two parts: Behind the Isthmus is modern, industrial Cádiz; on the other side is the romantic, historic part of the city. There are a number of important monuments and outstanding artistic works on display at various sites throughout the city, including the Museum of Fine Arts with its priceless collection of works by Rubens, Murillo, and other outstanding artists. The Archaelogical Museum has utensils from the Paleolithic and Neolithic Ages, along with other ancient historical pieces including the Anthropoid Sidonian Sarcophagus. This city offers regular sea connections to Barcelona, the Canaries, and other ports, and has constant service to the neighboring city of Puerto de Santa María. A bridge over the bay joins Cádiz to Puerto Real, and a modern highway allows the traveler to drive from Cádiz to Sevilla.

For further information on touring the wine regions of Spain, you can write to the Spanish National Tourist Office at one of the following addresses:

3160 Lyon St.
San Francisco 94123
(415) 346–8100

665 Fifth Ave.
New York 10022
(212) 759–8822

845 North Michigan Ave.
Water Tower Place
Chicago 60611
(312) 944–0215

Other sources of information are:

Mr. Antonio Gamiz, President
Spanish Wine Products
370 Lexington Ave., Suite 2213
New York 10017

Mr. Gerald Keller
Keller Haver, Inc.
Rioja Wine Information Bureau
770 Lexington Ave.
New York 10021

Portugal

You now are close to the southern border of Portugal, but to reach its winegrowing region you must travel to the farthest, northern tip of the country, to the Douro, Minho, and Dão regions in an area known as the Costa Verde.

The Douro and Minho regions produce a wine known as *vinho verde* or green wine, and the wines are trellised on trees and on pergolas around the little fields. In late summer, it is quite an enchanting sight, and the result is a light, golden and delicate wine peculiar to this region.

Another area, the Dão, produces vineyards in the heart of Portugal, sheltered both from the continental climates and the coast winds. Viseu is the capital of this district, and anyone chancing to visit the town and this lovely region should not fail to taste the delicious Dão wine at the Dão Winegrowers Federation headquarters, which are located here.

The greatest of all wine-producing regions of Portugal is, of course, the Douro region, and its port wine takes its name from the capital city, Oporto. According to Portuguese law, all wines called porto must be shipped either from Oporto or from Vila Nova de Gaia, just across the Douro River. Oporto gave its name not only to the world-famous wine, but at one time in history, to the country itself. This region formed part of the dowry of the Princess Doña Teresa when she married Henri of Burgundy in 1095. It was under their son that the country first gained its freedom and independence, taking the name of the region of Portugale.

Plan to stay in Oporto at least two days. On the first day, you can visit the ancient monuments and museum, including the Cathedral, the Pillory, the Stock Exchange and other architectural examples of the Romanesque, gothic, baroque, roccoco and neoclassical styles that abound in the city. At night you can visit a local tavern, and eat some traditional *Tripas a la moda do Porto* (Tripe a la Porto), a special dish made by the tripe-eaters, as the inhabitants of Oporto have been called since the fifteenth century because the city gave up all of its meat in order to supply the discovery fleets, leaving only the entrails or tripe for the inhabitants.

Another worthwhile spot to visit in Oporto would be the Solar do Vinho do Porto, at Rua de Entre Quintas, where you can taste Portuguese wine to your heart's delight.

On the second day you can visit a port wine cellar in Vila Nova de Gaia and take a boat trip along the River Douro. Of particular interest to the wine buff is the Museum of Ethnography and History, presenting the arts and culture of the region, including a reconstructed wine cellar among its exhibits.

For a closer look at the winegrowing regions, the visitor can rent a motor car and drive east along Highway 118 to Entre-os-Rios, skirting the north bank of the Douro, and then cross the river and travel the south bank to Lamego. South from Lamego, on Highway 2, you can travel 43 miles to the city of Viseu, a charming and quaint city with a fine museum and many interesting homes from the sixteenth and eighteenth centuries. Then, bending west, via Highway 16, you can view the mountain chain, Serra do Caramulo. From there, a little over 60 miles further, you'll reach the coast at Aveiro. From Aveiro, you can drive north by either highway 109 or highway 1, back to Oporto.

Another trip you can take takes you some 212 miles through the grandeur of the Serra do Geres and a number of quaint towns. You start from Oporto going to Braga, and then take Highway 103 towards the Serra do Geres and the upper reaches of the Cávado River. The mountain road brings you, after 75 miles, to Chaves. Not only do you go through spectacular scenery, but Chaves has been known since Roman times for the healing powers of its hot springs, and even today the waters are used for the treatment of rheumatism and digestive troubles. There are a couple of interesting castles in this area, including the ruins of the thirteenth-century Monforte Castle and the Bulideira, a huge "rocking" stone.

From Chaves, Highway 2 runs for 41 miles to Vila Real, probably best known for the seventeenth-century manor house of the Mateus family, which stands two miles away. Many excellent homes of the sixteenth and eighteenth centuries and an interesting cathedral from the seventeenth are situated at Vila Real. However, the house that appears on the label of the famous Mateus rosé wine bottles is a popular tourist attraction and familiar to thousands of visitors. It is open to the public, containing fine furniture and a small museum of the Counts of Vila Real. The gardens contain orchards and the vineyards from which the wine is produced.

From Vila Real, Highway 15 will take you a bit over 30 miles to Amaranto, and from that charming town on the banks of the river Tâmega, you will be 35 miles from Oporto.

Other sights you will enjoy while in this part of Portugal include the pastoral Peneda-Geres National Park, the gaming casinos in Espinho and Povoa do Varzim, the sandy dunes, and the mineral springs, possibly some of the richest in the world. For more information on wine touring, you may write to the Instituto do Vinho do Porto, Rua de Ferreira Borges, Porto. The telephone number is 26522–5 and the Telex number is 25337 P. Cable Inviporto. For further information on touring Portugal, write to the Portuguese National Tourist Office at one of the following addresses:

548 Fifth Ave.
New York 10036
(212) 354–4403

1 Park Plaza, Suite 1305
3250 Wilshire Blvd.
Los Angeles 90010
(213) 380–6459

Suite 500, Palmer House
17 East Monroe St.
Chicago 60603
(312) 236–6603

The
Social Life
of Wine

Wine in Restaurants

Mel Brooks is a funny man, a clever writer, and a successful film producer. He's also a customer of mine who takes his wine very seriously—at home and while dining. He has developed a technique for dealing with restaurants that goes something like this: Mel calls the restaurant and asks for information about the wine list. After he's gained a general idea of its type—poor, average, or great—he will decide on whether he is going to take his own wine to dine or not. If he and his wife, Anne Bancroft, decide they want a wine that's not listed, Mel will call the restaurateur to explain that he's bringing his own wine and to give his instructions on how he wants the wine to be served.

This isn't always easy to do, and being a movie star or V.I.P. does help. Restaurateurs are reluctant to lose the profit from in-house wine sales, and while they may say that they have no personal reluctance to allow outside wines in their establishment, they may tell you the law forbids it. Check it out.

In California, this statement would be false, and even if a restaurant had no wine license, it would still not be illegal for you to bring your own bottles to the restaurant. However, this is not permitted in New York state, and state laws will differ widely throughout the country. Every state has an alcoholic regulatory board that can keep you abreast of the state's statutes where you live or are traveling.

Naturally, like Mel, you must be prepared to pay a corkage fee for the privilege of the waiter's service and use of restaurant glassware. Make sure that you ask about the corkage fee before you enter the restaurant. This way, no one is faced with an embarrassing situation at the evening's conclusion. Be gracious and buy a bottle from the restaurant's own list, in addition to bringing your own.

Everyone of us, whether movie stars or wine merchants, frequents restaurants. The wine service, whether fancy or plain, can vary from lukewarm to enthusiastic (the latter is definitely in the minority). Learning what to expect from restaurant wine service, including selection and pricing, will spare you unrealistic expectations and expensive evenings full of frustration and disappointment.

Ninety percent of all Americans have their first experience with wine at a restaurant, and although I'd love to tell all of you that most American restaurant wine service is great, the facts are just the opposite. If you are dining out, however, here are my tips on what you should expect from your wine waiter in a fancy restaurant:

1. The waiter or sommelier should be able to give suggestions on the best wine to go with what you've ordered for dinner.
2. Whether it is the first or fifth bottle you've ordered, the waiter must allow you to inspect the label each time before he opens it.
3. After the waiter removes the capsule and uncorks the bottle, he should present you with the cork for your inspection.
4. The host will then be poured a small portion of wine. Only if it meets with your approval, will the waiter serve. In France, he pours in a counterclockwise position; in the United

States, he serves ladies first, over the left shoulder.

5. Cardinal rule: Never, never should you have to reach for a wine bottle. When the wine level is down to the last quarter, the waiter should repour.

6. When the first bottle of wine is consumed, the waiter should, if he knows his business, lean over the host, by the same shoulder from which he poured, inquiring as to whether he should bring more wine, and if so, what type.

7. The bottle should never be removed from the table without your approval—even if it has been completely decanted and all that's left is sediment.

Aside from wine etiquette, what should you be aware of while dining? In the first place, forget the rules about fair play and gamesmanship. In a restaurant, whether you are a wine merchant, Mel Brooks, or a layman, you are at the mercy of the limits of the wine list. However, you don't have to throw your hands up in despair. For instance, you can avoid the obvious restaurant money-maker: the house wine in a carafe with a peach at the bottom. The contents are not worth your dining dollar.

The price of wine in a restaurant should be no more than double what it sells for at the retail level. But you may dine at a den of forty thieves, finding yourself (if you are willing) paying three and four times what the wine is worth.

Some restaurants like Bern's Steak House in Tampa, Florida, are owned by people who love wine to the nth degree. He lovingly dedicates his 1,-139 page wine list to his wife, Gert, "who probably can't look at a bottle of wine without seeing a banker's face." Bernard H. Laxer is a rarity, a diamond shining among a myriad of rhinestones. So to the Laxers of this world I salute and give a toast. Unfortunately, most restaurant wine lists in this country are limited to generic wines, such as Pouilly-Fuissé or Chablis, and a motley crew of whites, reds, rosés, and sparkling wines, usually without much distinction.

Part of the problem is that restaurateurs are busy people with a lot of problems besides their wine lists, and they turn to a distributor for solace. This amiable fellow, in turn, may sell 40 restaurants within a 10-mile radius the identical list. In return for signing on with a given distributor, the restaurateur receives quantity discounts by buying from a single source—or at least this is the way it works in California. The dining spot receives a neatly printed wine list (another problem resolved) and both carefully

sidestep Federal laws prohibiting giveaways from distributor to restaurant.

I don't, for one minute, want to give you the impression that all fine restaurants are owned and staffed by cynics conspiring to cheat the consumer. But many restaurant owners don't have substantial knowledge about wines. Consequently, they rely on distributors who sell them the same products they've just sold a competitor three blocks down the street. If all of these people were serving and cooking for you out of one central kitchen, you would be outraged. The same outrage should be expressed by you, the consumer, when you find the identical wines at a number of the better restaurants in your city.

If you like to dine out and drink wine with your dinner, you will be rewarded by steadily frequenting at least three different restaurants of distinctly different character. One restaurant could be French; another Italian; and a third, more exotic. Learn their wine lists and cultivate relationships with the owners and/or the maître d's of these establishments.

One way of gaining the maître d's confidence might be to select one of your own wines and send a bottle to him with a friendly note. Ask him to try the wine and give you his comments the next time you frequent his restaurant. While dining there on another occasion, ask him if you can stock two or three bottles of the same wine you sent for his comments and offer to pay the corkage fee.

This ploy will pay off later, when you are trying to impress guests and can summon the maître d' to decork some of the wine you've stored at the establishment. It will really pay off when the restaurateur adds it to his list.

While this may not entirely save your pocketbook, here are some general Overstreet rules you may adopt when dining:

1. Whenever possible, choose a regional wine: on the East Coast, a selection from the Finger Lakes region; on the West Coast, a wine from California or Washington.

2. If it is a better-than-average restaurant, look for wines that are neither the most expensive nor the most cheaply priced. The first-growth wine of a fine vintage is the one that the restaurateur cannot afford to replace because it is no longer available, but gives prestige to his collection. The least expensive wine is the one he peddles most because it guarantees the restaurant the best deal. You don't know how the expensive wine has been stored so be cautious about buying this high-priced goodie at a dining

establishment. The middle-priced wine, however, often is the one representing the best bargain for the consumer. The wine may have been purchased and added to the list at the price before it went up. No restaurateur wants to be continually reprinting his wine list, so it is very possible that you may find a middle-level wine priced lower than retail.

3. Compliment a restaurateur on the wines on his wine list that are fine selections, or drop a note to the proprietor asking him to carry a particular wine. Be sure to send a copy of the note to the winery or supplier of that specific wine.

What about the way you return a restaurant wine? Rule number one: You don't have the right to return a bottle of wine just because you don't like it. Only two valid reasons exist for returning wine: If it's maderized or spoiled. The cork and smell will indicate a serious fault, and if this occurs, you should ask the sommelier or the owner to taste and smell the wine in front of you. If they disagree with your judgment or refuse to drink the wine themselves, decline to pay for your selection.

Generally, you won't find yourself embarrassed. A problem such as maderization or spoilage will be obvious to the management. In most instances, a restaurateur will be happy to provide you with a new bottle. But make sure that the fresh bottle is opened in front of you. Once the bottle is unsealed, it is up to you to give the sommelier proper instruction on how the wine should be served and whether it should be aired or chilled.

If you must order the house wine, ask the waiter what it is and if he says it is a jug wine, ask him to serve you from an unopened fresh jug. Because jug wine usually comes in a screw-top bottle that is constantly being opened and closed, drinking wine from an already opened jug can be like eating vegetables that have been repeatedly heated until soft and mushy.

Remember that adventure is the spice of life and that taking chances when you're out dining is a relatively harmless way of adding drama to your existence. You won't stray too far from safe ground if you choose a wine appropriate to the restaurant and culinary selection you are making. Happily sip when you've made a good choice and learn from experience when you've chosen a loser. In the final analysis, knowledge of the restaurant, its management policies, and its wine list will enable you to make fewer and fewer bad choices, gaining heightened pleasure when dining out.

Wine and Food

Wine and food go together like Nick and Nora Charles, but the subject, while seemingly simple, can become complicated by the increased use of off-beat spices, complicated sauces, and unusual or exotic game, fish, or poultry.

With today's exotic cuisine, repeating the traditional advice that red wine will go with red meat and white wine will be terrific with white meat won't do if the chef is planning a meal of chicken with a peanut sauce.

Here's your cardinal rule: The richer the dish, the richer the wine. Poultry, fish, or meat stuffed or covered with a specific type of sauce or dressing should be accompanied by a wine that is suitable for the sauce or dressing, not for the food itself.

And the richer the sauce, the fuller bodied the wine; the more complex the sauce, the more refined and complex the wine. At the end of this chapter, you'll find a list of gourmet sauces and my recommendations of the type of wine to serve with them.

Chicken with an orange glaze won't work with the dry white wine everyone says is perfect with poultry. Picture, if you will, a vicious tackle by Mean Joe Greene in football. The sauce will cream the chicken. But a Sauternes, normally a sweet dessert wine, will maneuver its way perfectly with the chicken, balancing your game. True, it is a bit of overkill, but you aren't creating a subtle gastronomical combination.

Chicken cacciatore, served with a lot of parsley and garlic, requires a robust red wine like a Barbera or something from the Nebbiolo grape like a Barolo. Both of these seasonings will fatigue your palate and shouldn't be consumed with rare or expensive wines.

Let us say you've decided to make a chicken that is to be roasted with raisins, apples, or apricots. In this case, as a novelty, you might choose a Sauternes or Barsac type of wine.

On occasions, you will downplay the wine, giving added emphasis to the dish. *Coq au vin* will be fine with a light red wine. But the same chicken, highly spiced in the Szechuan style, would marry far better with an inexpensive and pleasant Gamay, Beaujolais, or California jug wine.

The mention of *Coq au Vin* brings up the question of cooking with wine. You probably don't need to be told to stay away from cooking wines, which are an abomination. Loaded with salt and spices, they offend both the chef and the wine lover. Since

119

the alcohol content of any wine evaporates in the cooking process, you're left with the flavor. And if the flavor isn't good enough to drink, it's not good enough to cook with. (Of course, I'm not suggesting you use three cups of a first growth in a casserole, but you get the point.) Incidentally, it's a nice carryover of taste if the same wine used in preparation is served at the table.

The fat content of a dish will determine how full-bodied your wine should be, and for that reason, I suggest wines with higher acidity, such as Burgundian type red wines, for roast beef, steaks, and all fur-bearing animals such as rabbits. From the same region, the Montrachets and Meursaults, which are big, supple, creamy and buttery wines, are fine with fish dishes like salmon or trout. But with a leaner fish such as perch or with shellfish, a crisp light Chablis would be more appropriate.

Certain types of pâtés I've found delicious with Sauternes. This delectable, sweet wine is also outstanding with ripe fruit, especially a pitted type, and extraordinary with the right kind of fish.

Be imaginative in what you serve with soups and cocktail snacks. Dry sherries and Madeiras can be excellent with cocktail snacks, smoked salmon, or canapés. These same wines, or a Marsala, can be served with thick *potages*.

Some vegetables will accentuate your wine service, especially red wines, and when you are serving special vintages or classic growths, try to use these in your menu: lightly buttered beans; snow peas; new boiled potatoes; carrots; cauliflowers; string beans; French *flageolets*; wild rice; brown rice cakes; and lightly fried green tomatoes.

When you really want to show off your wines, you'll be giving a dinner of several courses. Don't despair if one of your guests is on a strict diet or is a diabetic: The Trocken-Diabetiker wines of Germany have, by law, a maximum residual sugar content of only 4 percent and are dry and refreshing.

Proper wine service has traditionally been white before red; dry before sweet; light before full; young before old; and least before best. Again, it ain't necessarily so. I have some tips that will make your presentation of a gourmet wine service far more impressive.

Handicap your dinner as if it were a football game or a horse race. It wouldn't be any fun to see Bill Shoemaker ride anything less than a thoroughbred or to attend a Super Bowl where the Pittsburgh Steelers are playing against a high school team. So don't match great wines with mediocre food.

People tend to be uptight when they arrive at a party, especially if they are meeting others for the

first time. I suggest a champagne Kir. It will enter the bloodstream immediately, and not only does Kir make the champagne very appealing, it also relaxes and stimulates the stomach. Kir, named for the late Canon Felix Kir, a former major of the city of Dijon, is a refreshing wine aperitif that comes in many flavors, including strawberry, bilberry, and raspberry. It is superb mixed with champagne at a ratio of one-third Kir to two-thirds champagne.

For the first course of this gourmet dinner, I'd serve a *foie gras* or *pâté* with a Sauternes, because the creamy texture of both is highly complementary. Next, everyone's palate would be cleared with a soup course, followed by a third course of pasta, served by itself in the Italian style. My fourth course would be fish, my fifth a *sorbet*, or sherbet, again to clear the palate, followed by the sixth course or main entrée. My seventh would be fruit and cheese, followed by an eighth course of dessert. Coffee should then be served, preferably stronger than norm and in demitasse cups, followed by a sweet champagne to round out the evening.

You are not serving dinner to Paul Bunyan or Pantagruel, so give each person a modest portion of each course. Wines should be chosen with an eye not only toward how they complement the particular food they are to be served with but toward your budget. You don't necessarily have to purchase Château d'Yquem, the most expensive Sauternes, or blow your wad on Dom Pérignon or Château Mouton-Rothschild. This type of multicourse dinner can, in fact, allow you to experiment with excellent wines from lesser-known wine regions such as Argentina, Chile, Australia, New Zealand, South Africa, Spain, and our own United States.

But most of us, even wine merchants, don't drink rare first growths with our workday meals. Your meatballs and spaghetti will blend beautifully with a full-bodied Spanish red Rioja, an Italian Grignolino, or a Gallo Hearty Burgundy—so will your occasional splurge of pizza or any other pasta-based dish centered on a red sauce.

Barbequed meat or meat loaf, two other American favorites, go nicely with Petite Sirah, an inexpensive wine produced quite well by a number of California wineries. If your supermarket doesn't carry Petite Sirah, try Zinfandel. It also is ideal with these types of foods.

Honest picnic fare like ham, salami, and other cold cuts or unsophisticated cheeses, are superbly married to simple Gamay Beaujolais, Beaujolais, Gamay, or Zinfandel wines. The Monterey Vineyard, Parducci, and Sebastiani are among many names you should look for on your supermarket shelf. For those who insist on a white wine, a crisp Sauvignon Blanc is also compatible.

Two California products, avocados and artichokes, are popular throughout the country and are abundant during season. How to serve them? Both, strange as it may seem, go very well with a dry, white Bordeaux type of wine. This recommendation is based, of course, on the two being served simply. The addition of a richer dressing would alter my choice.

Wine and Exotic Game and Fowl

Another food and wine marriage that is puzzling to many is selecting the right wine for exotic game and fowl. You may be the recipient of a hunter's bounty or have one in the family who keeps your freezer stocked with a year's supply of delectable meat, or you may decide to prepare an unusual game dinner. So here are my wine suggestions for game, wild birds, and other unusual meats.

Pheasant, foil-roasted and smothered in apricots, is a delicious accompaniment to the German Schloss Vollrads or Bernkastel-Doktor.

Partridge is a bird that is superb in a casserole with vegetables, especially mushrooms. The wine marries well with a heavy white Burgundy or a light Côte de Beaune. *Grouse*, another bird, I prefer stuffed with almonds and served with a lemon-butter sauce. It is ideal with a rich, old Meursault, almost maderized and turning brown.

Prairie chicken can be sautéed with fruit and is luscious with a Johannisberg Riesling.

We are fortunate in the United States, because tasty wild turkey is freely available. It is leaner than domestic turkey, and when roasted with chestnuts and juniper berries is absolutely savory. An acidic, light, red Gamay Beaujolais, or Beaujolais, or a Sauvignon Blanc would be a good choice.

Woodcock, a small, migratory bird that tastes exquisite, is great with lingonberry and orange-jelly sauce. With this bird, you'll want to serve a wine with a lot of acidity, such as French Colombard or still Champagne.

Quail is smashing breaded with cornmeal and sautéed with hazelnuts and grapes. Serve it with a white Graves, especially Château Haut-Brion Blanc or Château Carbonnieux, Sauvignon Blanc, or Pouilly Fumé.

Pigeon and *dove* are small, so I suggest you plan on a couple per person. These dark-fleshed birds can be cherry-roasted in foil and are excellent with a dry, complex Bordeaux type of wine, such as Saint-Estèphe.

Another bird that I put into a different classification, but still in the special-dinner category, is any water fowl.

Coot and *mud hens* are extremely savory. Plan on a couple of birds per person, braised in sherry sauce. I recommend a Burgundy, especially Côte de Beaune, Volnay, or Pommard. The high acidity of these wines go excellently with these birds.

Wild duck can be served in a variety of interesting ways. My favorite is pecan stuffing, which gives it a rich, nutty quality. For this type of bird I suggest a Burgundy, such as Nuits-St.-Georges, or a big, powerful Pinot Noir with a lot of "knitting" to its texture. Another way of serving duck is in a sauce of Grand Marnier. It is more traditional and gives the duck an orange flavor.

Beaver, a small game animal, is exquisite. There's a sort of tale about the tail and its purported delicacy. But forget it. Any muscle that is overworked will be tough, and this is the case with the beaver's tail. This 60-pound creature has dark, delicious meat and is ideal with a Rhône or Petite Sirah, Château neuf-du-Pape, or Hermitage.

Rabbit, more common, has white meat and a delicate flavor. Soak this meat in wine for about six hours. After that point, the wine may become sour. You can cook rabbit baked in a mayonnaise and Dijon mustard sauce. With this tangy sauce, I love to serve a white wine. I'd recommend a Chassagne-Montrachet or another quality Chardonnay. Another way of cooking it is with prosciutto ham. Rabbit prepared in this manner can be served with Semillon, Chenin Blanc, or Vouvray.

Opossum, a light-colored and tender meat cooked with cinnamon and Corton-Charlemagne is an unusual dish.

Another small game that will be the talk of your social season is *woodchuck*. It is scrumptious baked with winter squash and raisins and served with Madeira.

Raccoon, a dark-fleshed animal, has a mild flavor. If corn-fried with a sour cream sauce topping, I'd recommend a light-bodied red wine, such as a Volnay or Pommard.

Muskrat also has dark meat. Southern fry it with a fruit compote sauce and serve Vouvray Cour de Charmes or California Late Harvest Johannisberg Riesling.

Squirrel is tender, mild-flavored, and versatile. Serve it with Zinfandel, Beaujolais, or an Italian Bardolino or Valpollicella.

Now we come to the topic of big game and serious wine. With *deer*, you can serve a variety of dishes, including roasts, chops, or steaks. The way

I've enjoyed it is roasting it as I would a leg of lamb. This kind of meat can be served with a Pauillac or Napa Valley Cabernet. I'd advise you against a Sonoma County cabernet because it produces spicier, more pungent cabernets that are not harmonious with this type of meat.

Bear is mighty good, albeit rare, eating. It diets on apples, grapes, berries, and honey, and has a succulent taste. You can broil a bear steak with mushrooms, or pot roast it in red wine. The ideal wine for this delicacy is a St.-Émilion like Cheval Blanc with its "gout de terre," an intriguing counterpoint to the meat's sweetness.

With *mountain sheep* or *goat*, I'd stick to east European wines, such as Hungarian Tokay or Muscat. You can cook it similarly to venison, but goat meat will require overnight soaking in a vinegar solution fortified with cloves, cinnamon, mustard, salt, and pepper. Last but not least, *antelope* is excellent with Bordeaux red wines, and *roasted boar* will blend beautifully with a Côte de Nuits from Burgundy.

How to Keep Leftover Wine

You may have leftover premium wine after a party and decide that it is criminal to waste it—but what should you do?

You can make something worthwhile out of a leftover wine by making your own vinegar. In French cooking circles, it is often said that the easiest way to spot a great chef's kitchen is not by his copper and carbon knives but by the wine vinegar he uses. One of my customers (whose reported wealth by Fortune magazine was estimated at over $200 million) bottles his wine vinegar in tenths, or small splits, and sends his choicest batches to friends at Christmas. The surprising revelation to me was not that these token gifts were more highly prized than Gucci bags, but that one of the world's greatest chefs told me that it was one of the nicest gifts he'd ever received and that it made French vinegars anemic by comparison.

So here are some tips on how you can become a Vinegar Santa this Christmas.

1. Keep any leftover wine from a party or dinner; don't throw away the bottle.

2. Put three tablespoons of commercial vinegar or homemade vinegar from a previous batch into the bottle.

3. Cover the opening of the container with gauze or cheesecloth secured with a rubber band. Cover that with a removable bottle top or cork. Continue to add any leftover wines you have of the same type, red or white, until the bottle is full, pouring through the cheesecloth filter.

   Warning: Do not add jug wines, or wines with over 14 percent alcohol, or wines with technical defects such as too much sulphur or other spoiled overtones.

4. For a tangier or more exotic vinegar, add a pinch of tarragon, rosemary, garlic, cloves, or any spice you believe will give the vinegar a special touch.

5. Store the bottle without agitation or disturbance in a temperature ranging from 70° to 80°. When the jar is completely filled, recork and age as long as possible for maximum flavor.

Another simple trick that will allow you to keep your leftover wine is to drop marbles into the bottle until the level of wine reaches the top, after which you recork the bottle. The wine will stay fresh for three to four weeks. If you have leftover champagne, simply drop a metal object, such as a knife, into the bottle. This will keep the bubbles up to three days, provided the champagne is refrigerated and either recorked or covered with wax paper and a rubberband to keep it airtight.

Wine and Sauces

Aigre-douce (French) or *agro-dolce (Italian)*: a sweet-sour sauce often served with rabbit or braised meats; in Chinese cooking, you'll find a variant of it with chicken or pork. Wines: Chenin Blanc, Vouvray, Gewürztraminer, Alsace.

Albert: horseradish sauce, tinged with mustard and vinegar, served classically with beer. Wines: Rhône, Petite Sirah, Nebbiolo, Barolo.

Allemande: similar to sauce Veloute but enriched with eggs. Wines: St.-Émilion, Rhône, Morlot, Petite Sirah.

Almond: versatile sauce that goes with anything from fish to vegetables. Wines: Meursault, white Burgundy, Chardonnay.

Apple: a sauce made with a fruit puree base enhanced by spices and herbs; normally served with pork. Wines: Champagne, Anjou Rose, Johannisberg Riesling, Moselle, Sauternes, Chenin Blanc, Vouvray.

Aurore: similar to classic Bechamel sauce, with a dash of tomato puree. Wines: Médoc, preferably St.-Julien or Pauillac, California Napa Valley Cabernet Sauvignon.

Batarde: similar to Allemande sauce. Wines: White Burgundy, Sancerre, Chardonnay, Verdicchio.

Bavaroise: a wine vinegar and butter combo seasoned with horseradish and nutmeg; delicious hot sauce for shellfish and fish. Wines: Alsace, Chablis, Chardonnay, Verdicchio.

Bercy: same as Veloute sauce, made from a base of reduced fish stock and white wine, seasoned with shallots and parsley. Wines: White Burgundy, Chardonnay.

Beurre Noir: butter cooked nut-brown and served either with lemon juice or capers. Wines: White Burgundy, Chardonnay, Champagne, Verdicchio.

Bigarade: combines duck juice with orange and/or lemon juice, julienne strips of orange peel, and mashed duck liver. Wines: Côte de Nuits, Hermitage, Pinot Noir, Petite Sirah.

Bolognese: classic Italian tomato-base sauce with wine and herbs. Wines: Bardolino, Grignolino, Valpolicella, Beaujolais, Zinfandel.

Bordelaise: meat juice extract and red wine, with shallots, peppers, parsley and other herbs; served with grilled meats. Wines: Bordeaux, Cabernet Sauvignon.

Bourguignonne: mushrooms and red wine spiced with shallots, parsley, and bay leaf, with butter thickener; served with meats. Wines: Red Burgundy, Pinot Noir, Red Bordeaux, especially a Graves or St.-Émilion.

Bread: a British sauce of bread crumbs cooked in milk, onions, lemon juice, parsley, and diced ham. Wines: White Burgundy, Rosé, Gamay, Champagne.

Cambridge: another British sauce for mutton, made of mayonnaise, hard-cooked egg yolks, anchovies, capers, and mustard. Wines: White Burgundy, Chardonnay, White Graves.

Caper: pickled buds that go into a variety of dishes and can be served with a number of meats, fish, and poultry. Wines: If the dish is a fish base, use an Alsace, Gewürztraminer, or White Graves. If the dish has a meat base, use a St.-Estèphe or a Graves.

Chasseur: the hunter's sauce served with rabbit and game, made with white wine, chopped mushrooms, shallots, meat essence, and parsley. Wines: Puligny-Montrachet, Chardonnay, Loire, Sauvignon Blanc.

Chaud-froid: sauce made to mask cold foods; can be white or brown. Wines: For the white sauce, use White Burgundy or Alsace wine; for brown sauce, Red Burgundy, St.-Émilion, Pomerol.

Demiglaze: a basic brown sauce accented with sherry. Wines: Bordeaux, Cabernet Sauvignon, Nebbiolo.

Diable: primarily used to spice up meat or turkey. Wines: Lusty reds like Chianti, Zinfandel, Riojas, Nebbiolo.

Diplomat: a French classic sauce for fish. Wines: Chablis, White Burgundy, Chardonnay, still Champagne, Fino Sherry.

Financiere: similar to Madeira sauce enhanced by truffles, and chicken livers. Wines: Champagne, White Burgundy, Côte de Beaune, Burgundy.

Gribiche: sauce made from hard-cooked egg yolk base, with oil and vinegar, chopped gherkins and capers; ideal for shellfish and cold fish. Wines: Gewürztraminer, Alsace, Champagne, Sauvignon Blanc.

Laguipiere: chicken or veal stock and truffles marinated in sherry. Served with fish. Wines: Sauvignon Blanc, Pouilly Fumé, Fino Sherry.

Lyonnaise: onion puree cooked with white wine and vinegar, combined with demiglaze. Wines: Cabernet Sauvignon, Bordeaux, Red Burgundy, Pinot Noir.

Madeira: reduced brown stock and sauce enhanced by Madeira; served with roasted or braised meats. Wines: Red Burgundy, Rhône, Red Bordeaux, Pinot Noir, Petite Sirah, Cabernet.

Matelote: demiglaze sauce, particularly fine with fish; made from fish stock, red wine, and mushrooms. Wines: Beaujolais Red, Gamay, Chardonnay.

Mint: sauce served chiefly with lamb. Wines: Red Bordeaux, Cabernet Sauvignon.

Mornay: béchamel sauce with grated Swiss or Parmesan cheese. Wines: Champagne, White Burgundy, Chardonnay, Vouvray, and Chenin Blanc.

Nantua: type of Veloute sauce enriched with crayfish or lobster butter, tomato puree, white wine and brandy; served with shellfish. Wines: Chablis, Sancerre, Chardonnay.

Normande: similar to Veloute, made with reduced fish stock, mussels, oysters or clam juice, mushroom stock, egg yolks, and cream; served with fish. Wines: Chablis, White Burgundy, Alsace, Loire, Chardonnay, Verdicchio.

Parsley: melted butter, parsley, and lemon juice sauce; a favorite with fish dishes. Wines: Chablis, White Burgundy, Alsace, Loire, Chardonnay, Verdicchio, Soave.

Perigueux: French classic; truffles and Madeira added to a demiglaze. Wines: Red Bordeaux, Red Burgundy, Cabernet.

Piquante: brown sauce with capers, shallots, and pureed white wine; highly spiced with pepper. Wines: Red Bordeaux, Cabernet, Rhône, Rioja.

Poivrade: basic brown sauce tinged with wine vinegar and white wine, peppercorns, minced vegetables, and herbs; served with meat or game. Wines: Bordeaux, Cabernet, Red Burgundy, Pinot Noir, Nebbiolo.

Poulette: variation of béchamel, enriched with egg yolks and cream, seasoned with mushrooms, shallots; served with poultry. Wines: White Burgundy, Loire, Chardonnay, Sauvignon Blanc.

Provençale: tomato-reduced sauce with garlic and mushrooms. Wines: Valpollicella, Bardolino, Beaujolais, Gamay, Zinfandel, Nebbiolo.

Ravigote (cold): base of mayonnaise, chopped capers, and hard-cooked eggs; ideal sauce for cold fish and vegetables. Wines: White Burgundy, Chardonnay, Alsace, Loire, Chenin Blanc.

Ravigote (hot): made with béchamel, white wine, and seasoned with chevril and tarragon; served with poultry, liver, and kidneys. Wines: same as above.

Réforme: mixture of poivrade and demiglaze, made with chopped or julienne hard-cooked egg whites, tongue, truffles, mushrooms, and gherkins. Wines: Burgundy, Bordeaux, Cabernet.

Remoulade: made with mayonnaise, mustard, capers, gherkins, herbs, and mashed anchovy or anchovy paste. Wines: Alsace, Gewürztraminer.

Robert: onions, white wine added to sauce Espagnole, sharply seasoned with mustard and pepper; served with meats and steaks. Wines: Rhône, Barolo, Rioja, Petite Sirah, Chianti.

Soubise: béchamel sauce combined with onion puree and nutmeg; served with eggs, chicken, pork, or mutton. Wines: White Burgundy, Côte de Beaune.

Supreme: a version of Velouté, enriched with cream; ideal with poultry, especially boned and skinned chicken breasts. Wines: White Burgundy, Johannisberg Riesling, Moselle, Alsace, Loire.

Tartar: popular sauce for fish or cold chicken, made with hard-cooked egg yolks, oil and vinegar, snipped chives, and chopped onions; or made with mayonnaise, chives, capers and gherkins. Wines: White Burgundy, White Graves, White Rhône, Alsace, Verdicchio.

Verte: pureed blanched herbs like parsley, tarragon, sometimes basil, spinach, or watercress are added to mayonnaise. Wines: White Burgundy, Johannisberg Riesling, Chardonnay, Loire, Chenin Blanc.

Vin Blanc: another version of the Velouté sauce, made with fish stock, egg yolks, and softened butter; served mainly on fish. Wines: White Burgundy, Chardonnay.

Dessert sauces such as Chantilly, primarily whipped cream, are delightful with Sauternes or Champagne. Hard sauces take to ports and sherries, as do buttery brown, honey, caramel, butterscotch, and maple sugar sauces. Unusual sauces like Melba go well with Rieslings and Sauternes as well as Champagne.

The Wine-tasting Party

Once launched on the study and enjoyment of great wines, you'll want to be accompanied on your tasting adventures by others who are similarly inclined. A wine-tasting party can be a weekly get-together among a few intimate friends or a larger more formal tasting, with 20 to 60 people, perhaps featuring a lecturer.

The most important thing for the novice to remember is that frequency of tastings is essential. At least half a dozen of your first small sessions should deal with wines of known identity. You should learn the basic characteristics of different wine types and important varietals with good friends first, before you play Twenty Questions with the experts.

When judging the merits of a fine wine, taste it in relation to other wines, even if they're of a different type. You will learn a lot by tasting wines of the same vintage but from different areas; or from the same establishment but of different years. Taste superior wines, even if only occasionally. Look for the true characteristics of a district or winery as exemplified in the best wine of that area or château.

Drink with people who will exchange impressions with you and with whom you can share your tasting experiences so that you'll continue to learn without snobbery or self-consciousness. The camaraderie of a group of wine lovers (not wine snobs) is uniquely enjoyable, and the occasion shouldn't be spoiled by the feeling that you're unable to speak freely or relate to the other tasters.

Don't be intimidated by the pedant or expert. You need to learn to use words to describe wines, and they can vary from factual to fanciful. It will help your self-confidence to realize that even among experts there can be disagreement on such basics as whether a wine is full, light, or dry. Even professionals can be imprecise when it comes to the semantics of wine. Remember, you're becoming a taster, not a chemist. It's infinitely better for you to try to express your feelings about a wine, imprecise or not, than to sit through a tasting, your own or another's, without becoming a participant.

Tasting notes is an important tool that enables you to build a storehouse of sense memories. Include your mental pictures of images of aromas, flavors, bouquets. Later, a glimpse of old notes will help you to recall the characteristics of a particular wine. As Michael Broadbent puts it, "With wine, as with many other things, it is a matter of 'in one ear and out the other' unless specific action is taken to remedy the lazy human condition."

Compare your notes. Earnestly discuss what you like and don't like about a wine, and keep a clear mental picture of the qualities you look for in a specific varietal before you roam into more sophisticated experiences. Don't overload your group of wines to be tasted, especially if your guests are inexperienced tasters. Usually four to six samples can be tasted and compared without fatigue. (Experienced tasters are able to compare and evaluate several times that number.)

For a casual tasting party, allow at least half a bottle per person. At a disciplined and conducted tasting, one bottle will serve fifteen or more tasters. The number of glasses should correspond to the number of wines being tasted, especially if you are comparing particular varieties or château-bottled wines. If one glass must be used to taste different wines, as will occur at a large tasting, be sure the glass is carefully rinsed with water after each wine. Each glass should be filled to precisely the same height (generally, about one-third full) with each wine to be tasted.

In a *comparative* tasting, people state a simple preference among several wines, usually of the same variety but with no further restrictions. A *horizontal* tasting compares wines of the same vintage and area. In a *vertical* tasting, different vintages of a single producer's wines are evaluated.

The wines you select for a tasting should be of equivalent quality; if there is an odd man out in the group, whether a great wine or a decidedly inferior one, it will throw off your judgments. Similarly, if you are judging wines of the same types but from different growing districts, try to taste wines of approximately the same age. It isn't fair to judge a 15-year-old Burgundy Pinot Noir against its 3-year-old California counterpart. The difference in age will have a tremendous effect on the odor components and general quality, giving the French wine a definite advantage.

The order of tasting is based on elementary principles: dry before sweet, young before old, modest before fine. The order of tasting of reds over whites should be resolved by the relative weights of the wines involved, whatever the color. Light dry whites are better before fuller-bodied white wines loaded with heavy extract and residual sugar. Spar-

kling wines should be tasted separately for their own merits.

Hold your tasting, small or large, in a serene and peaceful environment—and indoors. An outdoor tasting may sound pleasant, but it will be a total loss as far as tasting goes. I remember an al fresco tasting held by a local wine writer in the Napa Valley that was attended by a number of California winemarkers. Shifting winds, the sunlight flickering through the trees, the various smells of the great outdoors, the cacophony of passing cars and twittering birds, all distorted the tasting experience. Not surprisingly, Robert Mondavi didn't recognize one of his own wines in a blind tasting and ranked it the lowest of the group. I'm told that Joe Heitz remarked to the host, "Thanks a lot for not having one of my wines at the tasting"; one of Mr. Heitz's wines had in fact been represented.

Your room should be well lit, but stay away from fluorescent lights or mercury arc bulbs because these produce artificial tints. Candles or incandescent lights are appropriate, but make sure there's enough illumination.

If you're going to pass out Monte Cristo cigars, do so after the tasting portion of the evening. This doesn't mean that you have to stop smoking to appreciate fine wine, but fighting a smoke screen while evaluating a wine will prove difficult. Don't spray your home, particularly the tasting room, with air fresheners or perfumes before the party, and don't heavily lade yourself with colognes or scent. Make sure your pet has been sent to the pooch or feline parlor for a shampoo—animal odors will easily throw off the scent of wine.

The best time for a tasting is before lunch or dinner, since you are more receptive when you're hungry. Don't serve cocktails or heavily spiced hors d'oeuvres. If you do serve food to clear the palate, make it something bland and unobtrusive: small pieces of French bread or Melba toast, carrots, or slices of apples. Avoid cheese: As the natural accompaniment to wine, it will improve even the worst wine.

For your own enjoyment, don't hold a winetasting party when you are physically exhausted, in bad health, or have a bad head cold. And for goodness' sake, forget the Listerine. Alkaline toothpaste interacts with the acidity of wine.

About equipment: There's no need to get elaborate. What you'll really need are a white (or better, gray) tablecloth and napkins, a few short candles for color evaluation, a pitcher with cool water (no ice cubes, please) and water glasses, spittoons in which to spill excess wine after each round, and pencils and pads at each place for making tasting notes. Have available plenty of glasses and several corkscrews.

I recommend that you use eight-ounce tulip-shaped glasses: These are big enough to allow you to sniff properly, and their shape, converging towards the rim, will retain and accumulate odors. Make sure your glasses are sparkling clean, without lint or water spots. Detergents and cleansers can easily leave odor traces. I suggest you wash them in hot water without detergent, rinsing them several times. Allow them to dry on a rack by their stems (which is also how they should be stored). Don't turn your glasses upside down on countertops, napkins or paper towels because their odors will cling to the glasses and influence the flavor of any delicate wine.

Try not to crowd your guests at your tasting table, and be unorthodox in your seating arrangements. Mix old and young, and don't necessarily go with the boy-girl formula or seat two old wine cronies together. Seat people according to the arrangement you think will be the most stimulating and a learning-enhancer.

Allow plenty of time for tasting, asking everyone to take a fifteen-minute break after an hour of serious evaluation. If you are having a speaker, plan on no more than two hours for sipping and listening. If the speaker is going to discuss six wines, calculate one and a half hours for the speaking portion of the evening. Have a wine assistant for every ten to fifteen tasters. This person should be responsible for serving his group. He can either pour at the table or bring out a tray with wines already poured without annoying the speaker or delaying the session.

By the time you're attending or hosting large and formal wine tastings, you're ready for more complex and subtle evaluation games that include a blind factor. At this degree of proficiency, participants are seated beyond peeking distance of one another and exchanges of opinions are prohibited. All samples are poured into identical glasses, and bottle sizes, shapes, colors, and foils are made unrecognizable (or, more simply, the bottles from which the wines are poured are kept out of sight). Unmarked glasses are set in front of the taster, designated from the left as Number 1, Number 2, Number 3, and so forth. (Needless to say, the taster should try to keep them in the same order before him as he tastes so as not to get hopelessly muddled.) The glasses are filled from bottles correspondingly marked. To avoid the value judgement implicit in coding your wines 1, 2, 3, etc., you might instead make your codes a random selection of two-digit numbers, 52, 38, 46, whatever, and so mark the glasses; another method is to tie colored ribbons to the glass stems and the

corresponding decanter. The taster is then free to move his glasses as he tastes. The object of course is to describe the wines as fully as possible.

The Duo-Trio game tests a taster's ability to identify a known wine against an unknown sample. It requires two wines and three glasses. One glass of each wine is poured into coded glasses. The one of the two wines is poured into a control glass and identified to the taster. He tastes the control, then the other two glasses. The object is to identify which of these holds the sample of the control wine.

A Head-On Comparison rates wines of a certain type or price range. The tasters rank the wines in order of personal preference in a blind tasting, the blind factor keeping the individual from being prejudiced by his own biases. Scorings are then compared.

Blind-Man, No Bluff tests the ability to identify wines by remembered characteristics without looking at the label. Any number of wines may be used. The participants are given a list of names of all the wines and samples of each in coded glasses. The object is to match the code number to the list.

In vino veritas. Games or no games, at a successful wine-tasting party, one in which the complexity matches the level of appreciation of your guests, the truth in the wine will be heard.

Wine and Children

Good manners, respect for others, and sensible use of food and drink is something that we're taught by our parents, or lacking that source, by the school or church. Children who are denied the knowledge of how to behave socially often experience rude awakenings as adults, when their everyday attitudes and manner are the basis for opinions formed by others. Many a failure of promotion on a job or self-consciousness with others can stem back to a lack of training in manners and social education as a child.

As with any other attitude about life, a child who sees his parents drinking wine at dinner in a sensible way isn't going to see this as something extraordinarily good or bad. It simply is a drink Mommy and Daddy have with dinner. However, a child who sees a parent drinking when he or she is emotionally upset, becoming violent or abusive, will learn that drinking wine or hard spirits is the way Mommy or Daddy relieve tension. In the future, your child may adopt heavy drinking as *his* way of dealing with tension—or become a teetotaler—but the parent's example certainly wields influence.

Those of you who are pregnant should consult

your obstetrician, the Salk Institute, or the Department of Health, Education and Welfare about Fetal Alcohol Syndrome and its dangers. Both the Salk Institute and H.E.W. have done intensive research into this subject. Studies conclude that overindulgence in alcohol during pregnancy can be dangerous to the unborn fetus, increasing the chances for a number of abnormalities during and after birth. While safe levels of drinking are unknown, it appears that a risk is established with ingestion of more than three ounces of absolute alcohol or six drinks per day. Between one and three ounces, there is still uncertainty, but caution is advised.

I've sent many of my customers with a new baby a bottle of wine for their child's 21st birthday. Not only am I insuring future customers for the Wine Merchant, but I think it is an inspiring way to teach children an important lesson about wine and life: that moments and things to be prized are often those requiring time to come into fruition. In an age of instant tea and instant gratification, this is one way to give a youngster a chance to look forward to drinking his own very special wine at age 21, with an object lesson in investing in the future and delaying enjoyment of a great experience.

We can also explain wine's living qualities. In this way, you are teaching your youngster that wine is a noble aspect of agriculture. It isn't something beyond his understanding and shouldn't be treated as a subject that is immoral or sinful.

You can dilute a glass of wine with water, allowing your child to take a sip or two depending on his age. You can discuss the different regions where wine is produced throughout the world and the role that it has played in the development of civilization. It can be a highly imaginative way of teaching him about your favorite hobby, important historical figures, and many other aspects of the social sciences.

Sharpen your child's appreciation of his own senses. Have him look for the nuances in the various colors of wine and the differences in aroma, and teach him to use his sense of taste, smell, and sight, and to appreciate not only wine but food.

If you are a connoisseur of wine, it is hypocritical to tell your child that "you shouldn't drink because it isn't good for you." We can give them the benefit of our own example, using wine and food joyfully and sensibly, not merely as a substitute for tranquilizers.

A study of first-generation Italians, Jews, and Chinese people living in the United States, shows these people are unlikely candidates for alcoholism, especially if they remain within their own milieu.

What is the common denominator among these groups drinking-wise? All three cultures make it easy for people within the group to drink sensibly. Drinking is done in a structured setting, whether a family meal, celebration, or religious ceremony. Sensible consumption is looked upon with favor, and drunkenness is considered a disgrace. Within all three cultures people eat while they drink, and children are taught to drink wine in a diluted quantity at an early age.

Unfortunately, Madison Avenue advertising campaigns have fooled many of us into thinking that drinking will make us more exciting, sophisticated, or intelligent. We have unreal expectations about drinking—especially hard spirits—and we transfer this unreality to our kids. The youth of a country will react to alcohol in the same way the adult population does. In countries like the United States, France, Sweden, and the Soviet Union, there is an escalating drinking problem. People drink casually, not always wisely, and there is a permissive attitude toward inebriation.

An example of how a culture can change is the Japanese. Prior to World War II, the Japanese were models of responsible drinking. Men had hot *Sake* with their food in the geisha houses, and imprudent drinking was frowned upon. Adopting the customs of their conquerors after the Occupation, the Japanese not only emancipated their women but also acquired our American way of drinking, substituting cocktail bars and hostesses for the former more gracious way of life. In conjunction with this change, drunkenness became more common.

There is no doubt that children whose parents are alcoholics face a greater risk of developing alcoholic problems. A study shows that they may also be more prone to develop other behavioral problems. Who were our role models when we were children? If these people drank heavily, with alcohol a problem at home, it is also likely that we as adults are now imitating their behavior. We are a society that has, until very recently, worshipped excess. We have given these signals to our youth, and they—full of precosity, adolescent exuberance, and energy—have reacted by equating "getting smashed" with being grown up.

As a wine buff I think we should teach our children to become students of the nuances of life, whether in a fine glass of wine or a strikingly beautiful sunset. Teaching them appreciation for all of life's small and large pleasures is perhaps, after they've experienced all of life's trials, the only real legacy we can leave them.

Wine
and the
Stars

I've never been one to peek furtively in the astrology column of my morning paper to check my favorable or unfavorable aspects. My only contact with the stars, in fact, has been in arguments with my wife, Ava. She is a believer who always ends a domestic argument muttering something about my "maddening Piscean vagueness." But doing business in Lotus Land makes it impossible *not* to notice astrology or its continuing fascination for *everyone* in Southern California, especially movie people.

As a wine merchant to many fabulous personalities, I have noticed that certain people tend to like the same wines or have similar logic in making their choices. I previously chalked this up to the fact that wines of the best caliber are able to interest anyone with taste and discrimination. However, my curiosity about this phenomenon was piqued further, when I sent a two-page questionnaire to my 10,000 customers, asking them to give me detailed information on their entertaining preferences, wine choices, and other information, including months of birth, sex, vocation, and race. I did this, not only in the interest of future purchases, but to explore the possibility that choices may be common among groups according to birth date, sex, race, and profession. Both the famous and not-so-famous responded (approximately one-third of my customer list) and the results tended to favor the astrological commonality theory more than any other factor, with certain general trends surfacing quite clearly for each group.

The first Aries celebrity customer that comes to mind when I think of Aries is Clare Boothe Luce, the famous playwright and former Ambassador to Italy. She happens to love Château Haut Brion and Pape

Clément, both fine Graves wines; and her enthusiasm for these wines was shared by another Aries, Thomas Jefferson, more than 200 years ago.

Rod Steiger
Aries

Aries who have responded to my questionnaire at the highest level seem to agree with Rod Steiger's predisposition to Chambertin and Bonnes-Mares, two of the greatest Burgundian red wines. For everyday drinking, they tend to agree with Wayne Newton, another Aries who enjoys inexpensive California whites for ordinary meals.

According to my survey, Aries will drink almost anything from beer to brandy, but in wines tend to express interest in those that are heavy and clumsy when young. In entertaining, they indicated an interest in informal parties. From the replies I received, if you are entertaining them, I suggest you be prepared for a blunt tongue and a large appetite that is not increased in diplomacy by additional booze.

However, they are strategists when it comes to the purchase and use of wines. The women from this group who replied tended to be professionals, and many indicated an interest in the female liberation movement.

Some Aries mentioned they disliked having someone else choose their wine while dining, and they tended to be more outspoken about their opinions on wines than the others. One of my favorite château owners, Baron Philippe de Rothschild, is a member of this sign and a perfect example of the independent and creative Aries personality.

If you are an Aries wine buff and want to plan a trip around your hobby, my suggestions for touring and drinking would be Capua, Italy, or Burgundy, France, both ruled by your sign. If you enjoy suki-yaki and the Japanese rice wine, Sake, go to Japan, also Aries-ruled. Other Aries wine-growing regions are Israel, Portugal, and Jugoslavia.

My Taurus customers are enamored of feminine, delicate and light wines, and they don't spare time or money in seeking to drink the finest.

One of my favorite Taurus customers, Gene Kelly, wrote me that he generally never bought wines on the recommendation of wine critics, but would try one bottle of a new wine, making his own ultimate decision before buying in greater quantity. He enjoys intimate sit-down meals and personally likes any of the great Burgundies or Bordeaux wines bottled in a good year. He also recommended that if you plan to travel to France, go in springtime when the Beaujolais is young. "I'm always delighted, and few Americans with whom I've spoken have had this experience," Kelly wrote.

Kelly concluded his letter by recalling that during the making of a movie, he was based for location shooting in the small village of Semur-en-Auxois, in the heart of the Burgundy wine country. "We had a ten-day shooting schedule, but torrential rains kept us mired there for six weeks. My gloom was dissipated by the hospitality of the local vintners who invited a few of the Franco-American group to be guests at the various residences. I received an education during those six weeks by listening and tasting—an education that could not be purchased. Along with it, of course, I learned an appreciation and love of fine Burgundy wines. God bless the Côte d'Or and its hospitable winemakers."

Gene Kelly is a typical Taurus in love with beauty, a quality that I've noticed in so many of my Taurus customers. He has an appreciation of the harmony between wine and food, suggesting California wines with most meals, and Chianti and Valpolicella with pasta.

Taurus wine buffs, at least those whom I've served, are a retailer's best friend, spending money on such rarities as out-of-season stemmed strawberries and Château Lafite-Rothschild. The latter, in fact, is the favorite wine of both Glen Campbell and Orson Welles.

Some of my other famous Taurus customers, like Barbra Streisand and Carol Burnett, enjoy Champagne and Montrachet, a magnificent white Burgundy, while another Taurus, Tom Snyder, the noted television interviewer, enjoys drinking still Champagne.

Others of the Taurus sign expressed interest in wines like La Mission-Haut-Brion, Cheval Blanc, and Château Figeac. The predominant type of entertaining favored was formal, whether with a large or small group of people, with the best of china used for the occasion.

For Taurus wine buffs, my traveling suggestions would be Cyprus, the third largest island in the Mediterranean Sea, home of a fine dessert wine, some white and red table wines, and a large quantity of fortified wines called Cyprus Sherry. Another Taurus-ruled area is the Greek Archipelago, where Taurus can try Greek retsina, Mavrodaphne, and the Muscat of Samos.

I've been fortunate to number many Geminis among my earliest supporters and customers, including Dean Martin, who likes Bernkasteler-Doktor, and Tony Curtis, who is extremely knowledgeable about wine and likes Romanée-Conti, the finest red Burgundy produced.

My overall impression of the Gemini palate is that these people aren't impressed with labels, but they do want wines to be assertive and consistently good. Joe Namath may like a Piesporter Goldtröpfchen; Bob Dylan, a St.-Estèphe; and the late Senator Hubert Humphrey, a Lafite-Rothschild, but

Gene Kelly
Taurus

130

snobbery wasn't the reason behind their choices. The best wine is usually consistently excellent and worth its price. Another Gemini, our 35th President, John F. Kennedy, had simpler but still consistent taste, preferring the California University of Davis hybrid, Emerald Dry Riesling.

Dean Martin
Gemini

Most Gemini customers indicated that they prefer buffets, canapés, and a lot of party activity. Many mentioned preferring wines with a bit of spritz, which would indicate that a Gemini wine vacation should begin in the Champagne district of France, perhaps at a little hotel and restaurant like La Touraine Champenoise (located at Tours-sur-Marne) or some other charming country inn of the area.

One of the funniest letters I received was from my good Gemini customer, Gene Wilder, who wrote that his favorite wine was a Brouilly, which is a Beaujolais, and that his next choices were 1967 Aloxe-Corton and 1966 Château Figeac. In lieu of these two wines, his other choices were a 1959 Richebourg, 1966 Bonnes-Mares, Domaine Comte de Vogüé, or a 1961 Château Petrus. Unlike most of his fellow Twins, he likes to entertain as intimately as possible, and always with candlelight, a good wine and fresh Brie. He said he dislikes large dinners because he is shy and feels uncomfortable with people he doesn't know. (Maybe there's a little Pisces in Gene?)

Wilder also related a story, which amply illustrates the Gemini predilection with consistency. The setting was a lovely Parisian evening in 1973. Mr. Wilder and a young lady went to dine at the famous or infamous Chez Denis. As Wilder relates, Monsieur Denis came to the table, and he and the couple discussed Bordeaux. Monsieur Denis told Wilder that he didn't believe in serving a Bordeaux wine that

was less than 20 years old, and Gene Wilder agreed to try a lovely old bottle of Haut-Brion. To his amazement, the wine arrived totally cold. When he asked Monsieur Denis about this odd state of affairs, the restaurateur told him that he believed in chilling all wines, red, white, or indifferent, and old Bordeaux as well as Beaujolais.

"I thought to myself, "Hmm . . . interesting," wrote Wilder. "It took 35 minutes before my Haut-Brion was near room temperature, and another ten before I felt that I was tasting the Haut-Brion as God had intended. Conclusion: *Stick to your guns, no matter in whose name you are given advice.*"

Geminis, according to my wife, are good promoters and publicists, and are often found in professions where they must sell a product or person through the written word. If this is the case, the theory is borne out by Gemini winery owners Baron Elie de Rothschild, Eli Callaway of Callaway Vineyards, Robert Mondavi of Mondavi Winery, and Jack Davies of Schramsberg, who are master promoters of their wines.

Moon children, those born with the Sun in Cancer, are supposed to be peace loving, romantic, moody, and inclined to gain weight. I must be a fortunate Pisces because my celebrated Cancer customers, Yul Brynner, Steve Lawrence, and Merv Griffin are trim and extremely jovial when they come into my shop. Brynner, a man of extreme vigor and energy, is especially fond of Gruaud-Larose, a St.-Julien, and I ship him this wine when he is on tour. He also has decided opinions on wine, including putting *one* ice cube in white wine to reduce the wine's acidity, and recently gave me some interesting insight into his actor's regimen and his personal use of wine. Mr. Brynner always has some Bordeaux wine available to him, and he doesn't drink this in the afternoon before a performance, since this time is spent napping and taking a steam at a gymnasium. After the performance, however, he drinks the red wine as he unwinds after the performance.

Charles Boyer was a very close dear friend of Brynner, and they would have supper together while performing in *Don Juan in Hell.*

"Our wives would be in bed, because after all, they couldn't stay up every night while we played in the theater, and yet we had the problem of having to bring ourselves to street-level for a few hours after the performance," recalled Brynner.

"Charles always told me to have a piece of cheese, maybe a Gruyère, with a glass of Bordeaux wine after the performance. White wine isn't as good because it will keep you awake rather than slowing up the body's mechanism. But a red Bordeaux is soothing, calming, very pleasant, and has a nutritious quality."

Brynner doesn't necessarily appreciate the white wine explosion because he believes, and I agree, that wine shouldn't be just gulped down without appreciating its taste. Currently, it is the quantity being poured down the throat that is being noticed, rather than the quality of the wine itself. He spoke with great feeling about the ultimate food and wine experience he enjoyed, the 150th anniversary celebration of Nicolas, the famous Parisian wine merchants, to which they invited 100 of the world's best chefs, along with a handful of other artists.

Brynner described going down an elevator, three floors underneath the ground, into the Nicolas cellars, and then walking into a room that stretched three city blocks in every direction, with a temperature of about 12° Centigrade. As he walked down each corridor, he noticed metal cages with built-in grills, containing in each cell, about 20,000 bottles.

Steve Lawrence
Cancer

He remembered each wine course with relish, starting with a young Beaujolais, a 1953 Cos-d'Estournel, a lovely La Mission-Haut-Brion, and concluding with two magnificent wines from 1934, a Château Margaux and a Château Cheval Blanc.

Brynner has a down-to-earth, refreshing sense of basics even though he is a connoisseur, and in spite of the Nicolas experience, he thinks "food freaks" are ridiculous. "I've seen people who are knowledgable and those who are maniacal. I have seen one actor, who shall remain nameless, arrive on location with a special black case,and it contained all the wines this man was going to drink for the two weeks of shooting.

"It is very nice to know about these things, but God help you when it becomes a necessity of life. In other words, I think it is nice to add a little salt and pepper to your life, but wine and food are only enjoyable as decorations in your daily necessity for food. But I think there is great danger in making this overly important."

Another wonderful friend who is a Cancer is Dan Rowan, of the well-known Rowan & Martin *Laugh-In* comedy team. When I asked him about his favorite wines, Rowan wrote what I believe to be a most compelling explanation of one man's wine preferences and how he balances these with his food.

"I imagine my personal interest in wine as a hobby dates back to the early fifties, a great time for California wines, and to my friendship with André Tchelistcheff, then winemaker at Beaulieu, and drinking those great Georges Latour Private Reserve Cabernets.

"I suppose one of the unending joys of wine collecting and drinking is the sharing of a great bottle with appreciative friends and discussing the relative merits of one bottle over another. There is happiness at the discovery of a new wine or being able to introduce friends to a wine they have never tasted which becomes their favorite.

"My own favorite wine is a Château Latour. Yet, I would be devastated if I could drink only one wine for the rest of my life, because there are so many that I enjoy. There are the German whites; the crisp bite of a strong finishing Chablis with stone crabs; the mouth-filling fulness of a Domaine Romanée-Conti with a game dinner; the nice palate preparing of an unpretentious Sancerre or Vouvray before dinner. I like too many of the world's wines to be restricted to one, but if I were, it would be to a Château Latour '61 or '45, although I've never tasted a vintage I didn't like. I've always thought Latour has an elegance and complexity no other Bordeaux wine has, at least for my palate and nose."

Other Cancers have been great wine collectors, including the late composer, Cole Porter, who enjoyed the light, white wine, Sancerre, and author, Ernest Hemingway, who drank a light rosé of Anjou. Most Cancers in my survey enjoy wines that are supple and generous. Steve Lawrence, for instance, always buys Puligny-Montrachet while Merv Griffin is another Lafite-Rothschild fancier.

Frequently mentioned by Cancers as favorite ways of entertaining are patio or costume parties, a romantic environment, and gourmet restaurants.

Lifting of diplomatic barriers with Mainland China may allow those of you who are Cancers to travel to that mysterious Cancer-ruled land, sipping some of China's rice wines. Closer to home, Cancer wine buffs can take excursions to the California wine country (ruled by your sign) or to other wine-growing regions such as Paraguay, Mexico, or Algeria.

Leo represents leadership, and like Jacqueline Kennedy Onassis, the dramatic, regal, and discriminating Leo man or woman is capable of setting trends and styles. Mrs. Onassis is said to maintain her size-six figure by eating one meal a day, consisting of a glass of champagne and a baked potato topped by a tablespoonful of beluga caviar. Whether it is true or not, it sounds like a wonderful diet, typically Leo in its luxurious tone.

Jacqueline Kennedy Onassis
Leo

Leos, like Napoleon, have classy taste. Napoleon is known to have ordered his troops to salute as they passed by Gevrey-Chambertin, his favorite wine estate.

Famous Leos who I've had the pleasure to .serve always have had elegant taste, and although they are label conscious, they want wines with depth. Robert Mitchum, for instance, likes caviar with Champagne or Le Montrachet; Lucille Ball likes Pouilly-Fuissé; Samuel Goldwyn, Jr., likes Château Palmer; and Alfred Hitchcock liked Haut-Brion Blanc, rarer than the red wine from the château, with a distinctive flavor. Natalie Wood, another elegant Leo woman, always chooses a wine with body, such as a Bordeaux or a velvety Cabernet Sauvignon. In white wines, she prefers a Germanic type of Johannisberg Riesling.

Most Leos in my survey definitely prefer quality to quantity, and I suppose the type of gesture that would impress them would be one combining generosity and flair, like perhaps giving or serving them your last bottle of 1953 Margaux, or a rare Chambertin or Clos de Vougeot. Most of my Leo customers indicate they definitely believe that they deserve the finest and admit to preferring entertainment on a grand scale, complete with elegant furnishings rather than anything more casual.

Leo wine buffs can follow the sun to Italy, especially Leo-ruled Rome, or to the island of Sicily. While staying in Sicily, you can experiment with Marsala, the sweet fortified wine made in northwest Sicily around the town of the same name. The wine, which is dark and tastes of burnt sugar, is a blend of an aromatic white wine, of *passito* made with dried grapes and fortified, and of grape-juice syrup.

Frederick de Chandon, the slim, aristocratic jet-setting chairman of the board of Moët & Chandon, Épernay, France, is a Leo. Another lion winemaker, quite different in personal style yet imbued with the same immense dignity and business flair, was the late August Sebastiani of the California-based Sebastiani Winery, famous for his striped bib overalls.

The next sign, Virgo, is the delight of a wine merchant because, for some inexplicable reason, most of my very fine wine collectors are either Virgo, Cancer, or Capricorn. The first famous Virgo who comes to mind is Bob Newhart, the comedian, who happens to prefer Piesporter Goldtröpfchen, a delicate German wine. Another Virgo, Sophia Loren, drinks a moderately priced champagne.

Another Virgo, Henry Ford II, chairman of the Ford Motor Company, expressed the discriminating viewpoint that is typical of the Virgo: "I personally do not often depend upon the advice of noted wine writers in selecting vintages. More frequently, I will hear of an exceptional vintage from a friend who has tasted it, purchased it, or on a rare occasion, even produced it. My favorite wines for both personal use and that of my guests are the noble red wines of the Haut-Médoc and particularly the '67 and '70 vintages of Château Lafite-Rothschild. If I have ever had a least favorite wine, I've tried to forget it. On occasion, I've been pleasantly surprised by excellent

Henry Ford II
Virgo

California wines of which I'd never heard until I tasted them."

Mr. Ford also mentioned the fact that he tries many fine local wines during his business travels, and "because many of these wines go perfectly with the characteristic national dishes, it is difficult to express a preference for the wines of one continent over those of another."

Most Virgos, like Mr. Ford, are not adverse to experimenting with wines of a particular region but will for their daily fare buy wines of traditional prestige. Peter Lawford, another Virgo, buys Italian Chianti, but only the best, Reserve Ducalle.

Virgos questioned in my survey tended to follow the astrological stereotype of being fastidious, brainy, and a bit formal. Most of them indicated they preferred formal entertainment, with first-growth Bordeaux wines, Sauternes, and Ports frequently mentioned as favorites.

Since Virgos are the natural critics, analyzers, and intellects of the zodiac, a trip from which they gain more knowledge about wine would be appealing. My suggestion would be a jaunt to Toulouse, France, ruled by Virgo, with an exploratory trip to Arbois, at the lower foothills of the Jura Mountains. This town is famous not only for its Rosé d'Arbois, but it is the birthplace of Louis Pasteur and the site of many of his famous wine experiments.

My Libra clients, whether Gore Vidal, Johnny Carson or Walter Matthau, are lovers of any wine classified as rare, imported, or delicate. Complexity is their key word when it comes to selecting a wine. Both Gore Vidal and Johnny Carson, by the way, enjoy the strawberry-preserve scented Margaux, along with Chassagne-Montrachet.

A noted Libra winemaker who makes a powerful, pungent Cabernet Sauvignon from California, a favorite of Andy Warhol, is Francis Mahoney of Carneros Creek Winery. Another Libra winemaker, Warren Winiarski of Stag's Leap Winery, makes perhaps the finest Cabernet Sauvignon produced in California. It caused a sensation at a Paris wine tasting in May 1976.

I received an hysterically funny letter from Walter Matthau, who confided that "the fact of the matter is: I don't particularly care for wine. I'm crazy about beer. I've tried for many years to develop a taste for wine, but I can't seem to get the hang of it. Oh, I'll order expensive wines in restaurants and give expensive wines to friends, but I can't tell the difference between a $350 bottle and one that costs $1.95."

As a footnote, Matthau pleaded that I do not

Walter Matthau
Libra

spread this around . . . "Please, Dennis."

I didn't promise *not* to, so here it is, world: *Walter Matthau really likes to drink beer.*

Most Libras in my survey, unlike Walter (who *does* buy fine wine), are epicureans to the nth degree. Many in the survey mentioned that the presentation is as important as the meal itself in their estimation. Many said they liked the St.-Julien wines, especially Léoville-Las Cases and Beychevelle.

Libra wine buffs planning a holiday might enjoy traveling to Australia, especially the Hunter River Valley, home of some fabulous and robust red wines. Another area of the world that is Libra-ruled and a wine producer, is Denmark, where they can visit Sealand, home of the national drink, Danish Cherry Heering.

Flamboyance, independence, and a bit of the iconoclast tipify my Scorpio customers. Like Linda Goodman's lizards and eagles, these people can really have extreme tastes, both high and low. Dick Cavett, for instance, likes a simple wine like Mateus Rosé, while the late general and President of France, Charles de Gaulle, liked Léoville-Las-Cases, a very fine St.-Julien, along with Mouton-Rothschild, of which he had many vintages in his cellar. Another Scorpio customer, Alan Ladd, Jr., likes Blanc de Blanc wines, while Burgess Meredith, a noted oenophile, will generally be found drinking California wines at his Malibu home.

It is perhaps typically Picassoish rather than Scorpioish, but Pablo Picasso, who was commissioned to design the 1973 Mouton-Rothschild label years before it was used by Baron Philippe, never picked up his five cases of the celebrated wine, even though this is the standard commission for anyone selected for this singular honor.

Most of the Scorpio customers responding to

the survey commented that they liked rather full-bodied and *macho* wines like Château Latour, Calon-Ségur, and the St.-Estèphe wines. Others, like the late Senator Robert F. Kennedy, said they enjoyed simple white wines.

Burgess Meredith
Scorpio

Scorpio, oddly enough for a water sign, doesn't rule any wine-producing region of the world. The closest area would be Scorpio-ruled Tokyo, Japan, where the Scorpios can visit a Buddhist Temple or sip some of Japan's famous Sake, or rice wine, accompanied by some sushi.

Scorpio winemakers may not be as numerically abundant as others, but Peter Mondavi of the Charles Krug Winery makes up for it in stature, producing sound, popular wines that are available at most fine restaurants throughout the United States.

My Sagittarius customers, I would say after studying the survey, are definitely label drinkers, preferring big name wines like Romanée-Conti or Barolo.

Frank Sinatra and Sammy Davis, Jr., for instance, are both Sagittarius and fans of Lafite-Rothschild. Jane Fonda likes Champagne, especially Dom Pérignon. Sagittarius Kirk Douglas prefers French Bordeaux and extends his choices to some second growths like Rausan-Ségla and Montrose. Typically of a Sagittarius, however, he chooses as his favorite Los Angeles restaurant, Chasen's, which has been voted one of America's finest restaurants but is one featuring a varied menu that includes its famous chili, with no *cuisine minceur* in sight.

Sagittarius people are, in fact, too busy or impatient for lengthy sessions in the gourmet kitchen, but are masters at the perfect steak to go with their favorite full-bodied red wine.

Jane Fonda
Sagittarius

Some interesting wine makers are born in this sign, however, including the famous oenologist, André Tchelistcheff; Joe Heitz of Heitz's Cellars; and Louis Martini, Jr., of the Martini Winery.

Sagittarius people, I'm told, love to travel, and if they happen to love wine as well, they can plan visits to Chile, Argentina, and Hungary, all ruled by their sign. In Hungary, they can observe production of the rare and sensual Tokaji Eszencia; or while traveling through South America, they can go to the heartland of Argentinian wine production, Mendoza, or visit Santiago, Chile, taking excursions to the wine-growing regions surrounding the capital, particularly the Maipo basin to the southwest.

One of the most interesting corollaries between wine preferences and astrological signs has to be the Capricorn's love of wines from the Margaux region of France. In fact, it was the overwhelming number of Capricorns who expressed a love for these wines that first made me suspect that there might indeed be a relationship between tastes and the signs.

My personal contact with people of the sign have included, among the celebrities, Danny Kaye, Elvis Presley, and Richard Nixon. Although Danny Kaye also likes Sancerre, Richard Nixon prefers Margaux, and according to my research, it was also enjoyed by Elvis Presley, Dr. Martin Luther King, Joseph Stalin, and Benjamin Franklin. Robert Stack, another Capricorn, is less specific in his wine-buying habits, but the late Henry Miller, the writer, was a devotee of La Mission, another powerful Bordeaux wine.

My personal conclusion about Capricorns is that they are serious people who aren't always easy to understand but who want to be taken seriously. Thus, their choice of wines would be those that are full of nuances and are feminine and explosive.

135

Most of these people reflected this sense of serious intent even in the way they entertain, preferring to consider the event as part of their need for status, and thus going all-out with elegant food and the most exquisite of settings, including fancy items like caviar and quenelles.

Maybe I'm exaggerating a little, but not much, and when the Capricorns settle down to an intimate dinner, it will be with tried-and-true friends, not casual acquaintances. They simply won't feel comfortable in a let-down-your-hair setting with someone they don't know intimately.

Richard Nixon
Capricorn

A distinguished Capricorn winemaker is Bob Travers of Mayacamas Winery of California, producer of an excellent Cabernet Sauvignon of a spicy, aromatic character.

Capricorn wine buffs planning a trip to a suitable wine country should try the Finger Lakes region of New York, named for four lakes: Canandaigua, Keuka, Seneca, and Cayuga, or venture further southwest to northern Mexico and Baja California.

In my own personal experience, an Aquarius person will make abrupt changes in his wine tastes, often making a choice based on the personality that owns the winery or dropping a preferred brand because he didn't like the political policies of the winery. Let me give you an example. Both the late Jack Benny and Ernest Borgnine have bought Château Haut-Brion from me, and both, on different occasions, mentioned they did so because Douglas Dillon, an American, owned this French château. Zsa Zsa Gabor, another Aquarius, came in one day and bought a white Burgundy bottled and shipped by Joseph Drouhin, the well-known Burgundian shipper. She told me that she was buying this wine because she'd met Mr. Drouhin and found him to be a charming man. Another Aquarius, Paul Newman, who likes the white Burgundy Le Montrachet, is also

fond of Coor's beer. He stopped drinking it because the company wasn't unionized.

Jack Lemmon, who likes Cheval Blanc, and Ronald Reagan, who likes Dom Pérignon, are two other Aquarius celebrities with excellent palates. Another Aquarius with an interest in wine who doesn't like to be pompous about it is Robert Wagner, who likes either Italian or French wines.

Paul Newman
Aquarius

Most of the Aquarius people who responded to my survey frequently stated that they liked ethnic or unusual foods, along with attending or giving unorthodox parties. Most of them rated Montrachet, La Tâche or a Pomerol like Petrus as tops on their list of favorite wines.

For an Aquarius who's planning a wine trip, I would suggest you explore South America, especially wine districts near Aquarius-ruled cities like Rio de Janeiro, Belem, and São Paulo, in Brazil, or those near Montevideo, Uruguay.

Aquarius winemaker Bernard Portet makes beautifully elegant Zinfandels and Cabernet Sauvignons at Clos du Val, off the Silverado Trail in Napa Valley.

I'm a Pisces, and I've been told that my sign is full of saints and drunks—and a meager number of middle-of-the-roaders. This, I'm afraid to say, holds true in our wine tastes, which can vary from the dregs to the heights of glory. If I could key in on any one quality of the Pisces, then I would say *vascillation* is the operable word, and while your Pisces friend may be crazy about an expensive first growth one week, he or she may switch to a jug wine the following month.

George Washington was one Pisces who was the exception to the rule, and according to his grandchildren, he was "extremely fond of fish dishes and

Don Rickles
Pisces

know that Dinah also likes a fruity red wine of California, Zinfandel. The last time I checked, Peter Fonda was drinking California Cabernet; Pamela Mason, Soave Bolla; Don Rickles, Chenin Blanc; and Jerry Lewis, Pouilly-Fuissé. This may all have changed since then, but these are typical Pisces tastes as of my last count.

We are, judging by my survey, fascinated with sensual, delicate wines, and Pisces, without a doubt, go heavy on fish and shellfish dishes and hearty soups like bisque and chowders (my personal favorite is New England clam), and they're suckers for costume parties or intimate romantic settings.

Luckily for Pisces, if we take a European wine tour, we'll be harmonious with such wonderful wine areas as Bordeaux, France, or Lisbon, Portugal. Especially delightful would be a tour of all the first-growth châteaux and, if we're in a working mood, a fortnight picking grapes during the Bordeaux harvest season.

one glass of Madeira with dinner.''

Elizabeth Taylor, another Pisces, can switch from beer to Champagne without thinking twice, and although Dinah Shore and Harry Belafonte both like Louis Roederer Crystal Champagne, I

The Wine Merchant's Wine Cellar

Each time I open the door to my wine cellar, I feel the same sense of excitement that must have gripped Lord Carnarvon upon entering King Tut's tomb. My wine treasures create more than a proprietary sense of ownership within me. They are relics of the past, and I focus on them almost in a sensual way, and not with mere intellectual curiosity. Having read about the exploits of the intrepid Carnarvon, I feel sure that he must have had the same sense of awe and wonder when he looked upon the possessions of the nineteen-year-old ruler of Egypt.

Like the Hindu teacher who taught his students to gaze with curiosity at the blade of grass, I too look upon my simple and complex wines with the same sense of joy. It doesn't take money to enjoy laying down wines; it *does* take the ability to think and be sensitive to the wine's meaning as a liquid time machine. This wine doesn't have to be fashionable or trendy to be beautiful. It is a living liquid, making its own statement independent of temporary public fancies, and is able to withstand the sieges of time.

I believe this is an important point: Look for uniqueness and potential greatness in the wines you put in your cellar. A quality of greatness in a wine survives fads or trends, and the wine should be able to improve and mature for at least ten years. A wine can be sound or fine and yet not last ten years. However, this wine cannot be considered great.

When I didn't have much money but realized the beauty of the blade of grass in my philosophy on wine, I decided to start my own small cellar. This was in my salad-and-bread days, circa 1966. I wanted to select one winery to collect and decided to lay down Cabernet Sauvignon type of wines because they are particular favorites of mine, with great aging poten-

tial. I chose the Robert Mondavi Winery because it was just going into the market with claret-type of wines and because I was intrigued by the label depicting the Cliff May-designed winery with its old California Mission-style architecture.

Intuitively, I decided that Robert Mondavi must be a man of extraordinary taste and sensitivity and that the wine he was going to produce would reflect something uniquely Californian in its identity. My choice in 1966 proved to be a sound one, and it is now amusing to take people into my cellar and watch their eyes widen when they see my collection of inexpensive California wines, of Mondavi and others, acquired to form a series of consecutive vintages. They are surprised becaue the collections are complete and made up of wines that a decade ago were inexpensive. Yet I think for novice oenophiles, this type of collection of one or two California wineries or of some other modestly priced wines can be a gratifying beginning and prove extremely educational.

You can't necessarily rely on the authority figures of wine when you are laying down unusual wines from lesser-known wine producing regions. Generally, the wine writers will give you information on the more established regions such as Bordeaux and Burgundy, or even California. However, if you study the subject a bit, you can find excellent wine producers in South America, South Africa, and Australia. Adding a few of the wineries from these countries to your wine stock can do much to make your cellar more interesting and distinctive than many that are stocked to the rafters with a lot of safe or traditional wines.

This is not to say that, if you can afford it, you

shouldn't lay down the fine Bordeaux or Burgundian wines. But a cellar should reflect a sense of curiosity, knowledge, and confidence about the owner, and a wider range of unusual, rare, or geographically out-of-the-ordinary wines certainly will add much to the cellar's interest, and to the collector's prestige as an oenophile.

While I thoroughly enjoy the wines of Château Mouton-Rothschild, I'm also enthralled with Baron Philippe de Rothschild's idea of having a different artist design the label for each year's vintage. That's one of the reasons I'm so proud of my Mouton-Rothschild collection dating from 1945 to the present. It is fascinating each year to see how each artist has left his or her imprint on the year's label, artistically depicting the special qualities they've perceived about Mouton in a personal, intimate way. These labels fill me with great joy, and something that could have been mundane has taken on new meaning for me and many others. It took the imaginative grasp of a strong personality like Baron Philippe to commission others to share their genius with the world through a bottle of wine. He started this back in 1927 with a bottling of the 1924 Mouton. The first label was designed by the French illustrator Jean Georges Carlu. The custom was not formalized as a yearly event until after the war in 1945. It was again resumed with the well-known Italian author on art, Philippe Jullian, in that first glorious year of peace.

No one, including the Baron, had any idea that the vintage would prove to be one of the finest of this century. Jullian's design incorporated tendrils of the vine in gold, and a gold letter V announced that at last the world was at peace and the voice of the turtle could be heard in the land.

For both the world and Baron Philippe it was a year of victory tainted with sadness. He had lost his wife in a concentration camp; fought in the Free French Resistance, and then found himself living at his own Château while rebuilding his life. Baron Philippe saw the production of great wine as a "divine collaboration between nature and man," and as only appropriate for such a majestic enterprise, he decided to again select a new artist for each vintage.

The designs reflected the individual vision of each artist: For 1958, Salvador Dali viewed Mouton-Rothschild as a playful ram; Pablo Picasso commemorated Mouton's elevation to first-growth status with a joyous bacchanal for 1973; for 1975, Andy Warhol created a dramatic double-image of the Baron.

The 1973 choice, Pablo Picasso was, according to the Baron, a matter of "fortunate destiny." The artist had been approached years prior to his death

and had drawn a sketch of a *bacchanalia*, or wine festival, as his design for the label. The only hitch was that Picasso postponed giving permission for the use of his sketch, and then suddenly died, in 1973, a month prior to Mouton's upgrading to a first growth. Baron Philippe went to Picasso's daughter, Paloma, and asked her for permission to use the label. She went to the other heirs and all agreed to give Mouton-Rothschild permission to use the label.

Baron Philippe looked upon the entire event as an ironic coincidence and said: "Mouton was legally classified in late June, and Picasso died less than a month later. Maybe the gods of Picasso and the gods of Mouton got together and decided this sketch should be held back for this special year."

Belgian painter Pierre Alechinsky, who designed the 1966 label, chose a goat figure to represent both "Mouton" and Dionysus, the god of wine. The glass reflected the three most important senses of wine: sight, taste, and smell. The upheld glass represented to them: "What is in the glass is only as good as one's refinement of these three senses."

Robert Motherwell was one of the American artists. He saw his concept as a stark black-and-yellow montage in which could dimly be detected the primitive dark figure of a ram. This theme emphasized the struggle between good and evil and the simpler viewpoint of primitive times.

Each year I look forward to Mouton-Rothschild's new vintage, as much for the artistic rendering as I do the wine. The marriage of art and wine is a pleasant one to be intermeshed and is expecially intriguing to me as a connoisseur. It reminds me that what is worth consuming is worth thinking about.

Many years after I'd started my first cellar, I was a guest at Mouton-Rothschild and was pleased to discover that Baron Philippe had a magnificent and quite complete collection of Almaden vintages and other California wines. This group is probably one of the least expensive in Baron Philippe's library of wines, but this doesn't faze the gentleman in the slightest. He is as curious about what is happening in California as he is about Pauillac. That, in my opinion, is an important attribute in any connoisseur— curiosity.

Some of my clientele begin collecting for their son or daughter's 21st birthday, and this is a lovely custom that I encourage. For me, however, each year requires a personal kind of celebration, and each new vintage I add to a collection is as if I were storing a liquid time machine. Something important always happens during those 365 days, and I capture my memories through the wine I open from each special year of my life.

A company that also follows this tradition is Möet & Chandon, who design and execute commenmorative labels marking special moments in world history. Twelve such labels have been produced. Included are the 1902 label for the coronation of King Edward VII (1898 vintage); the 1953 Coronation Cuvée of Her Majesty, Queen Elizabeth II (1953 vintage); the 1956 Cuvée for the wedding of Prince Rainier III of Monaco to Miss Grace Kelly of Philadelphia (1949 vintage); the 1960 Cuvée celebrating the wedding of the Belgium King Baudouin to the Princess Fabiola (1955 vintage); the 1971 special labeling of the 2,500th Anniversary of the Foundation of the Persian Dynasty; the 1976 American Bicentennial Cuvée (1971 vintage); the 1977 Silver Jubilee Cuvée of Queen Elizabeth II (1971 vintage); and the 1979 Millennium Cuvée of the foundation of the Parliamentary Government of the Isle of Man. Other commemorative labels have honored Simon Brothers Limited, former United Kingdom agents of Möet & Chandon (in 1935 with the 1926 vintage); in 1943, the bicentenary of Möet & Chandon (in 1935 with the 1928 vintage); in 1943, the bicentenary of Möet & Chandon with a vintage of the same year; in 1967, celebrated the wedding of Queen Margrethe of Denmark to Henri de Montpesat (1961 vintage); and in 1974, celebrated Prince Rainier's jubilee (1964 vintage).

Some of my wines are my "blue five-winged butterflies." They offer beauty only through my efforts to understand them. I buy these wines for what they offer me, not for what they are supposed to represent. I'm rewarded with enchantment only if I can curb my impatience. Never are they simply beautiful ornaments.

In this category is Vin Jaune, a specially made wine from Arbois, a wine region in eastern France near the Swiss border. It is an unusual butterfly that offers both a bizarre taste and a distinctive container. The bottle is called Clavelin. It is peculiar to this area of southeastern France near the Swiss border. The wine is made from a grape variety called Savagnin and is aged for at least six years in casks in a manner similar to sherry. To obtain Vin Jaune the grapes are harvested late and pressed in the same way as for white wines. The juice is then sealed in barrels and aged for six to ten years. A short time after the wine has been sealed, a film develops on top, sealing the liquid from air while the microorganisms, living on the oxygen in the environment, change the wine's color to an unusual yellow, enhacing the wine with its nutty fragrance, its strawlike color, and dried straw bouquet. Only 2,300 cases are produced from the entire appellation, and it isn't uncommon for the wine to last more than 50 years.

Another wine that stands out like an iceberg in a sea of flat, uniform wines is Madeira. The island itself rises out of the sea like a tiny 36-mile long jewel in the middle of the Atlantic, 360 miles from the coast of Morocco. The ancients referred to the island and its volcanic kin, Porto-Santo and the Desertas, as the Enchanted Isles. The island was covered with thick trees that were practically interwoven, and it was decided by Captain Joao Goncalves that the only thing to do was to set the island on fire. The fire lasted seven years, legends tell, and results were a deep rich ash soil into which settlers from all over Europe began planting vines.

Madeira became a famous stopping ground for sailors on their way to the New World who stopped for fresh water and food and to replenish the wine casks. By this time, the subtropical island had become famous for its wine, which was also a particular favorite of the American settlers.

The wine is made in a very odd way and is identical to the fumaria method used by the Romans. Originally, the wine, which is long lasting, was semi-pasteurized as it went through the heating process known as *estufagem* during its long voyages through changing seas and hot and cold climates on the journeys to and from the East or West Indies. It happened that when Madeira was shipped to India and other warm countries, it was noticed that the wine improved by being subjected to the ship's rolling motion and the sun's heat. Later, when the wines could not be aged in this fashion, the wine was placed in specially built stone lodges known as *estufas*, through which hot water pipes were run in order to give a constant hot temperature to the wine stored in casks inside these buildings.

The modern methods used to make Madeira include storing it in glass lined concrete vats with pipes running through them, while the wine's temperature is gradually raised to a warm temperature and then allowed to return slowly to a normal temperature.

Madeira can last an incredibly long time and Sir Winston Churchill commented on a vintage 1792 Madeira, which had been gathered when Marie Antoinette was still alive. My favorite Madeira of the various types—Sercial, Verdelho, Bual, Malmsey, Rainwater, Southside—is Bual, which is full and sweet and similar to the Bristol Cream Sherry. Some Madeiras, such as Sercial, can be partaken as aperitifs, and others like Verdelho are excellent with soup, particularly that of turtle. Malmsey is the sweetest and is excellent after dinner. Production from the minuscule island, 14 miles wide, is no more than

6,000 cases annually, and today, because the United States has forgotten its love for the wine, its customers are now in Scandinavia, France, Germany, Belgium, Holland, and Canada.

It is a shame, because this is the perfect warm-weather wine and is especially ideal for the Americans in the Sun Belt. Is anything more delicious than Madeira with morsels of pound cake? I doubt that anything can surpass this treat. And from the popularity of this island wine with our American forebears, it seems they tended to agree with me.

I have aristocratic lovelies like the 1921 Château d'Yquem extolled by H. Warner Allen and the 1900 and 1953 Margaux praised by André Simon. But their beauty is recognized by all connoisseurs, and the thrill of owning them is like possessing a Bentley or Rolls-Royce—half the fun is making the other fellow envious of your good fortune.

As you browse through my cellar, you may see the 1971 Montrachet from the Domaine de la Romanée-Conti, and the 1975 Château Petrus, as well as the 1945 Château Lafite-Rothschild. But these are expensive toys. If I weren't a wine merchant, I'd neither have access nor the funds to acquire them. Since these fashionable and classical wines are already known throughout the world, I'd like to end this chapter by giving you a list of the Ten most unique Wines of the world. Not all the wines on this list are expensive, but as a group they are difficult to find and worth seeking out.

Dennis Overstreet's Ten Most-Wanted Blue Five-Winged Butterflies

Bouzy Rouge: Red Bouzy is very popular with the Parisians and is rarely tasted outside of France. The wine comes from Montagne de Reims and utilizes the Pinot Noir grape to make a fine delicate red wine similar to a light red Burgundy.

Jura: Less than 2,000 acres produce this dry, strong, scented white wine of France. The most important wines of this district are those from Arbois. Château-Chalon, one of the most famous, is legally required to age six years in the cask, and it is the most notable Jura wine. Another famous wine of the area is L'Étoile, but this wine is extremely rare.

Condrieu: This wine is made in minuscule Château-Grillet, which is only four acres in size. It is the smallest French vineyard with its own *appellation contrôlée*. Condrieu is made from the Viognier grape unique to the Rhône Valley and is an unusually soft and fragrant white wine.

Quarts de Chaume: This is a small and outstanding wine region that was originally a huge estate that was divided into four parts. The 125 acres of Chenin Blanc make an intense and rich wine that is exceptionally long lived. Yearly production is 6,000 cases.

Eiswein: The Germans make this "ice wine" from grapes that have been frozen to 21° Fahrenheit. When the berries are pressed, the juice is rich in sugar and extract. This phenomenon occurs only twice in a decade, and as a result the wine is very expensive. Even more unusual is the Christ wine, which is Eiswein made at Christmas.

Mantonico: This is an amber dessert wine from the area of Reggio-Calabria, Italy, at the toe of the Italian peninsula.

Madeira: Under Portuguese control since 1419, Madeira has been famous for its wines for over 400 years. Colonial America was quite fond of this Portuguese-controlled wine, but western Europe is the biggest customer of the tiny island today. Madeira is a fortified wine, enhanced by brandy and blended similarly to the Solera system used to make sherry.

Moscatel de Setubal: This aromatic dessert wine is capable of lasting more than 100 years and is made by Señor J. M. da Fonseca, one of Portugal's richest men. The fortified wine is produced south of the city of Lisbon and is made from the Muscat grape. It has a distinctive Muscat flavor and aroma.

Tokaji Eszencia: Catherine the Great's favorite wine, this unusual Hungarian wine is probably the world's most enduring, and some Eszencia has been known to last more than 200 years and even longer. It is made from the luscious juice that drops through a goosequill by pressure crushing only. It is known for its restorative and aphrodisiac properties and is sold in limited amounts by the Hungarian government.

Moscato di Amabile: This is a slightly effervescent, creamy wine, similar to an Asti Spumante, made by one of California's prestigious pioneering winemaking families, the Martinis. It is available only at the winery.

Appendix

Glossary

acetic: Having the odor and taste of acetic acid or vinegar.

acid: The substance in wine that is mouthwatering, refreshing (tartaric acid), sometimes like raw cooking apples (malic acid) and detectable on the tongue, giving wine essential crispness and zing. "Volatile acids" (the acid of spoiled wine) rise up at certain temperatures and are more pronounced on the nose; "fixed acids" are the normal fruit acids: tartaric, malic, citric, etc.

aerate: To expose wine to air by filtering or bottling it.

aftersmell: An odor sensation, part of the *aftertaste.*

aftertaste: The lingering taste, odor, and tactile sensation that remain after a wine is swallowed.

alcohol: In wine, alcohol (the product of fermentation) is scarcely detectable on the nose, though it can be assessed by its "weight" in the mouth, by a sort of burning taste and, cumulatively, by its well-known effects on the head of the drinker.

Aligoté: Lesser white grape of Burgundy.

ampelography: Study of grapevine identification.

Amontillado: A particular style of medium-dry sherry.

apéritif: Drink taken before a meal to sharpen appetite. Many herbs, fruits, and flavoring agents added to wines; usually associated with Vermouths.

Appellation Contrôlée: On a label, indicates that the wine has been produced under a set of rigid rules and controls set up by the French government to assure quality. Regulations cover the types of grapes used, the amount produced, and the geographic origin.

aroma: The odor of fresh fruit that originates in the grape.

aromatic: Having a distinctive fruity odor, which is usually found in wines of certain varieties.

Asti-Spumante: Italy's most famous sweet sparkling wine from the Piedmont region. Produced from the white Moscato grape in the town of Asti near Turin.

astringency: The puckery sensation created in the mouth by young wines full of tannin.

bacterial: Term describing off-odors from bacterial action.

baked: The caramelized odor of sweet wines that have been heated too long.

balanced: Describes a wine in which all the tastes are present in their proper proportions.

banana: An overtone in the bouquet of wines made from frostbitten grapes; also a specific smell of old wine in poor condition.

Barbaresco: Lighter-bodied version of Italy's Barolo, also from the Piedmont region and the red Nebbiolo grape. After aging three to five years in the bottle, it acquires the autumn-leaf color the French call *pelure d'oignon.*

Barbera: Full-bodied red wine from the Barbera grape grown in the Piedmont region of northern Italy.

Bardolino: Excellent light red wine produced in the province of Verona. It is best when young and is paler and lighter than Valpolicella, a darker red wine made from the same grape grown in different soil, ten miles further east.

Barolo: Possibly Italy's finest red wine. Comes from the Piedmont area and the Nebbiolo grape. This powerful, full-bodied, and long-lived wine needs from 7 to 15 years of aging in the bottle.

Beaujolais Nouveau: One of the best-loved red wines of France. It is the first release of the young wine from the Beaujolais district in southern Burgundy. It can be released only past midnight on November 15.

bitter almond: The odor of cyanide resulting from poor filtration of wines treated with potassium ferrocyanide.

bitterness: The harsh taste that is detected on the palate, and on the back of the tongue; it is generally unpleasant. It can, however, be a desirable quality in certain wines (usually an acquired taste).

bodega: Spanish wine cellar, usually above ground.

body: The wine term that means substance. A full-bodied wine gives the impression of weight rather than lightness, which is not necessarily associated with a high alcohol content.

Bourgogne: Burgundy (Fr.)

breed: A distinctive and distinguished quality stemming from the combination of fine soil, *encépage* (the blending of different grape varietals), and the skill of the *vigneron* or winemaker.

Brunello di Montalcino: One of the finest Italian red wines. It is strong, high-flavored, full-bodied and is made from the Brunello grape grown in Tuscany. It is produced in a very small amount and can live up to 50 years.

bual (also *boal*): The leading grape variety of Madeira and the grape used to make sweet golden Madeira wine.

caramel: The odor of overly heated sweet wines, as is the case with some California sweet sherries.

carbon dioxide: Gas responsible for the sparkle of Champagne and sparkling wines and the tingle of spritzy or slightly effervescent table wines.

Catawba: American wine grape producing sweet wines with a grapey taste.

cave: A cellar located underground (Fr.).

cedarwood: Characteristic bouquet scent of many fine Clarets and Cabernets.

chai: Ground-level warehouse (Fr.).

Champagne: A particular wine made by a specific process using only a certain variety of grape grown in the Champagne country of France. Sugar levels: *Nature*—produced without a *dosage* of sugar syrup after fermentation; *Brut*—up to 1.5 percent *dosage* added; *Extra Dry*—up to 4 percent; *Doux*—up to 10 percent.

chaptalization: The addition of sugar to the wine must before fermentation to build up the alcoholic content.

Chasselas: White wine grape. In Switzerland, where it is called Fendant, it is the leading wine grape.

Château: According to French law, this term must not appear on the label with the name of the wine unless the grape was grown and the wine was produced only at the château's vineyards.

Chianti: An Italian wine from Tuscany, perhaps the most famous red table wine in the world. It is made from the San Gioveto and Cannaiolo grapes, plus a small amount of white Trebbiano and Malvasia grapes. Customarily packaged in a *fiasco* (straw-covered bottle).

clos: Walled vineyard (Fr.).

cloying: An excessively sweet wine, usually too low in acidity.

commune: French for a town or village.

Concord: American grape used for grape juice, jellies, and sweet, unsubtle wine

Corbières: A V.D.Q.S. *(Vins Delimités de Qualité Supérieure)* wine district of southern France

Côte de Bourg: Dry red wine area, across Gironde from Médoc.

cru: Growth (Fr.); when applied to wine it refers to a specific vineyard and the superior quality wine it produces.

cru classé: Classified growth, or vineyard, of Bordeaux.

cuvée: A blend of wines (from the French *cuve,* a vat or tank).

Dão: Light red and white table wine from Portugal.

Dégorgement: Process when making Champagne by which the sediment is removed from the neck of the bottle by freezing in brine.

degree-day: The unit of measure representing one degree of variation above or below a certain standard temperature.

domaine: Wine estate (Fr.).

dosage: Sugar syrup with an old-wine base (sometimes plus a little brandy), which is added to Champagne just before final corking to create bubbles by secondary fermentation; the sweetness is thus also increased.

Douro: River in northern Portugal that flows through the Port district.

dry: Lacking a sweet taste.

enology or *oenology:* The science of winemaking.

Entre-Deux-Mers: White-wine district in Bordeaux.

Est! Est!! Est!!! Light, semi-sweet white wine from the Moscatello grape grown in Montefiascone and Bolsena, North of Rome.

esters: Compounds formed of acids and alcohols that provide a combination of odors ranging from apples to tobacco.

extract: Soluble solids (excluding sugar) that add to a wine's body and substance; usually refers to the glycerin content in wine.

fat: Wine term that describes full body and high glycerol and extract content. If sweet, verging on cloying.

Finger Lakes: An important American wine region in northern New York.

finish: The end-taste. A wine cannot be considered well-balanced without a good finish, or a firm crisp and distinctive end. The opposite, a short or poor finish, will be watery, the flavor not sustaining and ending inconclusively. The correct degree of the right sort of acidity is a decisive factor.

Fino: A particular style of dry sherry.

flor: Flower (Sp.). Refers to the white, yeasty film that forms on top of some casks of Spanish sherry; these become Fino sherries.

Frascati: Light, almost dry wine produced in the Alban Hills near Rome and made from Trebbiano and Malvasia grapes.

Fumé Blanc: White wine made in California from Sauvignon Blanc grapes.

gassy: Wine term that describes the tactile (and often visual and auditory) sensation of carbon dioxide escaping from wine.

Gattinara: Italian red wine made from the same Nebbiolo grape as Barolo and Barbaresco, but in a different part of Piedmont. The wine is full-bodied, slow-maturing, and long-lived.

generic: Wine names that are unrelated to the wine's place of origin, such as *vin rosé,* sparkling wine, aperitif wine, etc. *Semi-generic* wines, such as California Chablis or New York State Sauternes, are so named because of their similarity to the wines of Chablis and Sauternes, France, and not to indicate their place of origin.

German Wine Descriptions:

Tafelwein: Table wine; light, pleasant, blended wine consumed mostly in Germany; cannot use a vineyard name.

Qualitätswein bestimmter Anbaugebiete (QbA): Reasonably good German wines that are made in good vineyards from grapes that do not reach the natural sugar content required for a QmP (the highest quality) label. These wines are checked by government laboratories and are allowed to have sugar added. They must come from certain regions and grape varieties and can use a vineyard name on the label. Each bottle carries an *Amtliche Prufnummer* (A.P.), an official government registration number.

Qualitätswein mit Prädikat (QmP): This is the designation for the highest quality German wines. All of these wines are government tested and must not be sugared. They are the finest estate wines, and five separate "predicates" or attributes are identified along with the designation of *Qualitätswein.* They are as follows:

Kabinett: Lightest and driest of Prädikat category.

Spätlese: Late-picked grapes that are left on the vine and picked after the regular harvest.

Auslese: More body and sweeter wine from specially selected extra ripe clusters of grapes.

Beerenauslese: Individually selected berries, luscious and sweet.

Trockenbeerenauslese: Produced from overripe grapes left on the vine until they are almost raisins. Very sweet, used mostly as a dessert wine.

Eiswein: Made from grapes harvested and crushed while still frozen.

Gigondas: Full-bodied red and rosé wines from Rhône village of same name.

Gironde: Département in southwest France containing within its borders practically the entire Bordeaux wine district.

Green Hungarian: Light wine from California (not colored green) that is usually blended.

Grenache: Good-quality wine grape used to make red and rosé wines. Widely planted in southern France, in the Rioja district of Spain, and in California.

Grignolino: Italian red wine from grape of same name. It is light-bodied and peaks young.

Gumpoldskirchen (One of the best white wines of Austria.

hardness: Severity due to the overprominence of tannin and, to a lesser extent, acidity.

Haro: Center of Rioja wine trade.

haut: High (Fr.), used in its geographical sense; not necessarily an indication of higher quality.

heady: High in alcohol.

heavy: More than just full-bodied: overendowed with alcohol and extracts. Sometimes referred to as *clumsy.*

hectare: Metric measure of area (2.47 acres).

hectolitre: Metric measure of volume (100 liters or 26.42 U.S. gallons).

herbaceus: Describing an odor, particularly of some varietal wines, suggesting the odor of herbs.

Hospices de Beaune: Fifteenth-century charitable hospital in Burgundy that owns many fine vineyards and auctions wines from them to raise money.

hot: Describing a fiery sensation, possibly pain, in the mouth or nose. Probably due to higher-than-normal ethanol content together with a low sweetness.

Hudson River Valley: Oldest winegrowing district in the United States, one hour from New York City.

hybrid: A genetic cross between two different grape varieties.

hydrogen sulphide: A chemical compound that produces rotten-egg-like smell that is disagreeable but harmless. Its appearance in wine is probably due to bad cellar treatment from old barrels or poor corks.

Kir: Popular aperitif made by mixing dry white wine with cassis liqueur.

Labrusca: The species of grape native to North America.

Lambrusco: Popular Italian wine from the Emilia-Romagna region, made from the grape of same name. Full, fruity, semisweet wine with some effervescence.

lees: The dregs or sediment left at the bottom of a cask after the wine is racked.

legs: Globules which fall down the sides of the glass after the wine is swirled, caused from heavy alcohol content falling in heavy sheets; wines low in alcohol fall thin.

Liter: Metric liquid measurement equalling 1.06 quarts.

Madeiras: Sweet or dry fortified wines. All Madeiras of Portugal, by the addition of high-proof brandy and owe their unique flavor to the fact that they are kept in special rooms called *estufas* at a high temperature for several months.

maderized: This term applies to a wine that has been stored in a warm place and exposed to oxygen. This creates a brown-tinged color plus the aroma and flavor of Madeira.

Malbec: Red wine grape variety used to soften French Bordeaux.

Manzanilla: Very dry style of Spanish sherry.

Marsala: Italian fortified dessert wine from Sicily, produced in dry and sweet varieties and in specially flavored versions (egg, almond, etc.).

mature: Giving the overall sensation, particularly in red wines, of a wine that gives no evidence of being too young or too old—one that has acquired its proper characteristics.

mellow: Soft, limpid, mature. No rough edges. Mellowness is normally associated with maturity and age.

mercaptan: The objectionable odor of methyl and ethyl sulfides.

Midi: Area in southern France that supplies much ordinary table wine.

Mise en bouteilles: Bottled (Fr.); this phrase on a wine label is followed by the name of the producer or shipper.

mouldy: Describes the unpleasant odor of wines made from moldy grapes or stored in stale, unclean casks.

mousy: Describes the bacteria-induced odor of wine made from late-picked grapes or low-acid musts; very disagreeable, and a

sign of bacteriological disease that usually affects only wine in the cask. Such wine smells and tastes flat yet acetic.
mushroomy: Describes the specific smell of some very old wines.

must: Grape juice or crushed grapes to be made into wine.

Nebbiolo: Outstanding Italian red wine from the *nebbia* (fog) grape, which ripens best and produces its finest wines in regions where it is very foggy.
négociant éleveur: The middleman who ships and sells wines.
Neuchâtel: Swiss white wine produced from the Chasselas grape.
Niagara: Popular Eastern United States grape from which is produced a sweet white table wine.
noble: Indicates stature and breed; a noble wine is a wine of towering elegance.

Oloroso: A particular style of sherry, used as a base for Cream Sherry.
organoleptic: Describes the evaluation of wine based on perception by the senses (taste, sight, smell) rather than laboratory analysis.
Orvieto: Light fruity white wine from Umbria, Italy. Available as *abboccato* (semi-sweet) or *secco* (dry).
oxidized: Said of wine that has developed a flat stale off-taste due to over-exposure to air; occasionally oxidized wine has an ammonia or vinegar smell.

pasteurization: The process of sterilizing wines by heating them to destroy any organisms that may be present.
peppery: Describes a sort of raw harshness, rather hard to define, due to immature and unsettled substances in wine that have not had time to marry. Occurs noticeably in young ruby and vintage port and many full young red wines; occasionally found in California white table wines. The origin is not known, but it may be related to a certain concentration of sulfur dioxide.
perfume: The fragrance of wine imparted by the grape, in contrast to its bouquet, which it develops as the wine matures.
petillant: Lightly sparkling (Fr.).
phylloxera: Insect that destroyed most of the world's vineyards in the nineteenth century.
pourriture noble: Noble rot (Fr.), which is the beneficent mold responsible for the unique flavor of Sauternes and Barsac. It forms on the skins of ripening grapes and causes a concentration of sugar and flavor that results in a high quality wine.
premier cru: First growth (Fr.); refers specifically to some of the best individual vineyards in Bordeaux and Burgundy
pricked: Describes an unpleasant sharpness due to excess volatile acidity that is indicated on the nose but particularly on

the palate; a sharp-edged, raw, almost effervescent quality.
puttonyos: Literally, baskets; used as a measurement to indicate the comparative sweetness of Hungarian Tokays.

raisiny: Describes the odor of semidried or wholly dried grapes. The same or a similar odor is present in wines made from overripe grapes.
rancio: Term used to describe the nutty flavor in sherries, or the sweet French dessert wines from Banyuls; also refers to the pungent taste of Madeiras, Marsalas, or Malagas.
Retsina: Greek wine flavored with resin.
Rioja: Finest wine district in Spain.
robust: Full-bodied, rough yet rounded.
rubbery: Describes the odor of some wines made from high-pH musts. Also called the *Fresno odor* or the *rubber boot* odor.

Sake: Colorless Japanese beverage made from fermented rice, served warm and sipped from porcelain cups.
Sangria: Spanish red wine with fresh fruits and soda water added.
Scuppernong: Native American grape grown in the South for full-bodied sweet wines.
sec: Dry (Fr.).
secco: Dry (It.).
sediment: The lees or deposits thrown off by a wine as it ages.
Soave: May be Italy's best dry white wine; from the Veneto region. Should be drunk very young.
solera: The maturing and blending process employed to make sherry.
Sommelier: Wine steward (Fr.).
sorbic acid: Not a natural grape acid but one that is sometimes added as a preservative. Its presence can be detected by a faint garliclike odor.
sour-sweet: A disagreeable taste, sometimes associated with the activity of lactic acid bacteria in sweet wines.
spicy: A distinctive odor, particularly of some varietal wines; for example, Gewürztraminer.
stagnant: Wines stored in casks that contain stagnant water acquire this unpleasant odor.
sulphury: Sulphur, in its various forms, not only has a very pronounced volcanic smell, but its presence can be detected physically by a prickly sensation in the nostrils and at the back of the throat, like a whiff from a sulphur match.

tannin: An essential preservative derived from grape skins during fermentation. Part of the maturation process consists of the breaking down of the tannin content; it is precipitated over a period by the action of proteins and becomes, with coloring matter, part of the deposit or crust left in the bottle. The presence of tannin dries the roof of the mouth and grips the teeth. It is a

particularly noticeable physical component of young red wine (Bordeaux in particular) that has a practical purpose: it cuts fatty foods and cleans the palate. Tannin is less of a factor in white wines as grape skins—the main source of tannin—are removed prior to fermentation.
tartness: A pleasant, sour taste in young wines.
tartaric acid: The presence of this fruit acid gives wine its healthy, refreshing tang and contributes greatly to its quality and crisp finish. Tartaric acid in the form of free acidity or acid tartrate of potassium is widely distributed in the vegetable kingdom, but its chief source is the grape.
tastevin: Shallow silver tasting cup used in Burgundy.
thin: Lacking body. *Watery* is a related term; *meager* is a similar but superfluous term.
Tokay: Sweet wine of Hungary.
Tonneau: Standard wine measure in Bordeaux. One *tonneau* yields 96 cases.

ullage: French term for air space in a bottle of wine caused by slow evaporation. Occurs when wine casks are not kept full or when bottle leaks. The wines are then usually oxidized, hence the oxidized odor of such wines.

Valpolicella: light fruity red Italian wine from the Veneto area. Enjoy when young.
varietal: term used in the United States for wines labeled by grape variety from which they are made; distinguished from *generic*.
Verdicchio: This Italian wine from the Marches region comes in the distinctive amphora bottle; it is pale, delicate, and dry.
V.D.Q.S. (or *Vins Delimités de Qualité Supérieure*): category of French wine that is one step below *Apellation Contrólée*.
Vermouth: A fortified white wine that is flavored with herbs and spices. The flowers of the wormwood shrub are what give Vermouth its distinctive aroma. Italy (Piedmont region) specializes in the dark, sweet variety, France in the pale and dry.
Vinho Verde: Literally, greeen wine; refers to young red and white wines from northern Portugal.
vinifera: Grape species responsible for most of the world's wines
volatile acidity: The acid of vinegar, which is present to a greater or lesser extent in all wine, but excess volatile acidity is undesirable and usually indicates the first step in acetic deterioration.

well-balanced: Said of a wine that has a satisfactory blend of the physical components: fruit, acid, tannin, alcohol and, to a lesser extent, of the intangible elements: breed, character, finesse.
woody: The odor of wine stored too long in oak containers or in too-new, improperly conditioned ones.

The Language of Wine

APPEARANCE

You may describe a wine as *brilliant* (sparkling in quality with no visible solids); as *clear* (no visible solids, but lacking sparkling quality); as *dull* (distinctly hazy with no visible suspended material); or as *cloudy* (large amount of colloidal material or suspended matter).

PRECIPITATION

Refers to a deposit of bitartrate of potassium in the form of small crystals in your young wine. Can appear in both red and white wine and resemble sugar or glass crystals. Indicates that there are certain minerals or nutrients in the wine and is found on the corks of premium bottles. Harmless.

SEDIMENT OR CRUST

Terms for different types of precipitation. Sediment can mean an accumulation of colloidal material, layers of yeast cells, cottonlike, fluffy sediment, or reddish brown precipitate. Crust can be a form of crystalline deposit, such as cream of tartar, or of granular deposit, which is a combination of tannin and pigment.

COLOR

White wines can be referred to as almost colorless, very light straw, light straw, light yellow, medium yellow, light gold, or medium gold.

Amber shades can be characteristic colors of higher alcohol dessert wines, sherries and vermouths. Very old cabernets also have an amber tint ranging from light, medium to dark amber.

Rosé shades can be described as pale or faded pink, light pink, medium pink (the color of genuine rosé wine), orange pink (peculiar to the Grenache Rosé), orange (result of oxidation of the pink color), light red, medium red (Burgundy, claret, Zinfandel) dark red (Petite Sirah, Alicante Bouschet, Salvador) or tawny. Amber can be characteristic of old red wine, an overoxidized wine or one exposed to high temperature. An onionskin color also is characteristic of over-oxidation of light red wines.

Note: Reds should give you clues as to the variety from which it is made, by their dryness, slightly bell pepper smell or overall balance.

ODOR AND AROMA

These characteristics are derived from the grape, and terms such as the following describe their lack or abundance:

VINOUS: Said of a wine with no individuality.
DISTINCT: Having an individualistic aroma that allows the wine to stand out
VARIETAL: Refers to a wine with a recognizable aroma that is characteristic of a particular variety. Following is a list of some varietal odors prevalent in red and white wines:

WHITE WINES

FLOWERY	*FRUITY*
ACACIA	APPLE
ANISE	APRICOT
CINNAMON	BANANA
FLOWERY VERBENA	LEMON
HAZELNUT	ORANGE
IRIS	PEACH
JASMINE	
LILAC	
LINDEN	
MAGNOLIA	
MINT	
RESEDA	
ROSE	
STRAW-BROOM	

RED WINES

FLOWERY	*FRUITY*
EUCALYPTUS	BILBERRY
LILAC	CHERRY
MOSS	CURRANT
PEPPER	KIRSCH
ROSE	PLUM
SEA WEED	RASPBERRY

CHARACTERISTIC AROMAS OF GRAPE VARIETALS

CABERNET SAUVIGNON	olive, eucalyptus, bell pepper
CHARDONNAY	fig, apple, or melonlike; ripe-grape aroma
CONCORD	fruity, foxy-sweet ripeness
GAMAY	flowery and fruity, like raspberry
GEWÜRZTRAMINER	fruity, linalool, floral
JOHANNISBERG RIESLING	dried apricots, raisins
MERLOT	brown sugar, Spanish olive
MUSCAT BLANC	fruity, floral, honey suckle
PETITE SIRAH	fruity, ripe-grape character; spicy
PINOT NOIR	mild aroma, unless very ripe; also described as pepperminty
SAUVIGNON BLANC	spicy, some herbaceous quality
SEMILLON	fig or melonlike aroma
ZINFANDEL	fruity, raspberry aroma; berrylike

WOOD AGING

Storage in wood tanks, casks, or barrels produces a desirable odor in wine, resulting from slow oxidation and the odoriferous substances extracted from wood. If present, in moderation, wood-aging bouquet adds to the wine's complexity.

BOTTLE BOUQUET

Occurs when the wine is sealed in its bottle and chemicals react to one another and cannot escape. It is the complex scent of mature wines and comes only from aging. Following is a list of the various associative smells used to describe the bouquets of red and white wines:

RED WINES		WHITE WINES
ALMOND	MUSHROOM	BAY LEAF
CEDAR	MUSK	CARAMEL
CLOVE	ORIENTAL SPICES	COFFEE
COCONUT		NUTTINESS
ENGLISH CANDY	RAISIN	RESIN
	RESIN	SPICE
HAVANA TOBACCO	SANDALWOOD	TOFFEE
	TRUFFLES	VANILLA

FERMENTATION ODORS

These occur with the prolonged fermentation of white wines at a relatively cold temperature, complementing the aromas derived from the grapes. Fermentation refers to the sugar breakdown by enzyme action in the yeast, which turns into ethyl alcohol and carbon dioxide, which in turn converts grape juice into wine.

SULFUR DIOXIDE

Recognized by its pungent smell that is irritating to mucous membranes. In higher concentration, it causes sneezing.

HYDROGEN SULFIDE

Smells like rotten eggs; results from the reduction of sulfur dioxide or of free sulfur.

MERCAPTAN

A smell reminiscent of garlic. The odor is due to chemical changes of hydrogen sulfide.

OFF-ODORS FROM SULFUR DIOXIDE

Result from extensive use of sulfur-containing components.

OFF-ODORS FROM BACTERIAL ACTION

MOUSY: Having pungent smell of moldy grapes or produced by storage in moldy container
ACETIC: Having odor of vinegar, produced by acetic acid bacteria
SAUERKRAUT: This odor tips you to the fact there is malolactic fermentation in the bottle

OFF-ODORS FROM EXCESSIVE OXIDATION

OXIDIZED: Smell resembling an overaged wine with a sharper tone
VAPID: Describes smell of wine that is flat and suffering from bottle-sickness
ALDEHYDIC: From overoxidation of table wines
OVERAGED: Odor occurs in overly aged white table wines

OFF-ODORS FROM FERMENTATION

HOT FERMENTATION: Referred to as a "pomace odor;" means wine was fermented at a high temperature in contact with the pomace, which is the mass of skins, seeds, and stems left in the fermenting vat after the wine has been drawn off.
STEMMY: Found mainly in imported wines; indicates too much contact of wine with green stems.
LEES ODOR: Occurs when wine that has remained in contact with the lees for too long absorbs the unpleasant descomposition products of the lees.
YEASTY: Yeast odor due to its undesirable growth in the finished bottle; much more yeastlike than similar fermentation aroma in young white wines.

OFF-ODORS FROM CONTAINERS

WOODY: Odor that occurs when wine absorbs the taste of the wooden container; common problem with California wines, particularly whites, when "too oaky."
STAGNANT: Improper cleaning of a wooden container prior to wine storage results in a stagnant odor caused by action of microorganisms in the water.
MOLDY: Odor wine takes on when it has either been stored in moldy cooperage or been made from moldy grapes.

CORKINESS: Indicates that mold-infected cork has been used as the wine's stopper or that mold settled in the cork's pores after bottling.

OFF-ODORS FROM ADDITIVES AND FILTER AIDS

SORBIC: Geraniumlike odor from an excessive amount of sorbic acid.
BITTER ALMOND: Odor due to over-blue fining to remove excess copper and iron from the wine.
CHARCOAL: Odor due to use of activated carbon in excessive quantities to reduce color. Its odor resembles that of an overoxidized young wine.
FILTER PAD: The peculiar "papery" odor absorbed by wine when the asbestos or cellulose filter pads are not properly prepared before use. It can be very intense in the first few dozen bottles coming off the bottling line. It appears only in filtered wine, when the wine is transferred from the filter to the filling machine and to the bottle.

OFF-ODORS FROM OTHER CAUSES

COOKED OR BURNT: These terms apply to wines such as sherries or dessert wines that have been overheated in excessively high temperatures.
RUBBERY: Dessert wines are described as such when the odor of a very high pH factor is present, usually due to oxidation.
SOPHISTICATED: Means that an unnatural flavor has been added to the wine to improve it.
FUSEL: This odor is sometimes present in fortified dessert wines containing a high level of alcohol.

TASTE

This is a very important aspect of wine enjoyment, especially in the more formalized setting of a wine tasting. Some terms used to describe various kinds of taste include the following:

FLAT, INSIPID: Wine of low acidity, uninteresting, or soft and mellow.
TART: Wine of pleasing freshness and balance with higher acidity
GREEN, ACIDULOUS, OR UNRIPE: Wine that is unbalanced because of excessive acidity.
SWEETISH: A negative term used to describe a wine that is sweet but unbalanced.
ASTRINGENCY: Pronounced in red wines because of their higher tannin content; less than 0.03 percent is present in white wines, resulting in less bitterness. Depending on the quantity of tannin, various terms are used to describe the astringent quality:

SMOOTH OR SOFT: Refers to a wine of low astringency.
SLIGHTLY ROUGH, ROUGH, VERY ROUGH: Indicates increasing astringency.
PUCKERY: Describes a wine with so much astringency it makes your mouth pucker.

FRUITY: Describes a fresh, tart and fruitlike young wine.
FRESH, CRISP, OR LIVELY: A young white wine possessing refreshing tartness and some effervescence can be described as such.
DELICATE: Refers to a light, subtle, fine wine.
PIQUANT: Indicates a light wine with a hint of spiciness.
TIRED: Describes a wine that has been processed excessively in its preparation—one that lacks fruitiness, freshness, and aroma.
COARSE: Suggests a poorly balanced wine in which astringency or acidity (or both) are excessive.

NUTTY: Refers to the nutlike impression (odor and taste) inherent in most dessert wines or well-processed sherries.
FLINTY: The dry, almost hard taste that is found in first-rate Chablis is described as such.
BOTRYTIZED: This term describes a wine that has been affected by the noble mold (*Botrytis cinerea*), which gives the German Auslese and the French Y'Quem their distinct and wonderful tastes.

FLAVOR

When applied to wine, this term refers to the complex impressions created on the palate when wine is worked over in the mouth.

HERBACEOUS

This characteristically refers to wines with the Cabernet Sauvignon family, which are often described as *weedy, peppery, smokey, leathery, minty,* or *spicy.*

WEIGHT OF WINE

This is determined by the alcoholic content of the wine and is described as follows:

WEAK, THIN, OR WATERY: A wine that is low in alcohol content
STRONG, ALCOHOLIC, OR HEADY: A wine with high or excessive alcohol content.

TEXTURE OF WINE

The several terms that can be used to described the way a wine feels in the mouth are as follows:

SMOOTH: A well-balanced wine of low astringency.
SILKY: A wine of fine texture, without bite.
VELVETY: A combination of smoothness and softness in a wine.
CREAMY: An extremely rich wine high in glycerol.
ROUND: Well-balanced wine without major defect.
ROBUST: A heavy-bodied, sturdy wine.

STATURE OF WINE

The level of development and maturity that a wine has attained and its overall quality can be described with the following terms:

GREAT: This adjective is reserved for wines of extraordinary quality, possessing perfect balance and superiority within their class.
FINE: This wine taster's term is applied to wines that show unmistakeable superiority. Although they are in greater abundance than great wines, they must excel in quality and stand out as exceptional.
COMMON OR *VIN ORDINAIRE:* Refers to sound, clean wines of ordinary quality for everyday use. In France, *vin ordinaire* appears on the label to designate a wine of unknown origin, one that was not produced under the *Appellation Contrôlée* or *V.D.S.Q.* designations. Many of the small local wines of any wine-growing district fit this category: a well-made Petite Sirah from California, a Vin Rouge from southern France, or any of the good drinking wines that are reasonably priced.

Vintage Notes

California

Year	Rating*	Remarks
1824		Joseph Chapman plants 4,000 vines in Los Angeles.
1833		Jean Louis Vignes's successful wine and brandy operation is well known throughout the state.
1850		California is admitted into the United States. Over 60,000 gallons of wine are consumed in the state.
1856		Kohler & Frohling begins exports of California wine to Europe, Asia, and Australia.
1858	17	Colonel A. Haraszthy encourages the planting of European vines. He becomes the director of the State Agriculture Society.
1861	19	Prices of vineyards soar from $15 per acre to $150 per acre. Governor Downey sends Haraszthy to Europe to conduct a viticultural expedition. The Charles Krug winery is established.
1865	19	Colonel Haraszthy returns from Europe with 100,000 vines. The California Senate refuses to pay him, suspecting him of Confederate sympathies. Phylloxera is attacking European vineyards.
1867	15	Sparkling Sonoma wine receives honorable mention at Paris Universal Expo.
1869	17	Wine cultivation increases dramatically with reports of devastation of Europe's vineyards by Phylloxera. Transcontinental railroad creates markets for California wines throughout the United States.
1876	18	Charles Lefranc Wine Co. enters wine for competition in the Philadelphia World Expo and receives the Diploma of Honor. A depression takes effect with wine selling for $.10 to $.15 a gallon.
1877	15	The ravages of a plague sweeping vineyards of California destroys most of Sonoma and Napa vineyards. Roots are grafted with New England vines. However, destruction will continue for two more years.
1880	19	Eugene Hilgard, Director of the Board of the State Viticultural Commission is starting to deal with problems and quality. Twelve million gallons are produced. Senator Seneca starts Valley View Winery, which will eventually become Beaulieu.
1880s		Plush period for the new American aristocracy aping their European peers in cultural and social terms. It is fashionable to establish a winery and cellar to become a gentleman farmer. This is a boon for the California agricultural scene, which benefits from the efforts of a host of entrepenurial personalities with an interest in making fine wine.
1884	18	A splendid harvest is reported. Paul Masson creates champagne. Napa valley wines, especially Inglenook's Napa Red, are rated as exquisite.
1886	15	The wine industry suffers its second economic depression as wine prices plummet to new lows. This results from poor quality of wine rather than from excess quantities.
1887	19	Inglenook debuts its first vintage and a magnificent new winery. Seventy-three years later, in 1960, Andre Simon opens a bottle of Cabernet from this vintage and winery, pronouncing it of an outstanding quality and as great as any of the pre-phylloxera Bordeaux he had ever tasted.
1889	19	Inglenook's Cabernet Sauvignon wins first prize at the Paris Exposition, being described in euphoric terms as equal to the Lafite-Rothschild. Other California wines are called equals to Schloss Johannisberg and Yquem. Another highlight is the opening of the wrought iron superstructure, the Eiffel Tower.
1890	18	An opulent vintage should be cause for celebration. However, depressed national economic conditions and production at one-half normal yield casts a negative cloud on the year's wine picture.
1892	18	Very good wine is made due to an excellent, hot summer. Wines from this vintage are tasted in 1971 and still preserve excellent varietal character. The Pinot Noir is particularly exquisite.
1895	17	California wines are in strong demand on the East Coast of the United States.
1897	20	Outstanding wines are produced, especially Cabernets and Pinot Noirs, which are still very good when tasted in 1971. The 1900s would be the first Golden Age for the infant California wine industry as the discovery of gold and other treasures of the state bring increased prosperity to the population and a greater opulence in life style.
1900	19	The Paris Exposition of 1900 creates international headlines, and California wines are compared to their French counterparts, winning three dozen gold medals. Paul Masson champagne wins the Honor of the Certificate Award and experts perdict that the native champagne will soon supersede the French bubbly.
1901	18	More awards for California wines at the Buffalo Exposition. From 1901 through 1915, six million European immigrants create exceptional demand for wines.
1904	18	An international jury of noted wine experts gather in St. Louis for the Louisiana Purchase Exposition. Among the tasters are famous *négociants* such as Kressman, Guestier, Perrier and Schyler. Grand Prize goes to Paul Masson's champagne.
1905	17	Newspapers of the day note that California is experiencing a new gold fever as its wines collect more gold medals at the Lewis and Clark Centennial in Oregon.
1906	16	The San Francisco earthquake destroys many wineries and their cellars.
1907	18	Outstanding native wines are made with California winemakers freely adopting the proprietary names of famous European châteaux on the wine labels. For example, it was not uncommon to find certain wineries

150   *Ratings are on a scale of 1 to 20, 20 indicating a wine of the highest quality; 10 and under, very poor.

Chateâu Mouton-Rothschild Labels, 1945-1976

Dessin inédit   de Henry Moore

Dessin inédit   de Dorothea Tanning

Dessin inédit   ...SE EN BO...   Alechinsky

Dessin inédit   de César

Mallarmé illustré   par Bernard Dufour

Dessin inédit   de Bona

Dessin inédit   de Joan Miró

Gouache de Marc Chagall réalisée pour le Mouton Rothschild 1970

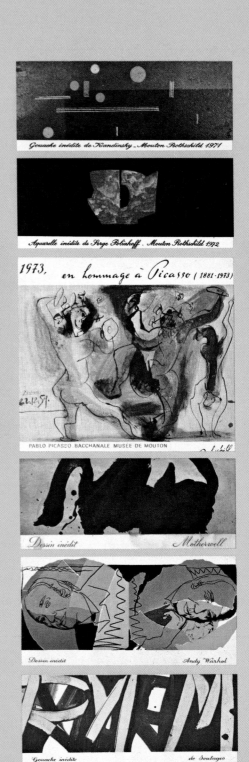

Gouache inédite de Kandinsky . Mouton Rothschild 1971

Aquarelle inédite de Serge Poliakoff . Mouton Rothschild 1972

1973, en hommage à Picasso (1881-1973)

PABLO PICASSO BACCHANALE MUSÉE DE MOUTON

Dessin inédit   Motherwell

Dessin inédit   Andy Warhol

Gouache inédite   de Soulages

Moët & Chandon Commemorative Labels

using the title Château d'Yquem on their own Sauterne-type wines, or any sweet white wine for that matter. It was in 1935 that the U.S. government abolished this practice, but even today certain terms are permitted, such as Burgundy, Chablis, and Rhine. The Sauternes of this year, by the way, were excellent.

Year	Rating	Description
1910	17	A cool long summer produces excellent white varieties such as Rieslings.
1914	18	Noted as an excellent vintage.
1915	16	The Panama Pacific Exposition held at the World Expo of San Francisco celebrates the opening of the Panama Canal. Grand Prize is awarded to Paul Masson's champagne, Oeil de Perdrix. An excellent vintage.
1916	18	A very fine vintage.
1917	17	Anna Held, the reigning superstar of the day, visits the Paul Masson estate and grabs headlines by bathing in champagne instead of her usual milk bath.
1919		National Prohibition.
1933	15	End of Prohibition. It is marked by a fair vintage and 800 wineries are launched. Quality is mediocre due to poor methods and lack of experience by the fledgling winemakers.
1934	16	An above-average vintage. Amateurish efforts by the new winemakers hamper the general overall production.
1935	17	An excellent vintage. Three gallons of dessert wine are being shipped throughout the world in ratio to one gallon of table wines. Definitely the Golden Age for fortified wines. I have tasted and sold the 1935 Simi Cabernet, and even though the wine was primitively made, it shows the breeding of the grapes used in that wine.
1936	19	Julian Street, noted wine expert, writes about the California Pinot Noir, calling it excellent and astonishing. The vintage itself is excellent. Beaulieu's Cabernet Sauvignon is set aside as the Private Reserve, Georges de Latour, by the new winemaker, André Tchelistcheff.
1938	18	André Tchelistcheff calls this a "very good vintage." However, overproduction of grapes causes Bank of America to encourage California wineries to increase brandy production, relieving the market's wine glut. Maynard Amerine and Albert J. Winkler classify California into five climate regions.
1939	18	Good vintage. Beaulieu's Burgundy, made of Cabernet Sauvignon Grapes, wins the Gold Medal at the Golden Gate International Exposition. Frank Schoonmaker encourages all wineries to use varietal labels.
1940	16	Quality varies. Extremely high demand for brandy. This is due to worldwide conflict.
1941	17	Very good vintage, producing delicious and delicate Cabernet Sauvignons.
1942	20	Outstanding vintage, producing very hard, tannic wines that 45 years later are just becoming drinkable. Truly a classic vintage.
1943	17	Very good vintage. Tasting of Cabernets in 1977 indicated they had not reached their maturity as of that date.
1944		No records available.
1945	16	Most wines are sold in bulk. Cool growing season with Chardonnays and Johannisberg Rieslings considered excellent wines.
1946	18	Very good vintage with the finest Pinot Noir ever produced in California marking the year.
1947	20	Outstanding vintage. Best of the forties. Prices drop dramatically throughout the state and the federal government initiates the set-aside program, asking farmers to store wines.
1948	7	A disastrous vintage due to excessive rains.
1949	17	Good vintage. President Truman encourages the consumption of domestic wines, serving Paul Masson wine at the White House.
1950	17	Good vintage of limited production because of an early frost.
1951	20	Frost again played havoc with harvest, reducing production. The vintage, however, is of outstanding quality.
1954	16	Good vintage that produces very tannic wines lacking in fruit.
1955	16	Very fine vintage showing excellent varietal character.
1956	16	Good-quality wine produced. James Zellerbach imports Burgundian oak barrels for his winery, Hanzell. This is a turning point for California winemaking because the old barrels add nuances to the wine.
1957	7	Disastrous vintage, due to poor weather conditions, especially rain.
1958	20	An outstanding vintage that produced intense, aromatic, varietal wines, especially Beaulieu, and Inglenook.
1959	17	Very fine wine produced. However, these wines now are fading.
1960	19	Outstanding vintage. This is a turning point for most wineries for vintage labeling, which was formerly long avoided because the wineries thought retailers would not want to carry additional inventory.
1961	18	Excellent vintage that produced rich, supple wines. However, they lack tannin.
1962	16	Fair but variable.
1963	14	A very light, somewhat poor vintage, producing thin wine. The wines of Sonoma are to be preferred.
1964	18	Damaging frost reduces the crop size. A warm summer creates wines of elegance, refinement, and charm.
1965	17	Produces lighter vintage than 1964 and is noted for its attractive aroma and softness. These are highly touted wines.
1966	18	Excellent vintage due to a very hot summer in which less than one inch of rain fell. Some red wine has a burnt character. This year marks the debut of Heitz's Martha's Vineyards wines, ushering in a new California style of winemaking, bold, masculine, and assertive.
1967	16	Begins with frost damage, followed by a very cool growing season, and rains at harvest. Overall, can be regarded as a fair vintage. One of the few vintages in which Charles Krug did not release their Private Selection. Also of note, California table wines equal the fortified wines in sales.
1968	20	Outstanding vintage. Probably the decade's best. The wineries of Napa, Sonoma, and Monterey all produce excellent wines. This is a true benchmark of standards for California wines. This was the first vintage in which mechanical harvesters were introduced. Special mention should be made of the Cabernet Sauvignon of Beaulieu, Inglenook, Souverain, and Louis Martini.
1969	18	Very hot summer creates high sugars, producing wines that are more masculine and assertive than the previous year's offerings.

Wine tasting is held at Buena Vista, focusing national attention on Robert Mondavi's Cabernet Sauvignon.

Year	Rating	Remarks
1970	19	Outstanding vintage created by spring frost, which reduces the crop's size, and a very hot summer that creates very thick skins on the Cabernet grape. This is to be a high water mark for California Cabernets, producing dramatic wines from Robert Mondavi, Chappelet, Beaulieu, and Heitz.
1971	16	Very good vintage. However, extreme September heat creates very high sugar and low acidity, a combination that results in very assertive, dark-colored wines that are rather flabby.
1972	7	Poor vintage similar to the 1948 disaster. Winemakers learn what their counterparts in the rest of the world already have learned. Nature can show its cruel side: late frost, very hot July, and a wet, rainy harvest. Created a total washout.
1973	17	Very good wines that are superbly balanced. Not as intense as past vintages. Record crops from a warm, even summer saw botrytized conditions appear in the vineyards at harvest. Stag's Leap Cabernet Sauvignon is produced this year and receives major attention at the 1976 Paris tasting held by Stephen Spurrier.
1974	20	Outstanding wine produced. This is the best vintage since 1968. Paul Masson Winery finally succumbs to vintage dating some of their wines.
1975	18	Overall good vintage and the coolest in memory. Grapes took much longer to become ready for harvest.
1976	15	This is the height of the drought. Extremely dry winter with one third of the normal rainfall; translates into half the usual production. It is a problematic vintage.
1977	17	This is the drought's second year. Small quantities are produced, but of excellent quality. This is the year that Christian Brothers starts to vintage date their wines.
1978	18	Very large, abundant crop. Very hot summer producing highly alcoholic wines; wines are characterized by raisiny, burnt character.
1979	16	Extreme heat is followed by rain and strong winds. Results in a difficult vintage. Were it not for modern technology, vintage would have been a disaster. Concluded with average wines without much aging potential.

Bordeaux

Year	Rating	Remarks
1770	16	Notes from an English tavern indicate this was of very fine quality.
1779	18	Thomas Jefferson writes this was an excellent vintage; especially Haut-Brion.
1784	19	A celebrated year sought after by Thomas Jefferson; especially Haut-Brion.
1795	15	Vintage not abundant, but good.
1796	12	Vintage not abundant. Results were mediocre, producing wines that were *maigre,* or thin.
1797	12	Vintage not abundant; resulting wines were mediocre or thin.
1798	19	Remarkable vintage. Margaux and Lafite were especially noted.
1799	11	Vintage not abundant and of poor quality.
1800	9	Vintage not too abundant, quality bad.
1801	14	Vintage not abundant, but quality passable.
1802	18	While French make Bonaparte consul for life, there are reports of an excellent vintage, average in quantity but marvelous in quality. Compares with 1798.
1803	18	Fine vintage.
1804	16	Vintage average in quantity and quality.
1805	12	Vintage abundant in quantity but mediocre in quality.
1806	13	Vintage of ordinary quantity and poor quality.
1807	16	Small crop of good quality.
1808	16	Vintage ordinary in quantity and quality.
1809	10	Small and very bad crop.
1810	14	Ordinary crop of passable quality.
1811	20+	Extremely abundant; a comet vintage at Lafite. A Russian ambassador introduces the practice of serving meals in courses in Paris, instead of placing many dishes on the table at once.
1812	14	Vintage extremely ordinary in both quantity and quality.
1813	10	Average quantity, quality flat and mediocre.
1814	17	A fair quality. Latour blended this vintage with others to reinforce their wines.
1815	19	The Waterloo vintage. Quite extraordinary vintage throughout. Russian troops who are in Paris introduce the word *bistro* for cafés by shouts at the waiters of "bistro, bistro" ("quickly, quickly").
1816	5	A fourth of the crop was harvested, and was wretched in taste.
1817	15	A fifth of the harvest was gained. It was extremely ordinary in quality.
1818	18	Half the harvest was gathered. Hard, good wine, gaining slowly in reputation.
1819	16	Vintage ordinary in quantity and quality.
1820	16	Half the harvest was saved, but quality was lackluster and the wine without much color.
1821	12	Quantity less than 1819. An insignificant, mediocre vintage.
1822	14	Early harvest began on August 27. Extremely ordinary quantity. Wines not good, dried up like corpses.
1823	9	Extremely ordinary vintage; the wines resulting were poor at best.
1824	10	Very small crop of poor quality.
1825	15	Ordinary quantity.
1826	12	Abundant quantity but poor quality.
1827	17	Abundant quantity of good overall quality.
1828	18	Vintage of ordinary quantity. The wine was full of elegance and grace of bouquet, the taste delicious.
1829	9	Crop of average size resulting in awful wine.
1830	9	Crop was small, the wine mediocre.
1831	17	Small crop but very fine.
1832	17	A very hot summer without a drop of rain from June to harvest.
1833	13	The crop was abundant, but the wine of no consequence.
1834	18	Another very small crop but very good.
1835	17	Abundant crop. Light, elegant, and smooth wine.
1836	12	Minimal crop resulting in disagreeable wine.
1837	15	Abundant crop producing exceedingly ordinary wine.
1838	13	Very small crop, poor wine.
1839	15	Vintage of medium quantity; ordinary wine.

Year		Description	Year		Description
1840	16	Abundant crop; good but average wine.	1885	8	Half of a normal harvest; quality was thin with much stench of mildew.
1841	17	Particularly smooth and rich. Very fine.			
1842	16	Minimal crop; ordinary wines.	1886	9	Two-thirds of a normal harvest. Light wines, still affected by mildew.
1843	9	Very small crop; extremely nasty wine.			
1844	17	Abundant crop; very good wine.	1887	12	Half of a normal harvest that saw very light wines with traces of mildew.
1845	12	Minimal crop; poor wine.			
1846	18	Extremely abundant. First vintage of Lafite bottled at the Château.	1888	17	This was the largest crop produced in the decade with fair quality. Margaux was singled out as the best.
1847	19	Abundant crop; exquisite wine.			
1848	19	Very fine. First of back-to-back vintages.	1889	17	Was the first good-quality wine the trade could sell.
1849	16	Average crop; ordinary quality.			
1850	16	Abundant crop; lightweight, ordinary wines.	1890	17	An excellent vintage that produced hard, long-lived wines.
1851	17	Average crop, good wines. Dead today.			
1852	17	Average crop. Very light but good wines.	1891	12	Small harvest producing mediocre, green wines.
1853–		Crops were destroyed by oidium.			
1857		Classification of 1855 takes place.	1892	19	Half the normal harvest, resulting in elegant, richly colored wines because of the heat wave that struck the area on August 15.
1858	16	Very abundant crop, very good wines (now dead) at high prices. The beginning of the Golden Age of Claret. Another comet vintage, enthusiastically received.			
			1893	19	A large production of excellent wines produced from an extremely hot summer. Picking of the grapes began on August 15th, the earliest in 150 years of record. These wines still are holding well today.
1859	15	Small crop; ordinary wines with a taste betraying the phylloxera. A corpse.			
1860	14	Light, not very good wines.			
1861	17	A very short crop due to May frost. Long lasting.	1894	9	A poor vintage due to a hot summer.
			1895	9	Another poor vintage. The wines were picked but turned to vinegar due to hot fermentation. Mouton and Lafite saved their vintages by dumping ice into the vats.
1862	16	Abundant vintage of medium-quality wines.			
1863	12	Passable quality, but did not mature.			
1864	19	Exquisite vintage, richer than 1862, blessed with large production. Fine bouquet and character; a complete wine.			
			1896	14	Were light wines from a poor vintage because of unripe grapes. However, the crop was quite large.
1865	20	Good quality, large quantity. A twin vintage reported to be one of the best to date, especially Lafite.			
			1897	3	A complete failure.
1866	10	Average production, very bad wines.	1898	17	A very small harvest due to the lack of rain and a dry hot summer; but good wines.
1867	15	Small crop, ordinary quality.			
1868	19	The highest price paid for Bordeaux wines. Powerful, intense wine.	1899	18	An excellent vintage that produced a large production that possessed tremendous flavor, depth, and color.
1869	20	Was probably the winner of the decade, if not the century. Well-balanced, rich wine. I personally consumed the Mouton and found it to have a nose of an old cigar box, very brown in color but extraordinary, even though fading.			
			1900	20	Excellent twin vintage with large yields. Much discussion took place as to which of three was the most outstanding: The Latour of 1900, the Haut-Brion of 1899, and the Margaux of 1900 have traditionally been considered the crown jewels of a great wine dinner.
1870	18	A very hard long-lived vintage with a large yield. A hot summer.			
1871	18	Excellent quality; remarkably good wine.	1901	7	Poor and unmarketable.
1872	16	Good quality, fair vintage.	1902	10	Poor and unmarketable.
1873	16	Fine but delicate wine.	1903	8	Poor and unmarketable.
1874	18	Good quality; a very large vintage.	1904	15	The first fair vintage of the century with a large crop. However, the wine lacked staying power.
1875	19	Excellent quality, drinkable and delicate from the onset. Continued to last even to the present day. Mouton was extraordinary. Possibly the finest of the period. Jack Rutherford's highest ranked wine. Another twin vintage.			
			1905	14	It was a small harvest that was well balanced.
			1906	16	A hot summer produced full-bodied wines from a very small crop. Lagune had the best reputation. A fair vintage that was extremely powerful.
1876	15	A light vintage that faded quickly.			
1877	16	André Simon's birth year. According to his notes some 20 years later, some wines were quite good, although uneven. Very light wines but still charming.	1907	11	Oidium affected the wines.
			1908	16	A small production that in general was quite good; a bit hard.
			1909	15	Quality wine produced; small yield.
1878	17	This was to be the last outstanding pre-phylloxera vintage. Greatly improved with time.	1910	3	One quarter of the normal harvest and one of the poorest vintages on record at Gilbey's, one of the largest shippers. They traced back over 100 years of records and could not discover a similar disaster.
1879	15	Small vintage producing ordinary wines.			
1880	16	Small vintage.			
1881	16	The quality was good. Phylloxera would ruin the vineyards until 1887.	1911	8	World War I caused late bottling. However, the quality was light in a small yield.
1882	14	Average vintage feeling the effects of mildew; produced light wines.	1912	15	Large crop that was affected by mildew and an excess of acidity.
1883	13	Average production of ordinary wines.	1913	11	Rather a thin, acid wine produced.
1884	6	Two-thirds of a normal harvest; wines were mediocre, with much mildew.	1914	15	A medium yield that produced good wines that did not last.
			1915	4	A poor vintage, half the normal harvest.

Year	Score	Description
1916	16	Big, powerful hard wines of small production that were good.
1917	14	Light wines that were good when consumed; a small yield.
1918	17	This vintage was hailed as excellent; a small crop.
1919	17	An excellent large crop that produced wonderful wines underrated by many.
1920	16	A very good quality vintage that was overlooked, yet offered much in a delicate austerity. Definitely still fine drinkable wine today.
1921	16	Extremely hot vintage that was most successful in St.-Émilion and Pomerol. Possibly the best for Cheval Blanc. Extremely successful for Sauternes.
1922	12	A huge production. The wines, however, lacked acidity.
1923	17	Although a small vintage, wines had beautiful charm and good color.
1924	18	On a special occasion, I had a 1924 Montrose and found it extraordinary. It was really a very good vintage.
1925	15	A good-sized vintage that was stemmy and green.
1926	18	Half the normal vintage; an October late harvest created, along with the devaluation of the franc, a very expensive vintage. The wines were hard and are just now beginning to fade.
1927	9	Very poor.
1928	20	Excellent wines; at the time hailed to be the greatest. The summer was very hot; a large plentiful crop. Lafite and Haut-Brion were somewhat disappointing. Lawsuits were brought against Lafite for pasteurizing their wine. Latour is, in my opinion, the most outstanding produced that year.
1929	20	Outstanding twin vintage. Rich and full-bodied wines with much sugar. Many consider Mouton the finest, but it is truly a cavalry charge with an abundance of great wine. They are still doing nicely in the eighties. Certainly the classic vintage of Bordeaux.
1930	11	Poor, light, thin wines.
1931	11	Poor, acid wines.
1932	14	Poor, acid vintage that started in mid-October.
1933	12	Light, lacking character.
1934	19	The best of the decade of the thirties. Pomerol and St.-Émilion were the most successful.
1935	14	A fair vintage that was quite variable.
1936	11	An uneven vintage that was fairly disappointing.
1937	12	This was the vintage coming under the control of the Appellation Contrôllée laws. An average quality vintage that was very hard. The last vintage to be shipped before the Germans overran France.
1938	14	Useful wines; some of average quality.
1939	14	Abundant vintage of light, flimsy wines lacking bouquet.
1940	9	Dull, uninteresting vintage.
1941	9	Thin and disappointing.
1942	14	Fair but undistinguished.
1943	16	The best of the wartime vintages. Rather on the light side.
1944		A large crop. The wines lacked body.
1945**	20	An excellent vintage that received much acclaim. Truly one of the great vintages of all time. The vintage suffered from a May frost that made it the second smallest in the century. The wines had an excess of tannin, which was responsible for the last of the old way of making wine, which was a prolonged fermentation on the skins resulting in a slow development. Many place Lafite as the finest; Latour certainly emulates the pre-phylloxera era.
1946	12	Average yield. Wines were green and did not mature; lacked body.
1947	18	An excellent vintage that had far more general qualities than the 1945. Much natural sugar was present due to this very hot summer. The areas that were particularly good were St.-Émilion and Pomerol.
1948	16	Good wines of merit, but surrounded by two outstanding vintages.
1949**	18	Wines of enormous concentration of flavor and body. They have started to fade. The best came from the Médoc.
1950	14	A very large production, although it was a wet summer. Some wines fared well, especially the St.-Émilions.
1951	8	A miserable, wet vintage that allowed chaptalization (adding sugar to increase the alcoholic content).
1952	18	A most attractive, fine vintage that had lots of tannin coming around quite well. Not as good in St.-Émilion or Pomerol. The older twin of this vintage lacked the charm of the younger.
1953	19	A late vintage starting in October. A large crop of excellent, well-balanced wines. Margaux and Mouton were the most notable. The Médoc did very well.
1954	9	A very poor vintage. Cold and wet.
1955	17	A plentiful crop that produced big powerful wines. Especially outstanding were Haut-Brion, La Mission, Cheval Blanc, and Petrus.
1956	6	A very poor vintage that saw frost destroy many vineyards in Pomerol and St.-Émilion. It was considered to be the worst disaster since phylloxera.
1957	17	A very poor summer and a late vintage drifting into October. Very hard wines were produced that still refuse to mature.
1958	13	A very small yield and another mid-October harvest. The wines ended up being very light.
1959	18	Delicious wines were made. A fine, hot summer, which was called the Vintage of the Century by journalists. The vintage possibly lacked acidity but continues to make up for it in softness and richness. Especially noted were wines of St.-Julien and St.-Estèphe. The phrase "an iron fist in a velvet glove" best describes this vintage.
1960	13	Wet weather that permitted chaptalization, making very drinkable wines.
1961	20	Outstanding quality, plenty of fruit, tannin, enormous bouquet. Generally accepted to be on par with the 1928, 1929, and 1945 vintages. Undoubtedly sensational wines made. Pétrus, Cheval Blanc, and Margaux were the most long lived.
1962	18	This was to be a disappointment in St.-Émilion and Pomerol. It was an abundant vintage that really received bad publicity only to later prove quite excellent. It upholds the adage that "you

**Baron Philippe de Rothschild believes that the greatest Bordeaux vintage is the 1949, on which he would bestow a 20; the 1945 he rates at 19½.

don't judge a Bordeaux until ten years of age.''

Year	Rating	Remarks
1963	6	A very poor vintage that was quite large.
1964	17	A very hot summer almost led this to become another Vintage of the Century. A downpour of rain in October spoiled the scenario. Late pickers, Mouton, Lafite, and Lynch-Bages were disappointing.
1965	7	A very poor, wet, cold vintage that made very light wines. A good deal of rot.
1966	18	A very fine well-balanced vintage that produced wines with great depth that are just beginning to show their classic potential.
1967	16	A light vintage that produced wines that had great finesse and distinction. Lafite was outstandingly delicate.
1969	15	A very good summer created much optimism. September produced heavy rains that resulted in light wines lacking fruit.
1970	18	A very good vintage with big rich wines that seemed quite forward and supple; classic style of distinctness.
1971	17	A lighter vintage, but of tremendous elegance. Pomerol, St.-Émilion, and Graves made wines even better than the 1970 vintage. Another ten years should determine whether it turns into a classic vintage; originally underestimated.
1972	12	A very acidic, dull vintage that was the result of
1973	15	the grapes refusing to ripen. A very large vintage rained upon at the last moment: resulted in light wines. Modern vinification methods permitted very good wines to be made out of this natural disaster and they were consumed early.
1974	16	A good vintage that was coarse, lacking in charm, and rather on the hard side. Late rains were responsible for thinning out the wine.
1975	19	A very warm summer created an awesome, huge vintage similar to the 1961. Excessive amounts of tannin have raised some eyebrows of concern in trade circles, among these predicting that it might outlive its fruit. Time will prove its greatness, which can only begin to show in 1990.
1976	18	A very hot dry summer and a light amount of rain at the end. Much softer than the 1975 but good depth and richness. Will eventually prove to be a worthy twin of 1975.
1977	16	Very wet summer produced generous light wines. Certainly much better than originally thought, and improving.
1978	18	Deep color, lots of acidity and fruit; a very fine vintage that needs aging time. Quite expensive.
1979	18	An excellent vintage not receiving much press. Very supple wines that will prove to be similar to the very good 1962 and 1970 vintages.

Burgundy

Year	Rating	Remarks
1753	16	The only note on this vintage comes from a French soldier prior to his departure for the Ohio Valley. He pronounced it good.
1755	16	Average wine reinforced with Rhône wines.
1757	16	French Indian War and Seven Year War with not much mention of the wines of Burgundy.
1766	16	Information unavailable.
1768	15	First appearance of Burgundy to be auctioned at Christie's.
1769	17	Reception of first Burgundy followed by second year of 400 cases.
1770	17	Two-day sale at Christie's and large tastings.
1771– 72	6	Potatoes are listed to be used in time of famine by Antoine-Auguste Parmenter. The diary of unknown author suggests that the 1771 and 1772 Burgundies would cure the emotional rigors of famine.
1774	16	A meager harvest creates unrest in France.
1775	17	Burgundies fetch higher prices than Bordeaux at five-day sale.
1778	17	The first mention of individual vineyards (Chambertin, Pomerol, Nuits-St.-Georges, Montrachet).
1779	17	French are attacked in Senegal by the British, says a diary of the day, along with mention of a good vintage.
1782	17	French are defeated in the Caribbean by the British; concern over wine trade upsets landholders.
1784	16	Peace treaty between France and Britain finds Burgundies reaching new lows in price.
1788	20	Possibly the greatest vintage of this century.
1791	19	Back-to-back outstanding vintages.
1794	17	Largest sale ever at Christie's: over 600 cases of Burgundy sold.
1795	16	Paris bread riots break out. Hoarding of wines creates a black market.
1798	16	Napoleon reports his fondness for Burgundy wines.
1801	16	Thomas Jefferson writes of the pleasures of Burgundy wines.
1802	17	James Watt, F.R.S., in his magnificent cellar, refers to the Nuits-St.-Georges as his prize.
1803	16	Napoleon Bonaparte writes of the pleasure of receiving wines of this vintage.
1806	17	Napoleon's brother, Joseph, requests Burgundy wines upon being placed on the throne in Naples.
1807	16	Concern grows for Britain's blockade of France's ports and the disruption of trade.
1808	17	Chambertin and Romanée wines demand highest prices to date.
1811	20	Possibly the greatest Burgundy produced in the century.
1815	18	The year of Waterloo. Chambertin is the outstanding wine.
1818	16	Allied troops leave France after Napoleonic Wars, educated to the taste of Burgundy wine.
1819	17	Information not available.
1822	17	Information not available.
1825	17	A very fine Burgundy vintage referred to in diplomatic papers.
1826	16	A fantastic vintage for Clos de Vougeot reported in a private diary.
1827	15	Auction prices show tremendous demand for Romanée wines.
1828	16	Auction prices for Montrachet indicates demand for white wines.
1832	17	Old trade papers refer to an exceptional Richebourg and Montrachet.
1834	17	Information not available.
1836	15	Sauce Béarnaise originates at Pavillon. Henry IV enjoyed sauce with French Burgundies.
1840	16	Information not available.

1845	17	First catalogued sales of Beaujolais by Christie's.
1846	19	Famine sweeps Ireland. Food and wine are sent from France.
1848	17	The wines of Romanée-Conti are extolled.
1849	16	News of the Gold Rush and fine wines are sent from California.
1858	16	Romanée-Conti wines bottled by Harvey's fetch record prices.
1859	17	A very good vintage and comments on a winemaking style that is changing to a lighter one.
1863	16	Information not available.
1864	18	Reported in 1976 to be still drinkable and elegant.
1865	19	An exceptional quality vintage; sometimes still found and drinkable.
1868	18	Clos de Vougeot and Romanée-Conti are celebrated for their fine richness.
1869	18	A very good vintage that is extremely long lived. The platinum vintage of France.
1870	20	An excellent, rich vintage that had a large yield.
1874	19	Full, fat wines that were produced in abundance.
1875	17	Long-lived wines that were elegant and stylish; characteristic of breeding.
1877	17	A vintage of good wines with an average yield. Highly enjoyed by Professor Saintsbury.
1878	16	A fair vintage that had a very large crop that could have been much better if vinification methods could have handled such a large crop.
1883	16	Wine was fast maturing; considerably enjoyable.
1884	17	Outstanding whites, especially Meursault.
1885	16	A very large crop brings about an attitude of confidence.
1886	17	A very good vintage with a small crop; delightful wine.
1887	18	A fair-sized crop that transformed reputations of Burgundy producers to quality image. Wines of the area broke new records for price. Clos de Vougeot in half bottles, reported by Christie's still to be good in 1964.
1888	16	A fair vintage with a very large crop.
1889	19	An excellent vintage that had an average-sized production. This was to be the last vintage of pre-phylloxera wines.
1890	16	A good quality wine with just a fair yield.
1892	18	Very good wines but minuscule production.
1893	17	Fine wine made, which still are very delicious.
1894	16	Good wines but minuscule production.
1895	16	Good wines but small yield.
1896	16	Saw the return of large yield and good wines.
1898	16	A fair quality and yield.
1899	18	Very good wines with a small yield.
1900	14	Thin and mediocre wines; an abundant yield.
1904	18	Good, even today, although extremely rare.
1905	17	Elegant, supple wine; now has faded.
1906	17	A fine wine with finesse and breed.
1907	14	Produced an average yield; wines were light.
1908	16	Supple and generous but lacked staying power.
1909	6	A very mediocre vintage.
1911	17	Small yield; wines with tremendous depth and austerity; still good.
1912	16	Elegant but lacked richness; large yield.
1914	14	Soft and fruity wines; now faded.
1915	20	Classic vintage. Everything was perfect; still exceptional; a small yield.
1916	16	A small yield but good wines.
1917	16	A small yield with good wines; a little high in acid.
1918	14	A very large yield that produced ordinary wines.
1919	20	Excellent wines, possibly one of the greatest. Small yield. This was to usher in what would be known as the Golden Decade of Burgundy.
1920	16	A small yield; light and lacking viscosity.
1921	17	A small yield with rich, full-bodied wines.
1923	20	Another blockbuster; deep, rich, distinguished wines of great flavor; still outstanding in the eighties.
1924	15	Soft, supple wine; already faded.
1925	14	Fair-sized crop with ordinary wine.
1926	18	Outstanding vintage with rich wines that still are holding.
1928	18	Perfect wines with fragrance and breed. Still fine.
1929	20	Tremendous richness, flavor, fruit; long lasting.
1930	8	Beginning of a slump; poor wines.
1931	9	Small crop; light thin acid wines.
1932	4	One of the worst vintages ever.
1933	16	Elegant finesse; wines with character.
1934	20	A classic, not to be seen until a decade later. Still outstanding today.
1935	16	A small vintage, consumed and not much mentioned.
1936	14	Light wines; undistinguished.
1937	15	Firm but average in overall quality.
1938	15	Acidic wines that were consumed.
1939	14	A small, undistinguished vintage.
1940		No information; rarely seen.
1941	12	Thin and disappointing.
1942	15	Supple; showed breed and style.
1943	16	Rich, full wines; still delightful.
1944	15	Light, pleasant, rather acidic.
1945	20	Frost the first of May created a small, intense harvest; an excellent vintage as in Bordeaux. Still a classic.
1946	14	Supple, light wines that matured quickly.
1947	19	A very hot year with many vinification problems. Those that succeeded were quite exceptional.
1948	15	A damp, cool vintage with a hot spell at the end; made a firm, hard wine.
1949	18	A drought year with rain just before the harvest produced the classic vintage that is wonderful now in the eighties.
1950	15	A large crop that produced satisfactory quantities of fine whites and variable reds.
1951	13	A thin, light mediocre vintage that lacked sun; faded by now.
1952	17	Might have been the greatest vintage of the century but lacked sunshine during the harvest. Very attractive wines when found. Lots of depth.
1953	17	Full, supple wines, which have already matured.
1954	15	A large crop that matured quickly and varied in quality.
1955	16	Another very large crop that had excellent balance and developed nicely in the bottle.
1956	12	A cold, miserable vintage. Thin, light wine; late harvest and low yield.
1957	17	A firm, intense, small harvest that resulted in sound, long-lived wines.
1958	15	A very large abundant harvest that did not last.
1959	18	A very big crop that was heralded the vintage of the century. Holding very well.

Year	Rating	Remarks
1960	12	A large crop that was weak in constitution. Very thin.
1961	18	Wine full of breed; a large crop that has great flavor.
1962	17	Another large crop; very supple and fine.
1963	12	Thin acid wines with abundance in production.
1964	17	Well-balanced, rich wine with exotic opulence.
1965	8	A rainy sunless year; a complete disaster.
1966	17	Elegant quality with large quantity.
1967	15	A frost in May responsible for light, average quality.
1968	8	A very wet vintage that produced rot and thin wine.
1969	18	An average harvest that produced excellent wines.
1970	16	A large yield with sound, attractive wines.
1971	18	A small yield, but outstanding wines; firm with lasting qualities.
1972	16	A year that yielded average quantities and many good wines.
1973	15	Light wines, rather thin.
1974	14	A variable moderate vintage for immediate consumption.
1975	13	A very wet vintage that will not last.
1976	18	An excellent vintage that saw the old practice of making longer-lived wines.
1977	14	A light, disappointing vintage.
1978	18	A magnificent vintage that parallels the outstanding 1971s.
1979	16	A good deal of hardship in the Clos de Vougeot area due to hail that ruined vineyards; in the Côte de Beaune very good wines were made.

Rhône Valley

Year	Rating	Remarks
1791	19	Possibly one of the oldest red wines ever offered at auction in 1978. Galbert was auctioned. It was described as beautiful, delicate, perfumed, very fine, and light in alcohol.
1795	17	Nathaniel Johnson notes that 1795 Lafite is reinforced with Hermitage.
1803	18	Very good.
1814	17	Beauvillier praised Hermitage.
1824	16	Henderson in *History of Ancient and Modern Wines* notes that Hermitage is being used to reinforce wines for shipment.
1825	17	Lanerthe, the wine of Châteauneuf-du-Pape, was on the wine list of Delmonico's in 1838.
1831	18	Sir Walter Scott praised Hermitage. André Simon praised this wine as one of the best old vintages.
1832	18	George Saintsbury referred to the wine of Hermitage as the manliest of wines. This vintage tasted in 1977 was still full of fruit. It was reported that not a drop of rain fell from June 6 until the end of the harvest with an extremely hot summer in both the Rhône and Bordeaux regions.
1846	19	Simon calls this the greatest Rhône vintage he had ever known.
1858	18	The great comet vintage.
1860	16	Cyrus Redding notes the majority of the vintage was sold to Bordeaux trade for strengthening Claret.
1865	20	A very fine vintage.
1869	20	One of the greatest Rhône vintages ever produced.
1875	20	Had tremendous amounts of sun, which produced a lasting vintage.
1877	18	Outstanding vintage.
1902	14	M. Loubet, President of France, is served 1900 Hermitage at the Court of the Russian Czar.
1904	20	An outstanding vintage of lasting quality.
1906	16	Very good, supple wine with good alcoholic strength.
1907	12	Rather thin and disappointing.
1908	9	Vineyards fell in disrepair.
1909	6	Poor.
1911	14	Average good wines; now faded.
1914	14	Delicate, good.
1915	15	A very good wine but small quantity produced.
1919	16	Very fine wine but seldom seen.
1923	16	Quite a superb vintage but delicate.
1924	15	Soft wines that were consumed early.
1926	18	Quite a good vintage
1927	9	Poor, acidic, flat vintage.
1928	17	Very good wines produced throughout the area.
1929	20	Outstanding vintage; the best of the decade.
1930	10	Poor vintage; dull and flat.
1931	14	Fair, undistinguished quality.
1932	14	Fair quality in a very poor vintage elsewhere.
1933	16	Good wines.
1934	16	Proved to be very fine, rich, well-balanced wine.
1935	11	Average quality, short lived.
1936	16	Good quantity but short lived.
1937	17	Hard and slow in developing.
1938	16	Consumed early.
1939	11	A rather poor vintage.
1940	6	Very poor wines.
1941	8	Another poor year.
1942	16	Supple wines, lacking acid.
1943	15	Light wines.
1944	8	A very poor vintage.
1945	17	Outstanding vintage throughout France.
1946	11	A poor quality and quantity.
1947	18	An extremely hot summer; full, sweet, rich wines.
1948	11	Very poor wine; rubberlike quality acid.
1949	18	A very hot vintage; drought conditions. Excellent conditions today.
1950	17	A large crop that saw wines in the South. Very good.
1951	11	Poor vintage.
1952	19	Outstanding wines; the best up to this point.
1953	18	Almost a twin vintage; rich supple wines.
1954	17	The wine matured very quickly.
1955	20	Possibly the most outstanding wines of the **Rhône** I have ever had.
1956	16	Fine wines with small yield.
1957	17	Very firm wines that have developed nicely.
1958	16	A rather large vintage.
1959	17	An extremely hot vintage that burned the grapes.
1960	16	Very good balance, of acid and sugar, made a very fine wine.
1961	16	Produced a good vintage but not outstanding.
1962	16	A small yield that is now showing very well.
1963	14	Not much character; rather thin wines.

Year	Rating	Remarks	Year	Rating	Remarks
1964	17	Proved to be highly overrated but sound wine.	1972	12	Rather thin and acidic.
1965	11	The harvest was quite good, unlike other areas.	1973	11	A very large yield, but quality was rather dull.
1966	16	Superb wines were made, blessed with good balance.	1974	13	The wines had more strength than 1973 but lacked fruit.
1967	18	Excellent wines were produced that are just beginning to show all of their promise.	1975	11	A disappointing vintage.
			1976	14	Rain swelled the grapes, responsible for thin wine.
1968	10	Pleasant wines; fading now.	1977	17	A full, rich crop with good aging potential.
1969	17	Some excellent wines in a small vintage.	1978	18	An excellent vintage that might prove to be the best of the decade.
1970	18	A large quantity along with good quality.			
1971	16	Average quality wines; lacked richness.	1979	18	A very large harvest with delicate, fruity wines.

Champagne

Year	Rating	Remarks	Year	Rating	Remarks
1743	16	A very good vintage.	1898	16	Developed very nicely, although hard and acidic.
1753	15	An agreeable vintage.	1899	18	An excellent vintage.
1758		Jean-Remy Moët is born.	1900	19	Back-to-back vintages of excellent wines.
1768	15	First appearance of Champagne at Christie sale on behalf of a gentleman of distinction.	1904	18	Exceptional quality.
			1906	18	Very good, almost to the quality of the 1904s.
1769	18	First sale devoted to wine and Champagne.	1911	20	Excellent, still holding quite well. Best since 1874.
1770		No information available.			
1771	12	Records indicate shipment of fine Champagne of M. de Pusseux.	1914	14	Made under immense difficulties at the start of World War I. A fine, well-balanced wine.
1772	8	Christie's auctions an Ambassador's cellar. Champagne sells for double the price of Claret and Burgundy.	1915	16	A very good wine.
			1919	17	Good, elegant quality. Krug made an outstanding wine.
1774	18	Outstanding vintage. Louis XVI insits on Champagne being the only beverage served to his beautiful bride.	1920	17	Good quality with full body.
			1921	18	Outstanding vintage with tremendous richness.
1783	17	A very fine vintage in Champagne.	1923	18	Surprisingly a great vintage in a ho-hum year elsewhere.
1788	19	Findlater's imports this very good vintage.			
1793	17	Shipments of Champagne are stopped when war is declared.	1926	16	Was very good. Pol Roger still good today.
			1928	20	Excellent. One of the finest Champagnes I've ever tasted, especially the Louis Roederer Brut.
1797	16	Stocks of Champagne, now fashionable, are depleted.			
1802	17	This marks the first year Champagne is officially permitted to be imported directly from France.	1929	18	Exceptionally fine quality.
			1933	16	Good overall vintage.
			1934	16	Very well balanced, abundant vintage.
1812		First mention of a merchant's label, Thackeray's Champagne.	1937	18	Excellent, very rich, with good color.
			1942	15	Fair quality.
1815	20	The Waterloo vintage, fine sparkling Champagne.	1943	17	A classic year, with much finesse.
			1945	19	Exceptional vintage. Big, overpowering wines that are very elegant. Very long lived.
1825	16	A very good vintage.			
1846	19	A great Champagne vintage.	1947	16	Fruity, very supple, with much character.
1857	20	Perhaps the greatest vintage of the 19th Century. Long lasting, dry and nutty. Still good in 1977.	1949	16	Fruity, quite firm, still quite good.
			1952	17	Very elegant and well balanced.
			1953	18	Excellent quality, long lasting, with rich fullness.
1858	18	Above average vintage. The famous Comet year.			
			1955	18	A fine elegant year.
1865	19	Excellent, fruity, rich wines.	1959	19	A powerful, fruity, heavy wine; developed quite well.
1868	18	A great vintage. Perrier-Jouet is highly sought.			
1870	18	A great vintage.	1961	18	Fine quality with a rich bouquet.
1874	19	The most celebrated vintage of the 19th century; excellent, rich, full bodied wines of fantastic color. Pommery & Greno Veuve Clicquot, Sillery are all avidly bought.	1962	18	A very good year that is elegant and fruity.
			1964	18	A fair vintage that was quite fruity.
			1966	18	A firm, elegant wine with good balance and finesse.
1880	16	An enormous wine of fine quality. First major appearance of Bollinger on the market place.	1969	17	A high amount of acidity but firm wine. Aging quite nicely.
1886	14	Appearance of Krug in salesroom.	1970	18	A fair vintage that is fuller and fruitier than 1969.
1887	18	Highest prices ever paid for any wine is obtained for Champagne.			
			1971	16	A fine, crisp vintage.
1889	19	Extraordinary, delicious vintage.	1973	17	Full bodied, perfectly balanced, and elegant.
1892	18	An exceptional vintage of excellent wine.	1976	18	Elegant and rich; should develop nicely.
1893	18	Saintsbury's favorite vintage. Some comments are that it was too ripe.	1978	12	A very poor small-sized crop.
			1979	18	Very good crop.

Cognac

Year	Rating	Remarks
1800	20	Oldest vintage in Hennessy's possession.
1811	20	Comet vintage. Seems to have had the effect of making all grape-producing areas outstanding.
1815	18	The Waterloo vintage. Not known as such in France.
1830	17	A very good vintage in the regions of Armagnac.
1848	19	A great year for Cognac and wine.
1858	20	A great year for Cognac and brandy areas.
1860	16	A very good year, but not truly great.
1865	19	An outstanding vintage for wine and Cognac.
1870	18	A very fine vintage; yield was small.
1872	16	A good vintage; average yield.
1874	16	A good vintage; small yield.
1875	20	An outstanding vintage; many felt it was too dear for distillation, especially since it would be the last great pre-phylloxera vintage.
1878	19	The crop was to be the largest before complete decimation by phylloxera.
1884	18	A very fine vintage; hardly any production.
1887	17	A fine wine produced a very limited yield.
1890	17	A fine wine; no signs of improvement production-wise.
1892	17	Fine Cognac with small production.
1893	20	An outstanding large crop with very hot weather and drought conditions. First grand vintage since phylloxera.
1895	16	A good quality but small production.
1896	16	A good quality, unknown production yield.
1898	16	Good quality Cognac.
1899	19	Great vintage plus a large yield.
1900	19	Became known as the Twin Vintages; outstanding for wine and Cognac because of such favorable weather.
1902	16	A fair vintage, but a very small crop.
1904	19	An exceptional vintage that had a very large yield.
1905	18	Fine quality with a large crop.
1906	20	Probably the best of the century, especially noted for Grande Champagne.
1908	16	Was good, but a small yield. Humid weather.
1909	15	Fair; a very small crop.
1910	16	Good Cognac, but very small crop.
1911	18	Fine to excellent with a large production.
1912	16	Fair quality with medium production.
1913	17	A good quality with a small production but strength; falls sharply.
1914	19	Excellent Cognac and large yield; harvest conditions became difficult because of the war.
1916	18	Very good quality; average production. War was taking its toll.
1917	19	Excellent; too dear for distillation; some of the finest Cognac ever made.
1919	18	Very good; hardly any yield. Women and children left to tend the vines.
1920	15	A good quality produced, but a small crop.
1922	16	A very large harvest with good quality.
1923	14	A moderate to average vintage.
1924	17	Sturdy fine wine; much cask time needed.
1926	16	A good-quality moderate yield.
1928	18	Classic vintage Cognac with moderate yield.
1929	12	Bad; cold frost conditions.
1930–34	6	Thin, watery wines. Mediocre.
1935	17	Large crop; excellent brandy.
1936	8	Severe frost at harvest resulted in varnish character to Cognac.
1939	17	Classic vintage Cognac; moderate yield.
1945	17	Very good, but frost destroyed most vines.
1946	16	Overall, a very good vintage.
1947	12	Too hot; grapes raisined and baked.
1948	16	A very good Cognac vintage.
1950	14	A large crop with moderate to fair quality.
1953	17	Good quality with abundant yield.
1961	17	Good quality; lacked rich fullness.
1962	16	Good quality; moderate yield.
1964	18	Surprisingly the best of the decade.
1969	16	Average quality and yield.
1970	16	A tremendously large crop with good quality.
1971	15	A good-quality average crop.
1972	16	Some are very good.
1973	14	A very large production; standard quality.
1974	14	Fair in quality.
1975	17	Very fine quality and a large crop.
1976	16	Good quality.
1978	17	Very good quality; will develop nicely.

Germany

Year	Rating	Remarks
1706	20	A vintage of the century!
1893	19	Frost on June 12 decimated crop. However, the reduced crop produced particularly full wines. Some of the Beerenauslese still drinking well.
1911	15	A good quality vintage.
1915	16	Good vintage with aging potential.
1917	17	A vintage with great keeping potential. Similar in many ways to the 1929.
1920	16	An excellent vintage; reasonably large crop.
1921	20	May have been "the vintage of the century." A small crop of superb quality; still discussed in hushed tones by those in the know.
1928	16	A large crop; many fine wines, although some a little out of balance (acidity a little high; some wines tasted hard).
1929	16	Quite a large vintage; some very fine wines made.
1933	17	A fine vintage; some outstanding wines made.
1934	18	As in much of Europe, a wonderful full vintage.
1935	14	A fine vintage.
1937	19.5	An outstanding vintage of reasonable size; fine, rich, well balanced. The last great German vintage before the ravages of World War II.
1938	8—10	A poor vintage.
1939	8—10	A poor vintage.
1940	8—10	Poor.
1941	5	A disastrous vintage; wines thin and disagreeable.
1942	14	A fine vintage, but a small crop.
1943	18	A very fine, rich, and intense vintage.
1944	14	A fine vintage.
1945	19	As in most of Europe, one outstanding vintage with a tiny production; the smallest vintage. Very few wines of Kabinett quality made. Many of the richer ones drinking well in the 1980s.
1946	17	A full fine vintage, but not quite the quality of the 1947.
1947	18	A very fine and rich vintage.

Year	Rating	Remarks
1948	16	A successful, useful vintage wines; well balanced if a little light.
1949	19.5	One of the fabled German vintages; huge rich wines produced from a fairly small crop. The balance of the wines was mainly excellent, and many are still approaching maturity.
1950	16	A good vintage of many fine wines. A fairly warm and dry summer produced some intense wines.
1951	15	Slightly larger vintage than 1952. A little patchy, but many particularly good Rheingaus made.
1952	15	A good vintage of fair size.
1953	19.5	A great vintage; small crop wines have remarkable intensity and balance. Many wines of Beerenauslese and Trochenbeerenauslese quality still only approaching their peak.
1954	10	A poor vintage; thin wines of little distinction made, due to a cool wet and overcast growing season.
1955	15	A reasonably good vintage with some full and intense wines made; a little patchy, however.
1956	9	A cold and fairly wet summer produced a vintage with few qualities and, worse still, with a long average production. 1956 produced an average less than half its nearest competitor.
1957	11	A medium-quality vintage of small production due to extremely hard frosts and poor flowering.
1958	15	A reasonably good vintage with a high production of good all-around quality wines.
1959	20	One of the finest vintages of the century: rich, intense, and well balanced, many wines still approaching their peak. Very high average temperature and low rainfall, combined with many hours of sunshine, produced a must of extraordinary intensity, weighing in at 91° Oe compared to 1975, which could produce only an average of 75° Oe.
1960	14	A very large vintage with many similarities to 1977. However, the wines tended to be even lighter.
1961	17	Many similarities with the 1962 vintages. However, higher temperatures and sunlight hours produced a richer and finer vintage.
1962	16	A medium-quality vintage, better than the 1963. Low rainfall produced a smallish crop, which unfortunately, due to low average temperatures, never ripened to full maturity.
1963	15	A medium-quality and medium-size vintage, although some full and robust wines were made.
1964	18	A great vintage with a small production. A long hot dry summer produced wines of unusual richness and depth. This vintage had a higher average must weight than even the 1975s—78° Oe.
1965	7	A cold and wet vintage with low hours of sunshine lead to one of the worst vintages of this century; some wines did, however, possess charm with an unusual steadiness and freshness.
1966	17	A very fine vintage indeed; many ripe and very elegant wines made.
1967	19	Many superb wines made, particularly from the Rheinhessen. A particularly ripe vintage with an average must weight of 75° Oe, identical to the must weight of the famous 1975s.
1968	10	A very poor vintage due to a short and wet summer; few wines of much quality made. Has many similarities to the 1956 vintage.
1969	17	A medium-sized vintage that produced fine wines, even if a little inconsistently.
1970	14	A very large crop making serviceable wines, but not much more. This vintage, on equal terms with 1973, produced extremely high yields per acre, almost double that of 1959.
1971	20	Superb vintage wines extremely well balanced with great aging potential; touted by many as the vintage of the century. Due to high average temperatures, low rainfall, and many hours of sunshine in the growing season, the must was particularly rich in extracts and high in sugar content.
1972	11	Not a good vintage. Many wines with excess acidity. A very low average temperature recorded in the wine-growing areas.
1973	15	A very large vintage of useful quality grapes that made lightist attractive wines. 1970 and 1973 share the dubious honor of producing the highest average yield per hectare.
1974	13	A medium-size crop of mainly medium-quality wines.
1975	19	A small vintage of outstanding quality; fine well-balanced wines produced; many not quite as rich as in 1976. However, the vintage was generally more consistent. The average must weight in 1975 was identical to that of 1967, another outstanding vintage.
1976	18	A small vintage of superb quality. Few Kabinett quality wines made; the production was mostly Spätlese and above. 1976 had the highest average temperature during the growing season in modern history, and also a remarkable amount of sunlight hours.
1977	14	A large vintage with very high yields per acre. The average temperature was reasonably high, but so were the hours of sunshine.
1978	13	Small vintage of very mediocre quality wines.
1979	16	A good and plentiful harvest of mainly Kabinett quality wines, although some excellent Spätlese and Auslese quality wines have been reported.

Italy: Barolo

Year	Rating	Remarks
1868	20	Outstanding vintage; one of the finest ever produced.
1869	14	A fine summer; good quality.
1870	13	A hot spell all over Western Europe; good quality.
1871	12	Remarkably good wine.
1872	12	A fair vintage.
1873	18	Very fine quality bordering on outstanding.
1874	9	A large undistinguished vintage.
1875	4	Poor to medium
1876	15	A light vintage that was extremely elegant.
1877	12	A fair vintage.
1878	4	Mediocre; a disaster.
1879	19	Outstanding quality; still talked about.
1880	8	A light wine that was acidic.
1881	13	A dull, quickly consumed vintage.
1882	9	A fair vintage.

Year	Rating	Remarks	Year	Rating	Remarks
1883	12	Overall good quality.	1935	16	A good wine.
1884	4	A disaster; poor weather.	1936		
1885	15	Fair quality; did not last long.	1937		
1886	18	Fine quality; a large yield.	1938		
1887	20	Outstanding; this is what the classic nebbiolo grape can be.	1939		Information too sketchy to have accurate vintage data.
1888	13	A very good quality.	1940		
1889	17	Distinguished wine that was quite elegant.	1941		
1890	16	Poor vintage; dull and flat.	1942		
1892	12	Quite good.	1943		
1893	4	Acidic poor wines	1944		
1894	20	Heralded as magnificent; magic weather conditions.	1945	19	Excellent vintage, full rich wines.
1895	17	A fine summer created good wine.	1946	14	Reported in a journal as equally unimportant as the granting of women's right to vote in Italy for the first time. I still question what that meant, but it was a lackluster vintage.
1896	8	Mediocre quality.			
1897	18	Proved to be fine rich wines.			
1898	20	Superb small vintage that was best of the decade.	1947	20	A truly outstanding vintage; probably the best in three decades.
1899	12	Fine delicate wine.	1948	8	Dull, undistinguished wines.
1900	13	Fair quality but did not last long.	1949	8	A wet harvest produced thin wines of no distinction.
1901	6	Light vintage that faded quickly.			
1902	4	A disaster partly because of miserable weather.	1950	12	A large production.
			1951	17	A fine vintage; many outstanding wines.
1903	12	Good quality and large vintage.	1952	17	Wine of great elegance and longevity.
1904	4	Disaster due to bad weather.	1953	4	A complete failure.
1905	19	Celebrated vintage that was truly outstanding.	1954	12	Very thin disappointing wines.
1906	17	Hot vintage; full bodied wine.	1955	13	A good well balanced wine but now it is losing its fruit and drying up.
1907	20	Huge crop with truly outstanding wines.			
1908	18	Small production that was excellent.	1956	8	Light wine that was pleasant when young.
1909	11	Fair quality; faded quickly.	1957	19	Wine of great finesse and aging potential.
1910	17	Excellent wines that were long lived.	1958	17	Stately elegance with rich depth and character.
1911	16	Well-balanced good wines.	1959	4	Very acidic and disappointingly thin wines.
1912	20	Very large crop that is even today outstanding wine.	1960	4	Twin disaster vintages.
			1961	20	Perfect weather created rich robust wines.
1913	12	Fine but not long-lasting.	1962	18	Somewhat overlooked because of the outstanding quality of the previous vintage.
1914	12	Delicate light wines.			
1915	4	Poor, acidic wine.	1963	10	Mediocre quality vintage, large production.
1916	9	Light but stylish wines.	1964	20	Fine well balanced vintage; full rich wines produced.
1917	19	Big, powerful, outstanding wines.			
1918	12	Soft wines consumed early.	1965	16	Very good but spotty vintage.
1919	20	Outstanding but seldom-seen wine; a small vintage.	1966	5	A very poor vintage.
			1967	16	Overall a very good vintage; now faded.
1920	14	Very good wines.	1968	18	Full bodied vintage, Some exceptional wines produced.
1921	11	Light wines; good when young.			
1922	19	Large production that was wonderful.	1969	16	Very good and abundant vintage.
1923	12	A very fine summer produced good wines.	1970	17	Excellent; overshadowed by the magnificent 1971s.
1924	16	Quite well balanced.			
1925	17	Very good quality wines that were overlooked.	1971	20	A great success producing the classic Barolo.
1926	10	Acidic and astringent.	1972	4	Disastrous vintage; crop declassified.
1927	20	Some say this was the benchmark of Italian wines because of its greatness.	1973	8	Short wines made, both in quality and longevity.
1928	15	Overlooked but quite good.	1974	17	A fine vintage; wines with good aging potential.
1929	20	Rich, full bodied wine. One of the finest wines I ever had was a Barolo from this vintage.	1975	8	A poor quality vintage for Barolo; wines of little body.
1930	15	Good overall quality.	1976	13	Only average quality wines were produced.
1931	15	Well balanced wines that were light.	1977	9	Poor vintage; thin insubstantial wines made.
1932	14	Good overall quality, rather on the light side.	1978	18	Good to exceptional wines produced.
1933	16	A small production but drinkable wines.	1979	18	Good to exceptional wines again produced.
1934	18	Excellent, rich well-balanced wines.			

Madeira

Year	Rating	Remarks	Year	Rating	Remarks
1789	17	A very good vintage, especially noted in the Cama de Lobos district.			singled out as especially sound.
			1806	17	A very good year for Cama de Lobos and São.
1791	18	An above-average vintage.	1808	19	Possibly the best Malmsey ever produced.
1792	17	Bual was especially pleasant.	1815	18	The Waterloo vintage noted for Bual.
1795	18	Tenantez was reported to be especially fine in a very good vintage.	1822	20	Excellent vintage especially Bual.
			1836	17	Sercial was probably the best produced in this staunch vintage.
1803	17	A very sterling vintage for Madeira.			
1805	17	Cama de Lobos and São and Martinho were	1838	17	Verdelho especially fine; generally overall

good quality.

Year	Rating	Remarks
1844	18	Bual, Verdelho, both were very sound.
1846	17	Terrantez, Bual, and Verdelho were quite satisfactory.
1851	17	Sercial, Malmsey, Bual were very good; the next ten vintages would be plagued by oidium.
1862	19	Outstanding vintage; the best ever for Terrantez.
1865	18	Extremely fine Madeira produced.
1868	19	Extremely fine vintage for Bual.
1870	18	A very small vintage that was especially good for Sercial.
1872	16	Generally fine throughout Madeira.
1873	18	A very good vintage, but phylloxera was responsible for a small crop.
1880	18	Should be referred to as the Malmsey vintage, for it was outstanding.
1883	18	Quite a small vintage, but extremely positive for Sercial.
1893	19	Seemed to be an extraordinary vintage everywhere.
1898	17	This was to be the first normal vintage since

phylloxera.

Year	Rating	Remarks
1900	18	A fine hot summer overall; very admirable vintage; noted for Verdelho and Sercial.
1902	17	Overall quality was fine. Verdelho was especially notable.
1905	16	A very small yield.
1906	15	Another small vintage. Malmsey most notable.
1907	15	Verdelho was most exceptional
1910	17	All the wines of Madeira were quite sound.
1914	15	A small vintage that generally made good wines. Probably most noted for Bual.
1915	16	Saw all the wines of Madeira quite agreeable.
1916	17	Malmsey was superb.
1918	16	A very good overall vintage.
1920	16	Quite good throughout Madeira.
1926	17	Bual was very fine.
1934	17	Verdelho was excellent.
1941	17	Malmsey and Bual especially fine.
1944	16	Generally very good overall year.
1951	16	Sound all-around vintage.
1954	16	Bual was especially good.
1956	17	Bual again is excellent.

Port

Year	Rating	Remarks
1815	19	The famous Waterloo vintage.
1820	20	Outstanding; rich sugar wine.
1834	19	Outstanding; a long lived-vintage.
1847	17	Excellent quality.
1851	19	Outstanding quality.
1853	16	Average vintage.
1858	17	A very fine, rich vintage.
1863	18	An outstanding vintage, especially Delaforce.
1864	16	Only Martinez declared this a vintage.
1865	17	Above-average quality.
1866	14	Only Martinez declared this a vintage.
1867	16	Above average.
1868	20	Outstanding vintage; practically every shipper declared.
1869	15	Croft was the only shipper to declare.

Year	Rating	Remarks	Shippers Declaring This Year a Vintage*
1870	17	Very good quality	Cockburn Smithes; Croft; Delaforce; Dow; Feuerheerd; Fonseca; Gould Campbell; Graham; Kopke; Mackenzie; Martinez Gassiot; Morgan; Offley Forrester; Rebello Valente; Sandeman; Smith Woodhouse; Taylor, Fladgate & Yeatman; Tuke Holdsworth, Hunt Roope & Co.; Warre
1871	14	Only Feuerheerd declared.	Feuerheerd.
1872	15	Average quality.	
1873	16	Very fine quality.	Burmester; Cockburn Smithes; Delaforce; Down; Feuerheerd; Fonseca; Gould Campbell; Graham; Kopke; Mackenzie; Martinez Gassiot; Morgan; Offley Forrester; Sandeman; Smith Woodhouse; Taylor, Fladgate & Yeatman; Tuke Holdsworth, Hunt Roope & Co.
1874	18	Martinez and Tuke declared.	Martinez Gassiot; Tuke Holdsworth, Hunt Roope & Co.
1875	20	Heralded as magnificent.	Cockburn Smithes; Croft; Delaforce; Dow; Feuerheerd, Gould Campbell; Graham; Kopke; Mackenzie; Martinez Gassiot; Morgan; Offley Forrester; Rebello Valente; Sandeman; Smith Woodhouse; Taylor, Fladgate & Yeatman; Tuke Holdsworth, Hunt Roope & Co.; Warre
1877	14	Only Sandeman declared.	Sandeman.
1878	17	Excellent.	Burmester; Cockburn Smithes; Croft; Delaforce; Dow; Feuerheerd; Fonseca; Gould Campbell; Graham; Kopke; Mackenzie; Martinez Gassiot; Morgan; Offley Forrester; Rebello Valente; Sandeman; Smith Woodhouse; Taylor, Fladgate & Yeatman; Van Zellers; Warre.
1881	17	A very good quality with a large yield.	Cockburn Smithes; Croft; Delaforce; Dow; Feuerheerd; Fonseca; Gould Campbell; Graham; Kopke; Mackenzie; Martinez Gassiot; Morgan; Offley Forrester; Rebello Valente; Sandeman; Smith Woodhouse; Taylor, Fladgate & Yeatman; Tuke Holdsworth, Hunt Roope & Co.; Van Zellers; Warre.

*Most port wines are blends of several years' harvests. Occasionally, a particular season's yield is so outstanding in quality that the shippers "declare a vintage." The port from such a year is not blended and is distinguished as Vintage Port.

1884	18	Very good quality, but a very small yield.	Cockburn Smithes; Croft, Delaforce; Dixon, Dow; Feuerheerd; Fonseca; Gould Campbell; Graham; Kopke; Mackenzie; Martinez Gassiot; Morgan; Offley Forrester; Rebello Valente; Sandeman; Smith Woodhouse; Taylor, Fladgate & Yeatman; Tuke Holdsworth, Hunt Roope & Co.; Van Zellers; Warre.
1886	15	Average. Only Martinez declared.	Martinez.
1887	18	Fine quality with a large yield.	Burmester; Cockburn Smithes; Croft; Delaforce; Dixon; Dow; Feuerheerd; Fonseca; Gould Campbell; Graham; Kopke; Mackenzie; Martinez Gassiot; Morgan; Offley Forrester; Rebello Valente; Sandeman; Smith Woodhouse; Taylor, Fladgate & Yeatman; Tuke Holdsworth, Hunt Roope & Co; Van Zellers; Warre.
1889	14	Fair quality; large crop.	
1890	16	Good overall quality; very large yield.	Burmester; Cockburn Smithes; Croft; Delaforce; Dow; Feuerheerd; Fonseca; Gould Campbell; Graham; Kopke; Mackenzie; Martinez Gassiot; Morgan; Offley Forrester; Rebello Valente; Sandeman; Smith Woodhouse; Taylor, Fladgate & Yeatman; Tuke Holdsworth, Hunt Roope & Co; Van Zellers; Warre.
1891	14	Fair quality.	
1896	18	Fine vintage; excellent today.	Burmester; Cockburn Smithes; Croft; Da Silva, A.J.; Delaforce; Dow; Ferreira, A.A.; Feuerheerd; Fonseca; Gonzalez Byass; Gould Campbell; Graham; Kopke; Mackenzie; Martinez Gassiot; Morgan; Offley Forrester; Rebello Valente; Sandeman; Smith Woodhouse; Stormont Tait; Taylor, Fladgate & Yeatman; Tuke Holdsworth, Hunt Roope & Co; Van Zellers; Warre.
1897	14	Only Dow declared.	Dow.
1900	18	Superb quality; very fine, delicate wine.	Burmester; Cockburn Smithes; Croft; Da Silva, A.J.; Delaforce; Feuerheerd; Fonseca; Gonzalez Byass; Gould Campbell; Kopke; Mackenzie Gassiot; Morgan; Offley Forrester; Rebello Valente; Sandeman; Smith Woodhouse; Stormont Tait; Taylor, Fladgate & Yeatman; Tuke Holdsworth, Hunt Roope & Co; Warre.

1901	14	Fair quality, large crop.	
1904	15	Fair quality, large crop.	Burmester; Cockburn Smithes; Croft; Da Silva, A.J.; Delaforce; Dow; Ferreira, A.A.; Feuerheerd; Fonseca; Gonzalez Byass; Gould Campbell; Graham; Kopke; Mackenzie; Martinez Gassiot; Morgan; Offley Forrester; Rebello Valente; Sandeman; Smith Woodhouse; Stormont Tait; Taylor, Fladgate & Yeatman; Tuke Holdsworth, Hunt Roope & Co.; Van Zellers; Warre.
1905	15	Fair overall quality, but a small yield.	
1908	18	Very fine quality; abundant yield.	Burmester; Cockburn Smithes; Croft; Delaforce; Dow; Ferreira, A.A.; Feuerheerd; Fonseca; Gonzalez Byass; Gould Campbell; Graham; Kopke; Mackenzie; Martinez Gassiot; Morgan; Offley Forrester; Rebello Valente; Sandeman; Smith Woodhouse; Stormont Tait; Taylor, Fladgate & Yeatman; Tuke Holdsworth, Hunt Roope & Co.; Van Zellers; Warre.
1910	14	Small-size crop with fair quality.	
1911	16	A very small crop, but very good quality.	Martinez Gassiot; Sandeman; Rebello Valente.
1912	17	Excellent quality; medium yield.	Burmester; Cockburn Smithes; Croft; Da Silva, A.J.; Delaforce; Dow; Ferreira, A. A.; Feuerheerd; Fonseca; Gonzalez Byass; Gould Campbell; Graham; Kopke; Mackenzie; Martinez Gassiot; Morgan; Offley Forrester; Rebello Valente; Sandeman; Smith Woodhouse; Sociedade Constantino; Stormont Tait; Taylor, Fladgate & Yeatman; Tuke Holdsworth, Hunt Roope & Co.; Van Zellers; Warre.
1914	15	A small sized harvest with fair overall quality.	Borges.
1915	15	Good quality; medium-size harvest.	
1916	15	A very large production with good quality.	
1917	17	A very good quality; large harvest.	Croft; Da Silva, A.J.; Delaforce; Ferreira, A.A.; Feuerheerd, Gonzalez Byass; Graham; Kopke; Rebello Valente; Sandeman; Smith

Year	Rating	Description	Shippers
			Woodhouse; Taylor, Fladgate & Yeatman; Tuke Holdsworth, Hunt Roope & Co.; Van Zellers; Warre.
1919	16	A fine quality; average yield.	Da Silva, A.J.; Delaforce; Kopke; Mackenzie; Martinez Gassiot; Offley Forrester.
1920	18	A good overall quality and small production.	Burmester; Croft; Da Silva, A.J.; Delaforce; Dow; Ferreira, A.A.; Feuerheerd; Fonseca; Gonzalez Byass; Gould Campbell; Graham; Kopke; Mackenzie; Morgan; Offley Forrester; Rebello Valente; Sandeman; Smith Woodhouse; Stormont Tait; Taylor, Fladgate & Yeatman; Tuke Holdsworth, Hunt Roope & Co.; Warre.
1922	17	Very good quality.	Borges; Burmester; Butler, Nephew; Croft; Feist; Fonseca; Gould Campbell; Kingston; Kopke; Mackenzie; Martinez Gassiot; Morgan; Offley Forrester; Rebello Valente; Tuke Holdsworth, Hunt Roope & Co.; Van Zellers; Warre.
1923	16	Fair overall quality.	Da Silva, A.J.; Offley Forrester.
1924	16	Good quality.	Butler, Nephew; Croft; Dow; Feuerheerd; Gould Campbell; Graham; Morgan; Offley Forrester; Ramos Pinto; Rebello Valente; Sandeman; Smith Woodhouse; Taylor, Fladgate & Yeatman; Tuke Holdsworth, Hunt Roope & Co.; Van Zellers; Warre.
1927	20	Outstanding quality.	Burmester; Butler, Nephew; Cockburn Smithes; Croft; Da Silva, A.J.; Delaforce; Dow; Feuerheerd; Fonseca; Graham; Kingston; Kopke; Mackenzie; Martinez Gassiot; Morgan; Offley Forrester; Quarles Harris; Ramos Pinto; Rebello Valente; Sandeman; Smith Woodhouse; Sociedade Constantino; Southard; Stormont Tait; Taylor, Fladgate & Yeatman; Tuke Holdsworth, Hunt Roope & Co.; Van Zellers; Warre; Wiese & Krohn.
1931	17	A very fine quality.	Burmester; Da Silva, A.J.; Martinez Gassiot; Offley Forrester.
1934	17	Very fine quality.	Butler, Nephew; Da Silva, A.J.; Dow; Fonseca; Gould Campbell; Martinez Gassiot; Offley Forrester; Quarles Harris; Royal Oporto Wine Co.; Sandeman; Tuke Holdsworth, Hunt Roope & Co.; Warre; Wiese & Krohn.
1935	18	Very good overall quality.	Adams; Burmester; Calem & Filho; Cockburn Smithes;
			Croft; Delaforce; Gould Campbell; Graham; Kopke; Mackenzie; Offley Forrester; Rebello Valente; Sandeman; Sociedade Constantino; Taylor, Fladgate & Yeatman; Tuke Holdsworth, Hunt Roope & Co.; Van Zellers.
1941	16	Generally very good quality.	Da Silva, A.J.; Sociedade Constantino.
1942	17	Fine quality.	Butler, Nephew; Croft; Da Silva, A.J.; Feuerheerd; Gould Campbell; Graham; Morgan; Offley Forrester; Robertson Bros.; Sandeman; Taylor, Fladgate & Yeatman; Van Zellers.
1943	17		Barros, Almeida; Burmester; Butler, Nephew; Feuerheerd; Tuke Holdsworth, Hunt Roope & Co.
1945	19	The vintage was bottled in Portugal and was quite outstanding, although small. Still developing in the bottle. A treasure.	Adams; Butler, Nephew; Croft; Da Silva, A.J.; Delaforce; Dow-Silva & Cosens; Ferreira, A.A., Sucrs; Feuerheerd; Gonzalez Byass; Graham; Kopke; Mackenzie; Martinez Gassiot; Quarles Harris; Ramos Pinto; Real Vinicola (Quinta do Sibio); Robertson Bros; Royal Oporto Wine Co; Sandeman; Smith Woodhouse; Sociedade Constantino; Taylor, Fladgate, & Yeatman; Tuke Holdsworth, Hunt Roope & Co.
1947	16	A lighter, more delicate vintage. At its maturity.	Adams; Cockburn Smithes; Calem & Filho; Da Silva, A.J.; Delaforce; Dow-Silva & Cosens; Quarles Harris; Real Vinicola (Quinta do Sibio); Robertson Bros; Sandeman; Smith Woodhouse; Sociedade Constantino; Tuke Holdsworth, Hunt Roope & Co; Ware.
1948	18	One of the hottest vintages recorded, lending to a burnt-nose sensation. The crop was small but full-bodied sweet wine.	Adams; Burmester; Butler, Nephew; Calem & Filho; Graham; Kopke; Mackenzie; Morgan; Taylor, Fladgate & Yeatman.
1950	18	Almost the opposite of the 1948. A delicate, graceful, feminine wine that is beginning to fade.	Adams; Cockburn Smithes; Croft; Da Silva, A.J.; Delaforce; Dow-Silva & Cosens; Kopke; Mackenzie; Offley Forrester; Quarles Harris; Real Vinicola; (Quinta do Sibio); Sandeman; Smith Woodhouse; Sociedade Constantino; Tuke

Year		Description	Shippers
1951	12	There was only one shipper who declared in this vintage.	Holdsworth, Hunt Roope & Co; Warre. Feuerheerd.
1954	14	Two shippers declared.	Burmester; Offley Forrester.
1955	19	A well-balanced wine that had good fruit and richness. Fine vintage, full and sturdy wine, only now at its best.	Adams; Burmester; Calam & Filho; Cockburn Smithes; Croft; Da Silva, A.J.; Delaforce; Dow-Silva & Cosens; Ferreira, A.A., Sucrs; Guimaraens & Co; Gonzalez Byass; Gould Campbell; Graham; Kopke; Mackenzie; Martinez Gassiot; Morgan; Quarles Harris; Ramos Pinto; Real Vinicola (Quinta do Sibio); Robertson Bros; Sandeman; Smith Woodhouse; Taylor, Fladgate & Yeatman; Tuke Holdsworth, Hunt Roope & Co; Warre.
1958	14	A fairly wet and late vintage that ended up producing excellent wine, elegant but without great concentration.	Burmester; Da Silva, A.J.; Delaforce; Guimaraens & Co; Kopke; Mackenzie; Martinez Gassiot; Offley Forrester; Quarles Harris; Sandeman; Sociedade Constantino; Warre.
1960	15	A very early vintage that started on Sept. 12 with rain shortly there-after. Great medium-body vintage of attractive, fruity wines; have developed reasonably quickly.	Adams; Burmester; Butler, Nephew; Calem & Filho; Cockburn Smithes; Croft; Da Silva, A.J.; Delaforce; Dow-Silva & Cosens; Ferreira, A.A. Sucrs; Guimaraens & Co; Gonzalez Byass; Gould Campbell; Graham; Kopke; Mackenzie; Martinez Gassiot; Morgan; Offley Forrester; Quarles Harris; Real Vinicola (Quinta do Sibio); Rebello Valante; Sandeman; Smith Woodhouse; Taylor, Fladgate & Yeatman; Tuke Holdsworth, Hunt Roope & Co.; Warre.
1962	16	Only one shipper declared.	Offley Forrester.
1963	20	Very fine vintage of full-bodied, rich, concentrated wine; among the greatest of the century. Can be ranked with 1945 and 1927. Most of the wines of this vintage will last and still improve to the year 2000.	Adams; Borges; Burmester; Calem & Filho; Cockburn Smithes; Da Silva, A.J.; Delaforce; Dow-Silva & Cosens; Guimaraens & Co; Gonzalez Byass; Gould Campbell; Graham; Kopke; Mackenzie; Martinez Gassiot; Morgan; Quarles Harris; Rebello Valente; Sandeman; Smith Woodhouse; Taylor, Fladgate & Yeatman; Tuke Holdsworth, Hunt Roope & Co; Warre.
1966	16	A very excellent vintage, although a small crop. Elegant, fruity, balanced, medium-body wine. Will develop faster than the 1963	Adams; Croft; Da Silva, A.J.; Delaforce; Dow-Silva & Cosens; Ferreira, A.A. Sucrs; Guimaraens & Co; Gould Campbell; Graham; Kopke; Mackenzie; Morgan; Offley Forrester; Quarles Harris; Rebello Valente; Sandeman; Smith Woodhouse; Sociedade Constantino; Taylor, Fladgate & Yeatman; Tuke Holdsworth, Hunt Roope & Co.; Warre.
1967	15	A very small yield, although excellent; Cockburn and Martinez preferred it to 1966.	Cockburn Smithes; Gonzalez Byass; Martinez Gassiot; Offley Forrester; Manual D. Pocas; Sandeman; Taylor, Fladgate & Yeatman.
1970	17	Perfect weather produced very mature wine. A vintage declared by most everyone; perhaps the best since 1963. Big, full, rich wine, extremely well colored; will live for many years.	Barros, Almeida; Borges; Burmester; Calem & Filho; Cockburn Smithes; Croft; Douro Wine Shippers & Growers' Association; Da Silva, A.J.; Da Dilva, C.; Delaforce; Diez Hermanos; Dow-Silva & Cosens; Feist; Ferreira, A.A. Sucrs; Guimaraens & Co; Gonzalez Byass; Graham; Hutcheson & Ca Lda; Kopke; Mackenzie; Martinez Gassiot; Messias; Morgan; Niepoort; Offley Forrester; Osborne; Quarles Harris; Manuel D. Pocas; Ramos Pinto; Real Vinicola (Quinta do Sibio); Robertson Bros; Royal Oporto Wine Co; Sandeman; Smith Woodhouse; Taylor, Fladgate & Yeatman; Vieira de Souza; Warre; Wiese & Krohn.
1972	16	Declared by two shippers.	Dow; Offley.
1975	15	A dry hot summer with some rain just before this harvest; attrac-tive wines with elegance and fruit certainly enough depth to last to the end of the century.	Declared by most of the shippers; Fonseca, Warre, and Graham will perhaps be the longest lived.
1977	19+	An excellent vintage; after a wet and cold spring and an indifferent summer, almost perfect conditions followed which made the wines full, rich and powerful; they will rank with the 1963 and 1945 as the best of post-war vintages.	Declared by all except Cockburn Martinez & Narol

Encépages of the Classified Growths _____

The *encépage* is the "secret recipe" of the proportions of wines from different grape varietals that will be blended in the cuvée. The great vineyards of Bordeaux are planted in the proportions of vines given below. Since each varietal is ready for harvest at a different time, these proportions may vary somewhat in the château's wine from year to year depending on weather and soil conditions; but in ideal circumstances, they represent what each château considers to be the blend that gives its wine its finest and characteristic identity.

First Growths

Château Lafite-Rothschild, Pauillac
    68% Cabernet Sauvignon
    18% Merlot
    13% Cabernet Franc
    1% Petit Verdot

Château Margaux, Margaux
    75% Cabernet Sauvignon
    25% Merlot
    (White wine: 100% Sauvignon Blanc)

Château Latour, Pauillac
    75% Cabernet Sauvignon
    15% Cabernet Franc
    8% Merlot
    2% Petit Verdot

Château Haut-Brion, Pessac
    55% Cabernet Sauvignon
    25% Cabernet Franc
    20% Merlot
    (Haut-Brion Blanc: Sauvignon Blanc and Semillon)

Château Mouton-Rothschild, Pauillac
    90% Cabernet Sauvignon
    7% Cabernet Franc
    3% Merlot

Second Growths

Château Rausan-Ségla, Margaux
    50% Cabernet Sauvignon
    35% Merlot
    10% Cabernet Franc
    5% Petit Verdot

Château Rauzan-Gassies, Margaux
    50% Cabernet Sauvignon
    30% Merlot
    16% Cabernet Franc
    4% Petit Verdot

Château Léoville-Las-Cases, Saint-Julien
    70% Cabernet Sauvignon
    15% Cabernet Franc
    15% Merlot

Château Léoville-Poyferré, Saint-Julien
    50% Cabernet Sauvignon
    50% Merlot

Château Léoville-Barton, Saint-Julien
    75% Cabernet Sauvignon and Cabernet Franc
    20% Merlot
    5% Malbec and Petit Verdot

Château Durfort-Vivens, Margaux
    65% Cabernet Sauvignon
    20% Cabernet Franc
    15% Merlot

Château Gruaud-Larose, Saint-Julien
    70% Cabernet Sauvignon
    20% Merlot

    5% Cabernet Franc
    5% Petit Verdot

Château Lascombes, Margaux
    60% Cabernet Sauvignon
    26% Merlot
    10% Cabernet Franc
    4% Malbec and Petit Verdot

Château Brane-Cantenac, Cantenac
    60% Cabernet Sauvignon
    20% Merlot
    17% Cabernet Franc
    3% Petit Verdot

Château Pichon-Longueville-Baron, Pauillac
    55% Cabernet Sauvignon
    45% Merlot

Château Pichon-Longueville-Lalande, Pauillac
    42% Cabernet Sauvignon
    36% Cabernet Franc
    14% Merlot
    8% Petit Verdot

Château Ducru-Beaucaillou, Saint-Julien
    65% Cabernet Sauvignon
    25% Merlot
    10% Cabernet Franc and Petit Verdot

Château Cos-d'Estournel, Saint-Estèphe
    60% Cabernet Sauvignon
    36% Merlot
    4% Cabernet Franc

Château Montrose, Saint-Estèphe
    65% Cabernet Sauvignon
    25% Merlot
    10% Cabernet Franc

Third Growths

Château Kirwan, Cantenac
    60% Cabernet Sauvignon
    25% Merlot
    15% Petit Verdot

Château d'Issan, Cantenac
    66% Cabernet Sauvignon
    34% Merlot

Château Lagrange, Saint-Julien
    60% Cabernet Sauvignon and Cabernet Franc
    38% Merlot
    2% Petit Verdot

Château Langoa-Barton, Saint Julien
    75% Cabernet Sauvignon and Cabernet Franc
    20% Merlot
    5% Malbec and Petit Verdot

Château Giscours, Labarde
    55% Cabernet Sauvignon
    30% Merlot
    15% Cabernet Franc
    10% Petit Verdot

Château Malescot-St. Exupéry, Margaux
    60% Cabernet Sauvignon
    30% Merlot
    10% Petit Verdot

Château Boyd-Cantenac, Cantenac
    69% Cabernet Sauvignon
    19% Merlot
    7% Cabernet Franc
    5% Petit Verdot

Château Palmer, Cantenac
    50% Cabernet Sauvignon
    40% Merlot
    10% Petit Verdot

Château La Lagune, Ludon
    50% Cabernet Sauvignon
    25% Cabernet Franc
    20% Merlot
    5% Petit Verdot

Château Cantenac-Brown, Cantenac
    70% Cabernet Sauvignon and Cabernet Franc
    30% Merlot

Château Calon-Ségur, Saint-Estèphe
    33 1/3% Cabernet Sauvignon
    33 1/3% Cabernet Franc
    33 1/3% Merlot

Château Ferrière, Margaux
    Cabernet Sauvignon
    Cabernet Franc
    Petit Verdot
    (Percentages not available)

Château Marquis-d'Alesme-Becker
    40% Cabernet Sauvignon
    30% Merlot
    20% Cabernet Franc
    10% Petit Verdot

Fourth Growths

Château Saint-Pierre, Saint-Julien
    63% Cabernet Sauvignon
    30% Merlot
    7% Petit Verdot

Château Talbot, Saint-Julien
    70% Cabernet Sauvignon
    25% Merlot
    3% Cabernet Franc
    2% Petit Verdot

Château Branaire-Ducru, Saint Julien
    40% Cabernet Sauvignon
    35% Cabernet Franc
    20% Merlot
    5% Petit Verdot

Château Duhart-Milon-Rothschild, Pauillac
    63% Cabernet Sauvignon
    18% Merlot
    15% Cabernet Franc
    4% Petit Verdot

Château Pouget, Cantenac
70% Cabernet Sauvignon
15% Merlot
10% Cabernet Franc
5% Petit Verdot

Château La Tour-Carnet, Saint-Laurent
79% Cabernet Sauvignon and Cabernet Franc
18% Merlot
3% Petit Verdot

Château Lafon-Rochet, Saint-Estèphe
80% Cabernet Sauvignon
10% Merlot
5% Cabernet Franc
5% Petit Verdot

Château Beychevelle, Saint-Julien
68% Cabernet Sauvignon
28% Merlot
4% Cabernet Franc

Château Prieuré-Lichine, Cantenac
50% Cabernet Sauvignon
40% Merlot
5% Cabernet Franc
5% Petit Verdot

Château Marquis-de-Terme, Margaux
78% Cabernet Sauvignon
13% Petit Verdot
9% Merlot

Fifth Growths

Château Pontet-Canet, Pauillac
83% Cabernet Sauvignon
17% Merlot

Château Batailley, Pauillac
75% Cabernet Sauvignon and Cabernet Franc
25% Merlot

Château Haut-Batailley, Pauillac
66 2/3% Cabernet Sauvignon
33 1/3% Merlot

Château Grand-Puy-Lacoste, Pauillac
75% Cabernet Sauvignon and Cabernet Franc
25% Merlot

Château Grand-Puy-Ducasse, Pauillac
44% Cabernet Sauvignon
44% Merlot
12% Petit Verdot

Château Lynch-Bages, Pauillac
70% Cabernet Sauvignon
17% Merlot
10% Cabernet Franc
2% Petit Verdot
1% Malbec

Château Lynch-Moussas, Pauillac
70% Cabernet Sauvignon
30% Merlot

Château Dauzac, Labarde
Cabernet Sauvignon
Cabernet Franc
Petit Verdot
Malbec
(Percentages not available)

Château Mouton-Baronne-Pauline, Pauillac
75% Cabernet Sauvignon
25% Merlot

Château du Tertre, Margaux
70% Cabernet Sauvignon

20% Merlot
10% Cabernet Franc

Château Haut-Bages-Libéral, Pauillac
89% Cabernet Sauvignon
9% Merlot
2% Petit Verdot

Château Pédesclaux, Pauillac
80% Cabernet Sauvignon
20% Merlot

Château Belgrave, Saint-Laurent
45% Cabernet Sauvignon
45% Merlot
10% Petit Verdot

Château Camensac, Saint-Laurent
60% Cabernet Sauvignon
20% Cabernet Franc
20% Merlot

Château Labory, Saint-Estèphe
40% Merlot
35% Cabernet Sauvignon
15% Cabernet Franc
10% Petit Verdot

Château Clerc-Milon-Rothschild, Pauillac
85% Cabernet Sauvignon and Cabernet Franc
15% Merlot and Petit Verdot

Château Croizet-Bages, Pauillac
60% Cabernet Sauvignon and Cabernet Franc
30% Merlot and Petit Verdot

Château Cantemerle, Macau
40% Cabernet Sauvignon
40% Merlot
15% Cabernet Franc
5% Petit Verdot

Directory

CALIFORNIA

Central Coast Wineries

Ahlgren Vineyard
20320 Highway 9
Boulder Creek 95006
(408) 338-6071

Almaden Vineyards
1530 Blossom Hill Rd.
San Jose 95118
(408) 269-1312

Bargetto's Santa Cruz Winery
3535-A No. Main St.
Soquel 95073
(408) 475-2258

Bertero Winery
3920 Hecker Pass Hwy.
Gilroy 95020
(408) 842-3032

David Bruce Winery
21439 Bear Creek Rd.
Los Gatos 95030
(408) 354-4214

Calera Wine Company
P. O. Box 342
Hollister 95023
(408) 637-2344

Carmel Bay Winery
P. O. Box 2496
Carmel 93921

Chalone Vineyard
Stonewall Canyon Rd.
The Pinnacles
Soledad 93960
(415) 441-8975

Channing Cellars
2157 Clinton Ave.
Alameda 94501
(415) 523-1544

Chateau Vintners
1688 Timothy Rd.
San Leandro 94577
(415) 352-5425

Concannon Vineyard
4590 Telsa Rd.
Livermore 94550
(415) 447-3760

Congress Springs Vineyards
23600 Congress Springs Rd.
Saratoga 95070
(408) 867-1409

A. Conrotto Winery
1690 Hecker Pass Rd.
Gilroy 95020
(408) 842-3053

Continental Vintners
Shandon Star Rte.
Paso Robles 93446
(805) 238-2562

J. E. Digardi Winery
3785 Pacheco Blvd.
Martinez 94553
(415) 228-2638

Durney Vineyards
Star Rte., Box 152
Carmel Valley 93924
(408) 659-4716

Enz Vineyards
1781 Limekiln Rd.
Hollister 95023
(408) 637-3756

Estrella River Vineyards
Paso Robles 93446
(805) 238-0751

Felton-Empire Vineyards
379 Felton-Empire Rd.
Felton 95081
(408) 335-3939

The Firestone Vineyard
Zaca Station Rd.
Los Olivos 93441
(805) 688-8940

Julius Firpo Winery
Sellers Ave.
Knightsen 94548
(415) 625-2915

Fortino Winery
4525 Hecker Pass Rd.
Gilroy 95020
(408) 842-3305

Frick Winery
3965 Bonny Doon Rd.
Santa Cruz 95060
(408) 426-8623

Gemello Winery
2003 El Camino Real
Mtn. View 94040
(415) 948-7723

Peter & Harry Giretti Winery
791 5th St.
Gilroy 95020
(408) 842-3857

Emilio Guglielmo Winery
1480 Main Ave.
Morgan Hill 95037
(408) 779-2145

Hecker Pass Winery
4605 Hecker Pass Hwy.
Gilroy 95020
(408) 842-8755

Hoffman Mountain Ranch
Adelaida Rd., Star Rte.
Paso Robles 93446
(805) 238-4945

Kirigin Cellars
11550 Watsonville Rd.
Gilroy 95020
(408) 847-8827

Thomas Kruse Winery
4390 Hecker Pass Rd.
Gilroy 95020
(408) 842-7016

La Purisma Winery
725 A Sunnyvale-Saratoga Rd.
Sunnyvale 94087
(408) 738-1011

Ronald Lamb Winery
17785 Casa Ln.
Morgan Hill 95037
(408) 779-4268

Live Oaks Winery
3875 Hecker Pass Hwy.
Gilroy 95020
(408) 842-2401

Llords & Elwood Winery
315 So. Beverly Dr., Suite 306
Beverly Hills 90212
(213) 553-2368

Los Alamos Winery
2635 Highway 135
Los Alamos 93440
(805) 344-2390

Paul Masson Vineyards
13150 Saratoga Ave.
Saratoga 95070
(408) 257-7800

Mirassou Vineyards
Route 3, Box 344
3000 Aborn Rd.
San Jose 95121
(408) 274-3000

Montclair Winery
910 81st Ave.
Oakland 94621
(415) 962-9492

Monterey Peninsula Winery
2999 Monterey-Salinas Hwy.
Monterey 93940
(408) 372-4949

The Monterey Vineyard
800 S. Alta St.
Gonzales 93926
(408) 675-2326

J. W. Morris Port Works
1215 Park Ave.
Emeryville 94608
(415) 655-3009

Mount Eden Vineyards
22000 Mt. Eden Rd.
Saratoga 95070
(408) 867-5783

Nepenthe Cellars
Scotts Valley 95066

Nicasio Vineyards
14300 Nicasio Way
Soquel 95037
(408) 423-1073/423-1578

Novitiate Wines
College & Prospect Aves.
Los Gatos 95030
(408) 354-6471

Oak Barrel Winecraft-Winery
1201 University Ave.
Berkeley 94702
(415) 849-0400

Ox Mountain
Route 1, Box 2Q
Half Moon Bay 94019
(415) 726-6465

Page Mill Winery
13686 Page Mill Rd.
Los Altos Hills 94022
(415) 948-0958

Michael T. Parsons Winery
170 Hidden Valley Rd.
Soquel 95073
(408) 475-6096

Pedrizzeti Winery
1645 San Pedro Ave.
Morgan Hill 95037
(408) 779-7380

Presenti Winery
Rte. 1, Box 169
(Vineyard Drive)
Templeton 93465

Rancho Sisquoc
Rte. 1, Box 147
(Foxen Canyon Rd.)
Santa Maria 93454
(805) 937-3616

Rapazzini Winery
4350 Monterey Hwy.
Gilroy 95020
(408) 842-5649

Martin Ray Vineyards
22000 Mt. Eden Rd.
Saratoga 95070
(415) 494-8922

Richert & Sons Winery
1840 W. Edmundson
Morgan Hill 95037
(408) 779-5100

Ridge Vineyard, Inc.
17100 Montebello Rd.
Cupertino 95014
(408) 867-3233

Rotta Winery
Rte. 1, Box 168
(Winery Road)
Templeton 93465
(805) 434-1389

Roudon-Smith Vineyards
513 Mtn. View Rd.
Santa Cruz 95060
(408) 427-3492

San Martin Vineyards Co.
13000 Depot St.
San Martin 95046
(408) 638-2672

Sanford & Benedict Vineyards
Santa Rosa Road
Lompoc 93436
(805) 688-8314

Santa Barbara Winery
202 Anacapa St.
Santa Barbara 93101
(805) 962-3812

Santa Cruz Mountain Vineyard
2300 Jarvis Road
Santa Cruz 95065
(408) 426-6209

Santa Ynes Valley Winery
365 No. Refugio Rd.
Santa Ynez 93460
(805) 688-8381

Sherrill Cellars
2975 A Woodside Rd.
Woodside 94062
(415) 851-1932

Sommelier Winery
2560 Wyandotte St.
Section C.
Mtn. View 94043
(415) 969-2442

P. and M. Staiger
1300 Hopkins Gulch Rd.
Boulder Creek 95006
(408) 338-4346

Stony Ridge Winery
840 Vineyard Ave.
Pleasanton 94566
(415) 846-2133

Sunrise Winery
16001 Empire Grade Rd.
Santa Cruz 95060
(408) 423-8226

Sycamore Creek Vineyards
12775 Ulvas Road
Morgan Hill 95020
(408) 779-4738

Tepusquet Cellars
Rte. 1, Box 142
Santa Maria 93454
(805) 937-2043

Turgeon & Lohr Winery
1000 Lenzen Ave.
San Jose 95126
(408) 292-1564

Vega Vineyards Winery
526 So. L. St.
Lompoc 93463
(805) 736-2600

Ventana Vineyards
P. O. Box G
Soledad 93960
(408) 678-2306

Conrad Viano Winery
150 Morello Ave.
Martinez 94553
(415) 228-6465

Villa Armando
553 St. John St.
Pleasanton 94556
(415) 846-5488

Vine Hill Vineyard
2317 Vine Hill Rd.
Santa Cruz 95065
(408) 438-1260

Weibel Champagne Vineyards
1250 Stanford Ave.
Mission San Jose 94538
(415) 656-2340

Wente Brothers
5565 Telsa Rd.
Livermore 94550
(415) 447-3603

Wine & The People
907 University Ave.
Berkeley 94170
(415) 549-1266

Woodside Vineyards
340 Kings Mtn. Rd.
Woodside 94062
(415) 851-7475

York Mountain Winery
Route 1, Box 191
(York Mtn. Rd.)
Templeton 93465
(805) 238-3925

Zaca Mesa Winery
Foxen Canyon Rd.
Los Olivos 93441
(805) 688-3763

Sonoma and Mendocino Wineries

Alexander Valley Vineyards
8644 Highway 128
Healdsburg 95448
(707) 433-6293

Bandiera Wines
155 Cherry Creek Rd.
Cloverdale 95476
(707) 894-2352

Buena Vista Winery
18000 Old Winery Rd.
Sonoma 95476
(707) 938-8504

Cambiaso Winery & Vineyards
1141 Grant Ave.
Healdsburg 95448
(707) 433-5508

Chateau St. Jean
8555 Sonoma Hwy.
Kenwood 95452
(707) 833-4134

Cresta Blanca Winery
2399 North State St.
Ukiah 95482
(707) 462-5161
(415) 956-6330

Davis Bynum Winery
8075 Westside Rd.
Healdsburg 95448
(707) 433-5852

Dry Creek Vineyard
3770 Lambert Bridge Rd.
Healdsburg 95448
(707) 433-1000

Edmeades Vineyards
5500 Calif. State Hwy. 128
Philo 95466
(707) 895-3232

Fetzer Vineyards
1150 Bel Arbes Rd.
Redwood Valley 95470
(707) 485-8998

Foppiano Vineyards
12707 Old Redwood Hwy.
Healdsburg 95448
(707) 433-1937

Geyser Peak Winery
3775 Thornsberry Rd.
Geyserville 95441
(707) 433-5349

Grand Cru Vineyards
1 Vintage Ln.
Glen Ellen 95442
(707) 996-8100

Gundlach-Bundschu Wine Co.
3773 Thornsberry Rd.
Vineburg 95487
(707) 938-5277

Hacienda Wine Cellars
1000 Vineyard Ln.
Sonoma 95476
(707) 938-3229, 938-2244

Hanzell Vineyards
18596 Lomita Ave.
Sonoma 95476
(707) 996-3860

Hop Kiln Winery
6050 Westside Rd.
Healdsburg 95448
(707) 433-6491

Husch Vineyards
4900 Calif. State Hwy. 128
Philo 95446
(707) 895-3216

Italian Swiss Colony
Asti 95413
(707) 894-2541

Jade Mountain
1335 Hiatt Rd.
Cloverdale 95425

Johnsons of Alexander Valley
8333 Calif. State Hwy. 128
Healdsburg 95448
(707) 433-2319

Kenwood Vineyards
9592 Sonoma Hwy.
Kenwood 95452
(707) 833-5891

F. Korbel & Bros.
Guerneville 95446
(707) 887-2294

Landmark Vineyards
9150 Los Amigos Rd.
Windsor 95492
(707) 838-9466

Martini & Prati Wines, Inc.
2191 Laguna Rd.
Santa Rosa 95401
(707) 823-2404

Mazzoni Winery
23645 Redwood Hwy.
Cloverdale 95427
(707) 857-3691

Mill Creek Vineyards
1401 Westside Rd.
Healdsburg 95448
(707) 433-5098

Nervo Winery
Independence Ln.
Geyserville 95411
(707) 857-3417

Parducci Wine Cellars
501 Parducci Rd.
Ukiah 95482
(707) 462-3828

Pastori Winery
23189 Redwood Hwy.
Cloverdale 95425
(707) 857-3418

Pedroncelli Winery, J.
1220 Canyon Rd.
Geyserville 95441
(707) 857-3619

Rafanelli Winery
4685 West Dry Creek Rd.
Healdsburg 95448
(707) 433-1385

Rege Wine Co.
26700 Dutcher Creek Rd.
Cloverdale 95425
(707) 894-2953

Russian River Vineyards
5700 Gravenstein Hwy.
Forestville 95436
(707) 887-2243

Sausal Winery
7370 Calif. State Hwy. 128
Healdsburg 95448
(707) 433-2285

Sebastiani Vineyards
389 Fourth St. E.
Sonoma 94576
(707) 938-5532

Simi Winery
16275 Healdsburg Ave.
Healdsburg 95448
(707) 433-6981

Sonoma Vineyards
11455 Old Redwood Hwy.
Windsor 95492
(707) 433-6511

Sotoyome Winery
641 Limerick Ln.
Healdsburg 95448
(707) 433-2001

Souverain Cellars
400 Souverain Rd.
Geyserville 95411
(707) 433-6918

Joseph Swan Vineyards
2916 Laguna Rd.
Forestville 95436
(707) 546-7711

Trentadue Winery
19170 Old Redwood Hwy.
Geyserville 95441
(707) 433-3104

Valley of the Moon Winery
777 Madrone Rd.
Glen Ellen 95442
(707) 996-6941

Vina Vista Vineyards
Chianti Rd.
Geyserville 95441
(415) 967-1824

Weibel Champagne Vineyards
7051 North State St.
Ukiah 95470
(707) 485-0321

Z-D Winery

Napa Valley Wineries

Beaulieu Vineyards
1960 Highway 29
Rutherford 94573
(707) 963-3671

Beringer Bros.
2000 Main St.
St. Helena 94574
(707) 963-7115

Burgess Cellars
1108 Deer Park Rd.
St. Helena 94574
(707) 963-4766

Carneros Creek Winery
1285 Dealy Ln.
Napa 94558
(707) 226-3279

Caymus Vineyards
8700 Conn. Creek Rd.
St. Helena 94574
(707) 963-4204

Chappelet Vineyards
1581 Sage Canyon Rd.
St. Helena 94574
(707) 963-7136

Chateau Chevalier
3101 Spring Mtn. Rd.
St. Helena 94574
(707) 963-2342

Chateau Montelena
1429 Tubbs Ln.
Calistoga 94515
(707) 942-5105

Christian Brothers Winery
2555 North Main St.
St. Helena 94574
(707) 963-2719

Clos Du Val
5584 Silverado Trail
Napa 94558
(707) 224-6387

Cuvaison Cellars
4560 Silverado Trail No.
Calistoga 94515
(707) 942-6100

Diamond Creek Vineyards
1500 Diamond Mtn. Rd.
Calistoga 94515
(415) 346-3644

Franciscan Vineyards
1179 Galleron Rd.
St. Helena 94574
(707) 963-3886

Freemark Abbey Winery
3022 St. Helena Hwy.
St. Helena 94574
(707) 963-7106

Heitz Wine Cellars
500 Taplin Rd.
St. Helena 94574
(707) 963-3542

Howell Mtn. Winery
150 White Cottage Rd. So.
Angwin 94508
(707) 965-2680

Inglenook Vineyards
Highway 29
Rutherford 94573
(707) 963-7182

Hanns Kornell Champagne Cellars
1091 Larkmead Ln.
Calistoga 94515
(707) 963-2334

Charles Krug Winery
Highway 29
St. Helena 94574
(707) 963-2761

Lyncrest Vineyards
White Sulphur Springs Rd.
St. Helena 94574
(707) 963-4736

J. Mathews Napa Valley Winery
1711 Main St.
Napa 94558
(707) 224-3222

Louis M. Martini Winery
Highway 29
St. Helena 94574
(707) 963-2736

Mayacamas Vineyards
1155 Lokoya Rd.
Napa 94558
(707) 224-4030

Moët-Hennessy
1743 Mt. Veeder Rd.
Napa 94558
(707) 224-2022

Robert Mondavi Winery
7801 Highway 29
Oakville 94562
(707) 963-7156

Mt. Veeder Winery
1999 Mt. Veeder Rd.
Napa 94558
(707) 224-4039

Nash Creek Vineyards
3520 Silverado Trail
St. Helena 94574

Nichelini Vineyards
Highway 128
St. Helena 94574
(707) 963-3357

Oakville Vineyards
7840 Highway 29
Oakville 94562
(707) 944-2457

Joseph Phelps Vineyards
200 Taplin Rd.
St. Helena 94574
(707) 963-2745

Pope Valley Winery
6613 Pope Valley Rd.
St. Helena 94574
(707) 965-2192

Raymond Vineyards
Galleron Rd.
St. Helena 94574
(707) 963-3141

Ritchie Creek Vineyard
4024 Spring Mtn. Rd.
St. Helena 94574
(707) 963-4661

V. Sattui Winery
111 White Ln.
St. Helena 94574
(707) 963-7774

Schramsberg Vineyard
Schramsberg Rd.
Calistoga 94515
(707) 942-4558

Silver Oak Cellars
915 Oakville Crossroads
Yountville 94599
(707) 944-8170

Souverain Cellars
Souverain Road at Silverado Trail
Rutherford 94573
(707) 963-2759

Spring Mountain Vineyards
2805 Spring Mtn. Rd.
St. Helena 94574
(707) 963-4341

Stag's Leap Wine Cellars
5766 Silverado Trail
Napa 94558
(707) 944-2020

Stag's Leap Winery
Stag's Leap Ranch
Yountville 94599
(707) 944-2792

Sterling Vineyards
1111 Dunaweal Ln.
Calistoga 94515
(707) 942-5151

Stonegate Winery
1183 Dunaweal Ln.
Calistoga 94515
(707) 942-6500

Stony Hill Vineyard
3331 North St. Helena Hwy.
St. Helena 94574
(707) 963-2636

Sutter Home Winery
277 St. Helena Hwy.
St. Helena 94574
(707) 963-3104

Trefethen Vineyards
1160 Oak Knoll Ave.
Napa 94558
(707) 255-7703

Veedercrest Vineyards
2203 Mt. Veeder Rd.
Napa 94558
(415) 849-3303

Villa Mt. Eden
Mt. Eden Ranch
Oakville 94562
(707) 944-2045

Yverdon Vineyards
3728 Spring Mtn. Rd.
St. Helena 94574
(707) 963-3266

FRANCE

WINE SOCIETIES

Alsace
Comité Interprofessionnel des Vins
d'Alsace (C.I.V.A.)
Pierre Bouard
8 Place de Lattre de Tassigny
68000 Colmar

Anjou/Saumur
Comité Interprofessionnel des Vins
d'Anjou et de Saumur (C.I.V.A.S.)
Yves Cariou
21 Blvd. Foch
49000 Angers

Beaujolais
Union Professionnelle des Vins de
Beaujolais (U.I.V.B.)
M. Canard
210 Blvd. Vermorel
69400 Villefrance sur Saône

171

Bordeaux
Conseil Interprofessionnel des Vins de
Bordeaux (C.I.V.B.)
Jean-Michel Corteau
1 Cours du XXX Juillet
33000 Bordeaux

Bourgogne/Macon
Comité Interprofessionnel des Vins de
Bourgogne et Macon (C.I.B.M.)
Raymond Cullas
B.P. 113 Maison du Tourisme
Ave. du Marechal de Tassigny
71000 Macon

Champagne
Comité Interprofessionnel du Vin de
Champagne (C.I.V.C.)
Joseph Dargent
5 Rue Henri Martin
51200 Epernay

Côte d'Or/Yonne
A.O.C. de Bourgogne (C.B.I.)
Lucien Rateau
Petite Place Carnot
21200 Beune

Côtes de Provence
Comité Interprofessionnel des Vins des
Côtes de Provence (C.I.V.D.P.)
G. Magrin
3 Ave. Jean Jaures
83460 Les Arcs sur Argens

Côtes du Rhône
Comité Interprofessionnel des Vins des
Côtes du Rhône (C.I.C.D.R.)
Pierre Ligier
Maison du Tourisme et du Vin
41 Cours Jean Jaures
84000 Avignon

Touraine
Comité Interprofessionnel des Vins de
Touraine (C.I.V.T.)
Madeleine Maurice
12 Rue Berthelot
37000 Tours

BORDEAUX

CHÂTEAUX AND NÉGOCIANTS

Ch. Ausone
33330 St.-Émilion
(56) 51 70 94
(The owners of Ch. Ausone also own Ch.
Belair.)

Ch. Batailley
33250 Pauillac

Ch. Beychevelle
St.-Julien
33250 Pauillac

Ch. Bouscaut
Cadaujac
33140 Bordeaux

Ch. Cheval-Blanc
33330 St.-Émilion

Domaines Cordier
10 Quai Paludate
33000 Bordeaux
(The Cordier family owns or controls

the following châteaux: Ch. Gruaud-
Larose, Talbot, Clos des Jacobins,
Lafaurie-Peyraguey.)

Ch. Cos-d'Estournel
St.-Estèphe
33250 Pauillac

Cruse et Fils Frères
124 Quai des Chartrons
33000 Bordeaux
(This firm owns also Ch. d'Issan, Haut-
Bages-Libéral.)

Ch. Ducru-Beaucaillou
St.-Julien-Beychevelle
33250 Pauillac

Louis Eschenauer
42 Avenue Emile-Counord
33077 Bordeaux
(This firm owns or controls Ch. Rausan-
Ségla, Olivier, Smith-Haut-Lafite.)

Ch. Giscours
Labarde
33460 Margaux

Ch. Gloria
St.-Julien-Beychevelle
33250 Pauillac

Ch. Haut-Brion
33500 Pessac

Ch. Langoa
St.-Julien-Beychevelle
33250 Pauillac
(The owners of Ch. Langoa own also
Léoville-Barton.)

Ch. Latour
33250 Pauillac

Alexis Lichine, S.A.
109 Rue Achard
33300 Bordeaux
(Mr. Lichine also manages Ch.
Lascombes, Lagrange, Prieuré-Lichine,
Coutet.)

Ch. Lynch-Bages
33250 Pauillac

Ch. Margaux
33460 Margaux

Ch. La Mission-Haut-Brion
3340 Talence
(The owners, Mr. and Mrs. Dewavrin, own
also Ch. La Tour-Haut-Brion, Laville-
Haut-Brion.)

Ch. Mouton Rothschild
33250 Pauillac

Ch. Palmer
Cantenac
33460 Margaux

Ch. Petrus
33500 Pomerol

Ch. Pontet-Canet
33250 Pauillac

Ch. Rayne-Vigneau
Mestrezat Preller
17 Cours de la Martinique
33000 Bordeaux

Baron E. de Rothschild
21 Rue Lafite
79009 Paris

Schroder & Schyler
97 Quai des Chartrons
B.P. 574
33006 Bordeaux

Ch. St.-Georges
St.-George de Montagne
33570 Lussac

Château-Vieux-Certan
33500 Pomerol

Ch. d'Yquem
33118 Sauternes

SHIPPERS

A. & R. Barriere Freres
Barton & Guestier
H. & O. Beyerman, S.A.R.L.
Birkedal Hartmann & Cie.
Albert Bichot
Borie-Manoux
Bouchard Pere & Fils
J. Calvet & Cie
Chantecaille & Cie
D. Cordier, S.A.
Coron Père & Fils
Cruse & Fils Frères
L. Danglade & Fils & Cie
A. Delor & Cie, S.A.
Descas Père & Fils
Dourthe Frères
Louis Dubroca
Dulong Frère & Fils
Louis Eschenauer
Gilbey, S.A.
Ginestet
Grenouilleau-Aurelien
Birkedal Hartmann & Cie
Nathaniel Johnston & Fils
Jouvet
Ed. Kressmann & Co.
Alexis Lichine & Co.
A. de Luze & Fils
Mähler-Besse & Cie
Marnier Lapostolle
Mestrezat-Preller
A. Moueix & Fils, Ltd.
Prats Frères
Les Fils de Marcel Quancard
Daniel & Alain Querre
Quien & Cie, S.A.
Baron Philippe de Rothschild
Schroder & de Constans
Schroder & Schyler & Co.
Maison Sichel
Woltner Frères

BURGUNDY

ESTATES

R. Ampeau, Meursault
Marquis d'Angerville, Volnay
Henri Boillot & Fils, Volnay
Domaine Bouchard Père & Fils, Beaune
Domaine Camus, Gevrey-Chambertin
Chandon de Briailles (Comte de Nicolay),
Savigny-les-Beune
Chapelle, Santenay

Domaine Clair-Dau, Bourgogne Rose
Marsannay
Domaine Cosson, Morey-St. Denis
de Courcel, Pommard
Delagrange-Bachelet, Chassagne
Domaine Drouhin-Laroze, Gevrey-
Chambertin
Domaine Faiveley, Mercury and Nuits-St.-
Georges
Domaine Felix Clerget, Pommard
Le Flaive, Puligny
Fleurot-Laroze, Santenay
F. Gaunoux, Pommard
P. Gelin, Fixin
Gouges, Henri, Nuits-St.-George
Jean Gros, Vosne-Romanée
Marquis de la Guiche, Chassagne
Henry Lamarche, Vosne-Romanée
Lequin & Fils, Santenay
Château Masson, Meursault
Prince de Merode, Ladoix
B. Michelot, Meursault
J. Monnier, Meursault
Chateau Noellat, Vosne-Romanée
Domaine Pidault, Santenay
Château de Pommard (Laplanche),
Pommard
Pierre Ponnelle, Beaune
Domaine de la Pousse d'Or (Potel),
Volnay
Ramonet-Prudhon, Chassagne
Rebourseau, Gevrey-Chambertin
Domaine de la Romanée-Conti, Vosne-
Romanée
Roumier, Chambolle-Musigny
A. Rousseau, Gevrey-Chambertin
Baron Thenard, Puligny and Givry
Domaine Trapet, Gevrey-Chambertin
Comte de Vogüé, Chambolle-Musigny

WINERIES AND NÉGOCIANTS

Marquis Jacques d'Angerville
Clos des Ducs
Volnay
21190 Meursault

Maison Bouchard Père et Fils
Au Château
21201 Beaune, France

Chanson Père et Fils
10 Rue du College
21200 Beaune

Joseph Drouhin
7 Rue d'Enfer
21202 Beaune

Maison Joseph Faiveley
Rue Tribourg
21700 Nuits-St.-Georges

Domaine Gaunoux
21630 Pommard

Jean Grivot
21670 Vosne-Romanée
(For an appointment write c/o Marquis
Jacques d'Angerville)

Louis Jadot
5 Rue Samuel-Legay
21200 Beaune

Jaffelin Frères
2 Rue Paradis
21200 Beaune

Domaine du Comte Lafon
Clos de la Barre
21190 Meursault

Domaine Laplanche
Château de Pommard
21630 Pommard

Louis Latour
18 Rue des Tonneliers
21202 Beaune

Domaine Leflaive
Puligny-Montrachet
21190 Meursault

Maison du Meursault
21190 Meursault

Comte de Moucheron
Domaine du Château de Meursault
21190 Meursault

Patriarche Père et Fils
5 et 7 Rue du College
21200 Beaune
(80) 22 23 20

Ropiteau Frères
21190 Meursault

Societé Civile du Domaine de la
Romanée-Conti
21670 Vosne-Romanée

Domaine du Comte de Vogüé
21770 Chambolle-Musigny

SHIPPERS

A. Barolet
Barton & Guestier
A. Bassereau & Cie
Albert Bichot
Boisseaux-Estivant
Bouchard, Aine & Fils
Paul Bouchard & Cie
Bouchard Père & Fils
Lionel Bruck
J. Calvet & Cie
Chanson Père & Fils
F. Chauvenet
Coron Père et Fils
Cruse & Fils
Charles Drapier & Fils
Joseph Drouhin
Georges Duboeuf
Dufouleur Frères
J. Faiveley
Maison Geisweiler
Jaboulet-Vercherre & Cie
Louis Jadot
Maison Jaffelin
Louis Latour
Leroy
Alexis Lichine & Co.
Liger-Belair & Fils
Lupé-Cholet & Cie
A. DeLuze & Fils
Mariner Lapostolle
Prosper Maufoux
Moillard-Grivot
J. Mommessin
J. Moreau

Morin Père & Fils
De Moucheron & Cie
Pasquier Desvignes
Patriarche Père & Fils
Piat Père & Fils
Albert Pic & Fils
Pierre Picard
Poulet et Cie
A. Regnard & Fils
Jules Regnier & Cie
Remoissenet Père & Fils
J. H. Rémy
Maison Antonin Rodet
Ropiteau Frères
Maison Sichel
Roland Thevenin
Maison Thomas-Bassot
J. Thorin
Charles Vienot
Pierre Ouver

CHAMPAGNE

HOUSES

Bollinger
Boite Postale 4
51160 Ay

Deutz
Boite Postale 9
51160 Ay

Charles Heidseick
46 Rue de la Justice
51100 Reims

Lanson Père et Fils
12 Blvd. Lundy
51100 Reims

Mercier
75 Ave. de Champagne
51200 Épernay

Moët et Chandon
20 Ave. de Champagne
51200 Épernay

G. H. Mumm
34 Rue du Champ-de-Mars
51100 Reims

Laurent Perrier
Domaine de Tourssur-Marne
51150 Tours-sur-Marne

Perrier-Jouët
24-28 Ave. de Champagne
51200 Épernay

Piper-Heidsieck
51 Blvd. Henri-Vasnier
51100 Reims

Louis Roederer
21 Blvd. Lundy
51100 Reims

Pol Roger
1 Rue Henri-Lelarge
51230 Épernay

Taittinger
9 Place St.-Nicaise
51100 Reims

Veuve Clicquot Ponsardin
12 Rue du Temple
51100 Reims

WINERIES

Alsheim
Dr. Reinhard Muth
Weingut Rappenhof
Bachstrasse 47
6526 Alsheim

Bad Dürkheim
Stumpf-Fitz'sches Weingut Annaberg
6702 Bad Durkheim-Leistadt

Weingut K. Fitz-Ritter
Weinstrasse Nord 51
6702 Bad Durkheim

Weingut Pfeffingen
Weinstrasse
6702 Bad Durkheim

Bad Neuenahr-Ahrweiler
Staatliche Weinbaudomane Kloster
Marienthal (ahr)
Walporzheimer Strasse 48
5483 Bad Neuenahr-Ahrweiler

Klosterstrasse
5481 Marienthal

Bad Kreuznach
Reichsgraflich von Plettenberg'sche
Verwaltung
Winzenheimerstrasse, Postfach 825
6550 Bad Kreuznach

Redolf Anheuser'sche
Weingutsverwaltung
Strombergerstrasse 15-19, Postfach 106
6550 Bad Kreuznach

Staatsweingut Weinbaulehranstadt Bad
Kreuznach
Rudesheimer Strasse 68
6550 Bad Kreuznach

Weingut August Anheuser
Brucken 53
6550 Bad Kreuznach

Weingut Carl Finkenauer
Salinenstrasse 60
6550 Bad Kreuznach

Bechtheim
Brenner'sches Weingut
Pfandturmstrasse 20
6521 Bechtheim

Weingut Richard Beyer
Pfandturmstrasse 12
6521 Bechtheim

Bernkastel-Kues
Gutsverwaltung Deinhard
Martertal
5550 Bernkastel-Kues

Weingut Wwe. Dr. H. Thanisch
Saarallee 31
5550 Bernkastel-Kues

Bingen
Weingut Villa Sachsen
Mainzerstrasse 184
6530 Bingen

Burg Layen
Schlossgut Diel auf Berg Layen
6531 Burg Layen

Weingut Dr. Josef Hofer Schlossmuhle
6531 Burg Layen

Castell
Furstlich Castell'sches Domanenamt
8711 Castell

Deidesheim
Carl Josef Hoch-sche Guterverwaltung
Weinstrasse 10
6705 Deidesheim

Dr. von Bassermann-Jordan
Postfach 20
6705 Deidesheim

Weingut Hahnhof
Weinstrasse 1
6705 Deidesheim

Weingut Reichsrat von Buhl
6705 Deidesheim

Durbach
Freiherr Zorn von Bulach
Graflich Wolff Metternich'sches Weingut
Grohl 117
7601 Durbach

Gutsverwaltung Freiherr von Neveu
7601 Durbach

Markgraflich Badisches Weingut Schloss
Staufenberg
Schloss Staufenberg
7601 Durbach

Eller an Der Mosel
Weingut Freiherr von Landenberg
Moselstrasse 60
5591 Ediger-Eller 2

Eltville
Freiherrlich Langwerth von
Simmern'sches Rentamt
Langwerther Hof, Postfach 15
6228 Eltville

Graflich Eltz'sche Guterverwaltung
Schloss Eltz
Eltzer Hof
Rosenstrasse
6228 Eltville

Verwaltung der Staatsweinguter Eltville
Schwalbacherstrasse 56-62, Postfach 169
6228 Eltville

Erbach
Schloss Reinhartshausen
6229 Erbach

Filzen
Weingut Edmund Reverchon
Saartalstrasse 3
5503 Konz-Filzen

Forst
Eugen Spindler
Weingut Lindenhof
Weinstrasse 55
6701 Forst

Geisenheim
Hessische Forschungsanstalt für Wein-und
Obstund Gartenbau
von Ladestrasse 1
6222 Geisenheim

Grunhaus
C. von Schubert'sche Gutsverwaltung
5501 Grunhaus-Mertesdorf

Haardt
Weingut Muller-Catoir
6730 Neustadt 13

Hattenheim
Domanenweingut Schloss Schonborn
Hauptstrasse 53
6229 Hattenheim

Hochheim
Domdechant Werner'sches Weingut
Rathausstrasse 30
6203 Hochheim

Weingut Konigin Victoria Berg
Mainweg 2
6203 Hochheim

Weingut der Stadt Frankfurt am Main
Aichgasse 11
6203 Hochheim

Ihringen am Kaiserstuhl
Versuchs und Lehrgut für Weinbau
Blakenhornsberg
7811 Ihringen

Johannisberg
Furst von Metternich Winneburg'sches
Domane Rentamt
Schloss
6225 Johannisberg

G. H. von Mumm'sches Weingut
Schulstrasse 30
6225 Johannisberg

Landgraflich Hessisches Weingut
Im Grund 1
6225 Johannisberg

Kiedrich
Weingut des Reichsfreiherrn von Ritter zu
Groenesteyn
Schloss Groenesteyn
Oberstrasse 19
6220 Rudesheim

Weingut Dr. Weil
Muhlberg 5
6229 Kiedrich

Kirchheim
Emil Hammel u. Cie., Weingut und
Weinkellerei
Weinstrasse Sud 4
6719 Kirchheim

Kleinbottwar
Weingut Brussele, Schlosskellerei Graf
Adelmann
Burg Schaubeck
7141 Steinheim-Kleinbottwar

Kreuzwertheim
Furstlich Lowenstein-Wertheim-

Rosenberg'sches Weingut
Rathausgasse 5
6983 Kreuzwertheim

Langenlonsheim
Weingut Erbhof Tesch
Naheweinstrasse 99
6536 Langenlonsheim

Lorch
Graflich von Kanitz'sche
Weingutsverwaltung
6223 Lorch

Mainz
Verwaltung der Staatlichen
Weinbaudomanen Mainz
Ernst-Ludwig-Strasse 9
6500 Mainz

Meersburg
Staatsweingut Meersburg
Seminarstrasse 8
7738 Meersburg

Neckarzimmern
Freiherrlich von Gemmingen-
Hornberg'sches Weingut Burg Hornberg
Burg Hornberg
6951 Neckarzimmern

Niederhausen
Staatlichen Weinbaudomanen
Niederhausen-Schlossbockelheim
6551 Oberhausen

Weingut Jakob Schneider
Winzerstrasse 15
6551 Niederhausen

Nierstein
Weingut Gustav Adolf Schmitt'sche
Wilhelmstrasse 2
6505 Nierstein

Weingut Burgermeister Anton Balbach
Erben
Mainzerstrasse 64
6505 Nierstein 1

Weingut Franz Karl Schmitt Hermannshof
Mainzerstrasse 48
6505 Nierstein

Weingut Freiherr Heyl zu Herrnsheim
Mathildenhof
Langgasse 3
6505 Nierstein

Weingut Geschwister Schuch
Oberdorfstrasse 22
6505 Nierstein

Weingut J. und H. A. Strub
Rheinstrasse 42, Postfach 11
6505 Nierstein

Weingut Louis Guntrum
Rheinallee 57
6505 Nierstein

Weingut Winzermeister Heinrich Seip
Kurfürstenhof
6505 Nierstein

Oberwesel (am Rhein)
Weingut Heinrich Weiler
Mainzerstrasse 2
6532 Oberwesel

Oestrich
Julius Wegeler Erben
Gutsverwaltung Geheimer Rat
6227 Oestrich-Winkel, Postfach 1105

Ohringen
Furst zu Hohenlohe-Ohringen'sche
Schlosskellerei
7110 Ohringen Marktplatz

Oppenheim
Dr. Dahlem Erben KG
Weingutsverwaltung Sanitatsrat
Wormserstrasse 50
6504 Oppenheim

Weingut Carl Sittmann
Wormserstrasse 59
6504 Oppenheim

Osthofen
Alfred Muller
Weingut Weisses Ross
Friedrich-Ebert-Strasse 50
6522 Osthofen

Salem
Weinguter Max Markgraf von Baden
Schloss
7777 Salem

Schozach
Graflich von Bentzel-Sturmfeder'sches
Weingut)
7129 Schozach

Schwaigern
Graflich von Neipperg'sches Weingut und
Schlosskellerei
Schloss
7103 Schwaigern

Selzen
Weingut Kapellenhof
Okonomierat Schatzel Erben
Kapellenhof
Kapellenstrasse 18
6501 Selzen

Siebeldingen
Weingut Okonomierat Rebholz
Weinstrasse 56
6741 Siebeldingen

Sommerhausen
Weingut Ernst Gebhardt
Hauptstrasse 5
8701 Sommerhausen

Stuttgart
Wurttembergische Hofkammer-Kellerei
Holderlinstrasse 32
7000 Stuttgart

Trier
Guterverwaltung Vereinigte Hospitien
Trier
Krahnenufer 19
5500 Trier

Reichsgraf von Kesselstatt
Palais Kesselstatt
Liebfrauenstrasse 9
5500 Trier

Stiftung Staatliches Friedrich-Wilhelm-
Gymnasium
Weberbachstrasse 75
5500 Trier

Verwaltung der Bischoflichen Weinguter
Gervasiusstrasse 1
5500 Trier

Verwaltung der Staatlichen
Weinbaudomanen
Deworastrasse 1
5500 Trier

Weingut Thiergarten Georg Fritz von Nell
Im Thiergarten 12
5500 Trier

Trier-Eitelsbach
Karthauserhof Eitelsbach
Postfach 40
5500 Trier-Eitelsbach

Wachenheim
Weingut Dr. Burklin-Wolf
Weinstrasse 65
6706 Wachenheim

Wehlen
Weingut Joh. Jos. Prum
5554 Wehlen

Weikersheim
Furstlich Hohenlohe Langenburg'sche
Weinguter
Schloss
6992 Weikersheim

Weinsberg
Staatliche Lehr- und Versuchsanstalt für
Wein und Obstbau
Hallerstrasse 6
7102 Weinsberg

Wiltingen
Egon Muller-Scharzhof
5511 Scharzhof bei Wiltingen

Winkel
A. von Brentano'sche Gutsverwaltung
Brentanohaus
Hauptstrasse 89
6227 Winkel

Schloss Vollrads
6227 Winkel

Wurzburg
Bayerische Landesanstalt für Wein
und Gartenbau
Residenzplatz 3
8700 Wurzburg

Burgerspital zum Heiligen Geist
Theaterstrasse 19
8700 Wurzburg

Juliusspital-Weingut
Juliuspromenade 19
8700 Wurzburg

Zell-Merl an Der Mosel
Schneider'sche Weinguterverwaltung
Merlerstrasse 28
5583 Zell-Merl

SHIPPERS

Anheuser & Fehrs
Leon Beyer
E. Boeckel, S.A.
Deinard & Co.
Dopff
Dopff & Irion
Drathen

175

Export-Union Deutscher Weinguter
F. W. Langguth Erben
Jakob Gerhardt
Weingut Louis Guntrum
Arthur Hallgarten
Hauptkellerei Rheinischer
Winzergenossenschaften
Carl Jos. Hoch
Jacob Horz
Adolph Huesquin
F. Hugel & Fils

Ernst Jungkenn
Julius Kayser & Co.
Herman Kandermann
Leonard Kreusch
Langenbach & Co.
Richard Langguth
Rudolph Muller
Ferdinand Pieroth
Franz Reh, K.G.
Reichsgraf von Kesselstatt
Societé Vinicole Dist. Sainte Odile,

S.A.R.L.
Gustav Adolf Schmitt
Georg & Karl Ludwig Schmitt'sches
Scholl-Hillebrand
Schulz & Wagner
H. Sichel & Soehne
A. Steigenberger
F. E. Trimbach
P. J. Valckenberg
Wilhelm Wasum
Adolphe Willm

Index

180